SEX AND THE WEIMAR REPUBLIC

German Homosexual Emancipation and the Rise of the Nazis

Liberated, licentious, or merely liberal, the sexual freedoms of Germany's Weimar Republic have become legendary. The home of the world's first gay rights movement, the republic embodied a progressive, secular vision of sexual liberation. Immortalized – however misleadingly – in Christopher Isherwood's *Berlin Stories* and the musical *Cabaret*, Weimar's freedoms have become a touchstone for the politics of sexual emancipation.

Yet, as Laurie Marhoefer shows in *Sex and Weimar Republic*, those sexual freedoms were only obtained at the expense of a minority who were deemed sexually disordered. In Weimar Germany, the citizen's right to sexual freedom came with a duty to keep sexuality private, non-commercial, and respectable.

Sex and the Weimar Republic examines the rise of sexual tolerance through the debates which surrounded "immoral" sexuality: obscenity, male homosexuality, lesbianism, transgender identity, heterosexual promiscuity, and prostitution. It follows the sexual politics of a swath of Weimar society ranging from sexologist Magnus Hirschfeld to leader of the Nazi Storm Troopers Ernst Röhm. Tracing the connections between toleration and regulation, Marhoefer's observations remain relevant to the politics of sexuality today.

(German and European Studies)

LAURIE MARHOEFER in an assistant professor in the Department of History at Syracuse University.

GERMAN AND EUROPEAN STUDIES
General Editor: Rebecca Wittmann

Sex and the Weimar Republic

German Homosexual Emancipation and the Rise of the Nazis

LAURIE MARHOEFER

UNIVERSITY OF TORONTO PRESS
Toronto Buffalo London

ISBN 978-1-4426-4915-6 (cloth)   ISBN 978-1-4426-2657-7 (paper)

German and European Studies

Library and Archives Canada Cataloguing in Publication

Marhoefer, Laurie, 1978–, author
Sex and the Weimar Republic : German homosexual emancipation and the rise
of the Nazis / Laurie Marhoefer.

(German & European studies)
Includes bibliographical references and index.
ISBN 978-1-4426-4915-6 (bound). ISBN 978-1-4426-2657-7 (pbk.)

1. Gay rights – Germany – History – 20th century.   2. Gays – Legal status, laws,
etc. – Germany.   3. Homosexuality – Germany – History – 20th century.
4. Prostitution – Law and legislation – Germany.   5. Prostitution – Germany –
History – 20th century.   6. Sexual freedom – Political aspects – Germany – History –
20th century.   7. Germany – Social conditions – 1918–1933.   8. Germany –
Politics and government – 1918–1933.   I. Title.   II. Series: German and
European studies

HQ76.8.G4M37 2015   306.76'6094309042   C2015-902581-8

University of Toronto Press acknowledges the financial assistance to its
publishing program of the Canada Council for the Arts and the Ontario Arts
Council, an agency of the Government of Ontario.

**Canada Council
for the Arts**   **Conseil des Arts
du Canada**

**ONTARIO ARTS COUNCIL
CONSEIL DES ARTS DE L'ONTARIO**
an Ontario government agency
un organisme du gouvernement de l'Ontario

Funded by the   Financé par le
Government   gouvernement
of Canada   du Canada

Canadä

In memory of Rushin,
and to Mom, Dad, and Stephanie

Contents

Illustrations

Acknowledgments

Over the past ten years, this book has received the generous support of many institutions and people. First among these is Belinda Davis, for whose wholehearted encouragement and insightful advice over the course of many years I am very grateful. Thanks also to Temma Kaplan, Seth Koven, Matt Matsuda, the other faculty, and the staff of the Rutgers University–New Brunswick History Department. I am also grateful to Dagmar Herzog and Joan W. Scott, who read and commented on the dissertation from which this book emerged. I was fortunate to be an Andrew W. Mellon postdoctoral fellow at the Jackman Humanities Institute at the University of Toronto from 2008 to 2009. Thanks to Robert Gibbs of the Jackman Institute, to the staff, and to the 2008–9 fellows, especially Mareike Neuhaus. Thanks also to Doris Bergen and Jennifer Jenkins of the University of Toronto History Department. I owe a debt of gratitude as well to Jane Caplan and to the Modern European History Research Centre at the University of Oxford, where I was a research associate in 2012 and 2013. Thanks to other institutions that funded the project: the Maxwell School of Citizenship and Public Affairs at Syracuse University, including via the Appleby-Moser Fund; the Syracuse University History Department, including through the Pigott Fund; the Institute for Research on Women at Rutgers University; and the Deutscher Akademischer Austauschdienst (DAAD). I am grateful to the staffs of the archives and libraries where I worked, especially to the volunteers of the Schwules Museum and Spinnboden Lesbenarchiv. Thanks also to my students at Rutgers, the University of Toronto, and Syracuse, for teaching me about history.

A number of people read portions of the manuscript and improved it. Thanks to Belinda Davis, Thomas Knapp, Norman Kutcher, Kirsten

Leng, Allison Miller, Katie Sutton, and Richard Wetzell. Thanks also to the two anonymous readers for the press, both of whom went above and beyond the call of duty, much to the benefit of the book. Stephanie Clare read the whole thing; I am grateful for her cogent edits. Thanks to Christina Chiknas for research assistance and to Anne Schult for editing. Richard Ratzlaff, Lisa Jemison, and their colleagues at the University of Toronto Press cheerfully and gracefully shepherded this book through publication. Barbie Halaby edited the copy expertly and with diligence, patience, and good humour. Thanks also to the Lesben- und Schwulenverband Berlin-Brandenburg for allowing me to use the image discussed in the conclusion.

The book benefited from exchanges I had with other scholars; I would like to thank them, but unfortunately I have not kept track of them all. These interlocutors did, however, include the following people. Thanks to Kathleen Canning, Jennifer Evans, Geoffrey Giles, Ian Grimmer, Erik Huneke, Anthony McElligott, Katie Sutton, Annette Timm, and Richard Wetzell. As an undergraduate interested in queer history and politics, I was glad for the guidance of Robert Amdur, Eliza Byard, and Senta German.

At Syracuse, I was enormously fortunate to join a dynamic scholarly community that was also a very good place to be junior faculty and, in addition, afforded some good times that had nothing to do with scholarship. Many of my comrades in the history department, colleagues and friends, have helped with this project. Thanks are due especially to Susan Branson, Andrew Cohen, Albrecht Diem, Michael Ebner, Carol Faulkner, Paul Hagenloh, Samantha Kahn Herrick, Amy Kallander, Norman Kutcher, Chris Kyle, Gladys McCormick, Dennis Romano, and Martin Shanguhyia. I am also obliged to the history department staff for their support.

Thanks to good friends Kris Alexanderson, Agatha Beins, Tom Orlowicz Bellin, Leigh-Anne Francis, Jenny Kurtz, Tom Keck, Julie Gozan, Jordan Halsey, Jessica Anderson Hughes, Chloe Jhangiani, Allison Miller, Jennifer Miller, Peter Couvares, Rachel Schnepper, Christopher Sandersfeld, Diane Williamson, Niamh Duggan, and Des Almoradie. Heartfelt happy wishes, gratitude, and love to the Berliners: Erika Krech, Carla MacDougall, and Nili Shani.

The winter of 2013–14 was unusually cold. In its first month, we suffered a heartbreaking loss. What sustained me as I completed the final revisions to this book was friendship, and though this is a debt of thanks that I owe to a number of people, I want to mention in particular Samantha Kahn Herrick and Julie Gozan.

That winter also took my friend Rushin Desai. He was a guy with a big heart who heard a lot about this project over the years. He died far too young.

Love and thanks to my family: Barbara Marhoefer, Joseph Marhoefer, John Marhoefer, Jack Marhoefer, Grace Marhoefer, Mary Beth Gaiarin, Manu Gaiarin, Alex Gaiarin, Ben Gaiarin, Melinda Maher, Bob Maher, Joe Maher, Will Maher, and Maggie Maher. My parents, Barbara and Joe, supported my education and spent the decade I devoted to this book offering encouragement, good advice that I did not always take, and an impressive quantity of tabbouleh. There has always been much that I have admired in the characters of these two people; among other things, Mom has been a model historian, and Dad has been a model of assiduousness. Thanks, guys.

To Stephanie, my brilliant partner/lover/girlfriend: my gratitude and my love. This book would not have happened without you.

30 November 2014
Syracuse, New York

Abbreviations

BArch	Bundesarchiv Berlin-Lichterfelde
DDP	Deutsche Demokratische Partei (German Democratic Party, a left-liberal political party)
DFV	Deutscher Freundschaftsverband (German Friendship League, a homosexual emancipation group)
DNVP	Deutschnationale Volkspartei (German National People's Party, a conservative political party)
DVP	Deutsche Volkspartei (German People's Party, a right-liberal political party)
GdE	Gemeinschaft der Eigenen (Society of the Self-Owned/Special, a homosexual emancipation group)
GStAPK	Geheimes Staatsarchiv Preußischer Kulturbesitz
JfsZ	*Jahrbuch für sexuelle Zwischenstufen unter besonderer Berücksichtigung der Homosexualität* (*Yearbook for Sexual Intermediaries with Particular Consideration of Homosexuality*, a WhK journal)
KPD	Kommunistische Partei Deutschlands (German Communist Party)
LA	Landesarchiv Berlin
NSDAP	Nationalsozialistische Deutsche Arbeiterpartei (National Socialist German Workers' Party or Nazi Party)
SA	Sturmabteilung (Storm Troopers, a NSDAP paramilitary unit)
SPD	Sozialdemokratische Partei Deutschlands (German Social Democratic Party)

Vierteljahrsberichte   *Vierteljahrsberichte des Wissenschaftlich-humanitären Komitees während der Kriegszeit* (*Quarterly Reports of the Scientific Humanitarian Committee During the War*, a WhK journal)

WhK   Wissenschaftlich-humanitäres Komitee (Scientific Humanitarian Committee, a homosexual emancipation group)

WhKM   *Mitteilungen des Wissenschaftlich-humanitären Komitees* (*News of the Scientific Humanitarian Committee*, a WhK journal)

SEX AND THE WEIMAR REPUBLIC

Introduction: The Opening Night of the Institute for Sexual Science, July 1919

This is the story of the creation of a particular type of sexual freedom, one that liberated a majority of people while curtailing a disorderly minority. This form of sexual freedom came about because of the long decline of religious morality and the rise of science and secular notions of individual rights, democracy, and citizenship. It reached a short-lived high point in Germany between 1918 and 1933. Its establishment was the crowning achievement of a progressive coalition for reform that included the world's first homosexual emancipation movement. That achievement came at a price. Its history demonstrates the promises and pitfalls of movements for sexual liberation.

The setting of the story is the parliamentary democracy known today as the Weimar Republic, founded in the wake of the First World War and succeeded in 1933 by the Nazi State. The story begins on the evening of 1 July 1919, when a distinguished and eclectic group that included doctors, intellectuals, and politicians gathered in a grand mansion beside Berlin's Tiergarten park to hear a song of secular consecration for the new Institute for Sexual Science (*Institut für Sexualwissenschaft*).[1] Less than a year earlier, Germany's monarchy had fallen in the midst of revolution and defeat in the First World War. Some weeks before, a new constitution had transformed Germany into one of the world's most modern and democratic welfare states, at least on paper.[2] That summer evening, the song dedicated the Institute, the world's first independent institution for the scientific study of sexuality, to the healing of suffering.[3] When the singer, who was also the cantor of Berlin's largest synagogue, fell silent, the Institute's founder, the sexologist Magnus Hirschfeld, stepped forward to address the guests. Hirschfeld was then in his early fifties. At public appearances, he looked the part of a scientific expert, with his roundish frame clad in a dignified dark suit and a thick moustache dominating his square face. A pacifist who denounced racism and European imperialism, Hirschfeld courageously presented himself as the public face of homosexual emancipation at a time when to do so meant to compromise not only his reputation but also his safety.[4] After a public lecture the following year, he would be attacked and beaten by antisemites who objected to his politics and to his Jewishness.[5] On the Institute's opening night, Hirschfeld told the guests that the Institute's purpose was "two-fold: scientific research on all of human sexuality and love life, as well as the sexual life of all other creatures, and second, to make use of this research for all [*für die Gesamtheit*]."[6] The Institute's opening night was doubtless a moment of pride for Hirschfeld, and one of hope as well. In the Weimar Republic's early days, he believed that Germany's new democracy was about to vindicate his motto, "through science to justice." Science demonstrated that sexual anomalies such as homosexuality were rare, natural, "purely biological, not pathological,"[7] variations, similar to other naturally occurring and yet unusual conditions, such as colour blindness.[8] Thus laws like Germany's Paragraph 175, which banned sex between men, conflicted with science.[9] "What is natural cannot be immoral," Hirschfeld wrote.[10] "When state and society, family and individual persist in their old prejudice against homosexual men and women, a prejudice that is based on ignorance, then an injustice is done, one that has only few parallels in human history."[11] He called on his allies in the new government, the Social Democrats (*Sozialdemokratische Partei Deutschlands*, SPD), to quickly repeal the sodomy law. They declined to do so.[12]

The Institute for Sexual Science championed the principle that science rather than religious morality ought to dictate how state and society responded to sexuality. This principle was tested and revised in the crucible of the Weimar Republic. Though it was not a new idea, between 1918 and 1933 activists who championed reforms based on this principle had unprecedented influence. The Weimar Republic relaxed restrictions on media about sexuality, which proved crucial for the formation of mass political organizations of gay men, lesbians, and "transvestites" (*Transvestiten*).[13] It made most forms of female prostitution legal. Finally, in 1929, Germany came very close to repealing its law against male-male sex, Paragraph 175. All of these reforms proceeded from the principle that rationality and science, not religious morality, ought to guide the state's response to sexual behaviour. Yet the Weimar Republic did not simply bring liberation. It also moved to crack down on people whose

Magnus Hirschfeld (left) in the doorway of the Institute for Sexual Science, during the First International Congress for Sex Reform on the Basis of Sexology, 1921. Also pictured are Dr Klausner of Prague, with whom Hirschfeld is speaking, and Freiherr v. Reitzenstein. Photograph by Willy Römer. Bildarchiv Preußischer Kulturbesitz.

sexual choices most threatened traditional norms, especially male and female prostitutes who worked in public spaces. In addition, other forms of what conservatives called "immorality" could exist so long as they were curtailed, often through media censorship. The management of supposedly unruly sexualities was part of the transition to a sexual ethics based in science and rationality.

The Weimar Republic is still remembered for libertinism, and historians have recently argued that the Nazis capitalized on conservative discontent with Weimar-era reforms to laws on sexuality. But the rise of the

Nazis and the collapse of the Republic in the early 1930s were not part of the price paid for the sexual freedom that the Republic created. They had little to do with sexual politics. Rather, the main significance of this history is that it demonstrates a fundamental dilemma in the politics of queer liberation in the twentieth century.[14]

On the opening night of the Institute for Sexual Science, at least one activist for sexual freedom suspected that the strategy that it embodied was flawed. He would eventually conclude that the price for sexual freedom was too high. Kurt Hiller was a baby-faced, balding man in his thirties, who held a doctorate in law and came from a middle-class Jewish family. He was Hirschfeld's ally and a member of the leadership of the homosexual emancipation group that Hirschfeld had co-founded decades earlier, the Scientific Humanitarian Committee (*Wissenschaftlich-humanitäres Komitee*, WhK). Although no guest list survives, Hiller was most likely among those who gathered to open the Institute. If he was there, he listened to speeches and then went on a tour of the Institute along with the other guests. They visited the well-appointed consultation rooms, in which doctors would soon offer marriage and eugenic counselling to heterosexual couples, treat impotence and venereal disease, and dispense advice to homosexuals, transvestites, and other "sexual abnormals" (as sexology termed them). Guests paused amid the collections of the Institute's research faculties. There, they may have been shown objects from the collections: slides of the brains of "sexual abnormals," statistical tables about masturbation rates, or items that the English novelist Christopher Isherwood later claimed to have seen on his tour of the Institute, including "whips and chains" for S&M sex, photographs of "the sexual organs of quasi-hermaphrodites," and "lacy female undies which had been worn by ferociously masculine Prussian officers beneath their uniforms."[15] Hirschfeld may have offered erudite commentary on these artefacts, as he would do for visitors to the Institute in the years to come.[16]

Faced with this display of the science of sexuality, Hiller must have harboured some reservations. Like Hirschfeld, he privately had affairs with men but did not publicly claim a homosexual identity, instead referring to "homosexuals" in the third person in speeches and publications.[17] Some months before, Hiller had called on the WhK membership to "be honest with ourselves" that the scientific literature on homosexuality "is predominantly read by inverts," that is, homosexuals, and was doing little to convince the general public.[18] Hiller tried unsuccessfully to persuade Hirschfeld and others in the movement to adopt a new tactic: "inverts" ought to form "their own political party" and run for seats in the new parliament. He anticipated the system of proportional representation that the Constitution of 1919 established: as an estimated 1 per cent of the population, homosexuals could elect several Reichstag delegates if they voted as a bloc.[19] This idea, however, was not in keeping with Hirschfeld's strategy of winning over politicians and the public by conducting scientific research. Hirschfeld also dismissed a similar suggestion of Hiller's: a large number of homosexuals should publicly declare themselves.[20] This tactic of "mass self-denunciation" had been proposed and rejected by homosexual emancipationists for decades.[21] Hirschfeld called mass declaration a "utopian" fantasy; the "internal and external inhibitions" of the homosexual psyche would prevent a significant number of people from allowing themselves to be publicly identified as homosexual.[22] Only through science, he believed, could homosexuals achieve liberation.[23] Hiller's inclination to unapologetically claim public space and to deemphasize science would, by the end of the 1920s, lead him to defend male prostitutes against the compromise on sexual politics that the Republic ultimately endorsed, a compromise which was predicated on removing male prostitutes from public spaces. This book tells the story of how that compromise came into being and of Hiller's dilemma: were the terms of the compromise acceptable?

This dilemma, so clearly illustrated by the history of homosexual emancipation under the Republic, is an important chapter in the history of sexuality. Other studies have shown how queer activism in the nineteenth and twentieth centuries did not always pose radical challenges to the societies in which it emerged. In Britain in the 1950s and 1960s, discrete, elite, and respectable homosexual men distinguished themselves from public queer cultures and thus achieved the decriminalization of male-male sex in private.[24] Likewise, many women and men in post-1945 homophile groups in Europe and the United States took care not to threaten the broader political and social order.[25] Lisa Duggan identifies a "new homonormativity" at the heart of a late-twentieth-century brand of self-consciously conservative gay activism in the United States. She defines homonormativity as "a politics that does not contest dominant heteronormative assumptions and institutions but upholds and sustains them while promising the possibility of a demobilized gay constituency and a privatized, depoliticized gay culture."[26] To be sure, the Institute for Sexual Science and the reformist movement for sexual freedom of which it was a part did contest heteronormative assumptions and institutions – that is, assumptions and institutions that privileged a certain traditional version of heterosexuality, one that took for granted the exclusive existence of two sexes, male and female, respectively performing masculinity and femininity and naturally attracted to each other. At the same time, however, Hirschfeld and other leaders thwarted more radical strains of activism, activism by some of the very people whom they claimed to represent.

Yet the history of the Weimar era invites conclusions about queer activism that go beyond the insight that it often shies away from radicalism. German activists – Hirschfeld foremost among them – did much to set the terms of gay activism that remained in place throughout the twentieth century, and not only in Germany. They "invented" the concept of homosexuality as such.[27] They grounded it in the sciences of biology and sexology. They also pioneered tropes of later gay activism such as claims to respectable citizenship.[28] The gains of homosexual emancipation in the Weimar period were contingent on the renunciation by homosexuals and transvestites of an assertive public presence, though they did carve out a limited subcultural presence. This sort of bargain about public space was a key issue for later movements as well. Under the Weimar Republic, a movement based on these claims had real success in winning reforms – most crucially to censorship – for the first time in history. It was in the Weimar era that several characteristic components of twentieth-century gay and lesbian liberation were first put to use in the context of mass democracy. For that reason, movements that came later and that adopted similar positions faced a similar dilemma.

This book makes the dilemma of homosexual emancipation plain because it takes a queer methodological approach, generating a history of "immorality" rather than a history of just one faction of "immorality." The Weimar Republic is still associated in popular memory with sexual licentiousness. Historians have published a number of studies of sexuality and gender under the Republic. Existing studies are excellent and have enriched this one. They have, however, overlooked a crucial element of the big picture. This is because no work has considered the refashioning of gender and sexual norms under the Republic according to the terms in which Germans understood it at the time.[29] At the time, Germans believed this refashioning to be a single, capacious phenomenon. The vocabulary of the Weimar era expressed this comprehensive understanding. Conservatives lumped several forms of non-traditional sexuality together under terms like "immorality" (*Unsittlichkeit*) or "moral degeneration." Although reformers disagreed that these forms of sexual and gender expression were "immoral," they, too, used a single designation – "abnormal" – to denote many of them. The nomenclature reflects the fact that, to people at the time, particular forms of non-normative sexuality were intrinsically linked. "Immorality" or sexual "abnormality" was a social "problem" to be addressed as a whole. And in many respects, it was a single historical phenomenon. Thus, a reform of laws on female prostitution had important implications for the politics of male homosexuality. The censorship of "pornography," or media with sexual content, shaped lesbian subcultures. The goal of having better control over media about sexuality was cited as a reason to repeal the sodomy law. Only by taking a comprehensive view of "immorality," and by considering women *and* men, can a complete account be given of the Republic's sexual politics. Throughout the book, I borrow conservatives' favourite term – "immorality" – to denote this interconnected complex that included homosexuality, prostitution, gender non-conformity, and obscene media, as well as birth control and abortion.[30] I do not agree that these things are immoral but have sought to avoid littering the text with quotation marks, trusting that readers will remember that "immoral" is used strategically, in order to open up an analytic angle rather than to convey a moral judgment.

Historians have written on elements of immorality, but in isolation from one another. The literature has especially concentrated on heterosexual, reproductive female sexuality and female prostitution – that is, the selling of sex by women to men.[31] Few histories of homosexual emancipation concentrate on the pivotal Weimar period.[32] Moreover, much of that literature is largely about men; fewer studies of lesbians have been published.[33] Other aspects of immorality, such as transvestitism and male prostitution (the selling of sex by men to men), have received little attention.[34] Histories of censorship under the Republic largely ignore media about sexuality.[35] The only analysis of the Nazi Party sex scandal of 1931–2 in the context of the Republic's sexual politics was published by the Scientific Humanitarian Committee in 1932.[36] The existing literature does not portray the overall dynamic of the politics of immorality, a dynamic that Germans perceived quite clearly and according to which they tailored their responses to non-normative sexuality. This dynamic was one of compromise between moderate conservatives and moderate progressives, resulting in sexual liberation for some at the expense of others. To consider all forms of immorality together, and to elucidate the politics of homosexual emancipation in the process, is to take a methodological approach informed by queer theory. The making and remaking of "normal" is a useful site for a scholar's attention, as is the articulation and re-articulation of the distinction between "normal" and "abnormal," or, to put it another way, "those hegemonic social structures by which certain subjects are rendered 'normal' and 'natural' through the production of 'perverse' and 'pathological' others."[37]

This book also seeks to revise reigning understandings of the Weimar Republic. In the early 1930s, destructive political currents pulled the Republic under. In its place, the Nazis constructed a dictatorship. For many decades, historians have asserted that sex is part of the story of how democracy fell. Indeed, as chapter 6 argues in greater detail, after 1945 some of West Germany's leading historians expounded the idea that "immorality" in the Weimar period, including sexual impropriety, had cleared a path to power for Nazism. Gerhard Ritter, for example, argued in *Europe and the German Question* (*Europa und die deutsche Frage*, 1948) that the Weimar years were characterized by a lack of authority and by the resulting "brutalization and flattening [*Verflachung*] of moral sense" and the spread of "cultural decay [*Kulturverfall*], lack of faith, and moral nihilism."[38] Because of the feebleness of moral norms that otherwise might have stopped it, the profoundly immoral Nazi movement bloomed like a flame in hydrogen. Only in the post–First World War "atmosphere," Ritter wrote, was "the sudden expansion of the Hitler cult [*Hitlertum*] into a mass party comprehensible."[39] This notion of a link between Weimar-era immorality and Nazism was luridly illustrated in popular culture: the 1972 film *Cabaret* is a prime example. Although recent histories differ from the older notion of moral collapse apparent in Ritter's study and in work based on Christopher Isherwood's novels, they have asserted a number of theories about how sexual politics helped in a significant way to bring down the Republic. Yet in fact, sexual politics played no major role in the Republic's collapse.

This history of sexual politics shows not the unstable, conflict-ridden Republic so familiar from other histories, but rather a functional and durable democracy, at least until 1930, when the Great Depression hit and the final democratically elected chancellor, the SPD's Hermann Müller, fell. To be sure, sexual politics were divisive and polarizing. Conservatives and reformers were far, far apart on issues such as male homosexuality, media about sexuality, abortion, and birth control. Opponents of democracy on the right as well as the left charged that the Republic's flawed response to sexuality was another reason to overthrow it. But at the same time, contrary to what others have argued, sexual politics were not especially destabilizing to the Republic. Compromises on sexual-political questions proved more palatable to many more political players than historians have generally acknowledged. For example, the moderately conservative Catholic Centre Party (*Deutsche Zentrumspartei*) and the right-conservative German National People's Party (*Deutschnationale Volkspartei*, DNVP) – an officially anti-Republic party for much of its history – both voted with many Social Democrats in 1927 to decriminalize female prostitution. A leading figure in the right-liberal German People's Party (*Deutsche Volkspartei*, DVP) was a prominent proponent of repealing the sodomy law. Moreover, sexual politics played only a minor role in the rise of the Nazis. The toleration of sexual outsiders promoted by the coalition for reform ironically rescued the Nazi Party from a homosexual sex scandal at a crucial moment. But the NSDAP did not come to power thanks to the era's "decadence." Nor did it take advantage of a "backlash" against Weimar libertinism.

This study's assessment of the Republic as a functioning democracy, even when beset by bitter struggles among an array of political actors with dizzyingly divergent and conflicting ideas about sexuality, contributes to a growing literature that portrays the Weimar Republic as in fact relatively stable and relatively functional prior to the onset of the Depression.[40] This revisionist literature is in part a response to a theme that has characterized histories of the Republic for a long time: the identification of key causes of the Republic's demise relatively early in its life with the effect that even in 1919, the outlook for democracy seems retrospectively grim. Emphasizing elements that were present from 1919 and that helped bring down the Republic need not necessarily lead to the conclusion that the Republic had little chance at survival.[41] But in many recent studies it has.[42] Not all of the enormous literature on the Republic's fall deems it "doomed" from the beginning; for many decades, much of the German-language scholarship has been preoccupied with the events of Brüning's presidential regime of 1930–2.[43] Yet the sense of doom persists. It is also present in the retrospective accounts of exiles.[44]

Aside from ignoring over a decade of democracy between 1919 and 1930, this perception of doom from the outset does not allow for much agency on the part of Germans in the 1920s and early 1930s. If the Republic was fatally flawed from 1919, then Germans were merely passengers on a crippled vessel, rather than actors who abandoned democracy or fought to rescue it. The net effect is to make the period seem less important.[45] This is reflected in some studies of the homosexual emancipation movement that deny much significance to the Weimar period.[46]

Yet scholarship that identifies the Republic as doomed from the start – often with the central causal agent dating to 1919, such as the lost war, the Treaty of Versailles, or the Weimar Constitution – has been productively criticized.[47] While the prior scholarly consensus faulted the Revolution of 1918–19 for changing little, new studies have challenged this view, asserting that the Revolution was revolutionary in many respects, despite continuities between the old regime and the new.[48] For much of the period, the Reichstag was quite functional, and many of its members strived for compromise and civility despite their political disagreements.[49] Germans did act to change culture, society, and politics in the Weimar era, even if those changes were controversial and did not go as far as many progressives wanted.[50]

This book emphasizes the stability of democracy not to argue that there were no problems with Weimar democracy, but rather to urge historians to focus their attention on what actually destabilized democracy as opposed to asserting that a list of sometimes ill-defined phenomena did so. In recent studies, this list has included gender and sexuality.[51] In order to perceive democracy's weaknesses, there is a need to look at specific cases and issues. Democracy was at times dysfunctional. Just as importantly, perhaps, it was at times perceived as dysfunctional.[52] But for the most part, it was not dysfunctional over sexual-politics issues – the exception is abortion, as discussed in the conclusion. Immorality was controversial. But controversial political issues do not necessarily in and of themselves signal the irrevocable breakdown of a democratic system. In contrast to sexual-political questions, welfare policy – including unemployment insurance – was so polarizing and acutely contested that compromise proved too difficult, and democracy was destabilized as a result.[53] Moreover, the fact that more than a third of the electorate voted Nazi in 1932 was a hugely significant factor in the Republic's fall and in the rise of Hitler. But most of those voters were not motivated by a broad discontent with the Republic, including with its sexual politics, as some studies have asserted.[54] Rather, voters were radicalized, driven to the extreme parties, and drawn to the polls by specific issues, such as the economic crisis, the fear of communism, and the trauma of unemployment.[55]

The story of the Republic's collapse is in fact more profoundly frightening than the "doomed from the start" narrative would have it. The Republic seems to have been capable of surviving. It did survive long after many other interwar European democracies had succumbed.[56] It was brought down by a confluence of factors – among them I would highlight the Depression, the breakdown of the democratic process that began in 1930 and is in part attributable to the president and the arch-conservatives around him, the miscalculations of the leaders of several major political parties, and the swell of voters' affinity for the radical parties of the Left and the Right.[57] These causes seem, in retrospect, unsettlingly contingent, located in a relatively brief period of about two years. Even almost one hundred years later, it is imperative to understand how such a vibrant democracy, in which such a diversity of political opinion found expression – moreover a democracy that operated in a relatively tolerant, open society that was home to left-leaning innovations and intellectual and artistic achievement – fell so quickly into genocidal fascism. To do that, historians must be specific.

This study also argues for a lasting achievement of the Weimar era that had influence after 1933, not only in Germany but in other countries as well – that is, what I term the "Weimar settlement on sexual politics."[58] In particular, the fight for this settlement shaped the homosexual emancipation movement in ways that had an impact after 1933. In the years that followed, activists in Europe and North America looked to Hirschfeld and homosexual emancipation for inspiration, and the central principles of homosexual emancipation were repeated, often, by the end of the twentieth century, with some success. Although homosexual emancipation's origins lay in the nineteenth century,[59] it was under the Weimar Republic that homosexual emancipation's ideologies and strategies were first put to use in mass democratic politics with significant success.

The Players and Their Conflict

Across these pages, two major coalitions appear again and again, locked in political contention. Their struggle began in 1918–19, when war, revolution, and the Republic's founding seemed to commentators from across the political spectrum to have destabilized norms of gender and sexuality. As chapter 1 shows, in many respects the players and their stakes in the game were formed in the period before 1914, but war, revolution, and democracy changed them and changed the state that they battled to control. The coalition for reform included Hirschfeld and the WhK. It also included feminists and sex reformers. To them, including the guests at the opening of the Institute for Sexual Science, a new era of sexual morality and parliamentary democracy promised a better life and a more just society. In party politics, the German Social Democrats (the SPD)[60] largely backed the reforms for which Hirschfeld and his allies fought. Within the ranks of the SPD, advocates of women's emancipation, such as Louise Schroeder, took a leading role on issues of sexual politics. At times, reformers got support from the German Communist

Party (*Kommunistische Partei Deutschlands*, KPD), a revolutionary party to the left of the Social Democrats that had ties to Moscow.[61] The KPD was also critical of some reforms. This was no formal coalition. These factions did not agree on everything. Yet they generally shared a vision: the state's relationship to sexuality ought to be scientific and rational. In a new and democratic era, religious morality ought not to have a major influence on law and public policy.

Opposing the reformers were people who defended a vision of sexuality drawn from Christianity. They valued heterosexual marriage and decried the creeping influence of what they called immorality, which included homosexuality, prostitution, and supposedly obscene media, as well as extramarital heterosexual sex and the birth control and abortion practices that it entailed. They were wracked with anxiety that Germany would soon drown beneath a monsterous "flood" of "immorality." The Protestant historian and diehard monarchist Ulrich Stutz declared in 1920 that in Germany the "new Sodom and Gomorrah" had arisen, by which, he said, he did not only mean Berlin but other big cities too, such as "no-longer-holy Cologne."[62] Among those who took this view were members of the conservative women's movement, moderate politicians in the Centre Party, Protestant morality activists, and right-wing conservatives, this last group often being linked to the German National People's Party (DNVP). The National Socialist German Workers' Party or Nazi Party (*Nationalsozialistische Deutsche Arbeiterpartei*, NSDAP) took no part in the major battles of Weimar-era sexual politics because it did not enter the national political arena with any kind of force until the Great Depression hit Germany in the winter of 1929–30.

Throughout the Weimar era, conservatives struggled to remake the state in order to restore traditional morality, whereas reformers sought to use law and welfare policy to manage liberated sexuality for the public good. For example, they clashed in 1919 over the Institute for Sexual Science. The Institute owed its existence to the new democracy and to the Social Democrats whom the Revolution empowered. On the Institute's opening night, Hirschfeld said, "Our Institute can be called a child of the revolution."[63] The story of its founding demonstrates how 1918 changed the landscape of sexual politics. The kaiser had intended to use the building that later housed the Institute for an expansion of the opera house, but as Hirschfeld said in his speech at the Institute's opening, "war and revolution ended those plans" and "we were able to buy the building for our purposes."[64] To conservatives, the Institute symbolized all that was wrong with the Weimar Republic. A right-wing, antisemitic newspaper lost little time in denouncing it as a site of the "homosexual seduction" of youth that ought to be shut down for the "moral renewal of the German Volk" as well as in the interest of the national birth rate, particularly in view of the two million soldiers recently killed in the war.[65] The Prussian Welfare Ministry, which was controlled by the Centre Party, demanded a police investigation of the newspaper's claims. In response, the Berlin police, who were under the Prussian Interior Ministry (a Social Democratic stronghold), defended the Institute. Demonstrating the depth of support for the Institute in Social Democratic circles, a police official wrote that scientific research into "sexual life ... can only be welcomed" and defended the Institute's advocacy of the "not uncommon opinion that homosexuality is not a vice, but rather an inborn predisposition."[66] Under the Republic, the Institute suffered no further attempts to shut it down.

Scope, Limits, and Source Base

Before detailing the major battles over legal reforms, the settlement that they resulted in, and the role of that settlement in the rise of the NSDAP, it is necessary to clarify the scope, limits, and source base of this study: to whom do its conclusions apply, and on what sorts of research are those conclusions based? First is the question of whether the politics of immoral sexuality mattered. Gay subcultures have been identified as a marginal issue affecting only a minority of Germans.[67] But the debates chronicled in this book touched millions of lives. They delineated the boundaries of legal, respectable sexuality, not only for sexual "abnormals" but for "normals" as well. Second, this study is based on extensive archival research. Much of this was on government files at the *Reich* (federal) level, the *Land* (provincial) level in Prussia, and the municipal level in Berlin and Munich. I examined municipal records in Munich in order to avoid too much focus on Berlin. Munich in the Weimar years was the right-leaning counterpart to Red Berlin and was less tolerant of homosexual subcultures, though not completely closed to them. Prussia was Germany's largest province under the Republic, containing Berlin as well as a number of smaller cities including Cologne and Frankfurt am Main and home to about thirty-eight million people, three-fifths of the total national population of about sixty-two million.[68] Bavaria, with its capital Munich, was the second-largest province. It had a population of roughly seven million.[69] Archival sources for this study are, however, not limited to government files. They also encompass a wealth of published material – newspapers, magazines, journals, and books, including memoirs by some of the key actors. The published material details happenings in Leipzig, Hamburg, and elsewhere. My research did concentrate on certain forms of immoral sexuality and not others. It was especially focused on sexuality that Germans at the time deemed non-reproductive. Heterosexual reproductive sex has already been examined in detail by a number of historians. On the issues of birth control and abortion in particular, I have drawn on the excellent existing scholarship.[70]

The limited role that ideas about race and sexuality play in this study calls for comment. The political compromise I call the Weimar settlement employed, above all, class, "respectability," public-ness, and disability – particularly notions about mental disability – to distinguish among subjects. Race could also act as a fundamental distinguisher in Weimar-era sexual politics. But it came up relatively rarely in connection with the national politics of homosexuality, prostitution, pornography, abortion, and birth control. Antisemitism was central to the NSDAP's politics of immorality, but less so to that of non-fascist conservatives. Ideas about Africans and people of African descent were also important in Weimar-era sexual politics, but with respect to events that this book does not have occasion to discuss.[71] The sexual politics of blackness was most clear in what can only be described as a national hysteria about the supposed violent hypersexuality of black men that gripped white Germans in the early 1920s.[72] It was also apparent in calls during the Weimar era to sterilize the children of white mothers and black fathers.[73] In addition, the hegemonic discourse of race and sexuality in the Weimar years was such that relationships between black men and white women could be casually defined as intrinsically immoral. As an official of the Colonial Office put it in 1916, "A marriage between white women and natives of our colonies must be considered immoral [unsittlich] in the sense of the law, because the natives are at a lower cultural level and do not understand Christian marriage."[74] Ideas such as this one were alive and well after 1918: the Weimar Republic's bureaucrats sought, in several cases, to disrupt the marriages of black men and white women.[75] As Fatima El-Tayeb shows, whiteness was fundamental to how white Germans understood their sexuality.[76] Black Germans and black people living in Germany dealt on a daily basis with the racist notions that most white Germans held about their sexuality. Yet the Weimar settlement as expressed in legislation and in national debates largely assumed – incorrectly – that Germans were white.

A reader might raise another question about scope: the question of whether immorality was more abundant in urban spaces. Indeed, popular perceptions at the time associated immorality with the big cities.[77] And in some respects, the forms of immorality that the Republic came to tolerate were less available in rural spaces. Magazines for gay men, lesbians, and transvestites, for example, could be had by subscription in small towns but probably could not be purchased from a small-town magazine dealer. Gay bars and clubs were features of cities and towns, though meeting places and cruising spots were not limited to urban spaces. The reform to laws on female prostitution was more restrictive in rural places than elsewhere; it banned street soliciting in small towns. Yet the urban/rural divide was less solid than one might imagine. Lesbian culture was not limited to big cities like Berlin, Hamburg, and Dresden; lesbian events also took place in smaller cities like Barmen-Elberfeld (later Wuppertal), Bielefeld, Chemnitz, and Zwickau.[78] Homosexual emancipation groups with large male memberships were not restricted to Berlin and Hamburg: in 1932, the League for Human Rights (*Bund für Menschenrecht*) had active chapters in Braunschweig, Breslau, Mannheim, Weimar, Nuremberg, and Cologne, among other places.[79] Substantial portions of the major lesbian novel of the era, Anna Elisabet Weirauch's *The Scorpion* (*Der Skorpion*, published in three volumes between 1919 and 1931) are set in the countryside, and the book critiques the conservative, bourgeoisie notion that perversion resided exclusively in cities.[80] Relatively inexpensive travel, together with very high literacy rates, a thriving print culture, and a cheap postal service, all made homosexual and transvestite subcultures accessible to many people living in smaller cities, towns, and rural areas, although this was more true of those who had financial means than it was of those who did not. The public education campaign about venereal disease travelled around the country in exhibitions and films, showing up in small towns as well as at the 1922 Oktoberfest in Munich, where adults could view a display about how to avoid infection.[81] Not only were cultural representations of abortion politics widely consumed, but birth control, abortion, and the laws pertaining to them were "everyday" matters in rural villages.[82]

Chapter Outline

This book's first four chapters examine three of the major legal reforms that, to conservatives, raised the problem of immorality – for reformers, these reforms held out the possibility of a humane, secular, and scientific state response to sexuality. The first two chapters investigate censorship and how it affected gay male, lesbian, and transvestite subcultures.

Chapter 1 examines the battle over censorship in the Republic's early years. The Revolution opened a window of relatively lax censorship that people with progressive views on sexuality rushed to make use of; conservatives, for their part, believed that the Revolution and the diminishment of censorship had sucked Germany into a "swamp" of immorality. Though conservatives succeeded in reinstating censorship, they never got the strict censorship they wanted. Homosexual emancipationists, emboldened by the experience of war and revolution, fought for and won some space for their publications. Chapter 2, which looks specifically at lesbian and transvestite subcultures, examines how this constrained but nevertheless public sphere changed the homosexual emancipation movement. Media helped homosexual emancipation grow into a more diverse, mass movement. Yet although lesbian sex was not a crime, depictions of lesbianism were targets of censorship. Rather than a simple liberalization, this was a new mode of management or containment animated by the idea that queer sexuality ought to be kept out of the wider public realm and away from impressionable young people.

Chapters 3 and 4 investigate two legal reforms, on female prostitution and male homosexuality respectively, that, like censorship policy, opened up greater freedom of sexual expression within limits. As chapter 3 describes, in 1927, new legislation changed the state's response to female prostitution and venereal disease. Chapter 4 relates how in 1929, homosexual emancipation nearly achieved its central goal when a committee of the Reichstag voted to repeal the sodomy law. But sexual liberation came with conditions. It was to be exercised discreetly. Most reformers did not intend to entirely do away with the social stigmas on prostitution, pornography, and homosexuality; rather, they sought to conceal such sexual expressions in private. This move appealed to conservatives. It did not appeal to some female prostitutes, and it furthermore came along with new duties for heterosexual couples. It also split the homosexual emancipation movement, as activists struggled over how to react to a proposed crackdown on male prostitution that was a condition of the decriminalization of non-commercial male-male sex.

Chapter 5 begins a two-chapter investigation of the extent to which the relatively tolerant sexual politics of the Republic were connected to the rise of the Nazis. It examines the case in which they most clearly were: the 1931–2 scandal about the homosexuality of Ernst Röhm, a top Nazi. The allegations about Röhm's homosexuality were widely known at a time when the NSDAP made important gains at the polls. Moreover, press coverage demonstrates that some of the arguments that homosexual emancipation had made for decades had become widely viable: even right-wing journalists argued that Röhm's sexuality was not a matter of public concern. This does not necessarily mean that a majority of Germans agreed with homosexual emancipation by the early 1930s, but it does show that homosexual emancipation had succeeded enough that it was relatively easy for people to ignore the Röhm scandal if they wished to do so. Ironically, in this way, the vehemently homophobic NSDAP benefited from homosexual emancipation. Chapter 6 challenges the view that the Nazis came to power on a "backlash" against Weimar-era reforms to laws on sexuality. Contrary to much recent scholarship, I argue that the NSDAP did not gain significant numbers of voters thanks to its sexual politics. Neither did the politics of sex help it to attract the support of a formerly democratic party, the Catholic Centre Party. Yet, despite the fact that the evidence points to only a tertiary effect for sexual politics in the Republic's fall, the notion that sex brought down the Weimar Republic is a durable one, evident in the work of key historians after 1945 and in popular culture, and will probably persist; I examine, at the end of this chapter, why that is the case.

This book concludes that the Weimar Republic established a compromise on the politics of immoral sexuality. I term this compromise the "Weimar settlement on sexual politics." It offered liberation to many at the expense of a few and employed biology and psychiatry to define these few. It entailed new duties for citizens that had to do with sexuality, particularly with heterosexuality. It had limits. One of the settlement's central premises was that homosexuality, female prostitution, and non-scientific media about sexuality ought to remain out of most of the public sphere. The significance of the politics of sex under the Republic was not that it helped the Nazis take power. Rather, these sexual politics are significant because they demonstrate the first instance of a type of sexual liberation that became an influential model for the rest of the twentieth century and beyond.

1 Homosexual Emancipation, Censorship, and the Revolution of 1918–1919

In 1921, the Munich police shut down Café Zehner. The raid was one of several against cafés and bars that had become informal gathering spots for gay men (and probably some lesbians) in Munich in the years after the First World War.[1] But the closing of this particular café sparked a resistance movement. It inspired four men to found a political group, a group dedicated to what they described as the "fight for equal rights and for a just assessment of people who have a same-sex orientation," the Munich Friendship League (*Münchner Freundschaftsbund*).[2] The group's leader, a twenty-one-year-old veteran of the war named Richard Linsert, applied to register the Munich Friendship League in the city's official list of clubs. Unlike the informal gatherings that had taken place at Café Zehner before the raid, Linsert wrote, the new group would not shy away from "the light of day."[3] This alarmed the police. They claimed that the Munich Friendship League was nothing but a conspiracy of male homosexuals seeking "new victims" – adolescent boys.[4] When police blocked Linsert's application to register the League, Linsert hired a lawyer, who made a bold argument: in Germany's new democracy, men who loved other men had a right to organize in public. The lawyer asserted, "Here in the German Reich a person enjoys equality of rights." Included among the "rights of citizens" granted by the Weimar Republic's constitution, he claimed, was the right to associate in clubs such as the Munich Friendship League, the purpose of which was "a struggle for justice" by "same-sex orientated men."[5]

Linsert would go on to become an important leader of the homosexual emancipation movement. He fought to establish the Munich Friendship League because he and his allies believed that war, revolution, and democracy had engendered a new era, an era in which "homoerotics" could step out of the shadows and demand the equality that they, as citizens, were due. This sentiment inspired thousands of men in the years after the First World War. Max Danielsen, one of the editors of the important new homosexual emancipation magazine *Friendship* (*Freundschaft*), wrote that after "the world war swept disaster over the old world" and "unconquered, but broken, the German Volk collapsed ... A new age dawned! The hour of liberation is now or never, for us ... We, the ostracized, persecuted, and misjudged, are set aglow by a new age of equal respect and equality."[6] Belief in a new age inspired the founding of *Friendship* less than a year after the kaiser fell.[7] The magazine reached a national audience and became a vital means of organization for the "friendship leagues," homosexual emancipation groups like Linsert's that sprang up just after the war in Berlin, Düsseldorf, Frankfurt am Main, Stuttgart, Hamburg, Dresden, Kassel, and other cities.[8] The friendship leagues were the beginning of an important transformation of homosexual emancipation: it became a mass movement, and a more diverse one. Yet, as soon as *Friendship* hit street kiosks, conservative forces within the government tried to censor it. They put the magazine's staff on trial for violating the obscenity law.

This chapter is about the historical context of the Munich Friendship League and the larger friendship league movement of which it and *Friendship* magazine were part. That context was the Republic's early years, when a sense of historical rupture prevailed and when conservatives fought to establish strict censorship of media about sexuality in order to rescue Germany from a "flood" of immorality. After an initial section that reviews the sexual politics of the imperial period, in which Weimar-era debates had their roots, the chapter makes three related arguments about how the politics of sex changed in 1918 despite precedents before 1914. The first argument is that many Germans shared a widespread perception that war, revolution, and democracy had put transformative stresses on norms of gender and sexuality. This argument responds to a trend in the historiography of the Weimar Republic to portray the Revolution of 1918–19 as not so revolutionary. In fact, when it came to questions of sexuality and gender, people felt themselves to be in the throes of revolutionary change. This first argument also demonstrates a point of rupture between the Weimar period and the imperial period. The second argument is that 1918–19 brought a material change to government policies on the censorship of media about sexuality, a relaxing of censorship that conservatives fought to undo but never succeeded in entirely rolling back. Third, I argue that 1918–19 transformed homosexual emancipation: in the Weimar era, it grew into a mass movement that demanded equal rights and invoked a rhetoric of citizenship invigorated by the war. These three changes came together in the battles over *Friendship* magazine. The chapter's fourth section examines how homosexual emancipationists successfully defended *Friendship* and the rest of the queer press, carving out a limited public sphere in which to publish. The limits on that sphere are important – they resulted from the failure of homosexual emancipation to entirely defeat the chief argument made by censorship proponents, which was that media could seduce young people into homosexuality. This notion of seduction through media would continue to be key to Weimar-era sexual politics and especially to the politics of homosexuality. The persistence of ideas about seduction meant that despite relative media freedom, homosexual emancipationists would not have an easy time under the Republic, as a final section on the suppression of Linsert's friendship league demonstrates.

The Politics of Sex in Imperial Germany

Before the First World War, imperial Germany was the site of a wide-ranging and complex debate between people who thought Christian mores ought to govern gender and sexuality and people who thought that principles based in secularism, individual rights, and science ought to do so. It is worth presenting an abbreviated review of the sex and gender politics of imperial Germany because they were precursors to the Republic's sexual politics.[9] Many of the players and the issues that would form sexual politics under the Republic took shape under the kaiser, as Germans staged a debate on sexuality, gender, and the state that grew increasingly vehement just before the war. By 1913, Edward Ross Dickinson writes, issues of sex were "among the most contentious in German politics."[10] Parties to this debate all sought to enlist the state in the service of their agendas, as they would continue to do under the Republic.[11] However, 1918 brought important changes: a perceived new era of sex and gender, material changes to censorship, and the rise of a new phase of homosexual emancipation.

By 1900, a number of movements contested the gender and sexual order. Among these were the Social Democratic Party, which grew to become the largest party in the Reichstag just before the First World War, and the women's movement. Social Democracy's official agenda included women's suffrage, legal equality for men and women, and reforms to marriage and divorce law.[12] In his widely read book *Women under Socialism*, August Bebel, the party's leader, criticized Christian marriage. He argued that men and women needed satisfying sex in order to preserve their mental and physical health and that sexual satisfaction was a private matter.[13] The women's movement was diverse. It included middle-class Jewish women's organizations; moderate, conservative, and right-wing middle-class women's organizations; the Social Democratic women's movement; and a radical left wing that championed sex reform.[14] Although the agendas of the various women's groups varied greatly, many moderates and leftists advocated greater female participation in politics and social policy, better work conditions and professional opportunities for women, and legal equality. Some middle-class women's groups also worked to abolish state-regulated female prostitution. Like Social Democracy, women's groups involved many Germans. Just before the war, a national umbrella group of middle-class women's groups claimed half a million members.[15]

Late imperial Germany was also home to smaller, more radical groups that increasingly contended that science, not Christian morality, ought to be the central organizing principle of sexuality.[16] The German Society for Combating Venereal Diseases (*Deutsche Gesellschaft zur Bekämpfung der Geschlechtskrankheiten*) was a doctors' league that favoured a public health response to the problem of venereal disease.[17] Radical feminists in the League for the Protection of Mothers and Sexual Reform (*Bund für Mutterschutz und Sexualreform*) advocated the end of patriarchal marriage, better access to birth control, milder penalties for abortion (which was a crime), sex education in schools, easier divorce, and legal and social support for single mothers and their children.[18] Helene Stöcker, the League's leader, developed a philosophy of the "new ethic" (*neue Ethik*), a Nietzschean, secular code to govern sexuality in place of religious mores.[19] Later, under the Republic, Stöcker would have a direct influence on public policy through her leadership of the sex reform movement, which established municipal marriage and sex advice clinics.[20] She was moreover an influential figure in unaffiliated leftist intellectual circles and had a close relationship with Hirschfeld's Scientific Humanitarian Committee (WhK) and with Kurt Hiller.[21] Although much of what Stöcker advocated, such as real legal equality for men and women, did not come to pass under the Republic, she wrote in 1929 "we have in the last decade already begun to see the result of … the hard fight for personal freedom, for personal responsibility [*Selbstverantwortung*] in love and marriage" in the banishment of the old "darkness of prejudice" by the light of science.[22] The state, she argued, should only intervene in sexual life in order to protect mothers and children; otherwise, sexuality should be governed by "a new sexual culture" of "sexual responsibility," not by Christian morality or by law.[23]

Homosexual emancipation itself dated to at least the 1890s, if not earlier. Advocacy on behalf of male-male eroticism and against sodomy laws in German-speaking Europe has a very long history. Ideas that meet these rough parameters are evident in Heinrich Hössli's work in the 1830s.[24] The first medical studies in the German-speaking world of men who had sex with men came out in the mid-nineteenth century.[25] The most important early advocate of "man-manly love," the lawyer Karl Heinrich Ulrichs, began to publicly defend "Urnings" in the 1860s.[26] In the years around 1900, hundreds of books and pamphlets on homosexuality were published.[27] Among them was the first homosexual emancipation magazine, *Der Eigene* (*The Special/The Self-Owning Subject*),[28] which the twenty-one-year-old Adolf Brand founded in 1896. The following year, Magnus Hirschfeld co-founded homosexual emancipation's first organization, the Scientific Humanitarian Committee, and it presented its first petition to the Reichstag calling for the repeal of Paragraph 175.[29] Although this and subsequent WhK petitions did not succeed, their signatories included hundreds of notable men, including Albert Einstein and Thomas Mann, as well as a few women.[30] In 1903, Brand founded his own group, the Society of the Self-Owned/Special (*Gemeinschaft der Eigenen*, GdE).[31] Judged by its membership, homosexual emancipation was a tiny movement. In the summer of 1914, the WhK counted 105 members.[32] But homosexual emancipation received a lot of attention and had some high-profile allies. The WhK had one of its greatest successes of the imperial period in 1898, when SPD leader Bebel denounced Paragraph 175 in a Reichstag speech.[33] Hirschfeld gained a national audience as a controversial expert on homosexuality when a series of scandals implicated the highest levels of the kaiser's government in male homosexuality. These scandals were the Krupp suicide of 1902, followed by the accusations and trials from 1906 to 1909 known as the Eulenburg/Moltke Affair.[34]

Not surprisingly, conservatives opposed efforts to reform gender and sexuality. Some of the conservatives who fought what they perceived as the immoral condition of German society and culture under the kaiser went on to become important foes of homosexual emancipation after the war. The "moral purity movement" (*Sittlichkeitsbewegung*), which by 1914 had separate men's and women's as well as Protestant and Catholic groups, sought to eliminate female prostitution, to curtail "filthy" and "trashy" media, to suppress contraception and abortion, to discourage extramarital sex, to stave off calls for legal equality between the sexes, and to quash homosexual emancipation.[35] Their conservative, Christian perspective took sexuality to be a dangerous and potentially destructive force that had to be mastered by the individual and held in check by the church, the state, and the law.[36] They blamed both Social Democracy and capitalist materialism for immorality.[37] The moral purity groups were relatively small, with memberships in the thousands.[38] But their message appealed to many conservatives beyond their ranks. They also had political clout. Some of the Protestant groups had connections to right-wing, antisemitic politicians in the Reichstag, and the leadership of some of the Catholic groups overlapped with the membership of the Centre Party's Reichstag faction.[39] Their ideology remained relatively consistent under the Republic. And their concerns were not frivolous. Men in this movement believed that if Germans, particularly men, could not master their sexual desires and could not obey religious authority on sexual matters, their mastery over the rest of their human selves would falter. The nation would descend into anarchy. A disorganized and weak population would be unable to meet foreign threats.[40] Conservative women in this movement agreed with their male counterparts that women were inherently moral, while men were prey to animal lusts, though unlike many male activists, they thought women ought to have a role in addressing this problem in politics and social policy.[41] Particularly male activists also feared for the falling birth rate.[42] During the Weimar years, these anxieties were shared, to a certain extent, by many conservative Germans.

Thus many of the basic elements of what would become Weimar-era sexual politics were present under the kaiser. Some of the most important pressure groups had already been active for decades prior to the war: moral purity organizations, conservative women's movement groups, conservative politicians, the Catholic Centre Party, middle-class liberals and their political parties, members of the moderate women's movement, the Social Democrats, sexologists, sex reformers and radical feminists, and the homosexual emancipation movement. The issues that these players would struggle over in the Weimar period had already been raised by the 1890s, if not before: female prostitution; women's equality with men; censorship of "filthy" and "trashy" media; homosexuality; birth control, abortion, and the falling birth rate; venereal disease; divorce and marital law. Although all sides succeeded in shaping public policy to a certain extent, the conservative forces had an advantage in the years just before the war because they were increasingly united while their opponents were not; a note of triumph crept into their discourse.[43]

Yet the First World War upended norms of gender and sexuality in belligerent countries. In the aftermath of the war, defenders of traditional gender roles across Europe believed that they had to reshape masculinity and femininity in order to reconstruct their nations.[44] Germans, too, believed that the war and revolution had eroded traditional norms.[45] And in a material sense, they had: in Germany, war, revolution, and democracy created new actors in sexual politics, like the friendship leagues. War, revolution, and democracy also shifted the balance of power among the existing players, changing what was possible and inspiring bold visions of reform. Although imperial Germany had not been entirely repressive on issues of sexuality, after 1918 these questions would be decided in a parliamentary democracy with universal adult suffrage, and that, too, changed what was possible.

1918–1919: The Collapse of the Dictatorship of Tradition

The belief that the war, the Revolution, and the new democracy had ushered in "a new age" of gender and sexuality was not confined to Richard Linsert and his fellow homosexual emancipationists in Munich: it was widely shared and often expressed by people of diverse political commitments. That is, whether or not change was in reality all that dramatic, many people perceived a dramatic change. Change was, thus, affective and epistemological, and this perceived change had lasting effects. Peoples' experience of change shaped how they acted and ultimately shaped the state that they built. In 1924, the *Kölnische Zeitung*, a major conservative daily in the Rhineland that backed the DNVP, published a front-page article on this.[46] "Each era has a different erotic morality," the paper informed its readers. "Ten years ago, none of us thought possible some of what we live with today ... We have, doubtless, experienced a sexual revolution over the course of a certain number of years, and even if it has not done us much good, it is a reality."[47] This author, like many such commentators, was aware that norms of gender and sexuality had undergone profound changes well before 1918; he or she noted that nineteenth-century industrialization was in part "guilty" for sexual revolution. Yet, as was typical of Weimar-era commentators, the author focused not on the longue durée but on what he or she was experiencing as a dramatic, short-term transformation between 1914 and the mid-1920s.[48]

Readers familiar with the imperial period might question whether this was all that new, given that various voices in German society had been warning of the corruption of norms of gender and sexuality since the nineteenth century. But there was something new in 1918–19, or so commentators asserted. Even those who had complained of moral dissolution before the war spoke about how 1918 had changed the game. Take, for example, the West German Morality League (*Westdeutscher Sittlichkeitsverein*), one of the two major Protestant moral purity groups of imperial Germany, founded in 1885 by Ludwig Weber.[49] Just before the war, the West German Morality League's discourse was not unlike what it would become after 1918–19. In 1913, the club warned that though Germany had developed a more powerful industrial economy since the 1870s, it had lost "strict public morality."[50] Yet the war brought new concerns, like military brothels, fatherless youths, promiscuous women on the home front, and the effect of millions of battlefield deaths on the national birth rate.[51] And when the war ended, the sexual-moral circumstances did not improve. Quite the contrary. The West German Morality League's publications just after the armistice reflect the sense that the bottom had suddenly dropped out: 1918 brought "moral collapse."[52] "Now we sit in a swamp" of "disgracefulness and immorality," lamented the November/December 1918 issue of the League's journal.[53] Prior to the war, these activists had identified the Social Democratic Party as a cause of moral decline.[54] So it is not surprising that when the kaiser fell and the SPD headed a transitional government, moral purity activists foresaw the end of German civilization. At the West German Morality League's first meeting following the war, in the spring of 1919, one of its leaders declared that "immorality has won the field ... the true nature of people has been made plain by the Revolution. The beast in humanity was released and has become master."[55] As evidence of this, he pointed to "crime and the waywardness [*Verwilderung*] of youth," as well as "moral filth [*Schmutz*] in cinemas and theatres" and "trashy literature [*Schundliteratur*]." A 1919 club publication described a "moral emergency" in progress that menaced youth and the family: "racketeering [*Schieberei*] and profiteering [*Wucherei*]," "pleasure-seeking and dancing in their crassest forms," gambling, movies with sexual content, prostitution, venereal disease, and divorce.[56] The West German Morality League had been complaining of "moral decline" since well before 1918, but League members claimed – and apparently sincerely believed – that the war's conclusion and the Revolution had plunged Germany into a moral abyss the likes of which had not yet been seen.

As long as the Weimar Republic existed, people who took a conservative view of sex and gender – from moderates in the Centre Party to antisemites on the Far Right – blamed "moral collapse" on the First World

War, the Revolution, and democracy. The Centre Party organ *Germania* claimed in 1932 that although "the moral degeneration in our big cities" did not begin in 1918, "it is undeniable that in the post-war period, the loosening of morals stemming from liberalism continued to spread."[57] In the early 1930s, a Chemnitz court convicted a man of obscenity for promoting birth control. In its decision, the court reflected on historical change: "The four years of World War and the subsequent overthrow [*Umsturz*] of the state caused a moral waywardness [*Verwilderung*] to break out in many areas of society, undermining the appreciation for chastity and convention [*Sitte*]." Resolute in its optimism, the court concluded that, nevertheless, "the vast majority of the population is of a Christian-religious worldview and ... glorifies chastity as a virtue."[58] The anti-feminist author Max Bauer wrote, "In the post-war period ... the traditions of morals and morality are marginalized [*an die Wand gedrückt*], they are called quaint and petty bourgeois [*kleinbürgerlich*], and now they will never again be standards [*Norm*] in their customary forms."[59] Bauer acknowledged that this change had roots stretching back before 1918. Yet at the same time, he portrayed the post-war period as a distinctly bad age characterized by increasing female prostitution, jazz music ("nigger songs"), and the accoutrements of women's liberation – female suffrage, the pageboy haircut (*Bubikopf*), the flapper (*Backfisch*), and female cigarette smoking. An antisemitic version of this story was a favourite of the Far Right: "the Jewish November revolution" and Magnus Hirschfeld had set off a "homosexual plague" spreading across Germany along with other forms of moral decay.[60]

Given the intense interest during the Weimar period in "the politics of population" (*Bevölkerungspolitik*), and the attention of historians to that interest,[61] it is worth emphasizing that people who complained of "moral collapse" often did not relate their fears to the falling birth rate. Many conservatives agreed with population experts that the falling birth rate was a problem, especially in light of massive war casualties. But they cared as much, if not more, about the nation's spiritual character, and they did not always see the two issues as necessarily related.

Beyond conservative circles, people whose views on gender and sexuality ranged from moderately progressive to radical also perceived change, which they often met with a sense of hopeful possibility. Kathleen Canning writes that the trauma of defeat and revolution at the Weimar Republic's beginning "ripped open the fabrics of possibility and required that they be stitched together again and again throughout the 1920s."[62]

The sense of possibility in 1918–19 is apparent in the comments made by a diverse group of individuals. Radical feminist Stöcker abhorred the violence of the war and the bloody civil strife in Germany that followed it. Yet she also felt hope for the openness of the future. She wrote in the fall of 1918, "For the first time in world history, from this defeat on the battlefield, a truly new reconstruction of the world should emerge."[63] The novelist Vicki Baum remembered in the 1960s that the Revolution brought "immense relief ... great hopes and promises for a free, shining future in most quarters. Only a small minority of professional soldiers, diehards, and inexperienced young hotheads seemed to care about the lost war."[64]

Voices in Social Democratic circles also declared hopefully that these were new times. In 1919, an author in a Social Democratic women's journal presaged the far-reaching prostitution reform of 1927 when she called prostitution "a remnant of the old Germany, which burst asunder and which was filled with so much rot and decay," and avowed that prostitution "must no longer have a place in our young republic."[65] The Social Democratic organ *Vorwärts* described young middle-class women who were choosing the pageboy haircut (*Bubikopf*). The haircut was, supposedly, a sign that these women had "rebel[led] against the dictatorship of tradition," that is, against the militaristic ethos of imperial Germany, to which their parents clung.[66] *Vorwärts* wrote that these young women were influenced by "the new times," were "democratic," and were concerned for "the common good of all women and girls." The lesbian magazine *Girlfriend* (*Die Freundin*) reprinted *Vorwärts*'s story on the pageboy in order to make the point that what was really at stake for some young women was gender identity. "For many people, it's about taking control of their life and dressing as much as possible like a boy, because that's their natural predisposition. The parents would do much better if instead of complaining about the 'corrupt and crazy times,' they took note of the mental life of their children" and accepted them for who they really were, masculine young women and feminine young men.[67] Both of the authors who weighed in on the pageboy haircut claimed that the Revolution had overthrown a "dictatorship of tradition" in matters of gender and sexual expression. Of course, neither *Vorwärts*'s nor *Girlfriend*'s interpretation of what the *Bubikopf* meant purported to actually represent the voices of any young women with short haircuts. But "G.M.," a self-identified female homosexual and leftist who was a young woman in the 1920s, remembered many years later that in the Weimar era, "I personally had and experienced [*durchlebte*] a feeling of freedom, the Wilhelmine braids [*Zöpfe*] had fallen, the opinions and views of the parents were not valid anymore, at least not for me."[68]

Queer voices named 1918–19 as a moment of rupture, and for the better. Just after the Revolution, Hirschfeld wrote,

> From our standpoint, the great revolution [*Umwälzung*] of the last week can only be greeted with joy. The new era brings us freedom of speech and publication, and with the liberation of all who were formerly oppressed, we may with certainty assume that those upon whose behalf we have worked for many years will also receive an equitable assessment.[69]

Ruth Roellig, a leading light of Berlin's lesbian scene, wrote in 1928, "In these times since the Revolution a very significant change has arrived – people have become more tolerant – particularly in Berlin – with regard to these things that existed before and cannot be denied" [that is, male and female homosexuality].[70] In a 1931 lecture at a transvestite club, Marie Weis acknowledged that although not all that democracy had promised in 1918, such as press freedom and socialized industry, had come to pass, when Germany "transformed itself into a democratic Republic ... it seemed as if with the collapse of the moribund monarchy, dogmatic and conservative moral theology ceased to rule our lives."[71] A sympathetic observer of Berlin's transvestite scenes remembered that it was first "with the drastic political change [*politischer Umschwung*]" of 1918 that many transvestites had the courage to enter the public sphere.[72] Authors in *Friendship* magazine declared again and again that "the dawn of a new age has broken for inverts"[73] and that "our hour of freedom has come."[74] Many homosexual emancipationists, including Hirschfeld, assumed that the new Republic would treat them more equitably: they expected it to quickly nullify the sodomy law.[75] The new regime was, after all, initially dominated by the Social Democrats, who had long opposed the law. And surely such a law was incompatible with the freedom citizens enjoyed in a democracy. The Scientific Humanitarian Committee told the new Reich Minister of Justice in February 1919 that after the "great revolution," the sodomy law could no longer be tolerated.[76]

The expectations that left-leaning people held for the post-war era were not entirely unfounded. The Revolution shifted power towards reformers. It did so at the cost of conservatives. The new regime put Social Democrats, liberals, and in some cases Communists into key positions at the national, provincial, and municipal levels.[77] They threw their weight behind progressive feminist and sex reform causes. They funded municipal clinics that distributed information about birth control and abortion.[78] They backed Hirschfeld's new Institute for Sexual Science. They declined to strictly censor media about sexuality. The Weimar Republic was not a project of Social Democracy. Yet hopes for reform in the early Weimar years were not without some cause.

In short, although conservative Christian morality did not rule by fiat under the kaiser, and the Weimar Republic did not obliterate it, the landscape of sexual politics changed in 1918–19.[79] One aspect of this change was a shared sense of historical rupture. The perception of change was in and of itself a "real" historical phenomenon. Sex and gender radicals as well as conservatives shared the conviction that they were living in "new times." It influenced how they acted and shaped the politics of the Weimar Republic.

The Losing Battle for Strict Censorship

The fall of the kaiser and the Republic's founding set off a second change: censorship of media about sexuality grew more lax. This change was prompted by perceptions of a new era in gender and sexuality. It also helped to foment what conservatives decried as "sexual revolution." Though censorship of media with sexual content had not been all that strict prior to 1914, it had been strict under military government during the war, and the Revolution opened a window of media freedom. Conservatives fought to shut it.[80] They did this because they believed that media about immoral sexuality was spreading immoral sexuality, imperilling the nation. This section of the chapter argues that censorship changed in important ways after 1918 and that, ultimately, conservatives were unable to institute the stricter control that they wanted. As a result, media about sexuality circulated more freely under the Republic, although within limits.

The First World War empowered a well-established movement against "filth" and "trash" publications (*Schmutz und Schund*) that had thrived for decades in imperial Germany.[81] This movement, which overlapped with the moral purity groups, distinguished two kinds of bad media. "Filth" (*Schmutz*) was media with sexual content, not only explicit depictions of nudity and sex acts but also information about sex or sexuality, such as publications about birth control and homosexual emancipation. "Trash" (*Schund*) was frivolous and insipid fare, such as cowboy adventures and detective stories that supposedly glorified crime.[82] Under the High Command, the censors abandoned the precepts of the *Kaiserreich* and censorship became truly strict.[83] Military authorities closed loop-holes that had frustrated conservative censorship advocates before 1914.[84] They suppressed all kinds of media, from theatrical entertain-ments to reports of unrest among women about high food prices and scarcity, from pacifist sentiments to so-called trash publications.[85] They also suppressed print media that dealt with issues of sexuality regardless of the legal definition of obscenity, banning publications on homosexual emancipation as well as on flagellantism, fetishism, masochism, sadism, sexual hygiene, prostitution, free love, and sex reform.[86] The military went beyond existing law and banned not only the advertising of materi-als for birth control and abortion, but the sale of these as well.[87]

The Revolution and the war's conclusion disrupted the relatively strict censorship that had prevailed under military rule. When military author-ities abruptly withdrew, the police divisions responsible for enforcing the obscenity law were caught unprepared.[88] Military regulations that had suppressed objectionable media in wartime could not be retained in peacetime, as the federal government acknowledged later in its justifica-tion for a new, post-war law to protect youth from filth and trash.[89] Mili-tary censorship had covered far more material than Germany's existing laws did, and though police acted to enforce the laws on the books in the Republic's early years, the effect was often that they seemed to be doing little.[90] The police were also initially confused about the legal grounds of censorship under the new constitution.[91] The revolutionary era rang with leftists' declarations of the abolition of censorship.[92]

Just as the censors stumbled, publishers and artists who were inspired by their sense of a new era of freedom rushed to produce a wide array of media that dealt with gender and sexuality, from nude modern dance to new magazines for gay men. Contraceptive manufacturers hurried to take advantage of improved opportunities to distribute their products; they flooded newspapers with advertisements.[93] Because of the Revolu-tion, the Berlin police reported in 1919, "many assumed that political freedom also meant unbounded freedom for obscene press materials and accordingly, the most coarse obscenities came to be hawked on the streets."[94] A Berlin prosecutor wrote in 1921, "Nothing has been as demoralizing for the Volk as the inundation of the market since the abo-lition of the censor with obscene and lewd print media of different sorts. One filthy magazine is barely driven out of the public realm when more of the same character appear." In addition, books "of the lowest sort" were "thrown onto the market en masse" and pictures that depicted "sexual acts of a perverse nature" were sold on the streets.[95]

For film too, a window of relative freedom opened in the early 1920s. The Revolution abolished the *Kaiserreich*'s practice of vetting films prior to their release, allowing for the premiere of what was most likely the world's first gay rights film. This was *Different from the Others* (*Anders als die Andern*), directed by Richard Oswald and co-written by Magnus Hirschfeld, who appears in the film as himself. *Different from the Others* tells the unhappy story of a talented violinist driven to suicide by a black-mailer. The film's conclusion calls for the repeal of the sodomy law. It screened in theatres across Germany.[96] In Berlin, one of Germany's best-known crusaders against filth and trash, Karl Brunner, showed up at a screening, stood up in the middle of the film, and loudly denounced it as "swinish filth." The director Oswald shouted him down.[97] *Different from the Others* was one of a series of public education films (*Aufklärungs-filme*) that came out in the early Weimar period, to the consternation of censorship proponents.[98] Some of these films were genuine efforts to improve public health, in which doctors educated viewers about sexual matters like venereal disease and prostitution.[99] Others, like *Hyenas of Pleasure*, were less educational.[100]

Brunner and other conservatives were incensed by all of this media because in it, they saw a grave threat to Germany's future. The problem with filth, according to them, was that it was actually changing how Germans had sex – and for the worse. Though censorship advocates were a relatively diverse group, stretching from moderate, democratic conservatives in the Centre Party all the way to the Far Right, they shared an ideology that made the stakes of censorship politics seem very high: media about sexuality could awaken the wrong kinds of erotic feelings in a reader or viewer. This was particularly true if the reader or viewer was in the midst of puberty, when the sex drive was malleable. If the sex drives of adolescent males were awakened prematurely and pushed in the wrong direction, youths would grow into adults who sought out pornography, extramarital heterosexual sex, and female prostitutes. Girls who were corrupted in this way would disdain marriage in favour of casual sex with men. And the wrong kind of media could suck people of either sex into homosexual desire. Karl Brunner gave voice to this ideology. Brunner was a former secondary school (*Gymnasium*) teacher. Prior to 1914, he had gained a national reputation as a crusader against filth and trash. He had also worked as a film and literature expert for the Berlin police before the war, and he resumed this work after the war.[101] He called for strict censorship to protect young people – who were in the midst of the life stage of "moral development" – from "threatening print materials [*Schrifttum*]," which he held to be "chiefly guilty for today's 'sexual emergency' of our youth."[102] The essentials of the argument were present in imperial Germany as well.[103] The belief in media's corrupting influence had roots in what was initially a particularly middle-class notion of self-improvement through self-cultivation and education (*Bildung*), especially reading, which had gained a deal of influence by the late nineteenth and early twentieth century.[104] Reading inculcated moral sense. But the process could go dangerously awry. In 1920, the *Dresdner Anzeiger* reported on the film *Lili: Morality Portrait from West Berlin* (*Lili, Sittenbild aus Berlin W.*), which tells the tale of a female prostitute. According to the newspaper, "The entire film is a school of immorality, and it is suited to corrupt young girls."[105]

So censorship advocates leapt into action, campaigning, as they saw it, to save the nation. In 1920, a moral purity group, the Berlin League to Fight Public Immorality (*Berliner Verein zur Bekämpfung der öffentlichen Unsittlichkeit*), informed the Prussian government that "shamelessness" and "perversity" in public were "the order of the day in Berlin," from whence "the filth flows over the whole of Germany" in the form of "movies, theatre, dance performances, erotic and perverse literature and periodicals."[106] The group demanded stricter censorship. A coalition of conservative Catholic and Protestant women's groups in Königsberg called for a new law against trash and filth in 1919 because, "in the course of the last half year, a prevalence of trash and filth literature, dirty postcards and art folios has become disturbingly noticeable" and this material was now acting as a "poison" on "the spirit of the Volk."[107] In the Reichstag, members of the Bavarian People's Party (*Bayerische Volkspartei*, a regional offshoot of the Catholic Centre Party) called on the federal government to present a draft law that would "effectively fight the ever-increasing public immorality in publications, images and performances, in particular to protect youths against seduction and to protect the public from the dangerous drives [*gemeingefährliche Triebe*] of abnormally orientated [*anormal veranlagt*] persons," among whom they surely included homosexuals.[108] A similar plea came from the Centre Party faction in the Prussian parliament in 1925: did the Prussian government know that in theatre, cinema, and stage an "in-no-way-artistic 'nude cultural movement' [*Nacktkulturbewegung*] is underway" which "in particular" threatened "the well-being of youth?"[109] On this occasion, the Centre Party received what was a rather typical response from the Prussian Interior Ministry, which the Social Democrats controlled: since the war, there were indeed more and more nude performances in theatres, cabarets, and varieties, but what was needed to combat this was not government action but rather an improvement of the public's taste.[110] Police would not go beyond the current rules to place more restrictions on nude revues because if they did they would face "very sharp resistance from many in the public, particularly in the art world, theatre business and in the press."[111]

Though the Republic's initial years brought a window of relative media freedom, the Republic was not without provisions for censorship, and these were quickly put to use. The Constitution explicitly left the door open for a film censor and for future legislation to protect youth from obscene or trashy material.[112] Moreover, the law against obscenity, Paragraph 184, survived the Revolution and the founding of the Republic. Paragraph 184 banned the sale, distribution, and public display of "obscene" (*unzüchtig*) publications, images, or representations.[113] This covered media with sexual content, including the advertising of birth control materials.[114] In 1900, Paragraph 184 had been expanded to prohibit the manufacture, warehousing, advertising, and public promotion of obscene works as well as the distribution of them to any person under sixteen.[115] It was used throughout the Weimar period to censor many sorts of media that dealt with sexuality, including the homosexual press, as I discuss later. The Republic also had some provisions for the censorship of political material.[116]

Opponents of trash and filth also moved quickly to pass new legislation to control media. It took censorship advocates, led by Karl Brunner, two years to pass a cinema law, which created a national review board that vetted all films before they were released.[117] Under the new law, *Different from the Others* was quickly banned when a panel of experts warned that it threatened to seduce young men into homosexuality. The experts on the panel were three influential men: the prominent psychiatrist Emil Kraepelin, the sexologist Albert Moll, and Siegfried Placzek, a neurologist and sexologist who had published a widely read book on homosexuality and law.[118] All three played important roles in debates on homosexuality in the Weimar years. Yet even after the banning of *Different from the Others* and the re-establishment of pre-release review for all films, Germany's film censors remained among Europe's most tolerant.[119] By the mid-1920s, conservatives had also restricted radio licences to prevent objectionable content.[120] In 1926, they achieved their most important victory: the Law to Protect Youth from Trashy and Filthy Publications (*Gesetz zur Bewahrung der Jugend vor Schund- und Schmutzschriften*).[121] The Filth and Trash Law allowed for relatively mild censorship of material that did not meet the legal definition of "obscene" (*unzüchtig*), and therefore was not covered by the obscenity law, Paragraph 184. Any individual, private group, or government agency could complain about a publication. Committees of persons from the worlds of art and literature, publishing, youth welfare, and education reviewed the offending works. If a publication was found to be filth or trash – one key criteria here being that the work lacked artistic or scientific merit – and dangerous to youth, it was placed on a national list. Works on the filth and trash list could not be sold to people under eighteen or publicly displayed.[122]

These conservative victories were mitigated by the opposition of people to the left, who fought censorship in the name of artistic, intellectual, and sexual freedom. Debates about censorship in the mainstream press did not focus on pornography and other media with sexual content, but rather on efforts by Brunner and others to use the obscenity law to censor what was, to most observers, recognizably art or political expression, such as the play *Reigen* (*Round Dance*) and the work of the artist George Grosz.[123] Much of the opposition to censorship voiced by liberals and Social Democrats assumed that protecting youth from trash and filth was just cover for politically motivated censorship carried out by people on the right against artists and writers on the left.[124] This sums up many Social Democrats' concerns. They wanted to protect youth. But they feared that censorship measures intended to protect youth would be misused to infringe on artistic and political liberties.[125] Nevertheless, their opposition resulted in far less strict censorship than what people like Karl Brunner sought. Although a good deal of material made the national filth and trash list, including many homosexual emancipation magazines, the 1926 Filth and Trash Law did not satisfy advocates of censorship. Listed materials could, after all, still be sold. In addition, one of the two regional review boards, the one in Berlin, proved relatively tolerant. Activists like Brunner quickly claimed that the law was not working because, among other things, the Berlin board sometimes refused to list homosexual magazines such as *Friendship* and *Girlfriend* and sex reform magazines like *Marriage* (*Die Ehe*).[126] The regional board in Munich was far more conservative than the Berlin board.[127] But even in Munich, booksellers carried the lesbian magazines *Women Love* (*Frauenliebe*) and *Girlfriend*, as well as a magazine for gay men, *The Friendship Paper* (*Das Freundschaftsblatt*), even though the police infrequently seized some of them.[128]

Thus advocates of stricter censorship were unsatisfied by their victories, particularly when it came to print media. "The public sphere is flooded with works that hold marriage, motherhood, and family in contempt and expose youths to the most severe danger," the Reichstag factions of the Catholic Centre Party and Bavarian People's Party asserted in the winter of 1929.[129] By then, the Filth and Trash Law had been in operation for several years, and yet, apparently, it had made little difference. Some important figures were among the Centre Party politicians who put their names to the 1929 warning about media that was supposedly exposing young people to "the most severe danger," which ultimately resulted in no new censorship provisions: Adam Stegerwald, head of the Christian trade unions; Heinrich Brüning, future chancellor; and Helene Weber, the only female member of the Centre Party's Reichstag leadership and, after 1945, prominent in the Christian Democratic Union (*Christlich Demokratische Union Deutschlands*, CDU), long the major party in West German politics.

The Republic's supposed failure to avert the "flood" of filth and trash became a favourite accusation of the anti-democratic right against the Weimar state.[130] Not everyone who opposed filth and trash opposed democracy – the Catholic Centre Party was the most important pro-censorship, pro-democracy faction. But for critics of democracy, filthy media merely attested to the irremediable flaws of democracy more generally: it diminished social controls, which enabled the rise of immorality. A national expert on film wrote in 1919 that for months people in "reasonable circles" had complained of the "rapid flood" of trash films "that have flooded in under the protection of the newly won 'freedom.'" "The only good result of this," he wrote, "is that it is proof against the Constitution's general abolition of censorship."[131] Only a brand of authoritarianism similar to wartime military government would facilitate the censorship that Germany needed. What such opponents of democracy wanted was not a return to the *Kaiserreich*'s censorship policies but rather a return to the military regime's. Wartime censorship provided the ideal model for many conservative enemies of trash and filth.[132] Military censorship was "a pleasant technical step forward," according to them, sadly repealed with the Republic's founding like so many other "exemplary" military-imposed social controls.[133] Anthony McElligott argues that in general, the wartime dictatorship offered a model to conservatives in the Weimar era.[134] This was also true for censorship. For example, at the war's end, city governments begged the Prussian Ministry of the Interior to somehow retain the military orders against trash.[135]

Voices on the anti-democratic right also occasionally wove antisemitic themes into their rhetoric. One example took place in the early 1920s, when Karl Brunner's foes turned the tables on the "morality apostle"[136] by convincing the police in Frankfurt am Main to put Brunner's own publications on their informal list of trash. The publications in question were a series of pamphlets that Brunner had founded entitled "German Deeds" (*Deutsche Taten*), which glorified the heroics of soldiers in the First World War. Brunner's critics crowed when the apostle of censorship was censored. "What must these [German] deeds be," mused the *Frankfurter Zeitung*, "that they are included on such a list?"[137] In response, some of Brunner's right-wing defenders charged that a conspiracy of Jews in the publishing industry was attacking him because Brunner had disrupted their lucrative trade in filthy publications.[138] However, antisemitism was rarely, if ever, explicit in internal documents produced by Prussian and Reich government officials or in the mainstream press. For example, when in 1931 the Prussian Justice Ministry warned a number of newspapers, including those owned by the Mosse publishing house, to stop running coded advertisements for prostitutes, bureaucrats did not refer in their memos and reports to the fact that the Mosses were a very high-profile Jewish family, although the Nazis who lobbied the Prussian government for tougher prosecution of the Mosse concern certainly did.[139] But even though antisemitism was rarely explicit in public anti-filth discourse aside from that of the *völkisch* Right, the rhetoric common to many censorship crusaders about "profiteering" (*Wucherei*)[140] and "unscrupulous speculators" fattening their purses by selling trash and filth to the masses at times sounded a lot like wartime accusations against Jews of economic exploitation, and doubtless served as encoded antisemitism for some of those who heard it.[141] In the imperial period, Protestant men's moral purity groups displayed a casual antisemitism in their rhetoric; it seems probable that after 1918, such notions persisted in these circles.[142] They do not, however, seem to have been shared by people beyond the Right, and they were not prominent.

In short, the Revolution of 1918–19 brought relaxed censorship, and under the Republic, more media with a wider variety of sexual content was published. Advocates of censorship, who were a diverse and not-always-unified group, sought throughout the Weimar years to make censorship stricter. They succeeded. But they never made it as strict as they wanted. The next section examines what this meant for homosexual emancipation.

The Transformation of Homosexual Emancipation after 1918

A new phase of homosexual emancipation unfolded in the Weimar Republic's initial years. The war and the coming of democracy inspired men who loved other men to insist that the new state recognize their full rights as citizens.[143] They took advantage of more lax censorship to publish new magazines. They fought off subsequent attempts to censor their magazines, thus helping to create the more open media climate that ultimately prevailed under the Republic. This more open climate allowed homosexual emancipation to flourish and to diversify. (The next chapter examines how women and transvestites made use of this freer media climate.) Nevertheless, homosexual emancipation still faced staunch opposition and internal problems, as the conclusion of the story of Linsert's Munich Friendship League shows.

Though claims to citizenship by homosexual emancipationists were not new during the First World War,[144] the war imbued citizenship claims with a new power. Kathleen Canning argues that from the final years of the war through the mid-1920s, "languages of citizenship" assumed a particular "resonance and promise" and "citizenship became a new object of desire, a social identity Germans *wanted* or aspired to fulfill" (emphasis in original).[145] She shows how this was true for a politically diverse group of people linked to the women's movement. The war experience prompted a general rethinking of the individual's relationship to the state.[146] This politicized women. It also politicized gay men. From their posts in the muddy, freezing trenches, homosexual soldiers looked forward to a post-war era in which the state would recognize their service and respect their rights. In 1915, a self-identified homosexual soldier wrote a letter to the WhK expressing his

> firm hope, that after the war our Fatherland will extend its protection to homosexual men. Many went and risked their lives, many lost their lives, and some will yet lose their lives, and should those who come back once again be persecuted by that unfortunate Paragraph 175? We must and we will be victorious, and the Fatherland will grant us the victory of a "final deliverance" [*endgültigen Erlösung*].[147]

The war brought a passionate self-assurance and an invigorated discourse of citizenship to homosexual emancipation, and the movement carried these things into the revolutionary era. People who had sacrificed for their country – who had lived through the destruction of their friends, lovers, and their own bodies – believed that now, the "Fatherland" must recognize the rights to which they, as citizens, were entitled. In December 1915, the partner of "S." died of his wounds in a hospital somewhere in Russia. In a letter to the WhK, S. described how his partner, "my dear, good, true heart's friend" (whose name S. did not give), had not wanted to go to war against people he viewed as "fellow humans." Yet he did, and he died far away and alone, plagued by thirst and pain. "We were to spend our lives together," wrote S. He ended his letter with the following observation on his lover's sacrifice:

> He laid down his life ... for the Fatherland, which persecuted him because of a natural orientation that he could not help. That persecution injured his sensitive soul deeply. It is deplorable that because of a short-sighted law, the Fatherland still makes it impossible for good citizens [*Bürger*], upright people with excellent character traits ... to feel that they are equal with others. It is deplorable that the Fatherland ostracizes them or condemns them and treats them as pariahs, simply because nature saw fit to organize them differently than ordinary people ... [P]eople who by nature are orientated towards the same sex perform their duty and their part fully and completely. It is finally time *that the state treat them in the same manner that they treat the state*.[148] [emphasis in original]

After the war, authors in *Friendship*, which became the chief organ of the new friendship leagues, took up this discourse of homosexual citizenship. "The state must recognize the full citizenship rights of inverts," wrote an author in *Friendship* in 1919. He demanded not just the repeal of Paragraph 175 but also the opening of all civil service positions to people who were known to be inverts.[149] A Leipzig friendship league asserted in 1923 that Paragraph 175 persecuted "many thousands of German citizens [*Staatsbürger*]."[150]

The friendship leagues inaugurated a distinct phase of homosexual emancipation because they made it a mass movement, the world's first such mass movement. They had roots in the older groups, the WhK and the GdE, and their memberships overlapped with them.[151] But mass organization was not a strategy that either the WhK or the GdE adopted. After 1918–19 the WhK concentrated on extending its political influence by persuading legislators and civil servants. Hirschfeld was convinced that a "mass organization" of homosexuals would fail because "homosexuals ... are almost entirely lacking in feelings of solidarity; there is barely another class of people [*Menschenklasse*] that has less interest in organizing around common legal and social interests."[152] In contrast, the friendship leagues proceeded from the assumption that in a democracy, a large contingent of citizens who demanded something of the state ought to be heard and heeded. The friendship leagues were mass organizations.[153] The League for Human Rights (*Bund für Menschenrecht*) became the largest of the homosexual emancipation groups, with about 100,000 members, among them 20,000 to 25,000 women.[154] *Friendship* authors discussed the political power that a relatively large group could wield in a democracy. They debated an idea Hiller had raised in the WhK, where it had been dismissed: whether homosexuals ought to elect their own representative to the Reichstag or form their own political party.[155] By 1920, the friendship leagues had banded together to found a national umbrella group, the German Friendship League (*Deutscher Freundschaftsverband*, DFV).[156] This was a new kind of homosexual politics, something Hirschfeld recognized: he wrote that the DFV was "mobilizing the homosexual masses."[157]

Seizing on what they described as a new era, friendship league activists created change by publishing. In the fall of 1919, Karl Schultz published 20,000 copies of the first issue of *Friendship*, a weekly.[158] For him, and for many others, the new democratic era was marked in particular by a key feature: more lax censorship. "In our censor-free times, the Revolution has brought us the opportunity to advocate our cause as freely and as openly as ever," wrote a *Friendship* author in early 1920. "We must use it!"[159] In its first two years, *Friendship*'s content reflected the politicized atmosphere of the friendship leagues. Its front page was most often devoted to political polemic in favour of the equal rights of "inverts" and to debate about tactics. *Friendship* covered the various trials of its staff members who were periodically charged under the obscenity law. It also ran readers' letters, of which it apparently received a flood.[160] The magazine's focus on politics was not exclusive. There were some short stories, such as a tale of romance involving an ex-soldier newly back from the war.[161] Poetry ran as well; so did the occasional scientific item. But the focus was politics.

The post-war moment saw the founding of several new homosexual emancipation periodicals. By the end of the 1920s, over twenty periodicals written for and by transvestites, homosexual men, and lesbians were on sale at newspaper kiosks in big cities across Germany, and by subscriptions in small towns in Germany and beyond: "an absolute flood of homosexual journals has appeared," Hirschfeld wrote.[162] In their early years, these publications took advantage of relatively lax and disorganized censorship under the Republic.

The way in which authors in *Friendship* named the Republic's early years "censor-free times" for homosexual emancipation, as well as the proliferation of homosexual magazines after 1918, might seem surprising given how famously lax imperial Germany was in its censorship of homosexual emancipation literature.[163] However, though the imperial regime had been remarkably tolerant of print media that discussed homosexuality, it did have limits. The publication in question had to have scientific or artistic merit, and if it only circulated to an expert audience or to a closed circle of subscribers, so much the better, as far as the police were concerned.[164] The WhK and the GdE had both produced periodicals; both primarily circulated them to their memberships, not to the general public. Berlin police stopped the sale of WhK pamphlets at newspaper kiosks in 1902.[165] The Weimar-era magazines for lesbians, gay men, and transvestites differed from homosexual emancipation periodicals of the *Kaiserreich* in that they did not claim to be scientific publications and they circulated publicly. They were for sale at kiosks on the streets of many cities rather than to a closed circle of subscribers. In addition, censorship had grown stricter during the war, when officials squashed certain articles in Hirschfeld's journal, the *Yearbook for Sexual Intermediaries*.[166] As the trial of *Friendship* demonstrated, it was not a given that the Republic would allow the new homosexual emancipation press leeway. Activists had to fight for it.

Homosexual Emancipation and the Politics of Censorship in the Early Republic: The Trial of *Friendship*

Changes wrought by war, revolution, and the coming of democracy – the perception of a "sexual revolution" that was either an opportunity or a problem, new media freedoms, and a more assertive, mass homosexual emancipation movement – came together in the 1919 trial of *Friendship*. In a Berlin courtroom, Karl Brunner and his allies in the battle to staunch the flood of filthy media struggled against the friendship league movement and against Hirschfeld, who defended *Friendship*'s right to exist. The trial of *Friendship* provided a strong example of how important the idea of seduction was to opponents of homosexual emancipation, and how homosexual emancipationists would need to somehow overcome it or circumvent it if their movement was to survive.

In the fall of 1919, highly placed opponents of filthy media moved swiftly to suppress *Friendship* as well as Adolf Brand's *Der Eigene*, which had recently resumed publication. They initially used harsh wartime measures, but they could not retain these for long under the new Republic. The same month that *Friendship* debuted, the Foreign Office exhorted the Berlin police to stop the "distribution of every pamphlet that fosters pederasty [*Päderastie*] and other degenerations of sexuality ... [which are] flooding not only Berlin and the other big German cities, but also the largest centres of German traffic in neutral foreign nations." The Foreign Office blamed "the most shameless business speculation" for "exploiting the newly won press freedom in Germany."[167] Shortly thereafter, Gustav Noske, the SPD Defence Minister (*Reichswehrminister*), banned *Friendship*, its publisher, Schultz, changed the magazine's name to *The Friend* (*Der Freund*) and continued to publish.[168] But heavy-handed wartime measures could not be transposed into peacetime, even to control the homosexual press, and it did not take long for Noske to lift the ban.[169] Police tried to keep Brand from publishing by threatening him and by seizing his magazine.[170] Authorities also used a more subtle wartime measure, paper rationing, in an attempt to suppress *Der Eigene* and *Friendship* until the fall of 1920, when these regulations went out of effect.[171] When that happened, officials, including Brunner, called on prosecutors to charge the magazine's publishers under the obscenity law, Paragraph 184. Some personnel in the prosecutor's office were against this. They argued that the cases would fail because the magazines did not meet the legal definition of obscenity.[172] Contributing to their misgivings was the emerging laxity of courts in obscenity cases. One court had recently ruled in favour of the publishers of a sex reform periodical, *The Gallows* (*Der Galgen*). The allegedly obscene material in that case included a denunciation of the injustice of the sexual double standard – that is, that young men were expected as a matter of course to have premarital sex, while young women were subject to public disgrace for doing the same thing. The magazine also questioned whether abortion ought to be criminal. The court held that the people behind the magazine had "a right" to have a public discussion of such matters and that that right "cannot be denied" even if the intended audience was popular rather than scientific.[173] The failure of the case against *The Gallows* was indeed a bad sign for Brunner, but he and other bureaucrats within the Prussian government nevertheless pushed for prosecution of the homosexual magazines, and they prevailed.[174] The publisher Schultz and another member of *Friendship*'s staff went on trial first, in the summer of 1921.

Prosecuting *Friendship* was an absolute necessity – a national priority – according to Brunner and other advocates of censorship, because the magazines were creating more homosexuals. This notion was just another version of the general idea promoted by campaigners against filth and trash: that media corrupted minds. But it is worth examining in some detail because it related to the primary argument against homosexual emancipation made in the Weimar years, which was that it was spreading homosexuality. Brunner commissioned fifteen medical experts to evaluate the following question: "Is it possible that people with normal sexuality could be lured into homosexuality through reading and example, especially while they are in puberty?"[175] The experts found that the answer was yes.[176] They for the most part denied that homosexuality had a biological cause, although they acknowledged that a small minority of people who sought same-sex sex might be born homosexuals. What was far more decisive than biology, however, was "the influence of concepts." This was particularly true for young people, "in whom sexuality is not very strongly developed." Young people might become homosexual through personal experiences, such as "mutual masturbation in boarding schools" or "drunken sexual excitement in the lack of normal cohabitation possibilities" or seduction by homosexual individuals. In addition, homosexuality could "develop ... through the suggestions of sexual psychopathological publications." As an example, the experts considered Richard von Krafft-Ebing's *Psychopathia sexualis*, one of the most important works of nineteenth-century sexology. The book had undoubtedly exerted an "unhealthy" influence on Germany's youth: "As certain as it is that the wide distribution of Krafft-Ebing's *Psychopathia sexualis* in its time led to more sexual anomalies, it is likewise certainly expected that the distribution of homosexual propaganda will have a similar effect."[177] And media magnified the danger of seduction, because through media sexual "abnormals" could reach far more teenagers than they could through personal contacts. Here, the authors of the report were on solid scientific ground. Many psychiatrists warned of the dangers of seduction into homosexuality.[178] Leading experts, like the psychiatrist Kraepelin and the sexologist Moll, agreed that reading the wrong thing could make a person into a homosexual; thus, German culture ought to promote heterosexuality, in the interest of national survival.[179] In the course of a pivotal debate in a Reichstag committee on the sodomy law (discussed in chapter 4), Rudolf Schetter of the Centre Party warned that thanks to new publications, "homosexuality" – which he deemed a threat to "the family, marriage, [and] the strength of the Volk" – was "tearing through the ranks of young people."[180]

It was above all teenaged boys for whom censorship proponents feared, and they feared that homosexual corruption would make them into bad members of society and bad citizens. Many argued that the age of consent (*Schutzalter*) should be set higher for men than for women because teenaged boys were more susceptible to homosexual seduction than were teenaged girls.[181] Teenaged boys were, in addition, a demographic that was supposedly embroiled in a wider crisis in the 1920s. The war destroyed two million men who would otherwise have helped to raise the teenagers of the Weimar years. Lacking male supervision, teenaged boys were supposedly at risk, yet the nation's vitality and military strength depended on them.[182] Discussions of the dangers of homosexual seduction singled out boys over girls. Placzek, the neurologist and sexologist, penned a rather hysterical anti-homosexual tract, *Homosexuality and Law* (*Homosexualität und Recht*), that was frequently cited by opponents of homosexual emancipation.[183] Placzek wrote that "the male homosexual has a predilection for youths, indeed, for lads [*Knaben*]."[184] Homosexual seduction in males, Placzek wrote, "hinders normal sexual activity or makes it totally impossible."[185] He argued in addition that homosexual sex feminized men and made them bad citizens. He described how the homosexual man "lacks a strong sense of honour" and "strength of will." Such men "happily use the feminine weapons of intrigue, hypocrisy, and lying" and have a "passion for gossip."[186] Placzek considered these traits indicative of failed citizenship. They caused treason: he claimed that homosexual diplomats had probably revealed more than a few national secrets.[187] According to another author, homosexual seduction was a "confusion of conscience" that feminized a man and moreover deteriorated his moral barriers against crime and violence. As a consequence, he then learned to enjoy these depravities.[188] Such a man would engage in antisocial mayhem, as had the notorious mass murderer Fritz Haarmann.[189] He would grow weak-willed and deceptive.[190] Referring to an important duty of citizens, military service, this author wrote that such men could not be soldiers because they could not be trusted with weapons.[191] This idea of homosexual men (at times conflated with Jewish men) as inherently bad citizens, traitors to the nation, was an international discourse evident across Europe in the nineteenth and twentieth centuries.[192]

At *Friendship*'s trial in Berlin, the magazine's defenders set out to establish that it was not seducing young men into homosexuality. But they did not entirely succeed. Hirschfeld appeared as an expert witness and asserted that homosexuality was a non-pathological, biological condition. Other experts called by the defence backed him up: no magazine had the "wizardly power" to seduce people into homosexuality.[193] Hirschfeld was not alone among prominent sexologists of the Weimar era in citing a biological basis for homosexuality. Both Moll and Iwan Bloch thought that heredity could contribute to homosexuality; both held non-biological causes to be important as well.[194] But Hirschfeld's work was unique in the way that he entirely discounted environmental factors. This was probably not incidental to his experiences fighting censorship. For example, in the case at hand, it was only by entirely dismissing environmental factors that *Friendship*'s supporters could argue against Brunner and company. Hirschfeld appeared as an expert witness in many censorship cases.[195]

At *Friendship*'s trial, the prosecution's expert witnesses disputed Hirschfeld's argument, and Hirschfeld's contentions about a non-pathological, biological disposition unaffected by environment did not exactly succeed. *Friendship* lost at the trial court level. Schultz got six weeks in jail and the second defendant, a former publisher of the magazine, got two weeks in jail.[196] They were convicted of breaking the obscenity law as well as the anti-pimping statute (Paragraph 180) because supposedly the magazine's personal ads constituted pimping. Prosecutors used the pimping law to go after newspapers that ran coded personal ads offering massage and language instruction, which were really ads placed by sex workers seeking clients.[197] By the early 1930s, these ads were so ubiquitous that even the Centre Party's *Germania* ran them; its editorial staff probably did not realize that "Spanish instruction" did not mean learning to speak Spanish.[198] Brand, tried later on the same grounds as Schultz, was comparably lucky. Although convicted of obscenity, he got a 5,000 mark fine, not jail time.[199]

When *Friendship*'s lawyers appealed the convictions to Germany's highest court, the *Reichsgericht*, the high court used the case to set an important standard for what the homosexual press could and could not publish. The high court emphasized that articles about homosexuality were not necessarily obscene. It considered "obscene" only those articles that "drag homosexual *sexual* intercourse into the foreground by depicting it" and in which homoeroticism "characterizes the entire article" (emphasis in the original).[200]

Though homosexual emancipationists recognized the *Friendship* case as "a trial of extraordinary importance" that not only mattered for the magazine itself but was also "of decisive importance for the whole movement to abolish Paragraph 175," they do not seem to have recognized the high court's decision as a vindication of their right to publish, which is understandable.[201] It was not an immediate victory for *Friendship*, and it heralded bad times for the magazine. The high court upheld the lower court's decisions: the issues of the magazine in question were obscene. Schultz and the other defendant had to serve their sentences. The high court also endorsed the claim that young people could be corrupted by the magazine, especially by its personal ads, which the court thought referred clearly to same-sex sex. The ads, the court wrote, "must be viewed as a grave threat to young and inexperienced persons, persons who can easily be seduced into illicit sex [*Unzucht*]." A few years later, a second obscenity case, this one spearheaded by Brunner as well, nearly destroyed *Friendship*.[202] That 1923 trial resulted in a large fine for one of *Friendship*'s editors, Max Danielsen, and threw the magazine into financial turmoil.[203]

Friendship had another problem in 1923: the friendship league movement split when Friedrich Radszuweit rose to the leadership of the national organization, the German Friendship League, and his flagship magazine, the *Journal for Human Rights* (*Blätter für Menschenrecht*) eclipsed *Friendship*. Radszuweit renamed the national group the League for Human Rights. Most, although not all, local groups also changed their names. The national group designated Radszuweit's *Journal for Human Rights* its official organ, and local groups were required to subscribe.[204] Radszuweit built the League for Human Rights into the Weimar Republic's largest homosexual emancipation organization. When he took over the friendship league movement, he was in his mid-forties and well established, having made his money as a textiles dealer before the war.[205] He used his personal wealth to lay the foundations of what became his homosexual emancipation publishing empire. The Friedrich Radszuweit Publishing House (Friedrich Radszuweit Verlag) developed a stable of homosexual emancipation magazines, including the *Journal for Human Rights* and the League for Human Rights's magazine for women, *Girlfriend*. Radszuweit also produced magazines for homosexual men – *The Island* (*Die Insel*) and *Eros* – and *The Transvestite* (*Der Transvestit*), which appeared as a section in *Girlfriend*. *Friendship* ultimately survived the crisis of 1923. A faction remained independent of Radszuweit and continued to use the German Friendship League moniker for its national group, and *Friendship* magazine stayed afloat. But the League for Human Rights became the larger, more influential group.

Despite *Friendship*'s subsequent travails, the Reichsgericht's decision in the *Friendship* case was an important victory for homosexual emancipation. The high court's decision expanded the sphere of press freedom for homosexual emancipation. It rejected the principles of military censorship. The decision gave the homosexual press more latitude to publish than it had enjoyed even prior to 1914. Before the war, *Friendship*'s publishers would have had to prove that their magazine had artistic or scientific worth. In *Friendship*'s case, this would have been tough: most of its content was political polemic, neither particularly scientific nor literary. But the Reichsgericht decision made no mention of *Friendship*'s literary or scientific merit.[206] Rather, the high court simply forbade depictions of same-sex eroticism. This ban on erotic material was more restrictive than it may seem on its face. Much of the material that the high court found obscene in the *Friendship* case only suggested same-sex sex. In a short story that the court singled out as obscene, the same-sex sexuality consists of nothing more than the following: two men kiss in a bedroom, and one entreats the other to stay with him.[207] However, the court's decision made it impossible for local authorities to use the obscenity law (Paragraph 184) to squash the new homosexual magazines, so long as their publishers avoided eroticism, which they duly tried to do, including in their personal ads. The *Friendship* case seems even more significant when one considers the context of the early Weimar years. The high court faced a new, self-assertive mass movement for homosexual emancipation that was fast making publishing one of its primary endeavours. Even to simply return to pre-war standards in this new era would have been a victory for homosexual emancipationists.

After the *Friendship* case, more and more magazines for gay men, lesbians, and transvestites went into production, though they had to fight censorship. Police continued to seize lesbian and gay men's magazines for obscenity under Paragraph 184, often on account of their personal ads. *Girlfriend* had been in publication for only about a year when police charged it with obscenity and seized copies.[208] They eventually dropped the charges. This lack of success was somewhat typical. Most of the homosexual and transvestite press evaded Paragraph 184 prosecutions most of the time.[209] The 1926 Filth and Trash Law proved more useful than Paragraph 184 for censoring homosexual magazines. Following the law's passage, homosexual emancipation publications frequently wound up on the filth and trash list. A 1928 application on behalf of youth welfare workers to list *Friendship* called it "powerful propaganda" for homosexuality and charged that it was responsible for "a terrible" and "unmistakable ... increase in homosexuality in present times."[210] But right-leaning critics of the Filth and Trash Law were correct that it lacked sharp teeth. It is unclear how much being placed on the filth and trash list actually harmed publications. Putting a publication on the list forced readers to ask for it by name at kiosks or bookstores, since listed publications could not be displayed. To ask for *Friendship* by name would be to risk publicly identifying oneself as a homosexual to the person working at the kiosk and anyone standing nearby, something most of *Friendship*'s readers had to avoid. One reader of the lesbian magazine *Girlfriend* made sure to always buy it at a street kiosk where no one would recognize her. Carrying the magazine home "was like you had a bomb in your bag," she said.[211] However, being on the filth and trash list did not affect a magazine's subscribers. Radszuweit, who by the mid-1920s was the leading homosexual emancipation publisher, denied that the list even hurt his business.[212] Given how hard Radszuweit fought to keep his publications off of it, he must have been putting a brave face on things. On balance, the Weimar Republic's censorship of media about sexuality was relatively lax. Yet the obscenity law and the Filth and Trash Law did push queer publications out of the public eye, containing them in a restricted space that especially young people were supposed to be unable to access.

The Suppression of the Munich Friendship League

Greater freedom to publish, within limits, did not mean that homosexual emancipationists would have an easy time in the Weimar years. Paragraph 175 prosecutions actually increased slightly after the war.[213] But this was not because the Weimar state was cracking down on male homosexuality.[214] Nor was it because, as the Munich police claimed, homosexuality itself had increased after the war.[215] Rather, gay male culture was far more accessible and public in the Weimar period and drew in more men, who were more confident and assertive and who ran into more trouble with the police. Linsert's story is a good example of this. And the rest of the story of the Munich Friendship League demonstrates some of the problems facing gay men in the Weimar years. It also gives an example of the infighting in the homosexual emancipation movement, now split between four national groups and a host of local groups.

Munich was not nearly as open to queer subcultures as was Berlin. Berlin police had tolerated queer bars even before 1918. The Berlin police department put the word out that any man being blackmailed under the threat of Paragraph 175 ought to contact them and need not fear prosecution.[216] In contrast, throughout the Weimar years, Munich police harassed gay men and transvestites and seized queer publications, although despite their efforts, Munich residents could still buy queer publications at bookstores and kiosks.[217] They also sought out and seized dildos, such as the eleven they referred to as "copies of the male member (for the purpose of female masturbation)," confiscated in 1924 and 1925.[218] Unlike Berlin police, who largely looked on as a network of queer bars and clubs flourished, Munich police aggressively raided bars and clubs known to be queer.[219] In 1920, they arrested 305 men for alleged homosexuality; police ensnared these men in raids on public toilets.[220] In 1921, Gerhard Daniel came to Munich seeking wealthy "gentlemen" (*Kavaliere*). He found meeting places difficult to locate and the Munich police "very strict" with male prostitutes like himself. His impressions, related in a letter to a friend, are confirmed by the fact that the police intercepted his letter and began surveillance of the one queer meeting place that he had managed to find.[221]

When Linsert applied for official recognition of the Munich Friendship League, the police went after him and its other members.[222] Police received a tip from Linsert's landlady that Linsert had spent the night with a man whom he apparently met at a meeting of the Friendship League. Police interrogated the two and subjected them to humiliating examinations of their bodies for signs that they had broken the sodomy law.[223] The two denied violating Paragraph 175; that is, they denied having had anally penetrative sex. They admitted, in the words of police, to "mutual masturbation." This was not enough to charge them with sodomy, but police did report the incident to the official body that was reviewing Linsert's application to register the Munich Friendship League. They claimed it proved that the club was merely a meeting place for homosexual men, as Café Zehner had been, and that the Friendship League was moreover a scheme to seduce adolescent boys.[224] The application to register the Friendship League was denied. Linsert appealed the decision and lost.

Around the same time, the Munich Friendship League ran afoul of Friedrich Radszuweit, who was now the head of the national organization of friendship leagues. Linsert was initially a Radszuweit ally. In the spring of 1923, he was listed on the front page of the *Journal for Human Rights* as one of two people to contact about founding a united, international movement of "homoerotics" (*Homoeroten*) – the other was Radszuweit himself.[225] But Radszuweit's leadership brought more centralized, national control over the friendship leagues.[226] Linsert and the members of the Munich Friendship League apparently opposed this. They called for the leadership of the national League for Human Rights to expand beyond Radszuweit and his trusted lieutenant Paul Weber to include people who were not based in Berlin.[227] Radszuweit did not welcome these suggestions. In a letter to members of the Munich Friendship League in the winter of 1923, he mocked them for wanting independence from the national group, implied that the police harassment they were facing was somehow their own fault, and threatened to disband the Munich group.[228] The threat implied that he had the power to do so, which he did not. In any event, by this time Linsert was done with Radszuweit and with the League for Human Rights. He was not, however, done with politics, or with homosexual emancipation. He would eventually put his talents in the service of the Communist Party and Hirschfeld's Scientific Humanitarian Committee, rising to the leadership of the WhK in a crucial moment. Chapter 4 recounts that story.

In 1918 and 1919, Germans perceived that war, revolution, and democracy had upended norms of gender and sexuality. Though conservatives reacted with anxiety, people with progressive views felt emboldened to overthrow the "dictatorship of tradition." After an initial moment of disorganized censorship and broader media freedom, the Weimar Republic settled into a practice of relatively relaxed censorship of media with sexual content. It did this despite the efforts of people who took a conservative view of gender and sexuality. Conservatives felt that Christianity ought to be recognized as the ultimate arbiter of sexuality and gender and that the nation itself was in peril because it was moving towards a secular and science-based approach to sexuality. One aspect of this peril, they claimed, was the ability of media about unacceptable forms of sexuality, such as homosexuality, to spread these sexualities, especially to adolescents. Though they used the existing law against obscenity, Paragraph 184, and passed new legislation, such as the 1926 Filth and Trash Law, members of the conservative coalition were not entirely successful in suppressing all discussions of sexuality in media. In the war's aftermath, gay men were inspired by a newly resonant discourse of citizenship to found new homosexual emancipation groups, the friendship leagues. These leagues confronted conservatives in a struggle over whether and to what extent new homosexual emancipation publications would be censored. They won a restricted public sphere for magazines like *Friendship*. Homosexual emancipation publications were nevertheless bound by restraints, such as the Filth and Trash Law, which often kept *Friendship* and similar publications from being publicly displayed or sold to minors. This move to contain homosexuality and to keep it from spreading, while allowing some public space for homosexual subcultures, would come to characterize the Weimar state's response to homosexuality and to other forms of immorality.

2 Lesbianism, Reading, and Law

It is only out of curiosity that Hilde and her fiancé go one night to the "infamous" café, down a flight of stairs in a disreputable neighbourhood.[1] Among the other people there – two young men sitting close together on a sofa, a few regulars at the bar – the good-looking waiter draws Hilde's attention. His name is Heinz. He sports "imperceptibly powdered mutton chops" and moves about in a manner that Hilde finds somewhat feminine. Heinz recognizes Hilde as a newcomer and sells her a magazine, *Girlfriend* (*Die Freundin*), which happens to be the very magazine in which this story of Heinz and Hilde appeared in 1930. Hilde reads *Girlfriend* so that she can "understand" the café and its occupants, which "was not difficult for her" because "she was not one of those women who immediately rejects anything that is not in accord with the moral code of the bourgeois [*bürgerlich*] law book." Hilde's first visit to the café is chic slumming. Guides to Berlin advised tourists to take in the city's homosexual and transvestite bars; when a reporter took a famous American actor on a tour of "Berlin's underworld," they of course stopped at a homosexual club.[2] But later Hilde returns to the café alone. After some difficulty gathering the courage to go inside, she does, and passes the evening listening to "sweet and sentimental" gramophone records with Heinz and "falling a little in love" as he tells of "the film and cabaret stars who belong to the 'others'" and of "his boss, a famous transvestite." In the course of this conversation, Hilde somewhat belatedly realizes that Heinz, the "nice young man," is also "one of the others" – is, in fact, "a young woman." Their romance proceeds with alacrity, with Hilde overcoming any hesitation she might feel on account of her fiancé as she takes Heinz's hand. "What beautiful, wondrously beautiful hands" Heinz has, and hands are "her weakness." They kiss. Heinz's kiss is "more tender, more feathery, and indeed more erotic" than a man's, "and as she

Ads for bars and clubs on the back page of *Girlfriend* magazine, 8 October 1930. Lotte Hahm is pictured in the advertisement for her Violetta club at the top of the page.

realized this, she knew in an instant that Heinz was a woman, and more than that, was the woman who had unlocked Hilde's love."

Hilde's story is fiction, but elements of it corresponded to real life. One is the centrality of *Girlfriend* magazine to Hilde's progression from a fashionable young woman out for an evening of voyeuristic slumming with her male fiancé to a fashionable young woman in love with a masculine woman or transvestite. Chapter 1 showed how in the wake of the First World War, an emboldened homosexual emancipation movement fought for media freedom, and the new democratic state granted it a restricted public sphere. This chapter demonstrates how important that restricted public sphere was. It examines lesbian and transvestite subcultures to show how relative media freedom facilitated their growth; media could even enable a person to become a lesbian or transvestite and to join these subcultures, as the magazine does in Hilde's story.[3] The Weimar state's response to this media reflected its centrality: containing media was more of a priority for politicians and bureaucrats than was suppressing lesbian sex. An introductory section of the chapter surveys lesbian and transvestite subcultures. It examines the growth of these subcultures and the definitional work done by their members regarding the relationships between lesbian and transvestite identity categories. It also examines the politics of these subcultures: the intellectual leaders of lesbian and transvestite movements sought a limited public, subcultural queer presence, which they used notions of rights, citizenship, and respectability to claim. These were not radical left politics, but neither were they homonormative. The chapter moves on to make two arguments specifically about these lesbian subcultures. Gay men were the focus of chapter 1, and here the analysis focuses on lesbians; yet these conclusions were most likely true for gay male and transvestite subcultures as well. The second section of the chapter shows how vital the homosexual print culture that flourished after the Revolution of 1918–19 was to lesbians. Because media was so important, the stakes of censorship politics were very high for members of the subculture. The chapter's final section takes up a debate within the history of sexuality in Germany about why lesbian sex was decriminalized while gay male sex remained criminal. It argues that in the Weimar period, though lesbian sex was not a crime, the state's relationship with lesbianism was nevertheless one of regulation and containment. This was accomplished through censorship policy. This arrangement was typical of the Republic's emerging response to homosexuality, both female and male: to tolerate it in a small group but to contain it in restricted spaces and in small adult populations. It is moreover characteristic of the settlement on sexual politics that parties reached under the Republic, a settlement that established a type of sexual freedom by keeping certain forms of immorality out of the wider public sphere.

Lesbian and Transvestite Movements under the Weimar Republic

The Revolution of 1918 and the advent of democracy opened up space for a greatly expanded and more public subculture of women who sought romance with other women.[4] The Weimar years not only saw the debut of Germany's first magazine for and by lesbians, they saw the publication of three different such magazines.[5] These magazines ran original serialized novels, short stories, poems, and essays by hundreds of female authors.[6] For the most part they were the products of publishing houses owned and run by men, but their editorial staffs were female.[7] One of the two major magazines for women was *Girlfriend*, which was published by Friedrich Radszuweit's company, was founded in 1925, and became a weekly with a circulation of about 7,000.[8] *Girlfriend* temporarily changed its title to *Single Women* (*Ledige Frauen*) in 1928 to avoid censorship. A name change made the magazine seem, to the casual observer, like a new publication, and the magazine could thereby avoid trouble for a time. The other major magazine for women was *Garçonne*. It was associated with the German Friendship League (DFV), which survived in a much-diminished form independent of Radszuweit's League for Human Rights. *Garçonne* debuted in 1926 under the title *Women Love* (*Frauenliebe*) but changed its name, first becoming *Women* (*Frauen*), then *Love and Life* (*Liebe und Leben*), and in 1930, *Garçonne*.[9] In 1931, *Garçonne* was printed twice a month in runs of 5,000 copies each.[10] In 1932, when the publishing house that owned it cut the magazine loose, *Garçonne*'s female editors kept it running for about ten more issues, apparently funding it with their own money.[11]

In 1928, a Berliner named Ruth Roellig published what was probably the world's first lesbian guidebook. *Berlin's Lesbian Women* (*Berlins lesbische Frauen*) is an insider's description of the city's network of cafés, bars, and social clubs for lesbian women and for transvestites, whom Roellig described as "women who prefer to appear in men's clothing."[12] Roellig herself was a fixture of these social scenes. She lived with her girlfriend in an apartment that served as a gathering place for artists, making a living as a writer and occasional secretary.[13] As noted in chapter 1, Roellig begins *Berlin's Lesbian Women* by describing how since the Revolution "people have become more tolerant."[14] Indeed, her book surely would not have escaped censorship even in imperial Germany, let along under military rule, and moreover could not have been published in a country with stricter censorship, such as Great Britain. The rise of the "penny novel" (*Groschenroman*) and relaxed censorship brought the publication of something like thirty novels by women featuring homosexual themes. Anna Elisabet Weirauch's extremely popular *The Scorpion* seems to have minted this genre. It was followed by Maximiliane Ackers's *Girlfriends* (*Freundinnen*, 1923), Grete Urbanitzsky's *The Wild Garden* (*Der wilde Garten*, 1927) and others. Of this body of literature, Christa Winsloe's play about love in a Prussian boarding school, which was filmed as *Mädchen in Uniform*, is perhaps the best remembered.[15]

Unsympathetic observers noticed that lesbian subcultures were far more visible in the Weimar years than they had been previously. Though this was largely because of the growth of lesbian subcultures, these observers attributed it to a simple increase in lesbianism itself after the war. This assertion was a species of the more general claim that immorality was on the rise, especially in urban spaces. "Currently Germany is indeed experiencing a boom of lesbianism [*Lesbiertum*] ... along with other perversions and perversities,"[16] wrote Th. von Rheine of the late Weimar years. Rheine was one of a crop of self-appointed experts in lesbianism. These experts authored books for general audiences called "moral histories" (*Sittengeschichte*) that revealed the titillating details of "abnormal" sexualities to a curious, assumedly straight public.[17] Politicians echoed the claim that lesbianism was increasing. During a committee debate over whether to abolish the sodomy law, Paragraph 175 (discussed in chapter 4), a DNVP Reichstag delegate said that "knowledgeable observers of behaviour and conditions in big cities report that this vice [*Laster*]" – that is, "lesbian love" – was, like male homosexuality, "increasing dramatically."[18]

The rise of mass organizations also opened up more space in the homosexual emancipation movement for women. Before the war the WhK had had female members, some of whom identified as homosexual. Women had written for its *Yearbook for Sexual Intermediaries* and spoken on lesbianism at WhK annual meetings. But the WhK remained focused on Paragraph 175, which did not apply to women, giving little attention to lesbianism and neither attracting nor seeking a significant female membership.[19] By the late 1920s, the German Friendship League and Radszuweit's League for Human Rights had women's chapters across Germany, in cities from Bremen to Zwickau, and in Vienna too.[20] Radszuweit especially made a concerted effort to bring women into his group. He and the lesbian/transvestite organizer Lotte Hahm tried to found a national, independent women's group, the League for Ideal Women's Friendship (*Bund für ideale Frauenfreundschaft*). It was to be an umbrella group for local women's groups, including the social clubs, though it did not last.[21] Like the WhK, the League for Human Rights' focus was the repeal of Paragraph 175. This may account for the gender imbalance in its membership. In 1926, of about 39,000 members of the League for Human Rights who responded to a survey, only 780 were women.[22] Women also organized independent of the male-led homosexual emancipation organizations. Selli Engler founded her own magazine, the *Journal of Ideal Women's Friendship* (*Blätter Idealer Frauenfreundschaft*), and organization, the Ladies-BIF-Club (*Damen-BIF-Klub*).[23] Until *Garçonne*'s editors took it over in 1932, Engler's was the only magazine for women independent of a publishing house and organization headed by men. The magazine probably lasted only two or three years; it is unclear how successful the Ladies-BIF-Club was. After her magazine folded, Engler remained active in the existing movement, working on *Women Love*, then on *Girlfriend*.[24] Elsbeth Killmer and others started the League for Women's Rights (*Bund für Frauenrecht*), which was supposed to replace the women's division of the League for Human Rights but did not succeed.[25]

Though women's political groups did not thrive, a somewhat different form of organizing did: women's social clubs. They had some precedent in the years before the First World War, when private social circles disguised themselves as bowling societies or savings clubs and met in certain bars and were occasionally busted by the police.[26] One of the most prominent leaders of social clubs for girlfriends and transvestites under the Republic was the dashing Lotte Hahm. Then in her late thirties, she was often pictured in advertisements for her events on the back page of *Girlfriend* in a suit and tie with her short hair slicked across her brow. She led Violetta, a Berlin social club that in 1926 boasted 400 members; she also served as leader for three other social clubs.[27] Social clubs like Violetta required dues. They arranged entertainment, much of which was advertised in the lesbian magazines and open to non-members. One of the most anticipated events was Hahm's annual summer moonlight cruise. In 1930, it sailed up the Spree to a beach hotel on a lake, where a room was reserved for a cabaret performance.[28] Hahm had set the price low, hoping that "those with less means can sail with us."[29] Later that year, Hahm's Violetta club celebrated its four-year anniversary with a week of events for girlfriends at the American-style dance palace Magic Flute (*Zauberflöte*). These included a free evening party, a transvestites' ball, another ball and cabaret, and a "night party" at which "surprises" were promised.[30]

The fact that social clubs enjoyed a lot of success while more explicitly political groups did not led some commentators to deride lesbians as apolitical.[31] Because the sodomy law did not apply to female-female sex, lesbians had been lulled into "passivity," charged a 1925 article by Radszuweit and Aenne Weber.[32] At the time, Weber edited *Girlfriend* and led the women's division of the League for Human Rights. She and Radszuweit urged homosexual women to join men in fighting Paragraph 175, since the campaign against the sodomy law was also a struggle against the "pariah" and "second-class" status of homosexual people in general. Women could join the battle, they wrote, by subscribing to *Girlfriend* and by reading the *Journal for Human Rights*, which carried more political news.

Historians, too, have deemed the social clubs apolitical. In his pioneering 1975 history of homosexual emancipation, James Steakley writes that the "flowering" of homosexual male and female subcultures under the Republic hurt the political movement because "it was far easier to luxuriate in the concrete utopia of the urban subculture than to struggle for an emancipation which was apparently only formal and legalistic."[33] Historians have taken a similar line on women's participation in politics under the Republic more generally. Women's lower rates of voting and constrained roles in party politics have led some historians to argue that many middle-class activists turned from the political to the "social" – that is, to involvement in social reform and welfare, including in welfare for prostitutes, which indeed female activists dominated.[34] In both cases, a relatively narrow definition of "politics" has the effect of dismissing this "social" organizing as unimportant.

Yet for lesbians – indeed, for all sexual outsiders – the "social" and the "political" were intertwined. This point is related to a broader argument that Kathleen Canning makes: the investment of women in what have been classified as "social" issues did not mean that they had given up making claims on the state. Far from it.[35] A more expansive definition of politics, drawing on feminist scholarship, identifies as "political" the fight to establish a limited public sphere in order to make queer communities and lives possible in new ways, not only because it entailed confrontation with the state's censorship policies, but also because it was a struggle for the survival of queer subjectivities. This was the explicit goal of Hahm and other organizers. Roellig wrote that above all, the club Violetta's mission was "to offer the same-sex-loving woman a kind of home ... to align love with understanding, to shield 'differently orientated women' [*andersgeartete Frauen*]"[36] from prevailing prejudice. This was a politics of "shield[ing]" women from stigma and hatred. For the most part, lesbian organizing did not take as its goal the reform of the world outside of the subcultures that activists built, whether through parliamentary politics or public education, although some authors in the lesbian press wrote explicitly political articles, elaborating a feminist critique of national politics and calling for the amelioration of the pervasive hostility in general society against the "Sapphic" minority.[37] But the fact that the subcultures existed and were so accessible through magazines and local branches in cities across Germany was due to political change. And activists in lesbian circles had to defend their subcultures, chiefly against censorship. They made rights-based claims to do so. Karen (Käthe André-Karen[38]) wrote in *Garçonne* that "organizing people of our kind" would both "help them gain their rights and their reputation" and "make their lives easier."[39]

The public spaces and print media culture of the Weimar Republic also proved hospitable to a movement of transvestites, which Katie Sutton describes as "one of the first examples of public activism by and for trans-identifying individuals anywhere in the world."[40] Both the German Friendship League and Radszuweit's League for Human Rights formed groups for transvestites.[41] Like the League for Human Rights and the various women's groups, transvestite organizing deployed notions of middle-class respectability.[42] Transvestite activism had roots in the years before the First World War, just as homosexual emancipation did. Hirschfeld had introduced the concept of transvestite identity to the general public in his 1910 book *Transvestites: The Erotic Urge to Cross-Dress* (*Die Transvestiten: Eine Untersuchung über den erotischen Verkleidungstrieb*).[43] Yet 1918 brought important change, and transvestites took advantage of relatively lax censorship under the Republic to create a more visible and accessible subculture.[44] From the mid-1920s until the early 1930s, two transvestite magazines ran as inserts in lesbian magazines: *The Transvestite* (later *World of Transvestites/Die Welt der Transvestiten*) was an addendum to *Girlfriend*, and *The Transvestite* (*Der Transvestit*) was a column in *Garçonne*.[45] Recurrent themes in the transvestite magazines included beauty, fashion tips, and calls to political action. One of these was penned in 1928 by Werner Kn., who called on "comrades" (*Artgenossen*) to let go of their inferiority complexes, to stop cowering, and to fight for their rights as "citizens" and for "liberation."[46]

This is a very early instance of people organizing around what was then a relatively new category of gender or sexual identity. Given that trans identities would go on to have tremendous import in twentieth- and twenty-first-century movements for gender and sexual liberation, it is important to take a close look at what "transvestite" meant to the people who self-identified as such. In transvestite magazines, one common theme was the debate about what the identity category "transvestite"

Transvestites in front of the Institute for Sexual Science during the First International Congress for Sex Reform on the Basis of Sexology, 1921. Photograph by Willy Römer. Bildarchiv Preußischer Kulturbesitz.

meant. Authors disagreed over whether it denoted people who only wished to dress in the clothing of the other sex, people whose true sex was not their birth sex and who had transitioned to their true sex or wanted to do so, or both of these groups. By the 1950s, sexology considered the former "transvestites" and the later "transsexuals."[47] But in the 1920s, people disagreed and used "transvestite" to describe a variety of states of being. The category was fuzzy in the 1920s because at that time, older models of homosexuality as being synonymous with gender inversion were still in use, while at the same time, newer ideas about homosexuality being independent of gender expression and related exclusively to sexual object choice were gaining traction.[48] In addition, other questions were at play, such as those concerning how profound the condition of transvestitism was. Was it relatively superficial – a form of clothing fetish practised in private – or did it concern the core of a person's being and every corner of a person's life?

One author who took the latter view suggested replacing Hirschfeld's coinage "transvestite" with "trans-sensible" (*Transsensible*) because the typical transvestite did not just want to dress like the opposite sex, but rather "primarily has the urge to live in the role of the other sex."[49] Toni Fricke was one such person. An early mainstay of the transvestite section in *Girlfriend* magazine, she lived as a woman. She hoped to win legal recognition of the femaleness of her body by having her blood tested for female hormones.[50] But a dissenting group held that transvestitism was less a feature of the self and more about clothing.[51]

In the transvestite magazines, the most prominently represented views were those of male-to-female individuals who sought relationships with women and who considered themselves heterosexual men; they understood transvestitism as cross-dressing rather than as gender transition.[52] The perspectives of male-to-female transvestites who sought relationships with men were noticeably absent from the magazines, with rare exceptions, such as the short story "Kurty Is My Darling's Name!" about the transvestite Kurty, who wins the love of an understanding male scientist.[53] Male-to-female people who sought relationships with men, such as the fictional Kurty, seem to have been marginalized within transvestite organizations.[54] They were not always made to feel welcome in the homosexual emancipation movement either.[55] Masculine and/or male transvestites (that is, female-to-male people) were also under-represented.[56]

Transvestites faced problems that lesbians and gay men who did not cross gender boundaries did not face. Simply cross-dressing could get a person arrested. German police considered the wearing of the clothing of the opposite sex to constitute gross public indecency, and for decades transvestites of both genders had complained about police harassment.[57] After the publication of Hirschfeld's book *Transvestites*, transvestites approached him and asked his help in securing police permission to cross-dress in public. Some also tried to change their names. With the help of Hirschfeld and other sympathetic doctors, in the decades before the First World War, Germans secured a number of police permits to cross-dress, or "transvestite passports" (*Transvestiten-Reisepass*), as they became known.[58] People also sought to change their bodies to conform to their true sex, sometimes on their own and sometimes with the help of doctors. An early report of a surgery in the German-language scientific literature was of a 1905 case in the Netherlands, where a married father carried out a self-castration and then attempted a breast augmentation, apparently with the help of his wife.[59] After the war, surgeries were performed at Hirschfeld's Institute for Sexual Science.[60] Identity documents also posed problems for transvestites.[61] A male transvestite who lived as a man in Berlin but had identity documents that still listed his birth name, Hedwig, found it impossible to get a job. He wanted a masculine job, but no firm would hire "Hedwig" for such a job.[62] Berthold was a male transvestite who had lived as a man for years and had an important job where everyone thought he was a man. He struggled for years to legally change his name. He hoped to marry his girlfriend after the name change became official.[63] The Weimar Republic alleviated this problem to a certain extent: 1919 regulations made it easier to change one's name.[64]

Lotte Hahm sought to unite transvestites and lesbians in one political movement, an effort that ultimately prompted more collective work on the definitions of identity categories. Hahm may have considered herself a transvestite and seems to have certainly considered herself a lesbian or "girlfriend." She at times used the first name "Lothar" and always wore men's clothing in the photographs and drawings of her in *Girlfriend*.[65] Hahm's club Violetta was known for its parties for male and masculine transvestites.[66] In seeking to organize transvestites and lesbians together, she had Radszuweit's support. Radszuweit wanted male-to-female people to find homes in lesbian groups rather than in those of gay men, probably because he saw respectable, masculine gay men as distinct from feminine men, whose overt presence he believed would harm the movement.[67] By 1930, Hahm was leading a transvestite group that held events for transvestites regardless of their gender expression or birth sex.[68] Female transvestites (that is, male-to-female people) recognized Hahm as a leader and source of valuable information. One advised neophytes that when they arrived in Berlin, they should contact Hahm to learn how to buy women's clothing and how to cultivate a feminine figure.[69] But Hahm's efforts to build a coalition seem to have failed. In 1932 a masculine woman wrote in *Girlfriend* magazine's transvestite section, "We homosexual women ... [w]e masculine women ... are not transvestites, with very few exceptions ... We want to remain women." She asserted that for the majority of lesbians who wore jackets, shirts, and ties, clothing was merely about "hitting a masculine note." "Transvestite" to her meant that one wanted to live not as one's birth sex but as the other sex. She expressed frustration about the transvestite-lesbian coalition Hahm had worked to build, alleging that male-to-female transvestites frequently hit on masculine lesbians at joint events.[70] Apparently caving to this pressure, only a few weeks later Hahm promoted a free Sunday night gathering "only for our women," for "girlfriends" to discuss "questions of particular interest to us."[71]

As the conflict between Hahm and others in lesbian and transvestite circles shows, the range of gender expression among women and female-to-male people in lesbian subcultures defied easy categorization. Male and masculine transvestites frequented lesbian social clubs.[72] Ruth Roellig described them as a distinct "genus" within lesbian circles.[73] Some of these female-to-male individuals had a concept of transvestitism like Fricke's: they sought to live as their true, male, sex.[74] Others were just "hitting a masculine note."[75] "Transvestite" meant different things to different people.

Lesbian and transvestite movements were based in claims to citizenship and respectability, at least according to the people whose views were represented in the lesbian and transvestite magazines. The program was, first, to assert that lesbians and transvestites were citizens and that they had a right to a public presence – that is, to subcultural spaces and to publications. This was expressed in the oft-sung anthem of Berlin's homosexual bars and social clubs of the Weimar era, the *Lavender Song* (*Das Lila-Lied*). It begins with a defence not of a biological type but of culture: "All we want / is this culture / so scorned by everyone." It ends by declaring that "we have the same rights!" and "we don't suffer anymore – rather, they must suffer us!! [*Wir leiden nicht mehr, sondern sind gelitten!!*]."[76]

Second, authors in the lesbian and transvestite press urged their comrades to behave respectably and to avoid overt challenges to norms of gender and sexuality and to decorum in general. Transvestite authors rejected prostitutes, emphasized the patriotic service of transvestites in the Great War, and implored their compatriots not to wear gaudy jewellery.[77] For many transvestites, the key goal was to conform in public. Indeed, to do otherwise was economically disadvantageous, not to mention downright dangerous. Hirschfeld and others used the ability of transvestites to pass as an argument for the transvestite passports. In one such case, Hirschfeld argued for a female-to-male person to be allowed to wear men's clothing because the person "incit[ed] public annoyance" and "always attracted attention" when he wore women's clothing on the street.[78] But when he dressed "as a man" the public "disturbances" stopped, and police did not have to intervene.[79] That is, this person was less of a "public annoyance" when he wore men's clothing; he thus ought to be allowed to do so. This was what the person wanted, and it was also good for society, Hirschfeld alleged: this transvestite's abnormality was not visible to the public when he dressed as a man. But beyond the possibility of passing, transvestite authors also believed that when they claimed rights and a certain amount of public space, they took on a "duty" to meet the standards of respectability and to maintain a low profile in public. "When we demand that the public acknowledge us," wrote one, "we have a duty to dress and conduct ourselves publicly in an inconspicuous manner."[80] Authors in the lesbian press emphasized respectability and public decorum, as Marti Lybeck shows.[81] A persistent theme in this form of respectability was the denial or sublimation of one's unruly sexual passions in favour of a purer, ideal love. Sexual desire had long been considered inappropriate for bourgeois women.[82] Women's social clubs excluded supposedly disreputable elements, such as prostitutes.[83] Hahm banished feminine and female transvestites who worked as prostitutes from her transvestite club.[84] As Sutton notes, this was the ethos of gay and lesbian activism in this period, an ethos that George Mosse describes as a project to "bend the bars of the cage" rather than to demolish the cage entirely.[85]

Scholars are increasingly using the notion of homonormativity to analyse such relatively constrained challenges to the sex/gender order. Yet what was at work in lesbian and transvestite subcultures in the Weimar years was not homonormativity according to Duggan's definition. Duggan argues that homonormative political movements do not "contest dominant heteronormative assumptions and institutions."[86] But lesbian and transvestite subcultures did directly challenge norms of heterosexuality and of gender. At the same time, however, they were not all that radical. Transvestite and lesbian subcultures held out the possibility of a relatively constrained queer culture, a subcultural formation that was not private but that followed the tenets of respectability. Given what a challenge queer sexuality and gender non-conformity were to the mainstream, this could never be depoliticized. But opinion leaders in the Weimar-era movements sought to invoke respectability in a way that would, they hoped, take the sting out of the confrontation they posed to the mainstream. I would characterize these movements not, therefore, as homonormative, but rather as restrained, respectable, and civic-minded.

It is important to note that these relatively moderate politics did not appeal to all of the people who moved in lesbian and transvestite social and political circles. One example is working-class women whose politics were more radical than the generally Social Democratic–flavoured politics of the lesbian magazines and of Radszuweit's League for Human Rights. The League for Human Rights was officially neutral in party politics, but *Girlfriend* urged votes for the SPD, with the German Communist Party a second choice.[87] Class distinctions were important in lesbian circles, although lesbian social scenes were not completely segregated along class lines. Certain bars catered to working-class women, such as those in Hamburg near St Pauli. A woman who frequented them, "Gerda Madsen," said they were for the "daughters of the working class" (*Arbeitertöchter*) rather than "bourgeois" (*bürgerlich*) people.[88] Class mattered in Berlin's bar scene as well, though in some clubs mixing prevailed.[89] For some working-class women in lesbian social scenes, political issues of lesbianism as presented in homosexual emancipationists organizations and media were less of a priority than were class politics. Madsen voted Communist. "The Sozis [SPD] were an old aunt's club [*Tantenverein*]" as far as she and her friends were concerned, she remembered. She had no use for the League for Human Rights because it was not far enough to the left.[90] In addition, the prostitutes whom movement leaders like Hahm sought to exclude lived their lives in a way that violated respectability; they circulated in lesbian and transvestite social scenes as well, but many probably did not back the bourgeoise organizations that derided them.[91]

Lesbian and transvestite subcultures flourished under the Republic. Leaders of these subcultures used rhetorics of rights, citizenship, and respectability to defend them, and doing so was a political act. It was a relatively less radical political act than others, but not a homonormative one: lesbian and transvestite subcultures challenged the sex and gender norms of their day.

What Slumbered Within Her? The Importance of Reading to Same-sex Desire

Beginning with the Republic's founding, homosexual emancipationists fought for media freedom. This section shows why media freedom was worth fighting for. The Republic's less-than-strict censorship made lesbian organizing possible, not only in logistical ways but also in conceptual ways. Censorship politics were one of the most important political questions for lesbian, gay, and transvestite subcultures: this point has, arguably, been underemphasized by historians of queer activism.[92] The stakes of censorship politics were high for sexual outsiders because publications made queer lives possible in ways that political groups or even social clubs, with their comparatively higher costs and more constricted geographical reach, did not. Magazines and novels, not organizations, were perhaps the most significant political intervention of the Weimar-era homosexual emancipation movement (which encompassed lesbian and transvestite groups). The women who produced the lesbian magazines, many of whom volunteered their time, thought they were improving, maybe even saving, lives.[93] Helene Stock wrote in *Girlfriend*,

> I call on all women: commit yourself to a serious deed. Don't just pursue your own pleasure while thousands of our sisters suffer in muffled despair. Help with enlightenment. Spread *Girlfriend* in factories and businesses. As soon as you have read the magazine leave it somewhere, ideally in a restaurant or on the train, the streetcar, or the bus, so that someone else will find it and read it.[94]

Roellig, the author of the lesbian guidebook, wrote of lesbians being doomed to sorrow "until through some lucky chance – by reading enlightenment literature or by meeting someone who feels the same way – they are delivered."[95] Transvestites, too, saw the magazines as a means to help other transvestites. Mimi wrote that she was thankful for the transvestite section of *Girlfriend* and that she purposefully left it lying on the seats of streetcars and trains so that it would reach others.[96]

The new women's magazines made it possible for readers to imagine queer lives for themselves. Magazines also transmitted practical information about how to be a lesbian, such as how to join a social club or find a bar or how to dress. *Girlfriend* and *Garçonne* announced club nights and parties. They ran political appeals, news, readers' letters, and debates on issues like sadism, bisexuality, the bob haircut (*Bubikopf*), and the nature of friendship.[97] The regular fare was short stories, poems, and serialized novels, not scientific tracts. Stories depicted female-female romance and drama. For example, in "The Girlfriend of Olga Diers," one night backstage the opera diva Olga encounters a young, destitute woman who has sought her out. Olga pledges to protect her.[98] In these stories of lesbian lives, the heteronormative disapproval of society was largely absent, lesbian communities grew and flourished, and women discovered their true natures and found true love.

Yet before one could seek to dress as a lesbian, or go to a bar, or imagine a different sort of life, one needed to understand one's own nature. One could do that by reading. In Hilde's story, which begins this chapter, Hilde knows the café before she goes there for the first time, but she does not know herself. Heinz, the handsome waiter, sells her the magazine, and through it, she gains a new understanding of the café. This understanding is crucial to Hilde's process of falling in love with Heinz, a process that climaxes not with Hilde's realization that Heinz is a woman – she realizes that well before the story's culmination – but with a sudden insight about herself: she loves a woman.

Some women who lived through the Weimar years came to recognize and understand their sexuality by reading. As an eighteen-year-old, Hilde Radusch moved by herself to Berlin. She found work as a telephone operator. She joined the Communist Party, eventually becoming a KPD city councillor. Her extended process of discovering that she was "different from the others" began at the train station one day when, intending nothing but a friendly bon voyage, she kissed an acquaintance and, unexpectedly, felt an erotic charge.[99] Seeking to discover what this strange kiss meant, Radusch read the novel *The Scorpion*. Many years later, Radusch wrote to the historian Claudia Schoppmann, "this book made an enormous impression on me ... For me the book was a revelation, I recognized myself in it."[100] According to Schoppmann, who interviewed Radusch and a number of other lesbians about their lives during the Weimar years, "literature often played an important role in triggering the self-awareness process in forming a lesbian identity."[101] This was the case for Freia Eisner, who realized, "Wow, I love women!" when she read another lesbian novel.[102] According to the author of a sensational exposé, when a group of lesbians were asked the cause of their lesbianism, a number said that they became lesbians "through reading."[103]

Reading could play such a role for transvestites as well. Elvira Karstens wrote in a letter to the editors of *Girlfriend* that for much of her life she did not realize that she was a transvestite. Growing up as a boy, she had been ashamed of her desire to dress in women's clothing and had fought against it. But as an adult she came upon *The Transvestite*, read the stories of other transvestites in its pages, and found "enlightenment regarding my nature."[104]

The moment of insight gained through reading was not always a happy one, however, taking place as it did in a society that stigmatized gender crossing and same-sex eroticism. "Branda" wept as she read the British novel of female inversion *The Well of Loneliness* (which is not a strictly uplifting book).[105] "That's where I really rediscovered [*wiedergefunden*] myself. That's how it was." The anguish was not about her sexuality itself, which "was not problematic to me. I found it totally natural." Rather, her tears were for the difficult position that society had placed her in as a same-sex-loving woman. The novel's depressing ending underscored this. The heroine, seeking to spare her girlfriend a life of social opprobrium, drives her into the arms of a man, who offers the girlfriend financial support and the respect of society. Having read this, Branda decided that the only way to ensure that she would not be parted from her girlfriend was to become financially independent. To do this she worked two jobs, one as a nurse and the other as a masseuse.

These stories about recognition, transformation, and reading did not necessarily refute the notion that various sexualities and desires had biological bases. Although the possible biological roots of sexual identity were not of great interest to many of the *Girlfriend* and *Garçonne* authors, some did incorporate them into their fiction, and many probably agreed with Roellig that "the inclination towards the same sex is inborn in most cases, and rarely acquired."[106] Accounts of reading and desire suggest, however, that a biological condition was not sufficient to make a woman a lesbian. Her self-conception, and how she acted on it, mattered. This is apparent in a short story that ran in *Garçonne*. As the story begins, its heroine, Loni, is living alone on a farm where she keeps chickens. One day, "a travelling woman" passes through and gives Loni a copy of *Garçonne*. Alone in her house that night, Loni reads it. As her eyes move across the pages, she feels a new physical sensation: "a deep passion filled her heart. A personal and intimate feeling grew in her. This was the first time that Loni had been able to read such a magazine. This new experience awakened in her all the tender and warm feelings that had slumbered within her." Loni must read more. She rushes to her desk and writes out an order for an edition of *The Well of Loneliness*, advertised in *Garçonne*. It arrives in the mail with another copy of *Garçonne*. Loni reads, and "the more she immersed herself" in book and magazine, "the more grew in her the desire, the yearning for love." But how to find love, isolated as she is on a chicken farm in the countryside? Happily, the magazine *Garçonne* can solve this problem too. Through its personal ads, "Loni met a beloved girlfriend, with whom today she has joy and happiness in the remote house on the edge of the woods where she tends her chicken farm."[107] It is not reading alone that leads Loni to seek "a beloved girlfriend"; something "slumbers within her" prior to the arrival of *Garçonne*. But, at least in this fictional piece, it is the magazine that opens up a new world to Loni. Otherwise, it seems, she might have lived out her life on her farm, tending her chickens alone.

Censorship proponents warned that lesbian media was "seducing" young women, but the ways in which women described attaining greater comprehension of their sexuality did not exactly match the unfriendly accusations about seduction. Conservatives warned of a sudden and unprecedented moment of transformation under the "wizardly power" of a book. But the interplay between reading and sexuality that these women describe is a process of becoming, a process in which reading might be a crucial step but was certainly not the only step. This was true for Radusch, for Eisner, and for the fictional Loni. Even if reading brought self-knowledge, it prompted further steps, such as the search for a girlfriend. Magazines could also assist with these additional steps. Margarete Knittel, who grew up in Berlin and worked as a stenographer and then as an official in a real estate management firm, was already dating women when she began reading *Garçonne* and *Girlfriend*. The magazines helped her to get over her "inhibitions." She visited a club for the first time; later, she met a long-term girlfriend through *Girlfriend*'s personal ads.[108]

Relative media freedom was important for lesbians and lesbian subcultures because publications were the parts of these subcultures that were the most easily approached. They were accessible to more people than were physical meeting spaces and events in bars, social clubs, and political groups. Publications were more available in rural areas than were meeting places, and helped to facilitate community building in smaller cities.[109] In addition, one needed money to take part in lesbian subcultures, and the Weimar period was one of economic insecurity, particularly for women. Oral histories conducted by Ilse Kokula with working-class women suggest that for them, the Weimar years were marked by economic strain and were less than golden.[110] Magazines were the most affordable part of the subcultures. An entry fee of 1 mark for a club or party was typical. *Girlfriend* cost 20 cents (*Pfennige*, pfg.) in 1924 and was still 20 pfg. in 1933, though that was not an insignificant sum. Madsen, who was one of the women interviewed by Kokula, said that when she first arrived in Berlin during the Depression and had no job, she paid 20 pfg. for a meal at a charity kitchen.[111] Yet she bought *Girlfriend* magazine, although very seldom. She and her girlfriend also went to a few social events, including a Christmas ball. "They did ballroom dancing," she recalled. "It was really fantastic."[112]

In cities where police were less tolerant of homosexual scenes, print media was also safer to access than were homosexual public spaces. Magazines were available by subscription through the post, making it possible for people who did not live near shops that carried them to receive them anyway. In addition, the circulation of magazines was apparently more difficult for police to control than were public spaces. Munich police were intolerant of homosexual meeting places. They were also more intent on seizing publications than were Berlin police, and perhaps partly as a result, not every magazine was on sale in Munich.[113] Raids on booksellers in Munich happened from time to time.[114] Yet police there could not keep homosexual and transvestite publications away entirely. In 1927, Munich police went to kiosks and bookstores to seize *Women Love* after a Berlin court deemed it obscene. But they failed. Although *Women Love* was only for sale in one neighbourhood, when police arrived to confiscate it, they found that, as they later reported, the issue in question was already five weeks old and "has been sold out for a long time."[115] *Girlfriend* (which an expert police reviewer noted contained a section for "transvestites – a name that I heard and read for the first time"[116]) and Radszuweit's *The Friendship Paper* for men were also for sale in magazine shops in Munich.[117] Police seized only one copy of *The Friendship Paper* per year in 1927, 1928, and 1929 and did not report successfully seizing *Girlfriend* or *Women Love*.[118] *Garçonne* was for sale in certain bookshops, and in 1932, a Munich woman advertised in it for a girlfriend.[119] That same year, a Munich transvestites' league advertised for members in *Garçonne*.[120] This was in spite of the fact that in the mid-1920s, Munich police arrested two men and harassed a third for wearing women's clothing.[121] In their arrests of transvestites, Munich police were not so different from Berlin police, who carried out a big raid in 1923.[122] Yet aside from word of mouth – which was probably important in a city with few public homosexual meeting points – buying a magazine or book may have been the safest, easiest way for a resident of Munich, whether a gay man, transvestite, or lesbian, to make a connection to homosexual and transvestite subcultures.

Publications had the power to reach across another kind of barrier as well: that of social stigma and the shame and fear that it caused. In a society where hegemonic norms held that lesbianism was disgusting and immoral, the sadness that a person might feel because of her outsider sexuality could make social scenes unattractive and inaccessible. In addition, a person might feel well-justified anxiety for her reputation and job if people found out about her sexuality. Despite considering her sexuality "natural," Branda expended a lot of anxious energy ensuring that it would not become common knowledge. She avoided Berlin's lesbian clubs. Their cabaret shows embarrassed her, and she feared that the police would burst through the door at any moment, which was improbable in Weimar-era Berlin. Branda had more use for *Girlfriend* magazine. She could not afford to buy magazines regularly, but when she could spare the money, she bought *Girlfriend* at a street kiosk where no one would recognize her. She locked herself in her apartment building's shared bathroom to read it. Branda wrote a poem and sent it to *Girl-friend*, and they published it, but under her real name, which caused her deep distress.[123]

The case of the lesbian press demonstrates the high stakes of censorship for lesbian subcultures. Transvestites' and gay men's subcultures had similar investments in media. The struggle to keep *Friendship*, *Girlfriend*, and other magazines from being seized under the obscenity law or placed on the filth and trash list was an important one. Relative media freedom under the Weimar Republic made queer lives more possible, and part of the Republic's reputation for sexual liberation is due to its less restrictive censorship. Moreover, although the sodomy law did not apply to female-female sex, that did not mean that lesbians had nothing at stake in political or juridical debates, despite what some activists claimed at the time.[124] In 1928, Irene von Behlau urged her fellow "girlfriends" not to forget censorship politics when they went to the polls.[125]

To Contain Rather than to Prohibit: Law, Lesbian Sex, and Censorship

The Weimar state responded to the fact that media was crucial for lesbian subcultures and could even be instrumental in the process of becoming a lesbian. It moved to curtail lesbianism chiefly through curtailing media. By the Weimar period, the omission of lesbian sex from criminal law, when taken in its broader context, seems not to reflect an utter lack of concern with lesbianism, but rather appears to be part of a different sort of state response to lesbian sex that was increasingly being applied to male-male sex and to other forms of immorality. Lesbianism could thereby be contained in a small, adult, most likely urban population. This approach to tolerating same-sex sexuality while limiting its public presence was seen by many lawmakers as ideal for male homosexuality as well, despite its heightened political significance. The strategy was part of a more general settlement on sexual-political issues hammered out by the opposing sides, the Weimar settlement on sexual politics, which is illustrated further in the next two chapters. It is the case that, as other historians have noted, lesbian sex did not disturb lawmakers in the ways that male-male sex did. It did not seem to disrupt citizenship because it did not involve that most freighted of political appendages, the penis. Indeed, many commentators did not think lesbian sex even counted as sex per se. At the same time, to an extent that other studies have not noted, lesbianism was perceived as a threat, as an unwanted condition that lawmakers feared would spread, especially to young women and especially through media. Many observers, including Reichstag deputies tasked with reforming the way that the federal criminal code responded to sexuality, felt that the dangers of lesbianism could be combated best through censorship, not through criminalizing lesbian sex itself.

Lesbian sex had never been a crime in unified Germany. It was a crime in the German lands prior to unification. For example, a woman was tried in Halberstadt and executed for committing sodomy with another woman in 1721.[126] But in 1851, the Prussian sodomy statute that had applied to female-female sex was quietly revised so that it only applied to male-male sex and human-animal sex. Upon unification, the new German nation adopted Prussia's penal code.[127] Historians have argued about why this revision happened, though the intriguing contrast between the decriminalization of female-female sex and the criminalization of male-male sex has drawn far less attention from the history profession than one might expect. Germany was not the only nation that criminalized male-male sex but not female-female. By the twentieth century, many of the European countries that still had laws against sodomy did not criminalize lesbian sex, although some, such as Austria, did. Though it has been asserted that the revision of the Prussian law was just an oversight, in fact the dropping of female-female sex from the penal code was an effect of a larger project to define the criminal act of "sodomy" as penetrative sex.[128] Moreover, the fact that women were not citizens made lesbian sex less of a concern for lawmakers.[129] In addition, by the first decade of the twentieth century, German lawmakers were reluctant to criminalize lesbian sex because they feared that if they defeated its epistemological evasiveness and defined it in law, they would call it into being.[130] These interpretations of the failure to criminalize lesbian sex, while doubtless correct, leave open a number of questions, such as why lesbian sex was perceived to be non-penetrative, why it evaded definition, and why, when the Republic fulfilled some of women's central claims on citizenship, there was less public agitation to criminalize lesbian sex than there had been under the kaiser.[131]

In the Weimar years, the logic of not criminalizing lesbian sex began with the assumption that it was not actually "sex," strictly speaking, or that it was a behaviour that fell short of the political and demographic significance of male-female and male-male sex.[132] "Sex" entailed penetration with a penis. At issue was not simply penetration. Dildos (*Godemiché*), defined by the Munich police in their handy lexicon of sexual deviancy as "artificial male member[s],"[133] were for sale in Weimar-era

Germany and were regularly seized by police.[134] They were illegal under Paragraph 270 of the criminal code, which banned the sale of "an object that is intended for obscene [*unzüchtig*] purposes."[135] But commentators on lesbianism did not seem to consider penetrative female-female sex with dildos, or for that matter with fingers or anything else, to actually be sex. Even the author of a "moral history" of lesbianism who claimed knowledge of penetrative lesbian sex acts – he recounts many tales of women penetrating other women with dildos or with larger-than-average clitorises – finally concluded that female-female sex was not really sex but rather was "mutual masturbation."[136] Penetration of a vagina with a clitoris was described as a "substitute for coitus"[137] but not coitus itself, apparently because for coitus, one needed a penis. Language about lesbian sex as a "substitute" for actual sex is common in descriptions written by non-lesbians.

The distinguishing of significant sex acts from insignificant sex acts by the former's involvement of a penetrating penis was well established in German law. Paragraph 175, the sodomy law, reflected it. German courts had struggled for decades to determine which male-male sex acts, exactly, were banned by Paragraph 175. Everyone agreed that the law's explicit prohibition of "unnatural sodomy" (*widernatürliche Unzucht*) covered penis-anus penetration (*Päderastie* or *immissio in anum*).[138] But what about other male-male sex acts, such as one man touching another's penis, or one man thrusting his penis between another's thighs? Confronted in 1880 with an accused who had lain on top of another man and achieved orgasm by rubbing his penis against the other man's legs, Germany's high court, the Reichsgericht, determined that the act that had taken place was an "analogue of natural intercourse" (*Analogon des naturgemäßen Beischlafs*) and that therefore Paragraph 175 had been violated.[139] From this developed a legal construct: "acts similar to intercourse" (*beischlafsähnlich*). It left masturbation decriminalized but applied to sex acts where one man ejaculated by putting his penis inside of another man's body or by rubbing it against another man's naked flesh.[140] Masturbation in this jurisprudence included not just the touching of one's own genitalia while a partner touched his own but also what was often referred to as "mutual masturbation" – the manipulation of one man's genitalia by another man. A 1913 Reichsgericht decision affirmed the legality of masturbation while confirming that, indeed, "masturbation" could include two people: it held that one man touching another's penis was masturbation, not "unnatural sodomy," the criminal act proscribed by Paragraph 175.[141] Hard-line opponents of homosexuality argued that Paragraph 175 ought to cover more acts, and indeed, sometimes men were able to beat Paragraph 175 charges if they could convince a court that they had gone no further than "mutual masturbation." As described in chapter 1, Richard Linsert and his partner did this when accused by Munich police. A few years later two other men in Munich beat a Paragraph 175 accusation in the same way, although even a failed prosecution often had devastating repercussions, like the loss of one's job, as in this case.[142]

The lack of a penetrating penis in lesbian sex thus led to a persistent difficulty in criminalizing it. This definitional problem came up when lawmakers in imperial Germany debated and declined to criminalize lesbianism. Some argued against doing so because lesbian sex could not, they alleged, be "similar to intercourse."[143] By the 1920s, lesbian sex had bewildered lawmakers in the German lands on this count for hundreds of years.[144] When the question of criminalizing lesbian sex came up in 1929, the Reich Minister of Justice advised against it because of the difficulties with the definition of "acts similar to intercourse."[145]

Because lesbian sex involved no penetrating penis in an unnatural or immoral sex act, it supposedly did not imperil the nation in the way that male-male sex did. For one thing, commentators averred that lesbian sex was not so appealing to women that they could not be won back to "normal" sex. Writing in the Republic's final years, the moral historian Rheine warned that lesbianism could "demoralize and destroy the Volk" by undermining the birth rate, masculinizing women, making them animalistic, and promoting the women's emancipation movement.[146] Yet he apparently thought that the wave of lesbianism spreading across Germany could be rolled back without too much trouble. This could be done without criminalizing lesbian sex, because lesbian sex was "nothing but mutual masturbation."[147] Rheine wrote that many women had female-female sex because they feared that having sex with a man would result in pregnancy or venereal disease. If reliable means of protection against venereal disease and unwanted conception were available, the number of lesbians "would sink considerably."[148] That is, lesbianism was a substitute for sex. If offered the real thing under agreeable conditions, many women would gladly take it. This is surely in part what Placzek, the authority on homosexuality and law, meant when he wrote that lesbian sex "does not interfere with the conditions necessary for normal sexual activity, or indeed make normal sexual activity totally impossible, as is the case for men."[149] In addition, lesbian sex seemed less threatening than male-male sex because, according to those knowledgeable on such matters, adult lesbians did not often seduce young women. Placzek made this point in his book. Although male homosexuals pursued youths,

> the homosexual woman mostly does not experience such a special need or primary interest in female children. This is a difference that is not only important for the protection of youth from seduction, and indeed recommends it … but also explains the fact that homosexual women remain free from the threat of law.[150]

Hermann Strathmann of the DNVP told the Reichstag penal code reform committee during its debate on Paragraph 175, discussed in chapter 4, that "the danger of lesbian love expanding through propaganda and seduction is not as great as is the danger of male homosexuality doing so" and that therefore lesbian sex ought not to be a crime. Strathmann had read Placzek – he mentioned him frequently in this speech. Since lesbians could not offer significant sex, their attempts at seduction would be unlikely to succeed.

In 1929, in the course of its debate on Paragraph 175, the Reichstag penal code reform committee briefly debated criminalizing female-female sex. The 1929 debate focused on the question of whether to decriminalize some male-male sex. But proponents of criminalizing lesbian sex put that topic on the table as well. They were a small collection of activists, authors, and politicians, including a Berliner named Emma Witte who appears to have made it her personal mission to see the law extended to lesbianism, explaining that she worked on behalf of right-wing women everywhere. Witte cited the dangers of lesbian seduction of the young, as well as the increasing visibility of lesbian subcultures.[151] Her quest failed. Even politicians who favoured retaining the criminalization of male homosexual sex dismissed the idea of extending criminality to female-female sex.

During this debate, politicians assumed that lesbian sex had little significance because it did not involve penetration with a penis and was unlikely to lure anyone away from heterosexuality permanently. Only a few speakers in the extensive debate on Paragraph 175 bothered to mention lesbianism. Rudolf Schetter of the Centre Party said the most about it. He was against extending the sodomy law to cover female-female sex. He also opposed another proposal on the table, to expand the sodomy law to cover more male-male sex acts. His reason was this: if the law were extended in both of these respects, "the perpetrators" would include "a large number of young people." Criminal proceedings against these male and female young people would do more harm than good; their homosexual liaisons would not otherwise mark them for life. "In youths, homosexual activity is often a preliminary stage in the development of a normal sexual orientation ... it is a vice that they jettison as soon as they leave puberty."[152] Schetter's view that young men and women often experimented with same-sex sexuality was remarkably common in a society so alarmed by the prospect of male teenagers veering into adult homosexuality.[153] According to the sexologist Iwan Bloch, young men and young women often had what he termed a bisexual phase, consisting of attractions to other youths or teachers of their own sex, especially in sex-segregated boarding schools. They nevertheless grew up to be perfectly heterosexual.[154] What is noteworthy is that the politician Schetter assumed that youthful same-sex relationships consisted of some sex acts and not others: current law did not cover these innocent dalliances because they did not feature "acts similar to intercourse." Only a particular kind of same-sex relationship warranted the law's opprobrium, in his view, and that was the seduction of young men by adult men, which he informed his colleagues was the cause of most cases of permanent, adult homosexuality.[155] These seduction relationships did include "acts similar to intercourse" and were, therefore, covered by the existing version of Paragraph 175. Female-female sex was comparatively harmless, in his view. It was neither penetrative nor likely to seduce. (Harmless as well were non-penetrative sexual relationships between teenaged boys.) Others agreed about lesbianism. The debate on Paragraph 175 included a discussion of whether the age of consent (*Schutzalter*) ought to be set higher for men than for women. Speakers on this question noted that the age of consent law had gender-differentiated functions. A Reich Ministry of Justice official explained that "the age of consent is a different issue for girls, because in their case the issue is not that their sex drive will be steered in the wrong direction, but rather that they be protected from the premature activation of the sex drive."[156] That is, the age of consent did not protect young women from the seductions of lesbians, which could steer their sex drives in the wrong direction. Rather, it protected young women from men, whose attentions might initiate the normal, heterosexual sex drive of a woman too early in her life. And the age of consent law need not protect women from other women. Lesbians, unlike men, were simply not imagined to be seducing young women, or indeed to be capable of doing so.

However, in discussions of censorship, lawmakers and policymakers asserted that lesbian seduction did happen, through media. Overall, the

Republic's laws pertaining to lesbian sex and lesbian media implied that publications about lesbianism were a greater danger to sexually "normal" women than was lesbian sex itself. The obscenity law (Paragraph 184) and the 1926 Filth and Trash Law were enforced against lesbian publications. The censorship boards established by the Filth and Trash Law ruled rather consistently that periodicals about lesbianism (particularly innuendo-filled personal ads) threatened to infect young women with lesbian desires, just as depictions of male homosexuality could seduce young men.[157] In 1928, an official in the Centre Party–controlled Prussian Welfare Ministry wrote,

It is a known fact in youth welfare circles that young people [*Leute*] and young girls at the age of development are for a period of time in a situation where the direction of their newly awakening sexual feelings is still unspecified, and can easily be diverted towards their own sex. The public debate on homosexuality, which is pushed upon [youth] through advertisements and commercial public displays, promotes such confusion. The result is serious damage to youth in body and mind. A terrible increase of homosexuality in present times is unmistakable. This is fostered by the mass distribution and public sale of homosexual magazines that have the character of propaganda ... [T]hrough their essays, advertisements and illustrations, they are suited to excite unnatural sexual lustfulness in developing youth ... There is a need to protect developing youth from these magazines, out of responsibility for the healthy development of the state and of society.[158]

This ministry applied in short order to have *Women Love* put on the filth and trash list because it "endangers youth above all."[159] The Berlin board that adjudicated on applications to include publications on the filth and trash list placed *Garçonne* on the list in 1930 because it threatened "particularly female youth."[160] The Berlin board adhered to the Reichsgericht's decision in the *Friendship* case. Publications on homosexuality were not objectionable per se: "The fact that it is a magazine for the discussion of homosexual questions does not come into consideration with regard to the question of whether it is filth or trash," the board held in a 1929 decision on *Women Love*. "*This* board does not judge erotic homosexual magazines differently from magazines that address heterosexual problems" (emphasis in original).[161] The Berlin board made the same point in other cases.[162] Yet lesbian magazines consistently made the filth and trash list and were occasionally seized as obscene under Paragraph 184.

Like men's magazines, lesbian magazines fought censorship. Rad-szuweit hired a lawyer to keep *Girlfriend* off of the filth and trash list in 1927 after a Hamburg youth welfare organization complained. Hiring a lawyer to argue before the censorship board was an unusual step for a publisher; Radszuweit did it several times. Radszuweit's lawyer complained about the "suppression of a minority," and a respectable, middle-class one at that. He described the members of the League for Human Rights as "mostly people from the middle class, who are themselves against prostitution, sexual slavery [*Hörigkeit*], and the influencing of minors." He called *Girlfriend* a scientific paper, which it certainly was not.[163] *Girlfriend*'s personal ads were the main issue, and Radszuweit's lawyer addressed this by pointing out that a host of other magazines had worse ads, including some heterosexual sex reform magazines and one of *Girlfriend*'s competitors, *Women Love*.[164] A few weeks later, the same Hamburg youth bureau applied to put *Women Love* on the list, too.[165] None of this swayed the Berlin board, which warned that *Girlfriend*'s personal ads could seduce heterosexuals into homosexuality.[166] *Girlfriend* ran personal ads for men as well as for women, so the board had both men and women in mind.[167] The board wrote that its decision was not a moral condemnation of homosexuality but merely a reflection of the fact that homosexuality was a "hindrance" to a person's social success and therefore ought to be kept from spreading.[168]

The Republic's overall position on lesbianism and law – that lesbian sex did not warrant criminalization, but lesbian media warranted censorship – followed a pattern that some Reichstag deputies advocated extending to male-male sex, as well. The idea was to leave individual homosexuals free of criminalization, but to prevent homosexuality from spreading to "normals," particularly teenagers, through media. This was a more modern, and more tolerant, approach to the "problem" of homosexuality that nevertheless threatened homosexual subcultures. As discussed in more detail in chapter 4, when the penal code reform committee debated Paragraph 175, Wilhelm Kahl, the committee's chair and leader of its moderate wing, argued for striking the law because doing so would drive male homosexuality from the public eye by removing the reason for homosexual "propaganda," which he warned could corrupt youths.[169] Speaking about men, Centre Party representative Schetter said that some individuals might have inborn inclinations towards homosexuality, and they were to be pitied. But the state ought to protect youths; it ought to prevent homosexuality from spreading like "a cancer on the welfare of the Volk."[170] Although Schetter opposed striking Paragraph

175 and Kahl favoured its abolition, the two men employed similar logic. The state could tolerate a few homosexuals, who might have innate inclinations, in constrained spaces, but the state must keep homosexuality from spreading throughout the public sphere. Control of media rather than criminalization of sex acts was the most effective way to do this.

Under the Weimar Republic, women formed lesbian organizations and created lesbian media. Transvestites did so as well. Media freedom was crucial to both movements. The Republic's response was to contain this media and these subcultures, in the interest of keeping lesbianism from spreading.

3 Female Prostitution, Modern Heterosexuality, and the 1927 Venereal Disease Law

In the mid-1920s in Hamburg, female social workers fought to rescue hundreds of poor and working-class women and girls from prostitution. The social workers administered a special brand of welfare called "welfare for the morally endangered" (*Gefährdetenfürsorge*). One of their best tools was a small institution, a forty-bed home (*Pflegeheim*) where "endangered" women could stay until they found respectable jobs. In one year, the Hamburg home helped 470 women find employment besides sex work, including posts in offices and factories.[1] But the social workers at the Hamburg home worried that they were not doing enough for the young women in their care. The young people needed education and culture. But local youth leagues and clubs did not want morally tainted girls as members, and the "endangered" girls found the "purity and naiveté" of the local youth leagues "foreign" and "boring."[2] So the social workers founded their own youth league at the home. It put on twice-weekly evenings of storytelling, game-playing, poetry, and lectures on topics like astronomy. There was also "factual, sober discussion of matters near at hand," such as the new law that would eventually revolutionize the way that Germany dealt with female prostitution, the Law for Combating Venereal Diseases (*Reichsgesetz zur Bekämpfung der Geschlechtskrankheiten*).[3] The women especially liked to sing. "It is remarkable," wrote one of the Hamburg social workers, "how many really musical girls are among the morally endangered."[4] The social workers hoped that these evenings of culture and fellowship would awaken a higher consciousness in their charges, that the girls would develop a sense of personal responsibility. Girls newly delivered to the home by the police sometimes mistrusted the youth league nights, calling them "forced conversion."[5] But dozens of young women participated, and for the social workers, the evenings had a happy glow.[6] Bent over paperwork in her room one

Prostitutes working, Friedrichstraße, Berlin. From WEKA (Willi Pröger), *Stätten der Berliner Prostitution* (1930).

night, a social worker heard "delicious, healthy, three-part singing, with a girl of extraordinary musical talent accompanying masterfully on the piano." The music, she wrote, "makes me feel deeply all the richness and worthiness of this home [*Heimatplatz*] for these restless lasses."[7]

Hamburg's home for "morally endangered" women and girls, and "welfare for the morally endangered" more broadly, was part of an ambitious effort undertaken by middle-class women to remake the manner in which state and society dealt with female prostitution. Social workers and their allies wanted "welfare for the morally endangered" to replace the system known as "regulation" (*Reglementierung* or *Kontrolle*). Regulation was police supervision of female prostitution in the interest of public health, a system that the women's movement argued degraded women and trapped them in prostitution. In 1927, the women's movement achieved its goal when the venereal disease law passed the Reichstag with broad support. The new law abolished regulation and made "welfare for the morally endangered" federal policy. It was a new, modern way to fight syphilis and gonorrhoea. Now, all Germans, male and female, would be responsible for preventing the spread of venereal disease. As Julia Roos notes, at a time when many nations were reinforcing restrictions on female prostitution, Germany essentially legalized it.[8] Supporters of "welfare for the morally endangered" and of the venereal disease law believed they were creating a form of sexual freedom. For the young women of Hamburg's home, this meant that rather than mandatory police supervision, they would receive the material support and ethical cultivation they needed in order to make better choices – better for them personally and better for society. Yet reformers also believed that not everyone was capable of making good choices in this new environment of freedom. Even the rosy evenings of song at Hamburg's home for the "endangered" were marked by the shadow of conflict between well-meaning social workers and resistant prostitutes. In one year, forty-three women ran away from the Hamburg home.[9]

This chapter, which intervenes in a well-developed historiography, is about the tension between freedom for many and management and surveillance for a few, a tension created by the 1927 venereal disease law. Historians of the 1927 law are somewhat divided as to whether it was coercive or emancipatory.[10] While remaining in accord, to a certain extent, with what other historians have argued, this chapter seeks to make an additional point. The venereal disease law was a step towards female emancipation, according to much of the women's movement. It created a new form of sexual freedom and put in place new welfare and public health benefits. The law was also interventionist. But it targeted a very small group. This small group did not even include all prostitutes, whose work took many forms, some of which were quite discreet. The law's interventionist measures, rather, targeted women whose sex work tended to be in the public eye. These were often working-class women who solicited clients on the streets. My point is that the coercive measures of the law that have been noted by some historians were directly related to the law's liberatory aspects. Indeed, they would not have existed without them: the policy's coercive measures produced its liberatory measures. This dynamic of freedom predicated on containment characterized the Republic's sexual politics more broadly. The relatively free sphere for homosexual emancipationist publications was critical to homosexual and transvestite subcultures, and the Republic tolerated it in part by ensuring that its public presence was minimal. The drive to curtail public immorality also shaped the reform of national policy on female prostitution and venereal disease.

The chapter builds this argument through four targeted interventions; it does not present an exhaustive history of either the 1927 law or female prostitution in Weimar-era Germany, both of which have been the topics of important studies.[11] The first section examines the feminist battle against regulated prostitution and the architecture of the 1927 venereal disease law. It argues that the law fulfilled much of what the woman's movement had wanted, greatly expanding a form of welfare that was emancipatory for women in several respects. The second section of the chapter looks at female prostitutes' opposition to the reform and at how the reform's advocates proposed to deal with female prostitutes who resisted it. The freedoms that the law established were predicated on a plan to abolish female prostitution and to contain the supposedly disorderly public sexuality of some female prostitutes, some of whom complained because they wanted to keep their jobs. Proponents of the reform argued that forms of mental illness and mental disability impelled these women to cling to prostitution. Together, these first two sections show that the freedom feminists envisioned in the 1927 law existed thanks to rather invasive forms of management and containment that were to be used against some prostitutes. The chapter's third section analyses the parts of the 1927 law that officially pertained to venereal disease rather than to female prostitution. The law essentially created a new legal duty to have what would in a later era be called "safe sex," that is, sex – assumed to be heterosexual sex – that did not transmit venereal infection.[12] This modern approach to heterosexuality also deployed coercive measures against a small minority in order to expand freedom of sexual expression for most people. The final section introduces a related issue lately raised by historians: the question of whether frustration with the venereal disease law's unintended consequences constituted a backlash against Weimar-era sexual freedoms that helped the Nazis come to power. It did not.

Replacing the Morals Police with "Welfare for the Morally Endangered": Feminism and the Architecture of the Venereal Disease Law

State-regulated female prostitution had long drawn the ire of European feminists. The system of regulation dated to the nineteenth century. Its logic was that prostitution would take place whether illegal or not and that the state ought to do what it could to protect public health from venereal diseases spread by prostitutes. Under the basic terms of regulation in Germany, if the police suspected that a woman was selling sex, they forced her to register with them. Once registered, she had to follow a litany of rules.[13] In some cities, registered prostitutes had to live in designated brothels. All registered women had to undergo regular medical exams for signs of venereal disease. If an exam showed a venereal infection, a woman could be forced into treatments that were only moderately effective and could be dangerous.[14] The battles of women's associations against regulated prostitution began in Great Britain in the 1870s, when Josephine Butler led a coalition of middle-class feminists and radical working-class men that succeeded in getting Parliament to end regulated prostitution.[15]

The opposition to regulation styled itself "abolitionism"; it was a key component of nineteenth- and early-twentieth-century feminism in European countries.[16] Butler and women who took up the struggle against regulation in other countries argued that police-supervised prostitution was bad for female prostitutes and detrimental to women in general. They denounced the system's sexist double standard: the male clients of prostitutes were not subject to police supervision or medical exams. Female prostitutes were the victims of a sexist society, driven into their line of work by employment and pay discrimination, by regulation itself, by the lack of safe housing for single women, by flawed religious moral education for youth, and by male exploitation.[17] Moreover, all it took to register a woman was police suspicion. Thus, technically any woman could be inscribed into an essentially extra-legal system against her will and without a trial. Once registered, it could be difficult for a woman to get her name struck from the police rolls. Anna Marx of Berlin unsuccessfully challenged her registration in 1914.[18] Marx appears to have married in order to escape registration as a prostitute, but police claimed that she was still selling sex and a court rejected her plea to be removed from the police list. In an analysis pioneered by Butler, feminists argued that this unjust system was symptomatic of the masculine and exploitative nature of the state.[19] The state, in their estimation, acted as a pimp, trapping women in prostitution for the benefit of men, while a patriarchal moral code looked on benignly. The feminist response to this – "There is only one moral for the two sexes" – is carved on Anna Pappritz's gravestone.[20]

Pappritz was among those most responsible for bringing abolitionism to Germany. She encountered Butler's movement while travelling in England, and in the 1890s, she set about founding a German branch of the International Abolitionist Federation. It was radicalism for a woman to take a public stand on prostitution in the 1890s, when polite society considered it improper for a respectable woman to even speak about the subject.[21] Pappritz was otherwise no political radical. Her sympathies lay with the liberal parties, and she distanced herself from the radical feminist and sex reformer Helene Stöcker, although like Stöcker, Pappritz envisioned new sexual norms.[22] Pappritz and her allies succeeded in getting many of the leaders of the women's movement to adopt the abolitionist position. The League of German Women's Associations (*Bund Deutscher Frauenvereine*) officially endorsed it in 1902.[23]

Abolitionism and homosexual emancipation were both reformist projects that drew support from the same political circles. The Abolitionist Federation supported homosexual emancipation's efforts to have the sodomy law repealed.[24] Enemies of abolitionism at times used accusations of homosexuality to try to discredit abolitionist feminists. These critics charged that the members of the women's movement who were seeking to rescue female prostitutes shared a taste for immoral sexuality with the women to whom they ministered. One self-appointed expert assured his readers that he knew of cases where "lesbian social workers" learned of lesbianism "in their profession" and that in addition, "among the women they work with – the prostitutes – there is a very high percentage of lesbians ... All in all, one finds this sort of tendency [i.e., lesbianism] in many women who professionally have something to do with prostitutes."[25] The assertion that many female prostitutes were lesbians was commonplace.[26] (Some female prostitutes did have female partners, although many had male partners.[27]) One attacker went so far as to name Pappritz in print as a feminist who hated men and marriage. He implied that she was a lesbian.[28] Pappritz never identified herself in public as homosexual. She did have a long-term relationship with Margarethe Friedenthal, an activist in the working-class women's movement.[29]

It is unclear how they defined their relationship, and female-female partnerships were not uncommon in the circles in which they moved; these partnerships were often not named as female homosexuality.[30] For a leader of a woman's organization, Pappritz was unusually willing to stand up for female-female partnerships. She and Helene Stöcker broke with most women's organizations in 1909, when they opposed a draft revision to the penal code that would have criminalized lesbian sex. In her comments on this draft law, Pappritz described female homosexuality as a "revolting ... sin." Yet, having thus distanced herself and her organization from lesbianism, she argued against the proposed law. Her contention was that many single women lived together for economic reasons and that if lesbianism were criminalized, their partnerships would unfairly fall under suspicion. Stöcker even acknowledged that sex took place in a minority of these female-female households.[31]

Pappritz and other abolitionists did not just want to end regulation: they wanted to replace it with a special brand of welfare. "Welfare for the morally endangered" was a bureaucracy of special welfare offices (*Pflegeämter*) and homes run by female social workers and dedicated to the goal of reforming prostitutes.[32] Various factions of the women's movement got involved in welfare work for prostitutes, including Christian and Jewish women's groups.[33] Various advocates of welfare for the morally endangered differed in important respects, such as whether they favoured secular, state-funded welfare or private religious welfare. Prior to 1918, they also differed in whether they wanted to abolish regulation, though after the war even conservative and Catholic women came around to the abolitionist position.[34] One of the chief activists in Catholic women's welfare work for prostitutes was Agnes Neuhaus of the Catholic Welfare League for Girls, Women, and Children (*Katholischer Fürsorgeverein für Mädchen, Frauen und Kinder*).[35] As a Reichstag delegate for the Centre Party, Neuhaus played a pivotal role in the 1927 reform. Before 1927, advocates of secular welfare struggled to establish welfare offices for the morally endangered on a city-by-city basis. By the mid-1920s, well before the new law, sixty-one cities had welfare offices for the morally endangered, including Hamburg.[36]

Under the Weimar Republic, abolitionism largely succeeded. The Revolution shifted power in favour of leftist and feminist reformers who backed abolitionism.[37] The SPD had taken an abolitionist stand before 1918, and its more substantial influence after 1918 helped to end regulation.[38] Women's enfranchisement also aided abolitionism.[39] Ultimately, women's greater influence over parliamentary politics under the Republic made the 1927 Law for Combating Venereal Diseases more radical and more feminist than it would otherwise have been and eased its passage.[40] As Julia Roos puts it, the 1927 law was a "major victory for bourgeois feminists and left-wing sexual reformers" over the sexism of regulation.[41]

In addition, the fact that post-war Germany was supposedly in the midst of an epidemic of venereal disease helped the reform pass. Commentators blamed the epidemic on the disruptions to sexual norms engendered by war and revolution. A wave of "venereal diseases" (*Geschlechtskrankheiten*), mainly syphilis and gonorrhoea,[42] had supposedly broken out among the troops during the war because of dissolute morals. In the words of one of the leading medical experts on venereal disease, "the tearing [*Herausreissen*] of hundreds of thousands, indeed millions of healthy young men from their normal living conditions, the long separation from their women and sweethearts, and the daily contact with women and girls of other countries and nations" had caused "sexual debauchery" and rampant infection.[43] After the war, experts claimed that heterosexual promiscuity and female prostitution, spurred on by the crisis in sexual morality as well as by bad economic conditions and social upheaval, were fanning the flames of the epidemic. The press complained of a "horrible increase in prostitution!" since the war and revolution.[44] The Communists blamed late-stage capitalism for spreading prostitution and venereal infections in the post-war period.[45] A delegate from the Bavarian People's Party declared in a speech to the Reichstag that Germany "has lost an extraordinarily precious wealth of ethics and morality due to the war" and "the best means of fighting venereal disease is the moral renewal and rebirth of our Volk."[46] (He nevertheless supported the 1927 venereal disease law.) Another delegate from a far-right, *völkisch* party complained that the moral strength of the German Volk had dwindled to the point that "one easily sounds ridiculous when one says, I am in favour of chastity until marriage."[47] In addition, venereal disease seemed a dire threat to the national birth rate.[48] According to the Reich Ministry of the Interior, it made men and women sterile, it triggered stillbirths, and it caused disabilities.[49] The members of the German Society for Combating Venereal Diseases, an influential group of reformist doctors, avowed that regulation did nothing to protect public health.[50] What was needed, they said, was "a modern and systematic fight against venereal disease."[51]

The 1927 venereal disease law was this modern and scientific public health response that almost all parties now agreed was necessary. The reform basically replaced police-regulated prostitution with welfare for everyone. In some cases, it did this quite literally. The city of Berlin simply took the approximately 5,500 city employees who had formerly regulated female prostitution and sent them to work at the city's clinics.[52] The new law took the primary responsibility for dealing with female prostitutes away from the "morals police," who had administered regulation. It gave it to welfare offices and to health departments. The law shut police-supervised brothels across Germany. It expanded the government's authority to find and treat people who had venereal disease. It subsidized medical care for venereal disease. It criminalized the knowing transmission of a venereal infection. Now all citizens, male and female, bore equal responsibility for preventing the spread of infection, and female prostitutes were no longer subject to a special system of policing that infringed on their rights. The law also granted greater, although still somewhat limited, means for individuals to protect themselves from infection by expanding access to condoms and other prophylactics, which had the side effect of making birth control somewhat more accessible.[53] In a concession to conservatives, the law also banned female prostitution in small towns and near churches and schools.

In parliament, the Law for Combating Venereal Diseases drew support from parties that rarely agreed. Social Democrats and members of the conservative German National People's Party (DNVP) voted for it. So did members of the Catholic Centre Party, the Bavarian People's Party, and the left-liberal German Democratic Party (*Deutsche Demokratische Partei*, DDP). It took a long time for this coalition to hammer out an acceptable compromise on the terms of the law.[54] One powerful factor that drove them to finally do so was the overwhelming support among women of all political persuasions for the repeal of regulation. Regulation was unpopular among women. Now that they had large female electorates, parties that had formerly supported regulation could no longer afford to do so.[55] And even in the right-leaning parties, influential women wanted to abolish regulation: the conservative Protestant leader Paula Mueller (later Mueller-Otfried) is one example.[56] Even some Nazis backed the law. Although the small, at the time relatively inconsequential, Nazi Reichstag faction voted against it, a major Nazi Party newspaper published a debate about the law that featured an argument in its favour as well as one against it.[57]

Welfare for the morally endangered as established by the 1927 law was a project of women's emancipation not only because of the sexism of regulation, but also because the institutions of welfare that the new approach established helped middle-class women gain footholds in certain professions. Pappritz and the Abolitionist Federation advocated the hiring of female social workers[58] and female psychiatrists and teachers[59] to staff the institutions of welfare for the morally endangered. Frankfurt, for example, increased its staff of female welfare workers tasked with the fight against venereal disease fourfold in the year after the law passed.[60] By 1927, the social work profession in Germany was overwhelmingly female, having been pioneered in the nineteenth century by women's movement leaders like Alice Salomon.[61] The idea was that women were best suited to rescue their fellow women from prostitution. Just before the 1927 law passed, Neuhaus told the Reichstag, "Today ... we are on the way ... to put just about the entire enterprise of this kind of work into the hands of women. And that is a good idea! Women's work done in a true spirit has the power to heal."[62] Here, Neuhaus drew on well-travelled maternalist feminist notions of women's role in public life arising from their motherly powers and unique moral uprightness. She understood motherhood as part of this. But she, like many of her contemporaries, thought that maternalism did not preclude careers outside of the home. "The recent development of women" was at its "highest and noblest," she said, when women entered the professions as teachers and social workers.[63] Many social workers worked with female prostitutes, and the 1927 law poured government funding into their efforts.

Maternalist feminism did much to inspire the construction of the European welfare state, including in this case.[64] The venereal disease law was a major welfare initiative, part of an expansion of Germany's welfare services in the Weimar era, although the Republic never lived up to the welfare commitments outlined in its constitution.[65] The law passed in 1927 amid a brief period of confidence in the economy. A few months later, the Reichstag passed one of the Republic's key pieces of welfare legislation, which established national unemployment insurance.[66] Welfare policy was contentious under the Republic. It often ran aground on an ideological rift over whether welfare services ought to be state-controlled or private, secular or Christian. Historians have identified the split between welfare advocates as ultimately detrimental to welfare and to democracy.[67] Yet these factions came together in 1927 to support the venereal disease reform. The law allowed for both public offices and private religious charities to take part in welfare for the morally endangered. Both kinds of agencies could receive referrals of prostitutes or suspected prostitutes from the police or health departments.[68]

Feeblemindedness and Female Prostitution: Prostitutes' Opposition to the Reform and Reformers' Responses

Despite the breathtakingly wide support that the 1927 venereal disease law found in the Reichstag, not everyone with an interest in female prostitution supported the new policy. Some female prostitutes wanted to keep doing sex work. But the intention of the 1927 reform was to abolish, or at least significantly cut down on, female prostitution, particularly forms of it that were visible to the general public, such as street soliciting. The conflict between some female prostitutes and the feminist social workers who sought to rescue them invigorated a discourse that identified recalcitrant prostitutes as mentally ill and mentally disabled. For "incorrigible" prostitutes, proponents of the reform planned confinement in welfare institutions, to be enacted through a proposed preventative detention law. This plan to manage the unruly, disreputable, and public sexuality of some female prostitutes made it possible, in the eyes of the venereal disease law's advocates, to dispense with religious morality and policing for the majority of people, who could be relied upon to make respectable choices.

There are signs of scattered opposition to the reform on the part of female prostitutes, especially those who were registered under the terms of regulation and who lived in brothels or worked the streets. One hundred and fifty-three Hamburg women petitioned their city government in vain to save the police-supervised brothels where they lived and worked.[69] Eight women who lived and worked in regulated brothels in Bremen petitioned in 1927 to stop the city from closing the brothels. Local feminist leaders dismissed their petition as a ploy by desperate women incapable of rejoining "respectable society."[70] The city closed its brothels. That same year, twenty-four registered prostitutes in Berlin sent a petition to the Prussian Welfare Ministry calling for regulation to be retained. Although the Welfare Ministry seems to have ignored the petition, it is a detailed description of these prostitutes' politics. They gave four civic-minded reasons in favour of regulation: public health, social well-being, efficient government expenditure, and the anti-crime effects of prostitution.[71] The mandatory doctors' exams protected public health, the authors of the petition wrote. Without police regulation, many "up-until-now respectable girls" would sell sex, but "inexperience and false shame" would keep them from paying attention to their venereal disease status. Medical authorities on venereal disease made the same argument: registered prostitutes knew how to deal hygienically with infection.[72] By making this point, the petition's authors defended their professional turf from women who sold sex without registering, the so-called clandestine prostitutes. A registered prostitute had a market advantage: she offered her customers the assurance that she was being regularly examined by a doctor. In addition, the petition's authors argued that prostitutes performed a valuable social role and saved the government money: "How many unmarried men are compelled to come to us, and those whose wives are handicapped through whichever illness. Single men cannot always have a relationship and marry as they are all at the moment suffering financially"; moreover, if men did form extramarital relationships rather than paying for sex, the result would be "children born out of wedlock" for whom state welfare would have to care. Finally, they argued, prostitution prevented sex crime: "How many more sex murders [*Lustmorde*] and sex criminals [*Sittlichkeitsverbrecher*] would there be" if prostitutes did not offer such men a way to satiate their overactive sex drives? The twenty-four women claimed, essentially, that prostitution was a job like any other. In fact, they claimed that it was more valuable to society than a lot of other jobs. Regulated prostitution, they asserted, served the national interest.

Prostitutes who opposed the reform were often working-class women whose sex work took particular forms that happened to be more visible to the public. Female prostitution was an economically diverse profession. Better-paid prostitutes tended to be more discreet: for example, one Berlin brothel connected sex workers to clients via the telephone, obviating the need for women to solicit on the street.[73] Forms of women's sex work that were more public – street soliciting and work in regulated brothels – were the focus of much of the public discussion of prostitution. Street soliciting was a lower-waged occupation, as was work in the regulated brothels. Moreover, social workers and police chiefly searched for "endangered" women and girls on city streets and in parks: thus, welfare clients tended to be women who did street soliciting. These women were disproportionately working class.

These working-class prostitutes were at odds with their mostly middle-class defenders in the women's movement. According to its feminist architects, the sexual freedom that the Law for Combating Venereal Diseases offered female prostitutes was the freedom *from* prostitution, not the freedom to *do* prostitution. Advocates of the new welfare hoped to "eradicate" female prostitution. They believed that new welfare services would help women find other jobs and that if offered the opportunity to do other kinds of work, women would leave prostitution. They dismissed

the claims made by some prostitutes that they had chosen their professions for sound reasons and preferred to keep their jobs and homes in
brothels. Speaking in the debate prior to the law's passage, Louise Schroeder, Reichstag delegate for the Social Democrats, told the parliament
that she was "completely convinced that prostitution is eradicable." She
continued, "I am convinced of this because prostitution just does not
belong in our contemporary society anymore." She called it atavistic,
"an evil that remains from the time of slavery."[74] Schroeder's view can
be taken as typical not only of Social Democrats but also of left-leaning
social workers. In addition to serving in the Reichstag, she was the director of Altona's office for welfare for the morally endangered.[75] Schroeder's colleague Julius Moses, an SPD spokesperson on health matters,
shared her sense that history had marched beyond female prostitution.[76]
He asserted that it was "a relict from the time of slavery, the time of
contempt for the woman and her work."[77] Neither Schroeder nor Moses
thought that the new law could singlehandedly end female prostitution.
They called for additional issues to be addressed, such as the problem of
alcoholism and the lack of job training and equal pay for women. However, the ultimate goal that their party claimed to be working towards
was the eradication of prostitution, which would, they believed, simply
reflect the modern era.

The new law was lauded by its supporters as a better way to get rid of
immorality in public, that is, female street soliciting. One of the central
principles behind the 1927 reform was that welfare was a more effective way to get female prostitutes off of the streets than were the police,
whom abolitionists claimed trapped women in prostitution by inscribing
them on their lists. The less contact endangered women had with the
regular male police, the better, according to abolitionists, although they
believed that special female welfare police could be useful.[78] Police themselves were, in some cases, sceptical that welfare would end female street
soliciting. Leipzig implemented welfare for the morally endangered on
the municipal level and closed its brothels in 1925, before the venereal
disease law passed. At the time, police cautioned of "the danger that
the girls would simply end up on the street."[79] But this did not happen,
according to supporters of the national venereal disease reform. The
city's welfare offices received municipal funds, the police sent the former
brothel inhabitants directly to the social workers, and Leipzig's "street
scene" (*Strassenbild*) did not get any worse.[80] A conservative voice who
backed the 1927 law around the time that it passed, Adolf Sellmann (the
leader of the moral purity group the West German Morality League),

described the closing of brothels in Leipzig as a success because it kept female prostitution out of public spaces: police sent the prostitutes to the social workers and therefore, "the street scene of Leipzig has in no way been altered through the abolition of regulation."[81] Even the author of the article published in the Nazi press in support of the venereal disease law argued that the new law would be superior to regulation at removing prostitution from public space. Although his party officially opposed the reform, he supported it because, he claimed, it would do more to combat street prostitution than regulation was doing.[82] Welfare for the morally endangered was supposed to rid Germany's streets of female prostitutes.

The problem with "eradication" was that some women who sold sex did not welcome efforts to shut down their profession. They were reluctant to find other jobs. Their reasons for recalcitrance varied. The registered prostitutes who lived in brothels and fought to save regulation likely feared losing both their jobs and homes at once, especially since many were supporting children.[83] Younger women who ran away from home and who were later picked up by the police and sent to the social workers may have feared being sent back to their parents.[84] Additional motives could have included resentment at the paternalism of feminists or, in the case of minors, fear of being sent to reformatories.[85] Most crucially, some women believed, despite prevailing moral norms, that prostitution was their best employment option. Some working-class women preferred prostitution to the long hours and measly pay of domestic service.[86]

Proponents of welfare for the morally endangered assumed that the relatively small group of incorrigible female prostitutes refused to give up sex work *in part* because of a biological predisposition that was probably hereditary but was in any event intractable. Their thoughts on this were influenced by academic psychiatry. From the late nineteenth century, German thinkers who were interested in criminology, many of whom were psychiatrists, generally held that an interaction of both environmental and innate factors motivated a person to commit a crime. By the Weimar years, most psychiatrists agreed that heredity and environment interacted in a complex way: in Richard Wetzell's words, "many criminals suffered from genetic mental abnormalities" and under pressure, they fell into crime "not because these abnormalities were directly criminogenic but because they handicapped their carriers in social and economic life."[87] Finally, although many psychiatrists were convinced of the hereditary sources of mental illness, most held that the hereditary sources of criminal behaviour were far murkier.[88] At the same time,

Weimar-era policymakers and the general public remained focused on the social causes of crime and on finding new welfare schemes to help offenders reform and rejoin society.[89] As did German psychiatrists and sexologists, advocates of welfare for the morally endangered rejected Cesare Lombroso's theory that inborn inclination was the singular cause of prostitution.[90] Rather they argued that both internal and environmental factors mattered.[91] A leading authority on criminal psychology, Gustav Aschaffenburg, wrote that the reason so many studies of female prostitutes had found "mental incapacity" (*geistige Minderwertigkeit*) among a high percentage of them was that just as plague would take the physically weakest members of the population, in "the battle of life" the "psychopathic characters sink into the swamp," that is, into prostitution.[92]

Abolitionists, too, believed that both innate and environmental factors mattered. They were generally more concerned with social factors. They thought welfare could make a difference. Pappritz wrote, "In most cases" endangered women "are not bad, but rather just badly behaved, they are misled young children, human beings who can be saved by timely intervention."[93] The project of welfare for the morally endangered overlapped with broader reforms, such as the Bielefeld System, that sought to use welfare for rehabilitation.[94]

Yet abolitionists believed that in a minority of cases, women were either too ruled by innate inclination to reform or too corrupted by the interaction of inclination and bad environment to turn back to a socially useful path. Katharina Scheven, a leading abolitionist, wrote that although Lombroso's "idea of born prostitutes should be rejected," it "contains a kernel of truth in the sense that naturally, a daughter of the Volk with an abnormal psycho-physical genetic factor [*Anlage*] searches for work with fewer moral inhibitions than does the healthy, normal individual."[95] This kind of girl also tended to resist rescue work, Scheven added. Moreover, welfare efforts on behalf of a girl whose brain "deviated from the average ... to a certain degree" would fail.[96] This was not strict biological determinism. But the belief that innate factors plus bad environments produced "incorrigibility" in some cases of crime, sexual disorder, and social marginality did dictate certain conclusions about the best uses of resources and the best ways to protect society.[97] These conclusions are apparent in welfare for the morally endangered. When the Depression hit and funds dried up, policymakers in other realms of welfare work, such as youth welfare, voiced the same idea: scarce resources ought not to be spent trying to reform people who were incapable of changing due to mental "abnormalities,"[98] as a Reich decree on child welfare put it.

As to what these mental "abnormalities" that helped to cause female prostitution were, a handful of concepts with roots in psychiatry came up again and again in public discussions. They are worth reviewing in detail because they also came up in discussions of homosexuality, as chapter 4 shows. One was "degeneration" (*Entartung*). Initially theorized by the nineteenth-century French psychiatrist Bénédict-Augustin Morel, degeneration was an undifferentiated morbidity that passed from parents to children, taking various, often worsening forms in successive generations. These included mental illness, epilepsy, and mental disability. Environment could supposedly exacerbate degeneration: parental alcoholism, for example, made the next generation worse. So did unhygienic living conditions. Morel's theory, in Richard Wetzell's words, thus "offered the advantage of combining both genetic and environmental factors in a single explanatory theory."[99] Degeneration captured the nineteenth-century European imagination, enjoying a hundred-year career as a conduit of anxieties about society and culture.[100] It influenced psychiatrists, including the founder of sexology, Krafft-Ebing, up until the First World War.[101] By the 1920s, German psychiatry had moved away from the theory of degeneration.[102] But it remained an important concept in lay discussions of sexuality and was still influential in sexology, including in Hirschfeld's sexology.

A set of mild mental disorders was also frequently linked to female prostitution. These disorders did not rise to the level of full-blown mental illness. They could, however, supposedly cause antisocial behaviour, including sexual disorder and crime. They were initially termed "psychopathic defects" or "psychopathic inferiorities," most often shortened to "inferiorities" (*psychopathische Minderwertigkeiten* or *Minderwertigkeiten*).[103] Prior to 1914, when degeneration theory's influence on psychiatry was strong, many psychiatrists linked these disorders to degeneration. Later, they pointed to other hereditary causes.[104] Into the 1930s, psychiatrists increasingly stressed the hereditary causes of mental illnesses and of the "psychopathic inferiorities," although they still investigated environmental causes as well.[105] Psychiatrists of the Weimar era preferred the words "psychopathy" and "psychopath" – which did not have the connotations that they now have in English – for these borderline abnormalities rather than "inferiorities," which was deemed derogatory.[106] However, both sets of terms appeared in the wider public discourse beyond academic psychiatry.

In addition, commentators on female prostitution often claimed that it had ties to "feeblemindedness" (*Schwachsinn*), a mental disability.

For example, in a 1918 debate in a Reichstag committee, politicians demanded that the state provide "protection for the feebleminded, who fall into prostitution in large numbers."[107] The concept of feeblemindedness was almost one hundred years old by the Weimar period and had gone through a number of permutations in the work of various psychiatrists.[108] By the 1920s, "feebleminded" generally meant a relatively mild disability that impaired higher intellectual functions but left more basic ones intact. One of the functions that feeblemindedness impaired was judgment about right and wrong, legal and illegal, and moral and immoral. Thus, the feebleminded gravitated to crime and immorality. A 1914 textbook on criminal psychiatry described how in school, children with this condition demonstrated problems with "comprehension" and an incapacity to internalize norms: "Admonitions and punishments have no effect."[109] In addition, "the flawed development of the power of judgment [*Urteilskraft*], in connection with an enhanced influence-ability [*Beeinflußbarkeit*] has the effect that" feebleminded children "can be exploited by healthy people for all possible purposes, including for things that people of complete mental facility would not be prepared to do."[110] Moreover, "feebleminded" people experienced acute sexual desire:

> the sexual lives of the feebleminded [*Schwachsinnige*] develop earlier and play a more conspicuous role than they do for normal people. As a result, the feebleminded engage in intensive masturbation or unusually early sexual intercourse. Their sense of shame is for the most part very scantly developed, and as a result, they often engage in immoral behaviour [*unsittliche Handlungen*] in public. Feebleminded girls [*schwachsinnige Mädchen*] fall extraordinarily easily into prostitution as soon as they are seduced.[111]

The author of a 1921 study of registered female prostitutes identified "feeblemindedness" in thirty-eight of the seventy women he interviewed.[112] Albert Moll, the influential sexologist, blamed all of these varieties of mental abnormality for female prostitution – "feeblemindedness," degeneration, "psychopathic inferiorities," and psychopathy. He described how women with these conditions easily slipped into prostitution out of a desire for fast money.[113] These same notions were at play when prostitutes and social workers encountered one another on the streets and in welfare offices. The director of Frankfurt's office for welfare for the morally endangered kept track of how many of her clients had "hereditary burdens" (*erbliche Belastung*) – fifty-seven in 1928.[114]

Gender affected feeblemindedness. It could occur in men or women. Experts on crime, welfare, and social policy often tied feeblemindedness in men to criminality. In contrast, feebleminded women supposedly gravitated to prostitution. The government of Saxony served up a blunt version of this idea in an effort to drum up support in the federal bureaucracy for a eugenic sterilization law. Referring to *The Yukes*, one of the better-known studies done in the United States of an "inferior" (*minderwertig*) family, a provincial official wrote that, "in the fifth generation, all the women were prostitutes and all the men were criminals."[115] The US family studies did tend to show this: *The Kallikak Family*, which was well read and well reviewed in Germany and also cited by this official from Saxony, is another example.[116] But the formula was too simple for many German experts, including Aschaffenburg. High rates of feeblemindedness were to be found among male criminals, he allowed, but environmental factors mattered.[117] Moreover, "whores," he wrote, were not the female counterparts of male criminals in general, but rather of certain males, "beggars and vagabonds" (*Landstreicher*).[118] Like female prostitutes, they lived in a state of "parasitism" on society.[119] They, too, exhibited high levels of mental abnormality, he wrote, and were "incapable of honest work, dulled to the fear of punishment," and "apathetic to everything."[120] Some experts also blamed feeblemindedness in men and boys for forms of sexual disorder that a normal "sense of shame" would prevent, such as public masturbation.[121]

In short, studies found high rates of conditions such as feeblemindedness, degeneration, and psychopathy among female prostitutes.[122] In some cases, social workers, feminists, and doctors assumed that such conditions produced incorrigibility. This necessitated a special response.

Abolitionist feminists envisioned long-term confinement for incorrigible prostitutes. Katharina Scheven of the Abolitionist Federation explained that a high percentage of young female prostitutes were "feeblemindeds" (*Schwachsinnige*) or "psychopaths." Although better environmental influences could reform many of these women, some would fall right back into prostitution unless confined "in special institutions, like physical cripples, the blind, etc.," where they could at least "do useful work in exchange for their support by the state." She wrote that "such individuals are born to be institutionalized [*Anstaltsmenschen*]."[123] Pappritz wrote that such women needed "suitable homes or work colonies" where they could be involuntarily committed "for long periods … for their well-being and for the protection of the public."[124] Both Scheven and Pappritz cited a study done by a female doctor in a welfare home (*Fürsorge-Erziehungsheim*) for girls that found a high percentage of "feeblemindeds" and "psychopaths," which the study's author blamed on "hereditary burdens" (*erbliche Belastung*) and degeneration resulting from parental alcoholism.[125] Pappritz noted, "These unlucky, hereditarily burdened women need a completely different treatment than do the normals ... We therefore need a preventative detention law [*Verwahrungsgesetz*] and a reform of the legal process of incapacitation [*Entmündigungsverfahren*]."[126] In a speech to the Reichstag, a female authority on welfare for the morally endangered explained that some of those who practised street solicitation and thereby offended public morality and decency would not stop, despite the threat of punishment. These people, she said, needed education and economic support. But in addition, in order for those methods "to be effective, a preventative detention law [*Verwahrungsgesetz*] for psychopaths, the feebleminded, etc. must be passed."[127]

Preventative detention (*Verwahrung* or *Bewahrung*) was a familiar concept in Weimar-era welfare politics. It was to be a powerful legal tool for making welfare compulsory, a new process for placing people into welfare institutions so that they could be educated and reformed, against their will if necessary. It had been developed in the pedagogical reform movement, but it was often proposed in the Reichstag as a means to address female prostitution.[128] Moderate-left welfare advocates called for replacing the old workhouses (which had their own compulsory detention provisions) with a new kind of institution. Here, the "asocial" would be confined by preventative detention and tended by social workers for long periods (some proposed lifelong confinement).[129] Some supporters of preventative detention also touted its eugenic benefits: it would be a means to institutionalized people with hereditary conditions during the periods of their lives when they were fertile, thus preventing them from reproducing.[130]

No preventative detention law passed under the Republic, despite broad support for such a measure and the introduction of several parliamentary bills that would have established it had they been approved by the Reichstag.[131] The SPD, Centre Party, left-liberal DDP, and conservative DNVP all backed preventative detention, as did many groups in the women's movement.[132] The Communist Party was the only major faction that opposed preventative detention on principle.[133] Several drafts of it failed to become law because of disagreements about financing; there was, in addition, a lack of consensus about whether the law would offer a broad definition of the types of behaviours that would qualify a person for preventative detention or a narrow one.[134] Even without preventative detention, in the Weimar years some local authorities used existing legal procedures for declaring adults mentally incapable (*Entmündigung*) to confine them, and in addition, people could still be confined in workhouses for limited stays.[135] And though preventative detention did not become law under the Republic, until the Great Depression and the breakdown of the parliamentary process in the early 1930s all political players acted as if preventative detention was a real possibility. The Centre Party and DNVP introduced a draft preventative detention law in 1928, and the German Society for Combating Venereal Diseases was still agitating for it in 1930, even as the economic crisis killed the prospects of another costly new welfare initiative.[136]

Advocates of the Law for Combating Venereal Diseases saw a preventative detention law as a companion reform, a necessary component of a wider scheme to end female prostitution. Agnes Neuhaus is credited with coming up with the idea of preventative detention in 1904 in the course of her welfare work with endangered women, and she was among preventative detention's foremost champions.[137] In a speech to the Reichstag in support of the venereal disease law just before it passed, she spoke of a preventative detention law as something that "will soon be a reality." She said it would be used to compel resistant female prostitutes "who are not capable of being responsible for their actions" to enter the welfare system.[138] The women's rights campaigner Marie-Elisabeth Lüders, then serving as a Reichstag delegate for the left-liberal DDP, also mentioned preventative detention in her speech to the parliament on the venereal disease law just prior to its passage. Her party supported the law, but she feared that the section of the law that banned prostitution near churches and schools and in small towns would be "misused" by the police to arrest female prostitutes. As did Social Democratic backers of the law, Lüders thought that the new system's success depended on having social workers, not police, interact with female prostitutes.[139] Thus, Lüders called for more social workers for the morally endangered and said that, in addition, "I hope ... that this preventative detention law will shortly become reality." Her party cheered this last statement.[140]

For some advocates of the law, such as Pappritz, preventative detention for some female prostitutes meant sexual freedom for other people. This was a freedom to make ethical choices about sexual expression rather than to have them dictated to one by religious morality or by the police. Pappritz praised the venereal disease law for bringing "freedom" to women, freedom not in the sense that the law legitimated "libertine" behaviour but rather in that it recognized how "sexual morality cannot be upheld through policing and criminal punishment, but only ... through the development of the ethical sensibilities of both sexes."[141] To Pappritz, sexual freedom meant doing away with policing as a way to uphold moral norms. Instead, she would introduce education and ethics as a way to uphold them. Yet the "moral norms" in question were not necessarily to be revised. And ethics and education instead of policing would only work if preventative detention made it possible to institutionalize the small number of resistant women, women who were incapable of making ethical choices about their sexuality. Therefore, in the same article in which she welcomed the "freedom" established by the new venereal disease law, Pappritz affirmed her commitment to a preventative detention law to be used on "asocial elements."[142]

The feminist project of helping women leave prostitution, a project that was made into government policy by the 1927 law, proceeded from a vision of a democratic welfare state. It advanced the cause of women's emancipation. It also exemplified the Weimar settlement on sexual politics: it established a form of sexual freedom that depended on constraining a relatively small group of working-class female prostitutes, who were supposedly incapable of making responsible choices in conditions of freedom.

Sexual Duties and the New Regime for Fighting Venereal Disease

One summer day in 1927, Emma Bunge found a letter from the Berlin police in her mail. It contained an order: she had to prove that she did not have a venereal disease or get treatment immediately. A sense of shock must have struck Bunge as she read the letter. She had recently been ill and had seen a doctor, who had initially suspected a venereal infection, but the doctor had quickly ruled this out, since, as Bunge later wrote, "I have not had sexual intercourse with anyone."[143] If she felt shock, it soon turned to anger. She had to spend money to get a certificate from a doctor attesting that she was not sick. Word of the accusation about her health, which Bunge called "a coarse injury to my honour," got back to her boss, who fired her. Bunge suspected that someone had maliciously made a false report about her to the police. She demanded to know the name of her accuser so that she could protect herself in the future; the police refused. They routinely kept the source of such denunciations secret from people who were denounced, although if denunciations turned out to be false, they often would name names.[144] In fact, a Dr Schmidt had told police that Bunge had given gonorrhoea to one of his patients.[145] Schmidt's patient apparently lied about Bunge. Bunge was not the only person with this sort of problem. In the first year after the venereal disease law went into effect, Frankfurt's office for welfare for the morally endangered, which ran a public venereal disease clinic, took in reports about almost 200 people who supposedly had venereal infections but who turned out not to be ill at all.[146] Bunge's case demonstrates the new duty attached to heterosexual sex by the Law for Combating Venereal Diseases, as well as the new surveillance measures put in place to make sure that people were fulfilling that duty.

This section of the chapter shows that with its ban on knowingly spreading venereal disease, the new law extended the freedom to make choices about sexuality to a majority of the population while moving to use coercive measures to contain a supposedly unruly minority. This was similar to the new law's response to female prostitution. In the case of the provisons on infection, the supposedly unruly minority happened to contain many of the same people targeted for preventative detention, including unrepentant female prostitutes. Yet there is a danger in over-emphasizing the reform's coercive aspects. The bulk of what the venereal disease law did was to provide health care.[147] Many benefited from the new system and had no contact with its surveillance provisions. At the same time, the law conformed to a particular logic: that is, that it was possible to offer expanded freedom of sexual expression to a large group of people so long as the sexuality of a relatively small group of people could be managed.

According to Sellmann of the West German Morality League, the venereal disease law created "a duty": "The person with venereal disease has the duty to be treated, even if he is not yet on his sick bed. If he does not, he can be forcibly sent for treatment."[148] Moreover, anyone who merely had good cause to assume that they were sick with a venereal illness had a legal obligation to seek treatment from a certified doctor. If they did not, they could be sentenced to up to three years in prison.[149] If health officials believed that the person posed a grave risk of spreading infection, they could call in the police to confine the person in a hospital ward, where he or she could be forced to undergo treatment.[150] The 1927 law was, thus, a "serious intervention in personal freedom," as Joseph Joos of the Centre Party put it in a speech to the Reichstag. Some, particularly liberals, complained about this.[151] But even many liberals agreed with Joos, who continued, "This intervention is justified. Society takes precedence over the individual. When the individual poses a danger to society, society has the right to hold him to account and to subject him to certain duties."[152] The duty in question came along with benefits that people took advantage of, like expanded access to prophylactics and health care.[153] The venereal disease law shows, in Annette Timm's words, "the degree to which questions of sexual propriety were considered central to the development of a new ideal of citizenship within the modern German state."[154] The law called on men as well as women to make sexual choices that would protect their fertility, in the interest of the nation. This was not the only effort at the time to use science and medicine to improve heterosexuality: it was concurrent with the campaigns of the left-leaning sex reform movement to teach Germans how to have mutually pleasurable, heterosexual marital sex that would result in eugenically fit offspring.[155] The venereal disease law was part of a modern approach to heterosexuality.

The law also established a new bureaucracy to make sure that the duty it engendered was being fulfilled. The venereal disease law charged health departments, social workers, and doctors with tracking down sources of infection in the population. Health workers questioned patients about their sexual partners. They collected reports from other agencies, doctors, and the public at large about people who seemed likely to spread venereal disease. They informed a person's sexual partners if he or she turned out to be ill.[156] The Prussian government directed health departments to investigate streets, nightclubs, and bars.[157] Doctors asked patients about their sexual histories.[158] They were legally obligated to report their patients to health departments if the doctor believed that the person's professional or "personal circumstances" made it likely that she or he would infect others.[159] Although the 1927 law directed clinics to ignore reports made by private persons, according to the staff of Frankfurt's clinic, "private persons" reported ten people to the clinic in one year.[160]

The new law also empowered health departments and clinics to compel people to be tested and treated. In the year after the reform passed, the venereal disease clinic in Frankfurt treated about 1,000 patients, and about 100 of them did not come to the clinic of their own volition but rather were identified by the clinic staff's investigative work and summoned to the clinic.[161] Likewise, Berlin's seventeen clinics had far more voluntary clients than clients who were reported.[162] According to an article on the Berlin clinics in the Social Democrats' newspaper *Vorwärts*, which was based on an interview with the official who oversaw the clinics, "compulsory medical treatment … is not often used. Although there are 6,000 prostitutes in Berlin, police help was required only 350 times to compel ill people to comply with a doctor's orders."[163] The number of cases of compulsory treatment was small compared to the overall number of patients. But compulsory treatment was happening. And, at least in the mind of this article's author, compulsory treatment was something that readers would expect to be used on female prostitutes.

The backdrop for these coercive measures was fear of dangerous, highly infectious, difficult-to-treat diseases. Syphilis and gonorrhoea did not always have obvious visible symptoms, making them easy to overlook and easy to hide.[164] Moreover, these infections were supposed to be quite contagious, capable of spreading through "kissing, sleeping together, eating, bathing, infected sponges, thermometers, chamber pots, sharing cigarettes, wind (musical) instruments, etc.," according to the Berlin Health Department.[165] A group opposed to the closing of regulated brothels in Altona warned that if female sex workers moved out of brothels and into regular apartment houses, they would spread infection to entire families via the communal toilets.[166] And with penicillin's availability to the public as a miracle cure still years away, treatment did not assure a return to full health.[167]

Above all, health officials, politicians, and doctors warned of the danger to the public posed by people who had "frequently changing sexual partners." This meant "promiscuous" men and women having non-commercial heterosexual sex. It also meant female prostitutes. Berlin officials pleaded with the Prussian government for help with the cost of treating large numbers of "venereal disease–suspected and frequently-changing-sexual-partners types of people" who needed care in the wake of the 1927 reform.[168] Officials warned against people who had a "reckless lifestyle" or "lack of judiciousness [Einsicht]."[169] The Prussian government warned officials to look out for "moral endangerment or waywardness" (Verwahrlosung).[170] It also encouraged health departments to require repeated testing for "people who are known to frequently change sex partners and who can therefore be expected to seek to mask a possible sexual illness by means of deception."[171] People had a powerful incentive for hiding infections, the Reich Ministry of the Interior cautioned: the "unchecked sex drive."[172]

A lot of the discourse around the 1927 reform pointed to the danger posed by a specific group of people with "frequently changing sexual partners": female prostitutes. This was despite the fact that officials suspected men as well as women of promiscuity, and that someone like

Emma Bunge, who does not seem to have been a prostitute, could be the target of an investigation. Now that female prostitution was legal and unregulated, police, health officials, and bureaucrats could not use the fact that a woman sold sex as a criteria to compel her to get tested and treated. Instead, they used coded language to designate female sex workers. They referred to them as women with "frequently changing sex partners,"[173] or women whose "profession or personal conditions ... seem ... to make the danger of infection particularly great,"[174] or women who might be violating the 1927 law's provisions against offensive public soliciting or soliciting near churches and schools,[175] or "former regulation [*Kontrolle*] girls without profession."[176] In its official guidelines on the new law, the Reich Health Department told doctors that infected "women who can prove no self-supporting profession and who are suspected prostitutes" should be given no chance to voluntarily submit to a doctor's treatment. For them, compulsory hospitalization "must be the rule."[177]

The Wiesbaden Health Department told Sofie Limbach to get tested for venereal disease in 1929 because they thought that she had "frequently changing sexual partners." Limbach got an exam, which turned up no evidence of infection. But the Health Department claimed that the exam had not been thorough enough. It ordered Limbach to come in for weekly medical exams. She protested that this was nothing but the reinstitution of regulation and hired a lawyer. The Prussian Welfare Ministry got involved and determined that the Wiesbaden Health Department had overstepped its authority by requiring Limbach to have regular exams. The Health Department could, however, order her to have a second exam, Prussian Welfare Ministry officials decided. They just could not schedule regular exams for Limbach by indefinite standing order.[178] This was no isolated incident. The federal government told doctors to avoid certifying that a patient had been treated and was no longer infectious if the patient "practise[ed] sexual intercourse with frequently varying partners" and if the patient gave cause to fear "that they will expose themselves over and over to the danger of infection."[179] This description was sure to be read by doctors as referring to prostitutes. With no certificate, such people could be required to come for regular exams. If a patient suddenly broke off treatment, doctors were to report her or him to local health officials, who might have the person confined for compulsory treatment.[180] In important respects, this system was nothing like regulation. For example, Limbach could live where she liked, and there could be no standing order mandating regular exams for her.

Yet Limbach's story shows that the new system did allow for rather close official oversight of the sexuality and health of some people. In practice, those people were often prostitutes. Martha Ardensee, Reichstag delegate for the Communist Party, said that although the law abolished regulation, her party doubted that it was going to bring real change, "because all of the regulations that are supposed to bring sick people to doctors are either exclusively or at least first-and-foremost intended for prostitutes."[181]

The classification "feebleminded" was also used by public health officials to identify people who ought to be watched closely and, if necessary, forced into treatment. The Reich Health Department's guidelines for doctors on the new law held that compulsory hospitalization was "especially advised for feebleminded and otherwise psychologically abnormal persons." Those hospitalized were only to be released once a doctor certified that they were no longer infectious.[182] People who had feeblemindedness, which many commentators linked to hereditary factors, supposedly lacked moral inhibitions. They could thus be expected to spread venereal disease. Public education efforts to inculcate a sense of national sexual duty would not work on the feebleminded.

In addition, certain men seemed to pose a particular threat to public health, just as certain women did. The fact that the 1927 reform made men's sexuality a public health issue by "treat[ing] the sexes the same," as the SPD's *Vorwärts* put it, was one of its great achievements, according to its supporters.[183] Frankfurt's clinic served factory workers and salesmen.[184] The new venereal disease regime did not, however, treat all men the same. Homeless or itinerant men, who were associated with sexual disorder in another context – that of male prostitution, as chapter 4 argues – seem to have been likely to fall under suspicion of harbouring venereal infection.[185] The Centre Party's Reichstag delegate Helene Weber urged health departments to pay attention to "wandering [male] youths."[186] In its book of directives for doctors on the venereal disease law, the federal government identified homelessness as a potential grounds for compulsory hospitalization.[187] In the years after the law passed, officials in Frankfurt claimed that they had large numbers of "young ramblers" (*jugendliche Wanderer*) passing through the city and sought funds to hire male welfare workers to fight the spread of venereal disease in this population.[188] The Reich Minister of the Interior warned of the "numerous cases of venereal disease among young ramblers," praised Frankfurt for tackling the problem, and suggested that compulsory treatment would be necessary for this population.[189] Frankfurt officials wanted to build a locked hospital ward for these "unemployed ramblers, a considerable number of whom are sick with venereal disease" and who would not stay under a doctor's care unless compelled to do so.[190] As I argued earlier, psychiatrists also identified high rates of feeblemindedness and other mental "abnormalities" in the population of homeless and itinerant men, "beggars and vagabonds" in the psychiatrist Aschaffenburg's words.

In short, health officials and social workers sought to apply the new coercive provisions of the venereal disease law to female prostitutes, many of whom could supposedly be expected to be suffering from feeblemindedness or psychopathy. Marginalized men, such as homeless men, were also suspicious; they too were thought likely to be afflicted with such conditions. After the law went into effect, one prostitute told Magnus Hirschfeld, "Whether the police are called morals police or health police, to us it's the same, they are the same 'bullies' as before, and also with the doctors that we must go to, nothing has changed."[191]

Unintended Consequences of the Venereal Disease Law: The Battle for the Streets

The venereal disease law did not, however, rid the streets of female prostitutes. In fact, it seems that street prostitution became more visible, at least in some cities. The year 1918 had mobilized female prostitutes, particularly those who worked on the streets and in brothels.[192] War and revolution made the discourse of citizenship and its entitlements meaningful for them as it had done for women in general and for gay men. Prostitutes banded together and spoke out against exploitative brothel owners and harassing police. Hirschfeld reported that during and after the Revolution, women formed prostitutes' counsels in many big cities "to fight for their natural human rights."[193] Prostitutes were thus a self-consciously politicized group. After 1927, some of them used the venereal disease law to assert that they had a right to work in public spaces.[194] For example, in 1930 Martha Schulz complained on behalf of "a large network of working-class prostitutes" whose place of business was the Alexanderplatz area of Berlin. Police were impeding their business by shutting down cheap hourly hotels where they took their clients.[195] Schulz and company's complaint did not stop police from interfering in their work. Officials in the Prussian Ministry of the Interior, which oversaw the Berlin police, assured Schulz that police acted well within the law when they closed these hotels, because the traffic to and from the rooms was disturbing the public.[196] Police – even, as here, the relatively tolerant Berlin police, under the direction of an SPD-controlled ministry – sought to protect public order. Schulz and other prostitutes were also facing off against a newly reconstituted public health bureaucracy charged with removing them from public spaces. Often, city officials, health workers, and police lost this struggle and were unable to keep what they called the "street scene" (*Straßenbild*) free of female prostitution. The obvious solution was the preventative detention law that almost all politicians agreed should be passed. But when preventative detention stalled, factions fell out over what they should do next. Should they give the police back some of their former powers to drive female prostitutes from public spaces? Or were the police part of the cause of female prostitution and therefore incapable of being part of the solution?

This problem of female sex work in public after 1927 sparked a debate, which this final section of the chapter analyses. The debate is worth examining because conservative opposition to female prostitution in public has been taken as a sign of a broader rejection of Weimar democracy, a backlash against the venereal disease law that helped to build support for the Nazis.[197] This backlash argument is a substantial piece of evidence for a broader assertion made by a number of historians, which is that the politics of sex contributed to the Nazi rise to power. Chapter 6 considers that broader argument. Here, however, the aim is not to critique the more general narrative but rather to look specifically at the controversy over the 1927 reform's unintended consequences, which included an apparent increase in female street soliciting. Though at times heated, disagreements about what to do about female street soliciting after 1927 did not contribute to a backlash against democracy and did not destabilize the Weimar Republic. They did, however, reflect the considerable importance that almost all parties assigned to banishing immorality from the public sphere. This was a central aspect of the Weimar settlement on sexual politics.

The 1927 venereal disease law's failure to curtail female street soliciting had been predicted prior to the law's passage by its critics, and after the law passed, it inspired more critics. Complainers voiced anxieties about how female street soliciting had moved out of designated streets and districts, where regulation had contained it, and into urban public spaces, where it was deemed inappropriate. Before the new law passed, police officials as well as some citizens' groups warned that it would spread female street soliciting throughout cities.[198] After the reform passed, critics charged that it had made the "street scenes" of cities worse. In 1928, a DNVP delegate told the Reichstag that people were saying that now, "prostitution is gaining the upper hand in public."[199] Citizens of Essen complained about female prostitutes on every street corner.[200] University administrators in Königsberg described "exceptionally active prostitution traffic" on a street where many students travelled to and from university buildings.[201] Because of the new law, they claimed, the police were helpless to clear the street. The basic allegation made by these critics was that the reform was worse than regulation had been at keeping street prostitution out of certain urban areas.

The 1927 law did not entirely divest police of their powers to restrict soliciting. It gave them some powers to arrest women for soliciting in public in an offensive way. It also banned the selling of sex by women near churches, schools, or places where children were living or were often present, and the selling of sex in towns of fewer than 15,000 inhabitants.[202] But critics charged that these powers were too limited.

Police, politicians, and advocacy groups sought to curtail female street prostitution in public spaces after 1927. Police in at least one city – Essen – continued to arrest female street solicitors in violation of the new law, until the Prussian Interior Ministry made them stop.[203] But the obvious solution was the preventative detention law. Addressing claims that female prostitution had moved into the public following the law's passage, Arnold Spuler of the DNVP told the Reichstag in 1928, "Admittedly, without a preventative detention law [*Bewahrungsgesetz*], [the venereal disease law] is indeed a torso," that is, a chest without arms. He said it was "high time" that the Reichstag passed preventative detention.[204] Also in 1928, members of the Bavarian People's Party made the same demand.[205] So did Helene Weber of the Centre Party.[206] But there was a problem: preventative detention was stalled and ultimately failed to become law.

In the absence of preventative detention, right-leaning and left-leaning advocates of the 1927 reform split over whether they ought to empower the police to suppress street prostitution. In 1932, speakers at a meeting of the Cologne chapter of the German Society for Combating Venereal Diseases praised the law for bringing many sick people in for care and empowering doctors and health departments. But, they said, police needed more power to ensure that "the streets remain clean."[207] Also in 1932, the Centre Party's Weber called for the venereal disease law to be revised so that street soliciting would be illegal, to "protect public order and morality" and to protect youth from the temptations of prostitution.[208] Left-leaning supporters of the law opposed these plans, although they did want to use the police for some tasks. Moderate leftist feminists like Louise Schroeder of the SPD and liberal feminists like Anna Pappritz of the Abolitionist Federation thought that prolonged contact with the police made it impossible for women to return to normal lives and that jail time hardened prostitutes against the ministrations of social workers.[209] But they supported the provisions of the 1927 law that put police in the service of welfare and public health – by the terms of these, the police were to hand women over to social workers and clinics rather than jailing them.[210]

This discontent with female street soliciting was not opposition to democracy. It was not even opposition to the 1927 law itself. The 1927 law was not intended by any of its architects in the parliament to establish a right to sell sex, let alone a right to sell sex in public. And almost no one made such arguments in its favour. Between roughly 1900 and 1914, abolitionists had advocated a liberal right to sexual freedom in private, and a speaker at a 1906 convention claimed that women had a right to sell sex.[211] But the argument that women had a right to sell sex was almost entirely absent from Weimar-era discussions of female prostitution. It was made consistently and loudly only by female prostitutes themselves. Politicians, activists, and journalists who backed the venereal disease law believed that it would "eradicate" female prostitution, including street prostitution, or at least suppress it. "Indecency [*Unzucht*] must no longer be recognized as a profession!" wrote Friedrike Weiking, head of Stettin's welfare office for the morally endangered, in 1921.[212]

In 1930, Agnes Neuhaus of the Centre Party made a speech to the Reichstag that is a useful illustration of the relatively specific and limited nature of conservative complaints about the venereal disease law. Neuhaus was a leading advocate of the 1927 law and of preventative detention, and voiced sentiments that were probably common to many of her fellow moderate conservatives. She spoke of "the horrible condition we have now on the streets of the big cities," which was "ten times worse than it was before the law passed." She demanded that female police officers be assigned to welfare offices, to add muscle to social workers' efforts. She wanted closer ties between welfare offices and police departments. She called again for a preventative detention law.[213] Neuhaus's plea for greater police involvement infuriated the SPD's Schroeder, who wanted to keep the police as far away as possible from endangered women and girls.[214] Yet had Neuhaus's proposals become federal policy, they would have constituted revisions to the 1927 law. They would have made people like Schroeder unhappy, but they would not have been a drastic change to public policy. The venereal disease law already included a role for the police, though Neuhaus wanted a more robust one. And Neuhaus's demand was not all that far from an idea backed by the mainstream bourgeoisie women's movement, in the form of the League of German Women's Associations, which was the development of female police forces staffed by professional women who ministered to the "endangered."[215] This speech by Neuhaus has been cited as a sign of backlash against the 1927 reform.[216] But Neuhaus was not calling for a repeal of the 1927 law or for a return to regulation. Nor was she calling for an overthrow of the Weimar Republic. She was calling for a revision of an existing law. She was signalling an area for possible future compromise, which Thomas Mergel argues was often the purpose of Reichstag speeches.[217]

In addition, speeches like Neuhaus's were a case of smoke but little or no fire: after 1927, female prostitution was not all that pressing of a concern for conservatives.[218] When in 1930 the Centre Party's Heinrich Brüning became chancellor under conditions that were only semi-democratic, he did not revise the venereal disease law. In addition, when the anti-democratic right came to power with Franz von Papen in 1932 and undertook cautious and limited moves against immorality in public (see chapter 6), there were no mass arrests of female street prostitutes. Only 172 women nationwide were convicted of prostitution-related offences in 1932.[219] At the same time, a lot of people were unhappy about female street soliciting after 1927. Female street soliciting was an overt form of public immorality, and opponents of democracy could easily lump their anxiety about it into an indictment of the immorality supposedly seeping throughout the public sphere. In 1933, the Nazis quickly suppressed street solicitation.[220] This heartened people who disliked street soliciting and helped to persuade them of the respectability of Hitler's regime. But, as chapter 6 argues, these conservatives were won over after Hitler became chancellor, not before.

Under the Weimar Republic, heterosexuality took on what reformers called a modern, rational form, one that respected the concept of equality between the sexes. Public education encouraged Germans to think about the nation's health and future as they made decisions about sexual expression. Women who did discreet sex work, which tended to pay more, were free to conduct business and need no longer register with the police. The less that they came into the public eye, the better. At the same time, the 1927 reform to laws on prostitution and venereal disease identified categories of people whom officials and activists assumed could not fulfil the new duties and therefore must not be allowed to abuse the new freedoms. For such people, social workers sought indefinite detention. The venereal disease law established policies of surveillance and compulsory treatment for them as well. Modern heterosexuality was implicitly a form of sexual citizenship.[221] Yet like all citizenships, it was defined by exclusions.[222] The next chapter examines how the logic of the venereal disease law was mirrored to a surprising extent by what at first might seem a very different reform, the proposed revision of the sodomy law. It, too, held out the possibility of greater freedom of sexual expression, on the condition that a disreputable and possibly dangerous minority be placed under stricter control.

4 Male Prostitution, Homosexual Emancipation, and the 1929 Vote to Repeal the Sodomy Law

Kurt Hiller might seem an unlikely defender of male prostitutes. The son of a man who owned a tie factory, Hiller grew up amid Berlin's Jewish middle class, got a doctorate in law, and by the late 1920s had made a place for himself as a leftist intellectual.[1] But he had a personal connection to male prostitution, as well as an intellectual reason to defend men who sold sex. The personal connection began around the time that Hiller turned twenty, in 1905. He had fallen into a deep but chaste love for a friend. The affair went badly when both sets of parents found out about it and forbade Hiller and the friend from meeting. Hiller was so distraught that he considered suicide. Arthur Kronfeld, a friend of his who later helped Magnus Hirschfeld to found the Institute for Sexual Science, talked him out of it. As the love affair dissolved, Hiller realized that the love he felt for his friend existed alongside, yet separate from, lust – an "animalistic desire," but not for the beloved; rather, the desire had no object in particular.[2] He learned that there were "certain places" in the Tiergarten where he might encounter men to whom he was attracted. One evening in October, Hiller found himself on a bench next to an older, "rakish and wiry" man whose face he could just make out in the glow of the streetlights. Hiller asked the man if he had muscles. Instead of answering, the man offered his upper arm. Hiller squeezed; his muscles were "like steel." Hiller thought, "Why not?" They went to the man's apartment, which was very small and clean. The man undressed. Tattoos decorated his muscled body, and although Hiller disliked tattoos, the sight filled him with lust. "We lay in bed and held one another, and I had scarcely pressed my yielding body hard against his splendid one than 'it was over.'" The man asked a low price. Hiller paid and never saw him again.[3]

That first evening in the park was representative of many that followed over the next three decades. Paying for sex became a part of Hiller's life. He believed that, as he put it in his memoirs, "the general criminalization of male prostitution is a scandal."[4] For Hiller, sex (in his words, "animal practice") grew distinct from the eroticism and loving devotion belonging to the mental and spiritual realms, "eros."[5] He loved various men with whom he had close, chaste friendships. He paid other men for sex.[6] This arrangement applied when Hiller met Richard Linsert, the young veteran of the First World War who had fought to found a friendship league in Munich in the early 1920s. In 1929, Hiller and Linsert had to decide just how far they were willing to go to defend male prostitutes. That year, the Reichstag nearly acceded to the paramount demand of homosexual emancipation: it came close to abolishing Germany's law against male homosexual sex or "sodomy" (*widernatürlich Unzucht*), Paragraph 175. Historians have interpreted the proposed reform as a sign of the Republic's toleration of sexual diversity.[7] Yet for some men who had sex with men, the repeal of Paragraph 175 would have meant harsher criminal penalties. Lawmakers voted to strike the sodomy law from the penal code in order to replace it with a new law that would have cracked down on male prostitution. The proposed reform bore striking similarities to the revision of Germany's laws on female prostitution and venereal disease. Like the 1927 venereal disease law, it would have offered sexual liberation to a large group at the expense of a small group of marginalized people, in this case male prostitutes. The push to revise Paragraph 175 also drew on a theme apparent in censorship politics: the revision of the sodomy law had merit, according to politicians, as a means to suppress homosexual "propaganda." What is most interesting – and often overlooked – about the proposed reform of Paragraph 175 is how controversial it was among the men who had lobbied for decades for the repeal of the sodomy law. Many homosexual emancipationists applauded the repeal of Paragraph 175. But not all did so. Hiller and Linsert believed that the repeal was but an illusion of liberation, and perhaps a dangerous one at that. Together, they transformed the Scientific Humanitarian Committee (the WhK) in order to fight the crackdown on male prostitution.

This chapter examines the position of the politics of male prostitution within homosexual emancipation, the proposed reform of Paragraph 175, and the bitter fight within the WhK that the reform occasioned. An initial section examines the nature of male prostitution in the Weimar years, homosexual emancipation's response to male prostitution, and Linsert's passionate fight against the criminalization of male prostitution. Although many male prostitutes did not consider themselves homosexual, the issue of male prostitution was a crucial one for the homosexual emancipation movement. The second section tells the story of the vote in the penal code reform committee of the Reichstag to revise Paragraph 175, elucidating how this reform was intended as a crackdown on the male prostitutes on whose behalf Linsert advocated and was in addition an attempt to drive homosexuality from the public sphere. These restrictions on male prostitutuion and on the public visibility of male homosexuality made the decriminalization of other forms of male-male sex possible. The third section examines the WhK's reaction to this. Was a crackdown on male prostitutes an acceptable price to pay for the decriminalization of sex between consenting adult men? The vote to reform Paragraph 175 coincided with Hirschfeld's abrupt resignation as head of the WhK, which left the organization largely in Hiller's and Linsert's hands. The WhK is increasingly cited as the first gay rights organization in history.[8] The resignation of its founder in the midst of a controversy, and its resulting near-demise in the financial turmoil that followed, has been largely forgotten or dismissed as insignificant.[9] But it was important: under Hiller and Linsert the WhK took a position that Hirschfeld's science did not support. The WhK's rejection of the proposed reform of the sodomy law was an early instance of a problem that has plagued many similar organizations: whether or not to endorse a settlement that liberates some at the expense of others.

The proposed reform of Paragraph 175 is moreover an instance of a more general settlement on sexual politics, as are the reforms that previous chapters examined, the Republic's policies on the censorship of media with sexual content and the 1927 law on venereal disease. This was the Weimar settlement on sexual politics. It brought greater freedom of sexual expression to a majority of sexual outsiders who were otherwise respectable citizens, while curtailing a disreputable minority and cordoning immorality off from the mainstream public sphere. The chapter's concluding section makes this argument.

Men's Sex Work and Richard Linsert

The cause of male prostitutes resonated in both of the two activist traditions to which Richard Linsert devoted his life: homosexual emancipation and communism. By 1923, with his friendship league suppressed (see chapter 1), he was ready to leave Munich. Hiller heard of his talents as an organizer and recruited Linsert for the WhK. Hiller was generally suspicious of democracy and dreamed of a political system where the best and brightest would lead the rest.[10] He dismissed Linsert's Munich Friendship League as "dilettantism"; a movement must be based in ideas, not on "the masses," he thought.[11] But when they met, Hiller found Linsert intellectual and well spoken. And Linsert was beautiful. He had an athlete's muscular body, yet Hiller perceived something feminine in his manner that recalled Adonis or a Rodin sculpture.[12] Later, Hiller noticed his elegant, powerful hands.[13] Hiller convinced Hirschfeld to make Linsert the secretary of the WhK, a job that came with a small salary and a post in the Institute for Sexual Science. Linsert proved himself indispensable. He co-authored several of Hirschfeld's books and published a few of his own. He worked with Hiller, Hirschfeld, and Kronfeld on the Coalition to Reform the Sex Laws (*Kartell für Reform des Sexualstrafrechts*), a committee that brought together groups advocating abortion rights, birth control, easier divorce, and homosexual emancipation, including Helene Stöcker's League for the Protection of Mothers and Sex Reform (*Bund für Mutterschutz und Sexualreform*) and the pacifist human rights group the German League for Human Rights (*Deutsche Liga für Menschenrechte*).[14]

In Berlin, Linsert also joined the Communist Party. He rose through its ranks to serve as a deputy of Hans Kippenberger, the head of the KPD's military bureau (*M-Apparat*), and as a person of some influence in the KPD militia, the Red Front Fighters' League (*Roter Frontkämpferbund*).[15] Linsert also worked with the KPD propaganda tsar Willi Münzenberg.[16] Münzenberg sought a popular front against fascism, fostered relationships with intellectuals of the unaffiliated left, and played an important role in KPD sexual politics in the early 1930s.[17] (Linsert apparently came from a working-class or lower-middle-class background.[18]) Hiller – who was a leftist and socialist but who rejected Marxism, the KPD, and the SPD – found that nevertheless he got along well with Linsert on political questions.[19] The KPD was receptive to homosexual emancipation, and Linsert was apparently able to shape the party line somewhat on that issue. The Bolsheviks had abolished sodomy laws in the Soviet Union; Stalin would later reinstate them. In the early 1930s, the KPD emerged as a major champion of radical notions of sexual freedom when it joined with sex reformers, feminists, and the SPD in the 1931 mass movement for abortion rights, rallying people with the slogan "your body belongs to you!"[20]

Men's sex work drew the ire of conservatives in 1925, when the federal Justice Ministry circulated a draft of revisions to the penal code that

called male prostitutes a "herd of criminality and of criminals" and proposed heavy prison terms, of between six months and three years, for
male prostitution.[21] Hiller blamed the DNVP for the harsh draft, which
also would have cracked down on abortion.[22] The proposal horrified
Linsert. He felt a deep sense of "duty" to and "brotherly solidarity" with
men who sold sex.[23]

To fight the draft penal code, Linsert undertook a massive study of
male prostitutes, run out of the Institute for Sexual Science. His goal was
to show that they were no "herd of criminals." His work accorded with
the official position of the WhK, which opposed the draft law's criminalization of male prostitution.[24] Linsert and his co-canvassers interviewed
300 men and asked 100 of them a more detailed list of questions. Of the
100, 59 had never been convicted of a crime. Linsert published this data
along with several testimonials against the criminalization of male prostitution from prominent women and men. One testimonial came from
Albert Einstein, who called the proposed law "prudery."[25] Linsert argued
that male sex workers were for the most part working-class men, often
young, reacting to "horrible economic distress" caused by the exploitative capitalist system.[26] As abolitionist feminists did for female prostitutes, Linsert called for welfare: male prostitutes needed unemployment
money and youth programs. Yet unlike abolitionist feminists, Linsert had
no plans to end male prostitution. He argued that although their work
was not pretty, it was honest in principle: these desperate men chose
prostitution over crime.[27] They were not hurting anyone.[28] A long prison
term would be the "ruin" of a man's "civic [bürgerlich] existence," making it impossible for him to reform and to return to civil society.[29] These
men were, besides, "entitled to the elementary right of every individual:
to be free to do with one's body what one sees fit, either alone or by
free agreement with other individuals who are capable of understanding and consenting. This right must only be restricted when its exercise
would damage or endanger another individual or society."[30] In this liberal defence of an individual right over one's body, Linsert gave voice to
an idea that Hiller had developed in his book *The Right Over One's Self*,
an idea that stood at the centre of much of Hiller's advocacy for homosexual emancipation.

Insofar as the views of men who sold sex themselves can be gleaned
from what was written about them by Linsert and others, male prostitution was, for many working-class men, a relatively casual act. At a bus stop
one autumn day in 1926, a Berliner noticed another man watching him.
He had heard his friends talk about this sort of thing and so recognized

the man as "a gay" (*ein Schwuler*). They spoke. The "gay" gave him money for cigarettes, and they arranged to meet later on the steps of a museum. But the man did not keep the date. Then he lost his job. After a few months of unemployment, he went to the bus stop, met an old gentleman, and earned 3 reichsmarks (RM). He began to do this regularly, meeting two or three men a day and making as much as 26 RM a week. "But when the weather is bad I make absolutely nothing," he said.[31]

The relative ease with which this man took up sex work owed in part to the fact that having sex with a man for money did not necessitate any conclusions about a man's sexual orientation or masculinity. Linsert found that most of the male prostitutes in his sample did not consider themselves homosexual. Only about one-third did. About one-third identified as completely heterosexual. Two of the men Linsert surveyed said they were selling sex to men in order to earn money to take women out on the town. Twenty-two of the men said they were bisexual. Almost all were working class.[32] The idea that having sex with a man did not necessarily make one abnormal may have been more available to working-class men than it was to men of other classes. George Chauncey found that in New York City in this same time period, a working-class man's gender expression marked him as "normal," and so long as he did not take on a "feminine" role in sex with another man, he could have male-male sex without damaging his reputation for "normal" masculinity.[33] German men, whether working class or not, were in a different position than were men in New York City. By the 1920s, Germans were far more familiar with the idea of homosexuality as an "orientation" or identity than were New Yorkers, thanks in part to several decades of activism by the homosexual emancipation movement.[34] Yet according to the science of the day, merely having sex with a man did not mean that one was homosexual. Psychiatry and sexology held that homosexual activity alone did not indicate the presence of homosexuality; indeed, many "normal," "heterosexual" men and women engaged in same-sex sex, especially during puberty and in single-sex environments like boarding schools and the military.[35] "Actual" homosexuality, in contrast, was a condition that marked the self on the most foundational level. Various psychiatrists and biologists pointed to gender variation or abnormal hormonal functioning as signs of the condition.[36] Many emphasized that "actual" homosexuals had a horror of the opposite sex.

Thus, "homosexuality" as it existed in public discourse in the Weimar era left a good deal of room for sexually "normal" people to engage in same-sex sex acts without being forced to doubt that they were normal.

By Hirschfeld's definition, actual homosexuals were men or women "who burn with a violent, pure, psychological love for persons of their own sex and only understand the merits of sex with their own sex, never or only against their will having sexual relations with the other sex."[37] This definition would not have applied well to "Otto," the erstwhile boy-friend of the English novelist Christopher Isherwood. Isherwood came to Berlin in the late 1920s because "Berlin meant Boys" – working-class boys.[38] The boys he met at the Cosy Corner bar sat about playing cards "with their sweaters and jackets stripped off and their shirts unbuttoned to the navel and their sleeves rolled up to their armpits," partly because of the intense heat thrown off by the bar's iron stove and "partly because they knew their bared skin excited their clients."[39] Most of them were unemployed. They traded sex with men for drinks and money. They also had their "girls."[40] Otto was a muscled, macho, working-class type who, Isherwood reported, "preferred women to men" but nevertheless embarked on a long, emotionally involved affair with Isherwood.[41] Their relationship was no simple exchange of money for sex. But Isherwood spent "more on Otto than he could well afford," buying him a new suit, among other things.[42]

Men's reasons for selling sex varied, as did those of women. Linsert's data shows this, although he drew different conclusions. Linsert empha-sized the unemployment and destitution that drove men to sell sex, and at times he seemed bound by the same assumption common to middle-class advocates on behalf of female prostitutes, to wit, that given other employment options, no one would sell sex.[43] Some sex workers were destitute, such as one young man who had run away from his middle-class family and ended up broke and sleeping in the Tiergarten. Another youth advised him to "go on the doll tour [*Puppentour*]." He met a "homo-sexual," who took him home and fed him, and they engaged in sex acts that the young man had already done at his boarding school. Eventually the young man's father fetched him home.[44] About a quarter of the men whom Linsert surveyed, however, gave other reasons for selling sex. For some prostitutes, such as Berlin's transvestite prostitutes, selling sex was a primary occupation.[45] But for other people, occasional prostitution was a ready source of spending money. Men in low-paying jobs, like clerks, tele-gram boys, and street sweepers, could make their lives more comfortable with a little bit of money to buy things like cigarettes and theatre tickets.[46]

Commercial sex was not an issue that homosexual emancipation could ignore. Many homosexual emancipationists saw it as something from which they ought to distance their movement. It was one of the most public and disreputable forms of male-male sex, and homosexual emancipationists who prized respectability – that is, most homosexual emancipationists – derided it.[47] *Friendship* magazine ranted against just the sort of Tiergarten cruising that Hiller enjoyed.[48] Yet at the same time, homosexual emancipation could not credibly claim to have nothing to do with male prostitution. Male prostitutes were men who had sex with men, and some, although not all, self-identified as homosexual. In addition, many "respectable," middle-class homosexuals paid for sex or engaged in relationships that had a commercial element, like Isherwood's relationship with Otto. Hirschfeld thought that the criminalization and stigmatization of male-male sex drove homosexual men to pay for sex: they had to keep their sex lives secret because of social scorn and the law, so they hired prostitutes.[49]

Hiller and Linsert's advocacy on behalf of male prostitutes was unusual among homosexual emancipationists. Most activists in the friendship leagues during their heyday in the early 1920s wanted to exclude disreputable elements like male prostitutes; so did Radszuweit.[50] Linsert saw the issue from an economic perspective, as did Hiller, and for both, the notion of a right over one's self and body made the selling of sex and homosexuality into the same political question. In addition, in Hiller's life commercial sex was a sort of supporting, companion piece to his friendship with Linsert that enabled it to grow into one of Hiller's primary emotional bonds. Hiller felt for Linsert a "loving adoration" that made him "unspeakably happy."[51] He does not seem to have told Linsert how he felt about him; the fact that Linsert had a boyfriend must have influenced this decision. Hiller kissed Linsert only once, awkwardly. They had been walking together one afternoon in the Tiergarten near the Institute for Sexual Science, and Linsert said something that struck Hiller as so astute that Hiller "grabbed his hands" and "bent over the right one and sealed it with my brotherly, joyful adoration. He was surprised and let it happen; if he was pleased or just allowing me to do it remains indeterminate."[52] Hiller seems to have had some hope over these ten years of friendship that with Linsert, he could unite the "animal practice" of sex and the ideal friendship of "eros," but gradually that hope faded.[53] He had sex with male prostitutes and chastely adored Linsert. The relationship with Linsert assumed such weight for Hiller that he wrote, "The meaning of my life was to a considerable extent bound up in this friendship."[54]

In 1929, Hiller and Linsert had to choose between defending the right of homosexual men to have sex in private and defending male prostitutes from a looming police crackdown. If they chose to defend male prostitutes, and if the sodomy law was not repealed, one of them would forsake a chance to see Paragraph 175's blanket criminalization of non-commercial sex between consenting adult men struck down in his lifetime, and the other would have to wait until he was an old man to see some of Paragraph 175's provisions abolished.

The Vote to Repeal Paragraph 175

Just before the global economic depression hit Germany, a committee of the Reichstag voted to strike Paragraph 175 from the federal criminal code.[55] The committee was in the midst of a controversy-provoking, marathon effort to rewrite Germany's entire penal code. Its membership included delegates from what were then the major parties in the Reichstag, among them Antonie "Toni" Pfülf and Julius Moses of the SPD, the Protestant theologian Hermann Strathmann of the DNVP, representatives of the left-liberal DDP, the right-liberal DVP, and the KPD, and, for the Centre Party, the former judge Rudolf Schetter and the former teacher, social worker, and organizer of Catholic welfare Helene Weber. The respected jurist Wilhelm Kahl of the DVP chaired the committee. Its vote on Paragraph 175 failed to gain the force of law before democracy collapsed in the 1930s. But in 1929, the national press reacted as if Paragraph 175 had fallen. The headlines ranged from "A Cultural Step Forward"[56] to "A Victory for the Corruptors of the Volk."[57] People assumed that the new penal code would not contain Paragraph 175.[58] Baskets of flowers arrived at the Institute for Sexual Science for Hirschfeld.[59] The vote was not, however, a simple repeal of the sodomy law. It was an effort to replace it. The day after the penal code reform committee voted to cut Paragraph 175, it approved Paragraph 297. This new law instituted criminal penalties for male-male sex in three instances. It outlawed sex between two men if one was under twenty-one and the other was not, if one party used a position of influence to pressure the other, or if one paid the other.

This reform was so polarizing for activists that it almost destroyed homosexual emancipation's oldest and most politically connected organization, the WhK.[60] Hirschfeld, by then a world-famous sexologist and Germany's foremost spokesman against Paragraph 175, resigned as president of the WhK, an organization he had co-founded and had led for thirty-two years. With Hirschfeld gone, a younger generation of WhK activists led by Hiller and Linsert warned that the penal code reform committee's vote "amount[s] to one step forward and two steps backward."[61] The step forward was the repeal of the blanket criminalization of male-male sex. The two steps backward were a higher age of consent (*Schutzalter*) for men than for women and the criminalization of male prostitution. Existing law ignored male prostitution; under the new law, a conviction could bring up to five years in prison.[62] Hiller went so far as to call the repeal of Paragraph 175 illusionary: "The decriminalization of sex between men is a pressing necessity for a free society, but a law like this is useless. It seems to bring decriminalization, but by criminalizing male prostitution (and by setting the age of consent at twenty-one years – what ridiculousness!) it makes decriminalization an illusion."[63]

Although many homosexual emancipationists greeted the vote as the victory for which they had long struggled, the man arguably most responsible for striking Paragraph 175 agreed with Hiller. He was Wilhelm Kahl, the penal code reform committee's long-serving chairman, an eighty-year-old law professor, and a widely respected liberal.[64] Kahl cast the decisive vote against the sodomy law.[65] His party, the German People's Party (DVP), was a moderate party that did not support homosexual emancipation. And Kahl made it clear that he also did not support homosexual emancipation as such, writing that striking the law was "in no way a recognition of homosexuality as a morally or legally [*rechtlich*] allowable act."[66] He wrote that the new law's provisions against "seduction" and male prostitution comprised "a considerable extension and sharpening of [Paragraph 175]." Kahl avowed that "homosexuality, under all circumstances, whether there's a disposition to it or not, is an exercise of the sex drive that goes against nature."[67] Nevertheless, his vote against Paragraph 175 violated his party's moral conservatism. The conservative press castigated him for it.[68] The vote may have threatened his political career. Following it, Kahl's party balked at nominating him for another term in parliament despite his gravitas, though the party eventually gave in and he returned to the Reichstag.[69]

Rather than an endorsement of homosexuality, Kahl portrayed his vote as part of a practical approach to reforming Germany's criminal code. He called Paragraph 175 a "failed" law for three reasons. One was a liberal argument very much like that made by Hiller and other homosexual emancipationists: homosexual sex injured no third party, and "adult people have free use of their own bodies."[70] A second was a practical argument: Paragraph 175 was rarely enforced and was anyway an ineffective way to stop male homosexuality.[71] But Kahl's most forceful argument was that Paragraph 175 caused evils more dire than homosexuality alone. These were "propaganda," homosexual seduction, and blackmail, which Kahl and others believed had an inextricable tie to male prostitution. "Homosexual propaganda" meant the media blitz coming out of homosexual emancipation organizations, which, Kahl and many others believed, actually spread homosexuality. They thought the media would stop if they removed its reason for existing, that is, Paragraph 175. In addition, Paragraph 297 provided for serious prison terms for male prostitution, for the seduction of a man under the age of twenty-one, and for a man who used his position at work to pressure another man to have sex. By replacing the old law with the new, Kahl sought to make it easier to police these "actual dangers to state and society."[72] Kahl's intention was not to liberate male-male sex; it was rather to restrict criminality only to forms of male-male sex that truly threatened society. Paragraph 297, which criminalized only certain kinds of sex between men, in Kahl's view would make for a better sodomy law: the revised law represented a "considerable extension and sharpening of [Paragraph 175]."[73]

Kahl's stand on Paragraph 175 reflected the growing consensus in public policy and – arguably – German society that certain types of immorality were tolerable so long as they remained out of the public eye. Both the Republic's censorship policy and the reform of the prostitution law had adhered to this convention. Kahl was clearly for keeping immorality out of the public sphere, as was his party. In the mid-1920s, he lobbied the Berlin police to shut down cabaret revues featuring scantily clad female dancers.[74] His effort to get rid of what he called "revolting propaganda for homosexuality" that could corrupt young people reflects this commitment.[75] Paragraph 297's prohibition on men over twenty-one "seducing" men under twenty-one – that is, the differential age of consent – similarly worked to contain homosexuality. Members of the penal code reform committee who voted to replace Paragraph 175 with Paragraph 297 voiced ideas similar to Kahl's: striking the law would get rid of "propaganda," while banning relationships between men under twenty-one years of age and older men would protect youths from being seduced into homosexuality. A Social Democrat explained that because puberty lasted longer for men than for women, the age of consent for men should be higher.[76] A Justice Ministry official said that according to the Berlin police, from ages eighteen to twenty-one the "sexual orientation … can easily be steered in the wrong direction" and that "adult homosexuals especially like to hit on [*sich heranmachen an*] minors."[77] Nevertheless, male homosexuals who did not seek to convert minors and did not seek the public eye did not deserve persecution.

Moreover, Kahl believed that the new law, Paragraph 297, would protect society from dangerous criminals: men who sold sex and committed blackmail. It was not that male prostitution itself was a severe threat to society. Rather, it was that it tended to attract dangerous, degenerate types. In 1926, Berlin newspapers reported the suicide of Otto Zöhn, a "happily married" bank clerk and father.[78] Zöhn wrote in a suicide note that he had killed himself to escape from a blackmailer, Aloys Dämon. Dämon was a skinny twenty-year-old, an occasional sex worker, and according to the court a "beggar and vagabond."[79] He had met Zöhn some months earlier at a train station. Zöhn probably initially paid him for sex. Later, Dämon threatened to expose Zöhn's homosexuality to his family and employer unless Zöhn gave him money. Press coverage of Dämon's subsequent trial was sympathetic to Zöhn, the respectable bank clerk. It presented Dämon as, true to his name, a "little devil" and Zöhn as a helpless victim. The press expressed the wish that Zöhn had had the "courage" to go to the police, "whose help in these matters is always discreet."[80] Other men who had been blackmailed by Dämon had gone to the police and apparently had not faced Paragraph 175 charges. They testified against Dämon at his trial, which resulted in a conviction for causing Zöhn's death.[81]

Dämon was the very type of young man from whom Kahl and the majority of his committee hoped to protect society by reforming Paragraph 175. Dämon was certainly not a sympathetic figure, so it is no surprise that the press was not kind to him. What is worth taking note of is the particular way in which the press presented Dämon, which was in keeping with a certain understanding of the connection between male prostitution and blackmail that politicians on the penal code reform committee shared. A reporter who covered Dämon's trial felt it worth mentioning that he was an impoverished street-dweller, a "beggar and vagabond." It would be important to mention this, since in popular perceptions, a young male vagabond was supposed to be quite likely to take up prostitution and blackmail. This was not because he was homosexual but because he was unscrupulous in his pursuit of easy money. The reform of Paragraph 175 was supposed to fight blackmail by cracking down on male prostitution. "The worst source of danger from male prostitution is blackmail," one liberal told his fellow penal code reform committee members.[82]

The homosexual emancipation movement welcomed anything that the government could do to prevent this sort of sexual blackmail. In the nineteenth and early twentieth centuries, blackmail was the scourge of middle-class and wealthy men who had sex with men, none of whom were in a position to make their sexuality public. Blackmail was common. Hirschfeld estimated that one out of three homosexuals had been black-mailed, and not only the wealthy but also men of the working class.[83] By 1920, Hirschfeld himself seems to have been the victim of more than one blackmail attempt.[84] Blackmail was illegal, but blackmailers' victims often could not afford to risk revealing their sexual interest in men by contacting the police. Some men who were blackmailed over male-male sex did go to the police, and in some cities, including Berlin and Leipzig, police would prosecute the blackmailer and not pursue a Paragraph 175 charge against his victim.[85] Yet being publicly identified as a homosexual could easily ruin a man's career, marriage, and social position. Even the leaders of the WhK who were homosexual wrote about "homosexuals" in the third person when they published in favour of homosexual emancipation. Homosexual emancipationist publications regularly reported the suicides of men who were victims of blackmail.

However, most male prostitutes do not seem to have been blackmailers. Some, like Dämon, were. Hiller, a regular client of sex workers, had only one dicey incident, which in any event was not blackmail: "a good-looking young man … was not satisfied with the agreed-upon honorarium, and asked for a much larger sum, and held my gold watch (which was my dead father's) until I handed it over." The next morning, Hiller brought the money and the prostitute gave the watch back.[86] Linsert asked seventy-seven male prostitutes their feelings on blackmail. Only nine of the seventy-seven seemed to have done it; fifty-one emphatically rejected it.[87]

But the close relationship between prostitution and blackmail that members of the penal code reform committee envisioned went well beyond the facts of what seem to be a minority of male prostitutes who blackmailed their clients or blackmailers who entrapped their victims by selling them sex.[88] Many of the delegates on the committee believed that blackmailers and male prostitutes tended to be the same men: young, jobless, heterosexual, urban men who suffered from forms of pathology and mental incapacity that were similar to those supposedly afflicting many female prostitutes. I discussed these forms of pathology and mental incapacity at length in chapter 3. They included degeneration, psychopathy, "inferiority" (*Minderwertigkeit*), and feeblemindedness. Young unemployed men in cities drew increasing public concern in the Republic's final years.[89] They were supposedly sources of crime and political radicalism.[90] Especially a subset of such men, those who were deeply impoverished and sought out public assistance, were of concern to experts in criminology and to the architects of the 1927 venereal disease law.[91] Blackmail was already illegal, but new, heavy prison sentences for male prostitution were another way to get at these men, who were supposedly not, by any means, homosexual.

The revision of Paragraph 175 reflected the central concept of what was then a reformist approach to penal policy: that punishments ought to be crafted with a view towards protecting society. This approach owed to the work of Franz von Liszt prior to the First World War. Liszt and his followers argued that punishment ought to fit the criminal rather than the crime, because the point of punishment was to protect society by keeping criminals from re-offending.[92] Liszt signed the WhK's first petition against Paragraph 175.[93] Under the Weimar Republic, reforms integrated welfare into criminal policy, promoting pardons and social programs over harsh sentences.[94] The reform of Germany's law on female prostitution reflected such an ethos in its preference for welfare and rehabilitation over imprisonment. In the early twenty-first century, Germany had one of the lowest incarceration rates in the world in part thanks to the influence of this reform movement after 1945.[95] Yet, in the 1920s, reformist approaches to penal policy encompassed the use of special measures to contain a small minority of supposedly un-reformable people. Preventative detention was one such measure. Although Kahl was initially a high-profile member of the "classical school" opposing Liszt and the reformers, the reformers influenced him, and he eventually adopted many of their ideas.[96] In 1930 he told a Dresden newspaper that the new penal code would do far more to take psychological differences among criminals into account. It would thus take a better approach to repeat offenders and increase public safety.[97]

Throughout the debate on Paragraph 175, members of the penal code reform committee asserted that male prostitutes were a particular type of criminal who warranted a special approach: they were unscrupulous "heterosexually inclined" men who were "simply making a business of using the pitiable abnormal dispositions of others for commercial purposes."[98] The press repeated this distinction: prostitutes were "criminal vermin" (*Gesindel*) but not homosexual; most homosexuals were not criminals, only "sad victims of nature" with their "unfortunately abnormal libidos."[99] Who were these reprobate heterosexuals who, in the words of one of the Centre Party's representatives on the penal code reform committee, "exploit homosexuality" in order to avoid "honest work"?[100] A government prosecutor explained that the disgusting nature of the sex that male homosexuals desired forced them into the hands of degenerate criminal types: "In the vast majority of [blackmail] cases the active partner [in the sex act] is a respectable person with a sick [sexual] orientation, while the passive one is often inferior [*minderwertig*], acting less out of inclination then out of calculation."[101] A Weimar-era psychiatrist likely would have swapped the word "inferior," which psychiatry had deemed pejorative, with the more neutral "psychopathic personality."[102]

The politicians knew that "degenerate" heterosexual men took up male prostitution and blackmail thanks to sexologists, psychiatrists, and legal experts. Moll, the sexologist, had claimed a relationship between blackmail and male prostitution since at least the turn of the century, when he described how degenerate, heterosexual men with feminine characteristics sold sex and practised blackmail.[103] In 1921 he wrote, "Homosexual prostitution is tightly connected to blackmail. Many male prostitutes make their livings more from blackmail than from prostitution."[104] A portion of male prostitutes was homosexual, but another portion was sexually "normal," according to Moll.[105] Placzek, the neurologist who had published on law and homosexuality, wrote that most male prostitutes were "born degenerate" and that "the male prostitute is almost always a blackmailer."[106] In a widely read article, Robert Gaupp, a psychiatrist at the University of Tübingen, readily identified male prostitutes as "heterosexuals" who took a passive role in anal sex, while real homosexuals took an active role.[107]

The image of male prostitutes as degenerate, blackmailing heterosexuals is particularly clear in Hirschfeld's work. He wrote that both environmental and innate factors drove men into prostitution, and that often the environment provided the tipping point. Yet, at the same time, most male prostitutes had innate "degeneration," causing "a dearth of the desire to work" and "the deadening of the normal feeling of shame."[108] He described how young, homeless, wandering men often took up prostitution and crime, not only out of destitution but because of a hereditary condition. They learned about prostitution and blackmail in places "where the poorest sectors of the population meet," institutions for welfare education (*Fürsorgeerziehung*), jails, and night shelters for the homeless (*Nachtasyle*), "where same-sex sex is frequently practised by the homeless themselves as a surrogate activity." There, men spread the word about how one could make easy money with prostitution and blackmail.[109] These young men "easily become acquainted with the close relationship of male prostitution to crime – namely robbery and blackmail – whereby they fall into temptation to sell themselves and at the same time to pursue a secondary, criminal purpose – an entice-ment which naturally appeals particularly to individuals with degenerate [*entartet*] and criminal dispositions."[110] This conflation of prostitution and blackmail is portrayed in the homosexual emancipation film *Different from the Others*, which Hirschfeld co-wrote. A blackmailer is the film's villain. At first, the film's hero mistakes this blackmailer for a male prostitute and, with hardly any hesitation, prepares to pay him for sex. This occurs wordlessly in the scene where the blackmailer and hero have their first romantic encounter: the blackmailer interrupts an embrace and asks for money, and the hero reaches for his wallet, as if expecting that the embrace will continue once he pays. The blackmailer corrects the hero's misapprehension: no, no, he wants a good deal of money, and the encounter will not continue; he is a blackmailer, not a prostitute.[111] The "degenerate" men who did sex work and blackmail were the coun-terparts of the "feebleminded" women whom the advocates of the 1927 venereal disease law feared could not be stopped from falling into pros-titution. These men were not homosexual: according to Hirschfeld, "the number of male prostitutes who are homosexually orientated is relatively small in comparison to those who are heterosexually orientated."[112]

This logic was so persuasive that a large majority of the members of the penal code reform committee backed the crackdown on male pros-titution. Communists voiced the only coherent counter position. They argued that male homosexuality was not normal, but not unnatural, and ought, like lesbianism, to be decriminalized.[113] They denied that seduction into homosexuality was a pressing social problem. They called Paragraph 297 a re-criminalization of homosexuality.[114] The KPD press trumpeted the party's support for decriminalizing male homosexuality.[115]

Mainstream scientific opinion supported the reform of Paragraph 175. Shortly after the vote in the penal code reform committee, a leading journal surveyed twelve important psychiatrists and specialists in law and medicine. They were overwhelmingly of the view that homosexuality was a form of psychopathic personality. They judged seduction a real risk, and they wanted the age of consent set higher for men than for women. They were, however, in favour of striking Paragraph 175 because they did not think it an effective means to combat homosexuality.[116]

Moreover, the vote to replace Paragraph 175 was no victory for Hirschfeld's model of homosexuality as an innate, biological but non-pathological condition. Several members of the penal code reform committee took time in their speeches to dispute the idea that homo-sexuality was present at birth rather than acquired. Kahl called homosexuality unnatural: "The sexual organs are intended for reproduction."[117] Hirschfeld's faith in the Social Democrats as the party of homosexual emancipation seemed misplaced when the SPD's Moses argued that it was unjust to criminalize homosexuality because homosexuals were "constitutionally ill" and that, in addition, Hirschfeld was wrong about seduction – a person could be seduced into homosexuality, though this did not justify keeping the sodomy law on the books.[118] The Reich Minister of Justice, Theodor von Guérard of the Catholic Centre Party, told the committee that although "Hirschfeld's group is of the opinion that the origin of homosexuality is not a psychic abnormality, but rather an inborn, constitutional and therefore unalterable orientation," the majority of sex researchers – like Moll, Placzek, and the psychiatrist Aschaffenburg – thought that homosexuality was inborn only in rare cases and could in fact be treated.[119] The psychiatrist Emil Kraepelin rejected the notion of innate homosexuality and linked it, rather, to psychopathy, arguing that it was acquired through masturbation, alcohol, and/or "seduction."[120] All of this demonstrated how far out on the intellectual fringes was Hirschfeld's model of homosexuality as inborn, immutable, and not pathological.

Judging by how the voting went, the reform of Paragraph 175 was intended foremost as a crackdown on seduction and selling sex, not as a decriminalization of male-male sex. There was far more support among committee members for the new law on male prostitution than there was for the decriminalization of male-male sex. The repeal of Paragraph 175 passed 15–13. Voting to repeal were the members of the SPD, KPD, the left-liberal DDP, and Kahl from the right-liberal DVP. Voting against were the conservative nationalists (DNVP), the Centre Party, and the rest of Kahl's right-liberal DVP. The vote on Paragraph 175 was contentious, and the men and women of the Centre Party who lost that day would revisit the question of Paragraph 175's fate later when they determined to clog up the entire penal code reform effort.[121] In contrast, the criminalization of male prostitution was not contentious. Only three members of the Communist Party voted against it.[122] One observer of the 1929 vote on Paragraph 175 wondered at how a decriminalization of male homosexual sex could, for Kahl (and for others), "fit perfectly together" with a measure against male prostitution so harsh that it was more an "outburst of fury" than a piece of legislation.[123] The answer lies in the perception of male prostitutes as dangerous degenerates from whom society had to be protected.

Hirschfeld's Resignation from the WhK after the Vote and Its Significance for Homosexual Emancipation

The vote on Paragraph 175 sparked a power struggle in the WhK that pitted Hirschfeld against Hiller, Linsert, and other WhK leaders. It resulted in Hirschfeld's resignation. This section of the chapter examines why Hirschfeld resigned and what his resignation meant for homosexual emancipation. Hirschfeld's departure from the WhK was significant. With the vote on Paragraph 175, the WhK faced a profound dilemma, one that would face many subsequent movements for gay liberation: was the liberation of respectable homosexual men at the expense of male prostitutes an acceptable settlement? Hirschfeld's resignation allowed Hiller and Linsert to dedicate the WhK to outright rejection of the proposed reform of Paragraph 175, even though the reformed law would have decriminalized many sorts of non-commercial male-male sex. They thus took the organization in a more radical direction, one that it probably would not have pursued under Hirschfeld's stewardship. Moreover, at the heart of the crisis in the WhK leadership was a question that would dog gay liberation movements throughout the twentieth century, that of the role of science. Did one need science to advocate for emancipation, as Hirschfeld argued? Or could other arguments, like Hiller's right over one's self, take its place? One's view on this could dictate one's position on male prostitution. Hirschfeld's science separated the fates of male prostitutes from those of homosexual men; Hiller's political philosophy united them. The issues of science, male prostitution, and the right over one's self came together in a crisis that in 1929 threatened to destroy the WhK.

At a meeting about five weeks after the vote on Paragraph 175, the WhK's executive committee endorsed Hiller's view on the proposed reform of the law. Although it contained "small improvements," it was "a considerable sharpening" of the existing sodomy law. Following this meeting, WhK leaders informed their members that in fact, "Paragraph 175 has not fallen!" Because of the proposed new law's various constraints on male-male sex, including on male prostitution, "The conclusions of the penal code reform committee with respect to homosexuality constitute one step forward and two steps backward. The demand that we have made for decades – that the law be applied in the same way to the homosexual minority of the population as it is to the majority – is in no way met. Our Committee must keep fighting."[124] At the same meeting of the leadership where the WhK determined to fight the proposed reform of Paragraph 175, Hirschfeld resigned.

The circumstances that prompted Hirschfeld's resignation were not made public at the time and have remained mysterious ever since, though the timing of his departure suggests that it had something to do with the vote in the penal code reform committee. Surviving sources that record the views of those who were there are very quiet about why Hirschfeld resigned, and historians have proposed a number of conflicting explanations for the crisis in the WhK leadership. The players in the struggle strove to keep the acrimony out of public view. The WhK continued to "venerate" Hirschfeld in public.[125] Hiller praised him in his memoirs and did not discuss the resignation crisis.[126] In a farewell letter to WhK members, Hirschfeld himself suggested only that he was leaving the WhK to devote more time to science and to the Institute.[127] A laudatory article in the WhK magazine by Karl Besser, a member of the leadership who also worked at the Institute for Sexual Science, identified a number of reasons for Hirschfeld's resignation: his poor health, his exhaustion from years of personal attacks, and the fact that his career had moved beyond the WhK and that he was, quite understandably, concentrating on the Institute and on his work as a sexologist.[128] Yet why did Hirschfeld resign when he did, just after the vote in the penal code reform committee? Besser offered the following explanation as to the timing of Hirschfeld's departure: "An external impetus for Magnus Hirschfeld to fulfil his plan to resign at the present moment was also the fact that the work of the Committee [that is, the WhK] to abolish Paragraph 175 (Paragraph 296) reached a certain stage ... in the penal code reform committee."[129]

The polite remarks about the resignation of the public face of homosexual emancipation from the organization he had led for thirty-two years concealed a bitter falling out. Friedrich Radszuweit, head of the League for Human Rights, wrote the following year that "in well-informed circles, it is known that Hirschfeld (*Sanitätsrat Hirschfeld*) did not voluntarily resign the presidency, but that rather he was forced to resign, despite all of the public sugar-coating of the matter."[130] Linsert later referred to "the critical November days of the year 1929" which "our movement ... had to undergo."[131] After he resigned, Hirschfeld fought with the WhK over the organization's finances and its office space in the Institute for Sexual Science. Hirschfeld had some control over WhK funds, either because the group was getting support from the Institute or because he had sunk his personal money into the organization.[132] After he left, in the February/March 1930 edition of the WhK's magazine for its membership,

WhK leaders wrote that they would undertake new efforts to raise money for the organization. They reported that one reason for the fundraising, which they pursued with "heavy hearts," was the fact that "the founder of our Committee, Dr Magnus Hirschfeld ... was forced by economic and political circumstances" to enact an "interim liquidation" of the WhK's business office.[133] The business office had coordinated the WhK's lobbying and had provided advice to WhK members in legal and medical matters. With the office closed, individual members of the leadership pledged to volunteer their time to continue these services.[134] More than a year after the business office shut, the WhK magazine reported, "in the last months a friendly understanding with Dr Magnus Hirschfeld has been reached, in which the personal relationships between him and some executive committee members have been renewed so that it can be assumed that the resolution of the financial disagreement between him and the WhK will take as quick and friendly a course as possible."[135] In the period after Hirschfeld's departure, the WhK was strapped for funds, in debt, and desperate for contributions from its members.[136] The fact that Hirschfeld apparently pulled some of the group's funding can only have contributed to this distress and may very well have been the central cause of it. Moreover, his resignation was accompanied by strains on personal relationships between himself and other WhK leaders that it took more than a year to resolve. Hirschfeld and the remaining leadership were not on friendly terms when he left, and the split threatened the organization's existence.

The immediate cause of the break between Hirschfeld and other leaders was a disagreement about the best way to lobby the penal code reform committee before it voted on Paragraph 175, which involved a question about whom to recommend to the politicians on the committee as an expert, scientific or otherwise, on homosexuality. In a narrow sense, the disagreement was about the "organizational-tactical leadership of our Committee," as Hiller described it several years later.[137] In a broader sense, it was about the position of science in homosexual emancipation and about Hirschfeld's leadership. The most detailed version of the story is in a letter that Linsert and the sex reformer Max Hodann wrote to a Swiss leftist and birth control advocate some months after the incident.[138] This is the story they recounted: Reichstag delegates who were friendly to the WhK suggested that the WhK give them the names of some experts – aside from Hirschfeld – who supported the repeal of Paragraph 175. The WhK should canvass opinion leaders as to their views on the sodomy law and discreetly, by word of mouth, convey the names of those who supported repeal to the friendly Reichstag delegates. They in turn would pass the names along to members of the penal code reform committee, who would be more likely to pay attention to what these experts said if their names did not come directly from the WhK. In this way, these expert supporters of repeal would seem objective rather than in cahoots with the WhK. Around the time that the WhK received this offer from the unnamed Reichstag deputies, Friedrich Radszuweit's League for Human Rights invited Wilhelm Kahl to an evening event in support of the repeal of Paragraph 175. It was held at the Magic Flute, a Berlin dance palace known as a homosexual and transvestite meeting place. The venerable Kahl attended the event, where he was shocked to hear a speaker say, "We do not ask for equal rights, we demand equal rights!"[139] Kahl wanted to grant homosexuals nothing of the sort. WhK leaders found out about the Magic Flute incident and immediately feared that their cause was in jeopardy. A spooked Kahl might vote to retain Paragraph 175. The WhK had to reach out to him again. After a five-hour debate, they decided to execute the plan suggested by the Reichstag delegates with whom they were in contact: they would discreetly convey the names of some experts aside from Hirschfeld to their allies, who would pass them along to members of the penal code reform committee, Kahl included. Hirschfeld allegedly went along with this decision, but, according to Linsert and Hodann, he was actually opposed to it. Hiller and some other WhK leaders were in the process of confidentially disseminating a list of experts when, Linsert and Hodann alleged, Hirschfeld covertly foiled their effort. Unbeknownst to most of the WhK leadership, they claimed, Hirschfeld sent his own letter to Kahl. In it, he named all of the experts on the list that the WhK was going to send to its allies, thus, in Linsert and Hodann's view, ensuring that no one would pay any attention to them. Other WhK leaders considered this a betrayal and forced Hirschfeld to resign. The gist of Linsert and Hodann's account is supported by the actual letter that the WhK sent to Kahl in the wake of the Magic Flute rally, which mostly conforms to the story they told.[140] In this letter to Kahl, the WhK repudiated the League for Human Rights and offered to set up meetings between the politicians on the penal code reform committee and "same-sex orientated people" who were of unquestionable "respectability." It recommended Hirschfeld as the "internationally recognized, leading scientific authority" on homosexuality. Finally, it named a series of men as additional experts: police officials, lawyers, law professors, doctors, psychiatrists, and medical professors. It is worth keeping in mind that Linsert and

Hodann's letter tells just one side of the story; the situation was probably more complicated. In any event, it seems safe to assume that the endorsing of experts aside from Hirschfeld by the WhK was a highly fraught procedure. Linsert believed, or at least claimed, that Hirschfeld acted to block Hiller and others from naming experts aside from Hirschfeld. The larger issue at stake here was about science's role in homosexual emancipation. Some of the experts the WhK planned to name had very different scientific positions from Hirschfeld's, and it appears that Hiller and his allies wanted to endorse the view that science was not necessary at all. The WhK's course following Hirschfeld's departure makes this apparent.

After Hirschfeld left the WhK, its propaganda reflected two major intellectual changes. The first was that the WhK's magazine began to include a greater diversity of scientific opinion rather than a singular focus on Hirschfeld's science, as Friedemann Pfäfflin notes.[141] Otto Juliusburger, a psychiatrist who took over the presidency of the WhK from Hirschfeld, believed that especially psychiatric opinion, such as Robert Gaupp's work, supported the repeal of Paragraph 175 and that the WhK ought to use it.[142] Gaupp was one of the experts the WhK named in the letter to Kahl. He had authored a widely read article in which he called for the repeal of the sodomy law on grounds very much like what Kahl later articulated in his speech to the penal code reform committee.[143] Although Gaupp supported repeal, he did not support homosexual emancipation's broader goals. He rejected homosexual emancipationists' claims that homosexuality was a natural human variation unrelated to pathology or degeneration and that homosexuals deserved equal rights. One can see why Hirschfeld might have hesitated to convey his name to the politicians. Gaupp criticized Hirschfeld. He also warned that 50 per cent of male homosexuals were paedophiles and called for homosexual emancipation literature to be burned in order to protect youth from "sexual corruption."[144] Juliusburger, however, did not last long as head of the WhK, and the organization's magazine reflects his influence much less than it does that of Hiller and Linsert. Moreover, there is evidence that the fight in the WhK leadership was foremost between Hirschfeld on one side and Linsert and Hiller on the other. Charlotte Wolff reports in her biography of Hirschfeld that a friend of Hirschfeld's recalled that Hiller, together with Linsert, was "the driving force behind the antagonism against Hirschfeld" and that this led to Hirschfeld's resignation.[145] Linsert and Hiller were responsible for another major change in the WhK's message: a move away from science altogether.

The second significant difference in WhK propaganda after Hirschfeld is the sudden challenge to the role of science in homosexual emancipation, not only to Hirschfeld's science but to all science. In the issue of the WhK's magazine that announced Hirschfeld's departure, WhK leaders published an argument about the irrelevance of science to homosexual emancipation. Its author was Arthur Kronfeld, the psychiatrist and friend of Hiller's who had long been involved with the WhK and had helped Hirschfeld found the Institute for Sexual Science.[146] Kronfeld wrote that the question of homosexuality's biological basis was "fully irrelevant" to the question of its legality. "Whoever ... assumes that proof of a constitutional basis of this kind is a prerequisite for the decriminalization of homosexuality makes a logical-methodological error" and "leaves open the possibility that if the proof of this fails, he will be promoting the criminalization of homosexuality." Rather, "the decriminalization of homosexual behaviour follows fundamentally from legal theory."[147] Prior to the vote on Paragraph 175, the WhK had considered enlisting Kronfeld to lobby the penal code reform committee and had canvassed him as to his views,[148] but he is not named in WhK's letter to Kahl. Yet with Hirschfeld gone, the WhK quickly published Kronfeld's argument – and Kronfeld's opinion was very close to Hiller's own. Hiller, too, favoured a sort of sexual liberalism and preferred arguments about individual rights and the state over those about biology or psychiatry.

A declaration of the independence of homosexual emancipation from science such as Kronfeld's article would have been unthinkable with Hirschfeld at the helm of the WhK.[149] Hirschfeld's life was dedicated to the principle "through science to justice" (*per scientiam ad justitiam*), which Hirschfeld's friends and lovers had carved on his gravestone after he died.[150] In 1929, Hirschfeld was unique among Germany's prominent, living sexologists in his unequivocal defence of homosexuality and other forms of "abnormal" sexuality.[151] He claimed that science proved that homosexuality was a non-pathological, biological variation and that therefore, it made no sense to criminalize homosexual behaviour. He himself touched on the question of what science's role in the movement ought to be in his brief farewell letter to the WhK membership, which was his only public comment on his reasons for leaving the organization. He argued in favour of a role for science, urging that the "weapon" of science be used "especially in the current moment of the decisive battle," and wrote that he would continue to use it, but from his position as the leader of his Institute, not from within the WhK.[152] And afterwards

Hirschfeld did devote himself to science, embarking on an international lecture tour that put him in the role of a public scientific expert.

Other evidence indicates that the crisis of the WhK was about the role of science in homosexual emancipation – particularly the role of Hirschfeld's science in the reform of Paragraph 175. In 1931, Friedrich Radszuweit, the head of the League for Human Rights, published a critical account of the lobbying of the penal code reform committee prior to the vote, which he called an "utter fiasco."[153] Radszuweit disliked Hirschfeld's scientific approach and had argued for years that science alone would not achieve the goals of homosexual emancipation.[154] He wrote that Hirschfeld gave people the impression that homosexuality was an illness and that homosexuals were "hermaphrodites" (*Zwitter*).[155] In contrast, the League's position as he described it was basically a liberal position, very much like Hiller's and Kronfeld's: "on the grounds of rights and of justice [*Gerechtigkeit*], Paragraph 175 must be struck down." Hirschfeld's scientific research was not, Radszuweit wrote, the foundation of the League's claim for equal rights. Rather, homosexuals injured no third party with their sexual behaviour, which therefore ought to be decriminalized. Homosexuals were not "sick" and were not abnormal, as Hirschfeld's science implied, but rather were "worthy citizens" (*vollwertige Staatsbürger*). But in any event, the League for Human Right's position was not heard in 1929, he claimed. The problem, Radszuweit wrote, had been Hirschfeld's control of the WhK. Although other WhK leaders had silently rejected Hirschfeld's method of claiming that homosexuals were "abnormalities" (*Abnormitäten*) and "hermaphrodites" (*Zwitter*) to justify the repeal of the sodomy law, "no one wanted to say anything, because they did not want to offend the old leader and pioneer." Though Radszuweit and his organization had rocky relationships with Hiller and Linsert – in Linsert's case, dating back to the days of the Munich Friendship League – Radszuweit seems to have heard some of the inside story about the crisis in the WhK.[156] A faction in the WhK – Kronfeld, Hiller, and Linsert seem likely candidates here – wanted to use a liberal argument against Paragraph 175, not a scientific one, but were prevented from doing so by Hirschfeld.

By the late 1920s, most homosexual emancipationists were not putting an exclusive emphasis on science, although they had not abandoned it entirely. From its outset, the friendship league movement's publications trumpeted citizenship and rights and devoted less space to biology and sexology. The articles, stories, and poems in the magazines for female homosexuals that were founded in the mid-1920s generally expressed a persistent disinterest in whether or not homosexuality had a biological basis. The League for Human Rights, as Radszuweit's comments suggest, greatly downplayed science in favour of a discourse of citizenship and equality of rights.[157] All of these activists stressed above all the image of homosexuals as respectable citizens. Hiller put forward an alternative model for homosexuals: they were not a group bounded by a shared biological condition; they were rather analogous to an ethnic or national minority, that is, a "sexual minority."[158] Radszuweit, Hiller, and others did not deny that homosexuality had a biological basis. But they reframed the question, focusing their efforts on making a point that was about law and the state, about liberalism and citizenship, rather than about biology. After Hirschfeld left, the WhK continued to argue that science demonstrated that homosexuality was an innate, constitutional condition.[159] But it also pursued other arguments.

Kurt Hiller had taken a dim view of "through science to justice" since at least 1919, when he urged Hirschfeld and the rest of the WhK leadership to acknowledge that rather than public education and science, homosexuals needed their own political party, or a mass public self-revelation by respectable homosexual people.[160] Hiller agreed with Kronfeld that homosexual emancipation followed from a liberal right to privacy and control of one's own body. Indeed, Hiller had expended a good deal of scholarly energy making this argument: it was the topic of his dissertation, which he published as a book. He wrote that the state only had the right to punish in order to protect the "worthy" interests of individuals or of society.[161] Otherwise, "the state may not interfere with individuals … in the shaping of their lives … even in cases of extreme deviation from the 'norm' – unless the activity of the individual collides with the interests of another individual, a grouping of other individuals, or perhaps with the whole, the society."[162] Although Hiller referred to science in his work, his primary interest was in the rights of consenting adults to make choices about their bodies. This applied to homosexuality, but it also applied to other matters, such as abortion and male prostitution. At times Hirschfeld also made this point about consenting adults and third-party injury. Yet in general, the thinking of each of the two men remained rooted in the fields in which they had trained: for Hirschfeld, medicine; for Hiller, law.[163]

Hirschfeld's work was deeply biological.[164] He was influenced by degeneration theory into the 1930s, though he always flatly denied that homosexuals were themselves degenerate. In examining Hirschfeld's use of the concept of degeneration, it is important to note that his interest in degeneration, as well as in eugenics, was not at all unique among progressives of the 1920s. I do not mean to reopen the debate about whether Hirschfeld's ideas paved the way for Nazi eugenics: they did not.[165] What Hirschfeld did was to draw on the scientific discourse of legal reform that was current in the Weimar era and to make it work in favour of homosexual emancipation. In his canonical *The Homosexuality of Men and Women* (*Die Homosexualität des Mannes und des Weibes*), Hirschfeld lent his support to the theory of his former student, the Dutch sexologist and WhK member Lucien von Römer.[166] Von Römer's theory was that homosexual children tended to be born into families that were sinking into degeneration, where they absorbed it like sponges, rescuing the family line. Hirschfeld quoted von Römer:

> In a family line where degeneration might be suspected, where the parents already display notable odd characteristics that however are not yet clearly degenerative, a homosexual child will be born. Most of these individuals are completely healthy and in many cases are even very capable, but they are not intended for further reproduction. They bleed off some of the current that would otherwise lead to degeneration, acting like the asexual blossoms of plants. The family line overcomes the degeneration thanks to this release, returning to full power in the healthy offspring of the normal siblings.[167]

Though von Römer's theory had assets, in Hirschfeld's view it was perhaps too complicated. He found a similar but simpler idea more persuasive: "that homosexuals, without themselves being degenerates [*Degenerierte*], constitute a substitution for degeneration … homosexuals serve nature as a preventative for degeneration."[168] As proof of this, Hirschfeld pointed to cases where a homosexual man or woman married a "normal" person. Most of these marriages were childless, he noted. When children did result, often they bore "the stamp of mental inferiority [*Minderwertigkeit*]." From the perspective of eugenics, Hirschfeld wrote, such marriages were risky.[169] He then offered ten brief case histories of homosexual men and women who married and produced children who had a variety of problems that pointed to the presence of degeneration. They suffered from mental illness or mental disability, took their own lives, became prostitutes, or displayed other signs of degeneration. He concluded that the marriages of homosexuals often produced degenerate offspring.[170] At the end of this passage, Hirschfeld left open the question of whether he or von Römer was correct but asserted that in any event, homosexuality was clearly part of the natural order, as were, for example, the sterile worker bees in a bee colony.[171] Hirschfeld thus denied that homosexuality was a form of degeneration yet maintained that in nature's scheme, homosexuality most likely had something beneficial to do with degeneration. Homosexuality was nature's way of preventing reproduction in situations where it was likely to result in inferior offspring. Hirschfeld avowed that homosexuals ought not to conceive. In the film *Different from the Others*, Hirschfeld (playing Hirschfeld) declares that nature did not intend for homosexuals to have children. Elsewhere he wrote, "from the point of view of producing a healthy generation – in other words, from a eugenic standpoint – the intercourse of a homosexual with a person of the opposite sex is more dangerous than the sexual relation natural to him."[172] He made similar points about transvestitism.[173] Hirschfeld's theories fit very well within the science and public policy of the Weimar era, in which, as this chapter and the preceding one showed, ideas about heredity and degeneration were current.

All of this became viscerally important in the fall of 1929 in part because science, particularly Hirschfeld's science, could colour one's views on male prostitution. Rejecting science as a primary platform for homosexual emancipation did not lead Radszuweit's League for Human Rights to defend male prostitutes: the League called for the criminalization of male prostitution along with the repeal of Paragraph 175.[174] But to Hiller, whether or not male prostitutes were homosexuals and whether or not they were degenerate was all immaterial: they had a right over their bodies that the state violated by criminalizing their sexual behaviour. To Hiller, the political question of male prostitution and that of male homosexuality were the same question of the individual's right over his body. And though he did not mention it in print at the time, Hiller's own life testified to the entanglement of male-male desire, love, and sex work.

Hirschfeld also opposed criminalizing male prostitution. His position on it was very close to the abolitionist feminist position on female prostitution, which he also supported. He believed that male prostitution, like female prostitution, had two causes: social conditions and biological predisposition. He argued for welfare to address the environmental causes of male prostitution and eugenic schemes to address the "degeneration and hereditary burdening" that also caused it.[175] Moreover, although he claimed that there was significant overlap between the population of male prostitutes and that of blackmailers, he denied that the two groups were one and the same. "Male prostitution and blackmail are in no way identical," he wrote, and it would be unjust to send "every male prostitute" to prison "just because some of them are guilty of asocial behaviour."[176] He criticized the proposed reform of Paragraph 175 in print, arguing that criminalizing male prostitution would force men who had formerly been prostitutes to become pimps instead, which would hardly be a move into a more savoury profession, and that in addition, a law against male prostitution would make possible a new injustice: the wealthy clients of male prostitutes could blackmail the prostitutes themselves.[177] At times, Hirschfeld sounded very much like Linsert and Hiller, claiming that male prostitution injured no third party and that destitute men chose it over worse crimes, such as robbery, fraud, and murder.[178] He could also seem somewhat internally conflicted, as when he wrote that the oft-repeated opinion that most blackmailers began their careers as male prostitutes was incorrect, and went on to explain that it nevertheless was the case that male prostitutes practised blackmail "quite frequently" as a casual side business. Though these casual blackmailers were to be distinguished from the worse sort of career blackmailers, the casuals made up three-quarters of all blackmailers.[179]

In any event, Hirschfeld and Hiller had different notions about what caused male prostitution and about what it had to do with male homosexuality. They had publicly differed on this issue as early as 1921, when, in a public debate, Hiller argued that bad economic conditions drove young men to prostitution while Hirschfeld emphasized that an innate disposition drove them into prostitution.[180] The difference between these positions mattered. Hiller's made commercial sex central to the homosexual emancipation movement by subsuming it into his notion of the right over one's self; Hirschfeld's made it peripheral. This was a more general question for homosexual emancipation – was the question of the legality of male prostitution connected in a meaningful way to the question of the legal and social status of male homosexuals? Paul Weber, who took over as the head of the League for Human Rights when Radszuweit died in the spring of 1932,[181] wrote in early 1933 that it was

> entirely correct, from a tactical standpoint, that we not tie our fight for our liberation to a fight for the equal rights of prostitutes. Our fight for the equal rights of homosexuals actually has nothing to do with this question and an activist organization of homosexuals cannot therefore represent the prostitutes, if it is serious about the struggle and if [it] ... wants to achieve something.[182]

Weber actually made this point in response to the essay that Hirschfeld had published arguing against a police crackdown on male prostitutes. And yet, though Weber favoured the crackdown and Hirschfeld did not, Hirschfeld's body of published work made it clear that he agreed with Weber about one thing: the question of homosexual emancipation was separate from that of male prostitution.

To Hirschfeld, the question of whether male prostitution ought to be legal had nothing to do with the question of whether male homosexual sex ought to be legal. He wrote that people often erroneously treated male prostitution as if it were part of the homosexual subcultures, like the homosexual press and homosexual clubs and bars. But in fact, "there is only a relationship between these things [that is, the subcultures] and homosexual prostitutes when the prostitutes are homosexual. However, for the majority of people in question, this is not the case."[183] Most male prostitutes were not homosexual; therefore, the issue of male prostitution had little to do with homosexual emancipation. In Hirschfeld's model, male prostitutes acted due to one biological condition, degeneration, plus environmental influences. Male homosexuals acted due to another biological condition, homosexuality, with environmental influences having no effect. Most male prostitutes did not have the condition called homosexuality. If one adopts Hirschfeld's perspective, the 1929 reform of the sodomy law does not seem like one step forward and two steps backward. It seems like progress for male homosexuals and an unrelated growing threat to male prostitutes, perhaps a necessary trade-off. After all, the repeal of Paragraph 175 only passed the penal code reform committee because of the new law intended to replace it, which cracked down on male prostitution. Someone with Hirschfeld's views would not necessarily think it imperative to pledge the WhK to fight the proposed reform of Paragraph 175.

There is evidence that Hirschfeld believed that the vote on Paragraph 175 was a victory, if a victory mitigated by the inclusion of a crackdown on male prostitutes that he did not support. Besser's tribute to him in the WhK magazine, quoted earlier, suggests as much.[184] In addition, in his farewell article, Hirschfeld perhaps implied that the fight against Paragraph 175 would end when Kahl's committee finished its work and the reformed penal code became law, writing that the work of homosexual liberation "we hope … will come to a good end in the foreseeable future."[185] Wolff, who interviewed members of Hirschfeld's circle, writes that in 1929, he felt "satisfied" with the "considerable progress" represented by the revision of Paragraph 175 and that he took no part in the

WhK's resolution to fight the reform, which was passed at the meeting where he resigned.[186] If one took the position that the vote in the penal code reform committee constituted a partial victory, one would lay out a path for the WhK moving forward that was very different from what the organization actually did and that would have done little to establish what Hiller called "the right over one's self." With Hirschfeld gone, Linsert's influence in the WhK grew, and the group resolved to fight the reform of Paragraph 175.[187] It denounced the crackdown on male prostitution and Paragraph 297's higher age of consent for male-male sex.[188] It also took steps to transform itself into a mass organization like the League for Human Rights, expanding its dues-paying membership and beginning to sell subscriptions to its magazine to non-members.[189] And though Hirschfeld later criticized the proposed new law against male prostitution, there was a significant difference between criticizing it and rejecting it as an "illusion" of "liberation" that the WhK must fight.

Had Hirschfeld been at the helm of the WhK after the vote on Paragraph 175, his worldview would not have led him to push the WhK to agitate so stridently against the proposed reform. Disagreements about the role of science in the movement triggered the power struggle that put him out of the organization. That power struggle was set in motion by events that happened before the vote to reform Paragraph 175. Hirschfeld's resignation does not seem to have centrally been about male prostitution. However, if Hirschfeld's science had remained the guiding principle of the WhK, it seems unlikely that the WhK would have categorically rejected the proposed reform rather than accepted it as a partial victory. Hirschfeld's departure left space for Hiller and Linsert to follow their politics, which contrasted with his. They took the WhK in a more radical direction, in defence of male prostitutes.

This account of Hirschfeld's resignation from the WhK differs from other historians' explanations, all of which attribute Hirschfeld's departure to a break between himself and Linsert and Hiller but which identify a number of competing explanations for that break. Among the explanations are personal animosities that manifested themselves in allegations about Hirschfeld having mismanaged WhK finances.[190] In addition, Hirschfeld's support for the SPD versus Linsert's for the KPD has been presented as the root of the conflict,[191] as has Hiller's manifest hostility to gender non-conforming homosexuals and transvestites versus Hirschfeld's support for them.[192] There is some truth to all of this. There were private allegations of financial mismanagement.[193] Hirschfeld and

Linsert backed the SPD and the KPD, respectively. In a 1932 essay in the WhK's magazine, Hiller denounced effeminate homosexuals, transvestites, and "hermaphrodites" as "monstrosities."[194] However, none of these issues had reached any sort of boiling point in the fall of 1929 when Hirschfeld resigned. Hirschfeld seems to have been a disorganized or lax manager,[195] but he had been relieved of his responsibilities for handling WhK monies as early as 1926;[196] although alleged bad financial practices may have been an issue in his resignation, they could not have been the decisive one. Linsert was a Communist, but he was no hard-line ideologue, and moreover, after Hirschfeld's resignation, the WhK's magazine showed no pronounced preference for the KPD.[197] Although gender was a point of contention between Hirschfeld and many homosexual emancipationists, including Hiller, it seems very unlikely that Hirschfeld was forced out of the WhK because of this. After Hirschfeld left, the WhK's magazine did not publish much material about gender conformity.[198] Hirschfeld's insistence that gender non-conformity was a defining feature of homosexuality had put him at odds with other homosexual emancipationists for several decades, and by the early Weimar years he had softened his position somewhat, allowing that gender non-conformity and homosexuality did not always coincide: not all homosexual men were effeminate and not all homosexual women were virile.[199] Hiller seems to have found some common ground with Hirschfeld on the question. In a 1927 speech, he praised Hirschfeld for demonstrating that gender non-conformity and homosexuality were separate.[200] A disagreement about gender existed among homosexual emancipationists and was reflected in the 1932 Hiller essay. But it was largely incidental to Hirschfeld's resignation. Furthermore, though historians have written a good deal about the differences between Hirschfeld and other leaders over gender, these differences were often also about science. Hirschfeld's prioritization of gender inversion in his model of homosexuality had irritated a number of other activists over the years, including Radszuweit, Adolf Brand, and Benedict Friedländer. Radszuweit criticized male homosexuals whose gender performance was not conventional, naming them, along with male prostitutes, as "the dregs of humanity."[201] He attacked Hirschfeld's scientific position, which he argued made homosexuals seem like pathological "abnormalities" and "hermaphrodites" (*Zwitter*).[202] This anxiety was about gender but did not reduce entirely to gender: to Radszuweit, the gender problem was a manifestation of the problem with science. Brand's complaints were similar.[203] Prior to the First World War, Friedländer had broken with the WhK because of its use of scientific arguments, which Friedländer associated with insufficient masculinity.[204] Gender non-conformity was an important issue among homosexual emancipationist, but it was not the only issue at stake and in any event was not as controversial in the late 1920s as it had been.

In summation: it is worth remembering the WhK's 1929 leadership crisis because it reveals divisions among homosexual emancipationists about the use of science and the place of sex workers in the movement. The fates of male homosexuals who did not do sex work were bound to those of male sex workers. The reform of Paragraph 175 passed because politicians defined "sick" but otherwise respectable homosexual men like Otto Zöhn in opposition to "degenerate" and criminal men like Aloys Dämon.[205] Hirschfeld's science helped to make this distinction. Indeed, for most of homosexual emancipation, the blackmailing male prostitute served as the biological homosexual's constitutive outside. The respectability and citizenship of the latter was defined against the dangerous criminality of the former. This formulation worked, at least from one perspective: the penal code reform committee voted to decriminalize consensual, non-commercial sex between male adults in private. As they had in the 1927 reform of the law on female prostitution, ideas about degeneration helped to reform Paragraph 175 in 1929, creating liberation for many men who had sex with men. The dilemma was whether this settlement was acceptable, and though it was for many homosexual emancipationists, it was not for Linsert and Hiller. They dedicated the WhK to fight the reform of Paragraph 175 because it cracked down on male prostitution, even though the reform contained what many others – including, apparently, Hirschfeld – perceived as important gains for homosexual emancipation.

Degeneration and Sexual Liberation: The Weimar Settlement on Sexual Politics

Degeneration and ideas about hereditary biological dispositions were useful to people seeking to change Germany's laws on sex. In the 1927 reform of the laws on female prostitution and venereal disease and in the 1929 reform of the sodomy law, ideas about degeneration defined the boundaries of citizenship. If one fell within those boundaries, one was granted greater freedom of sexual expression, on the understanding that one would make good choices and keep one's "abnormalities" out of the public eye and away from impressionable young people. If one fell outside the boundaries, as did some working-class female prostitutes and male prostitutes, one was believed incapable of making good choices. Both reforms were related and part of a broader progressive project: as early as 1919 the WhK saw the growing success of feminist abolitionism as heralding the success of its cause, the repeal of Paragraph 175.[206] And both reforms included rather strict controls on some people. In 1925, the WhK explicitly endorsed this scheme. That year, members of the Bavarian People's Party in the Reichstag made one of their familiar calls for censorship to protect "youths" from "seduction" and to defend "the general public from the sex drives of sexually abnormal people, which are dangerous to public safety."[207] In a response signed by Hirschfeld, Hiller, and other WhK leaders, the WhK agreed with the Bavarian People's Party in part. But it argued that it made no sense to characterize all "sexually abnormal people" as "dangerous to society." WhK leaders wrote,

> At the same time that new and stronger restrictions carrying the force of legal punishment are put into place against the sex drives of certain abnormally inclined people, who are dangerous to society, there must be a rescinding of legal regulations that cruelly and senselessly threaten the private lives of abnormally inclined people when it is not the case that they are dangerous to society.[208]

To put it simply, restrictions on some people could and ought to bring liberation for others. This is what I term the Weimar settlement on sexual politics. It apparently came to seem a mistake to Hiller.

Science, in particular ideas about degeneration and mental and physical disability, worked to produce liberation for many people in Germany during the Weimar years.[209] The settlement on sexual politics made Germany one of the states in the world most tolerant of some sexual outsiders, but it came at a price for other sexual outsiders. It is critical that the full history of these reforms be appreciated so that the memory of what they cost can also be appreciated.

In prison following Otto Zöhn's suicide, Aloys Dämon experienced these sexual politics. The bank clerk Zöhn ended up dead as a result of his relationship with the prostitute Dämon, but the meeting at the train station proved to have been unlucky for Dämon as well. Since prevailing discourse cast him as a degenerate criminal, prison officials could expect Dämon to exhibit symptoms of his flawed nature. In 1927, a prison doctor found him to be "mentally disturbed" and sent him to an institution.[210] Incidental to my argument but not to Dämon's story, he remained in

prison through 1933, when the Nazis put a harsh compulsory sterilization law in place. The following year, prison officials declared that "in
Dämon's case, the prerequisites for sterilization are present." Though
he and his sister begged that he be granted clemency and released from
prison, he was not, and it seems likely that he was forced to undergo a
sterilization operation – there are no further documents in the file after
the denial of a pardon.[211] I do not bring up Dämon's fate after 1933
in order to suggest strong continuities between mainstream Weimar-era
sexual politics and Nazi policies. It is, in the end, superfluous to this
study that Dämon was nominated for sterilization under the Nazi State.
What is not superfluous is that Dämon was defined as a degenerate criminal under the Weimar Republic because he engaged in prostitution and
blackmail. Dämon's society – that is, Weimar-era Germany – expressed
its condemnation in a particular way. The social and cultural trends that
culminated in his classification as a degenerate criminal also led to the
repeal of Paragraph 175. It was up to Dämon's contemporaries to decide
whether they could stomach the terms of this settlement.

5 "The Third Sex Greets the Third Reich!": The Röhm Scandal, 1931–1932

On 12 May 1932, the Social Democratic propagandist Helmuth Klotz went to the café in the Reichstag building to meet an SPD member of parliament. Klotz was drinking coffee alone at a table, his companion having been called away to a vote, when a handful of Nazi Reichstag deputies came in to the café to smoke. Some weeks before, Klotz had published letters written by Ernst Röhm, head of the Nazi Party paramilitary, the SA. In those letters, Röhm discussed his sexual affairs with men and his opposition to Paragraph 175. Now Klotz was in the wrong place at the wrong time. One of the Nazi Reichstag deputies who walked into the café that day was the blond, square-jawed Edmund Heines, a deputy of Röhm's. Heines was a violent man. He was already a convicted murderer, and later he would orchestrate a bloody campaign against Jews and leftists as head of the SA in Silesia.[1] Heines recognized Klotz. He cried out something to the effect of "Ach, that's the dog who faked the Röhm letters"[2] or "You're the hoodlum who published the pamphlet!"[3] Then he walked to Klotz's table and slapped him across the face. Two of Heines's fellow Nazi Reichstag deputies descended upon Klotz, punching him and striking him with a chair. A waiter and some other Reichstag deputies rushed in and dragged the Nazis off. The Nazis fled. Two police officers arrived on the scene. They told the shaken Klotz that they would escort him through the building so that he could identify his attackers. Klotz agreed. But when the police officers and Klotz left the café, they did not get far before a ring of Nazi Reichstag deputies surrounded them. The Nazis cried, "Get Klotz out of here! Out with the swine!"[4] Klotz and the two policemen were crushed at the centre of a growing throng of Nazis; fifty or sixty men pressed around them. The Nazis struck from all sides, raining blows on Klotz and the policemen. They dragged

Ein außergewöhnliches Bild: Schupo im Reichstag.

The Berlin police led by Bernhard Weiss enter the Reichstag in force to arrest Nazi deputies during the Klotz incident. This picture ran on the front page of the *Berliner Lokal-Anzeiger* on 13 May 1932. The caption reads, "An extraordinary picture: police in the Reichstag."

Klotz away from his protectors, pummelled him to the floor, and beat him bloody. Later, some witnesses said that they heard someone yell, "Let me in, I'll beat him to death."[5]

During this violence, the parliament was actually in session. News of the attack reached the president of the Reichstag, the SPD's Paul Löbe. Löbe took the floor in the parliamentary chamber and announced to his fellow deputies that Nazis had attacked the "journalist" Klotz in the Reichstag building. Löbe said he was therefore imposing the maximum sanction on the Nazi delegates, thirty-day suspensions, and that he had instructed police to arrest the accused attackers. The Nazi Reichstag delegation, which at the time totalled 107 men, responded with a roar of "Heil Hitler!" In that instant, Berlin's deputy police president Bernhard Weiss and a crowd of his officers appeared in the door of the parliamentary chamber.[6] The Nazis greeted Weiss, who was Jewish and a favourite target of NSDAP propaganda, with antisemitic slurs – "Isidor! ...

Jew!"[7] – and with more choruses of "Heil Hitler!"[8] Thirty police officers advanced on the pack of Nazi deputies. In the chaos, Löbe suspended the parliamentary session. Police arrested Heines and two other Nazi deputies. Later they also arrested Gregor Strasser, a member of the NSDAP leadership, who had managed to escape the police at the Reichstag building. The four NSDAP deputies went to trial in a Berlin courtroom packed with press and heckling Nazis.

This book's last two chapters investigate the extent to which sexual politics played a role in the Nazi rise to power. This chapter examines the case in which, arguably, they most clearly did: the Röhm scandal of 1931–2, a series of events that made questions about male homosexuality more important in national political campaigns than they had ever been before, or so wrote Paul Weber of the League for Human Rights.[9] First, the chapter tells the story of Röhm's political and personal life, culminating in the scandal and the brawl in the Reichstag. Then, it analyses the national press's reportage on the brawl in order to make two arguments about how the allegations of homosexuality affected the NSDAP. Historians have examined the Röhm scandal but have not considered how the attack on Klotz brought Röhm's sexuality to national attention.[10] Contrary to what other studies have asserted, most media did not report on Röhm's letters prior to the melee that began in the Reichstag café.[11] But the bloody assault put the scandal on front pages across the country. The highly public, persuasive allegations about Röhm's sexuality made it tough for the NSDAP to campaign as a party of moral renewal. (Chapter 6 argues that indeed, the NSDAP did not make claims to be a party of moral renewal a central part of its propaganda in the final years of the Republic.) The second argument in this chapter is that it is significant that the NSDAP weathered the Röhm scandal without too much trouble. Nazis feared that the scandal would damage their party's political fortunes just before the pivotal Reichstag election in July 1932. Historians agree that it did not, though they do not note that this lack of an effect is itself important.[12] The national media's relatively phlegmatic reaction to Röhm's sexuality demonstrates that by the early 1930s, it was quite possible for journalists at major papers to act as if credible allegations of the homosexuality of a public figure were not a matter of public concern. Röhm's homosexuality offered a narrative with which to attack the Nazis, but even staunch Nazi opponents refrained from using it and instead indicted the NSDAP for other things. It is difficult to imagine the national media in the 1930s in a country other than Germany reacting to a homosexual sex scandal about a leading politician with such restraint.

Ernst Röhm, on horseback at left, raising his arm, and his deputy Edmund Heines (directly to the right of Röhm, also on horseback) at a rally in August 1933. Photograph by Georg Pahl. Bundesarchiv.

Yet this was the Weimar settlement on sexual politics, reflected in the proposed reform of the sodomy law: homosexuality, if kept private by the person in question, could be tolerated. Ironically, in 1932 this benefited the vehemently anti-homosexual NSDAP.

The Röhm Scandal

Ernst Röhm was a military man. Raised in a middle-class Protestant family in Munich, he joined the Bavarian army and won distinction as an officer in the First World War. He had the top portion of his nose blown off in the process. Together with his thick neck, the mangled nose gave him a formidable look. Had 1918 not brought revolution, he probably would have made a career as an army officer. Instead he found an alternative career in anti-democratic and antisemitic radical-right politics. The year 1918 politicized Röhm. As he saw it, the Revolution's upending of the just social hierarchy and its dismissal of the privileges that he had enjoyed as an army officer had to be put right again.[13] He plunged into far-right politics in Munich, enlisting in a right-wing militia (*Freikorps*) unit and joining the German Workers' Party (*Deutsche Arbeiterpartei*) in 1919. Around the same time, one Adolf Hitler joined. They became friends. Hitler often went for meals with Röhm's family. In 1923, Röhm resigned from the army in order to devote himself full time to politics, that is, to what he thought of as the salvation of Germany.[14] He was an important early backer of Hitler and an asset to the tiny party, which soon changed its name to the National Socialist German Workers' Party. He had connections to the military and to important figures in right-wing, anti-Republican political circles. Convicted of treason for his role in the NSDAP's bungled Beer Hall Putsch of 1923 but not imprisoned, Röhm's profile was high enough that he published an autobiography, *The Story of a Traitor* (*Die Geschichte eines Hochverräters*). Many years later, this book sparked the friendship that led to his sexuality being splashed on the front pages of newspapers across Germany.

Through the 1920s, Röhm served in the leadership of the tiny and marginal NSDAP. Nazis were not major voices on any political issues, sexual or otherwise, until after 1929, when the Nazi Party began to win a significant slice of the national vote and a bloc of seats in the Reichstag. In 1928, Röhm abandoned the party, which polled 2.6 percent of the national vote that year, and left Germany to serve as an adviser to the Bolivian army. He hoped to restart his military career. But Hitler wanted Röhm back, and in late 1930 Röhm agreed to return to Germany to lead the "Storm Troopers" or SA (*Sturmabteilung*). The NSDAP's political fortunes reversed and it began to win more and more Reichstag seats. With the Great Depression's full force bearing down on Germany and bloody street violence between the Communist militia and the SA becoming a daily event in big cities, the Republic's fate was looking increasingly dim and certain voters were increasingly viewing Nazism as a viable alternative to the threat of Communist revolution. Upon his return as head of the SA, Röhm became a national figure, a leading fascist with strong credentials as a *völkisch* politician and military man. He had a top post in the Nazi Party, a friendship with Hitler, and a good measure of status because he had joined the party early and had seen action in the 1923 putsch.

This story of the rise of Röhm's political fortunes is shadowed by another story, that of a personal journey that might seem much at odds with his political career. In the years that Röhm spent helping to build the Nazi Party from a Bavarian movement of hundreds to a national party of hundreds of thousands, he came to terms with his sexuality and made a life for himself as a man who had sex with men. He kept this personal life carefully separated from his political career, though as it turned out, he was not nearly careful enough. Since his youth, Röhm had felt desire for men but had slept only with women. In 1924, when he was in his thirties, he realized that he was, as he put it in one of the letters that were later leaked to the press, "same-sex orientated [*gleichgeschlechtlich*]."[15] That year, he moved to Berlin to serve as a Nazi Party Reichstag deputy. NSDAP doctrine brutally rejected homosexuality. Nevertheless, Röhm hung out at homosexual spots in Berlin, including the famous Eldorado nightclub, known for its transvestite performers.[16] He joined Radszuweit's League for Human Rights and thus received, and perhaps read, its flagship magazine, the *Journal for Human Rights*.[17] Röhm believed that his desire for men was an innate part of him that society forced him to conceal. He resented being forced into deception.[18] Early on, he displayed a stubborn disinclination to hide his sexuality. Just a year after Röhm moved to Berlin, a man he had brought home from a bar tried to blackmail him. Röhm ignored the blackmail threat and reported the man to the police. News of this incident got back to Hitler, who did nothing.[19]

Nazism privileged heterosexuality and derided homosexuality. Adolf Brand, leader of the small homosexual emancipationist group the Society of the Special/Self-Owning (*Gemeinschaft der Eigenen*), polled the political parties about their stand on Paragraph 175 in 1928. The Nazi response is worth quoting at length. It leaves no doubt as to the party's unfriendliness towards homosexual emancipation and same-sex desire:

> It is not necessary that you and I live, but it is necessary that the German people live. And it can only live if it can fight, for life means fighting. And it can only fight if it maintains its masculinity. It can only maintain its masculinity if it exercises discipline, especially in matters of love. Free love and deviance are undisciplined. Therefore we reject you, as we reject anything which hurts our people.
>
> Anyone who even thinks of homosexual love is our enemy. We reject anything which emasculates our people and makes it a plaything for our enemies, for we know that life is a fight and it's madness to think that men will ever embrace fraternally. Natural history teaches us the opposite. Might makes right. And the stronger will always win over the weak. Let's see to it that we once again become the strong! But this we can only do in one way – the German people must once again learn how to exercise discipline. We therefore reject any form of lewdness, especially homosexuality, because it robs us of our last chance to free our people from the bondage which now enslaves it.[20]

These deeply anti-homosexual sentiments were regularly expressed by various NSDAP mouthpieces. Nazi Reichstag delegates railed against homosexuality. The party press threatened to sterilize gay men once in power.[21] (After the Nazis took power, they forced gay men to undergo castration.) Nazi leaders and Nazi propaganda charged that homosexual emancipation was a Jewish conspiracy to undermine the German Volk's morality.[22] Nazis frequently indulged in antisemitic castigation and mockery of Hirschfeld, whom *völkisch* thugs had beaten unconscious after his lecture in Munich in 1920.[23]

Yet Röhm's fascist politics did not entirely isolate him in Berlin's queer scenes in the 1920s. Other fascists and arch-conservatives counted themselves among Germany's homosexuals and homoerotics. Although only about 3 per cent of the more than 30,000 male members of the League for Human Rights who responded to a 1926 survey identified themselves as members of far-right *völkisch* parties (including the Nazis), about 21 per cent said they belonged to the conservative DNVP.[24] In the Republic's final years, the DNVP was increasingly right-wing and friendly to the fascists. Hirschfeld's WhK also had Nazis on its membership rolls.[25] However, the most likely home for fascists in the homosexual emancipation movement was Brand's Society of the Special/Self-Owning. The Society's longing for a male-dominated, pre-industrial world shared intellectual and cultural roots with fascism. Members of the Society openly espoused quasi-fascist and *völkisch* racist notions.[26] Röhm would have seen views similar to his own in the Society's celebration of virile, martial masculinity and bonds between men. As an antisemite, Röhm would have moreover appreciated the antisemitic views of various members of the Society. He most likely agreed with their rejection of Hirschfeld's model of biological homosexuality as feminizing and insufficiently spiritual.[27]

The chain of events culminating in the scandal began the day Röhm discovered the Society. One of the men in Brand's circle, Karl Günter Heimsoth, wrote Röhm a letter in 1928. Heimsoth was a psychologist and an antisemitic, *völkisch* nationalist who contributed to Brand's magazine, *Der Eigene*. His purpose in writing the letter was to inquire about a particular passage in Röhm's autobiography. In this passage, Röhm seemed to oppose Paragraph 175, although he was not explicit. Röhm wrote, "The struggle against the cant, deceit and hypocrisy of today's society must take its starting point from the innate nature of the drives that are placed in men from the cradle ... If the struggle in this area is successful, then the masks can be torn from the dissimulation in all areas of the human social and legal order."[28] The passage moved Heimsoth to reach out to Röhm. The fact that Röhm was known to many in Berlin and Munich's homosexual subcultures probably also inspired Heimsoth to write.[29] In his first letter to Röhm, Heimsoth asked whether he had perceived this passage correctly as a denunciation of Paragraph 175. Röhm had good reason to be cautious about this letter from a stranger. But he seems not to have comprehended the danger. Heimsoth's letter delighted him and he dispensed with all pretence, writing back, "You have understood me completely!"[30]

The two men struck up a friendship. They wrote letters for the next two years while Röhm was in Bolivia.[31] Heimsoth and Röhm had a lot in common. Both idealized their experiences as front soldiers in the First World War. Both had sought to prolong the front experience by becoming *Freikorps* fighters in the early 1920s. Both believed that the front experience ought to be the basis for politics. In the macho, battle-scarred Röhm, Heimsoth recognized Hans Blüher's male hero (*Männerheld*), loved and beloved by young men. He sought to win Röhm over to something like Blüher's vision of all-male institutions, such as the army, cemented by homoerotic bonding. German fascism already sought to create a *Männerstaat*, a state founded on bonds between racially superior men and martial masculinity. In Heimsoth's version the *Männerstaat* would acknowledge the universal bisexuality of people and the higher beauty and truth of homoerotic male love.[32] The truly important distinction for Heimsoth and for other men associated with Brand's Society was not between men who had sex with men and those who did not, but between masculine and feminine men. Heimsoth had published an antisemitic attack on Hirschfeld rejecting his supposedly effeminate model of homoeroticism.[33] Nazi propaganda also harped on the supposed effeminacy of gay men and claimed that Jews like Hirschfeld had masterminded the homosexual emancipation movement as an attack on the "Aryan" race. Since Heimsoth, Röhm, and others like them rejected both effeminacy and Judaism, they believed that their sexuality could be compatible with Nazi ideology.[34] Heimsoth hoped to change the NSDAP's policy on homosexuality through his friendship with Röhm. For his part, Röhm was intrigued by Heimsoth's ideas and apparently happy to have a correspondent with whom to discuss masculine homoeroticism. His letters frankly described his desires for men and narrated how he came to terms with his sexuality.[35]

These letters, and the scandal that they later fuelled, have been grist for an enduring myth about Nazism: that the NSDAP, and particularly Hitler, tolerated Röhm's sexuality because the ranks of the Nazi Party were filled with gay men or because there was a significant, friendly relationship between fascism and male homosexuality. Charges of male homosexuality in the NSDAP were put to use in the Weimar era chiefly by the Social Democrats and Communists and were kept alive by Hitler's enemies after 1933.[36] When Nazism fell, the stories transformed into a supposedly more sophisticated theory about how fascists tended to be homosexual and vice versa.[37] Although remarkably long-lived, mutable, capable of regenerating itself in various contexts, and even entertained at times by reputable historians, the myth of legions of gay Nazis has no historical basis.[38] The myth is nearly as old as the NSDAP itself: beginning in the party's early years, anti-fascists used allegations of homosexuality against it.[39] The Röhm scandal was grist for these accusations. The myth endured because after 1945, the exiled anti-fascist German Left had considerable influence on various fields of intellectual endeavour in Western Europe and North America; for example, assertions about the innate homoeroticism of Nazism surfaced in theories of totalitarianism, such as that of Theodor Adorno, as well as in New Left politics in West Germany.[40] But viewed in its historical context, Hitler's loyalty to Röhm during the scandal of 1931–2, which has been seized upon as evidence of Hitler's own homosexuality, does not seem all that unusual or remarkable.[41] It certainly does not seem indicative of homosexuality: as discussed later, major conservative, non-Nazi newspapers defended Röhm and implied that his sex life did not matter. To the larger point: there is no evidence that people who preferred sexual or romantic relationships with their own sex were any more likely to take part in the Nazi project than were people who preferred the opposite sex. Without the support of millions of the latter, the Nazis would never have taken power. In addition, the significant link between male homosexuality and German fascism is that German fascism employed violence and coercion in a project aimed to destroy male homosexuality.[42] Of course, one could be a homoerotic and a fascist at the same time, provided one was up to the mental gymnastics required to get around the NSDAP's official anti-homosexual position. There is no necessary connection between sexual radicalism and left-wing radicalism.[43] But homoeroticism was compatible with any and all political views under the Republic.

Indeed, the NSDAP was not all that accommodating of Röhm's sexuality. Whatever toleration existed was thin and fragile. His position within the NSDAP after his return from Bolivia was somewhat isolated and quite dependent on Hitler personally, and his sexuality only contributed to his lack of support within the party.[44] Röhm gave signs of his vulnerability in his very first letter to Heimsoth. He wrote that party ideologue Alfred Rosenberg was attacking him in print for his sexuality, although, Röhm claimed, generally the party had been forced "to grow accustomed to my criminal idiosyncrasy."[45] He also told Heimsoth that in Nazi Party circles, "I make no secret of my inclination."[46] In reality, Röhm compartmentalized his life, sharing certain things with trusted friends and allies.[47] His claim that the party had "grown accustomed" to his sexuality was wild optimism or self-delusion. Joseph Goebbels apparently did not know that Röhm was homosexual prior to the early 1930s: when accusations about Röhm's homosexuality came out in the *Munich Post* (*Münchener Post*) in 1931, Goebbels wrote in his diary, "Severe attack on Röhm because of 175 in the *Post* here. Is this supposed to be true? [*Was soll daran wahr sein*]?"[48] Other Nazis knew and used the information against Röhm, circulating rumours in an attempt to discredit him and Hitler.[49] As will be seen later, some of the leaks to the press concerning Röhm's sexuality in the Republic's final years came from inside the Nazi Party. Hitler did ignore Röhm's sexuality. He also defended him from intra-party attacks and stood by him throughout the public scandal.[50] Homophobia was not among Hitler's "major obsessions" as Geoffrey Giles writes, and Röhm was one of his first comrades in the Nazi movement, an "old fighter" who had braved the failed putsch by his side.[51] Hitler's photographer claimed in the 1950s that Hitler remarked in private that homosexual behaviour in a man who had been in the tropics, such as Röhm, meant something entirely different and that he, Hitler, had no interest in Röhm's private life so long as Röhm was discreet.[52] In addition, Röhm was a capable administrator of the unruly SA, had useful connections to the army, and was dependent on Hitler and therefore unlikely to buck his authority.[53] Hitler's indifference was, however, not a permanent state. In 1934, he used Röhm's sexuality to help to justify his murder, and afterwards, Giles argues, his anxiety about male-male eroticism grew more acute as he sought to legitimate in his own mind having ordered his friend's death.[54] Other Nazi leaders, like Heinrich Himmler, nursed livid anti-homosexual sentiments.[55] Yet Röhm was not alone in interpreting Hitler's forbearance as a broader Nazi "tolerance" of homosexuality. Prior to his murder, other gay men believed that the fact that Hitler had kept Röhm in a leading role despite the scandal of the early 1930s meant that homosexuals would be tolerated to a certain extent by the Nazi State.[56]

Röhm's double life grew unsustainable when he returned from Bolivia to head the SA. Now his fame and power were greater than they had ever been before, and Röhm had more enemies, both inside of his party and outside of it. Meeting men was riskier, something Röhm seems not to have immediately appreciated. Soon after he returned to Germany, another blackmail attempt by an unemployed Munich waiter prompted a police investigation, word of which reached the newspapers.[57] There was enough press hinting at Röhm's homosexuality by the winter of 1931 that Goebbels complained in his diary that the Nazi Party had become known as "the Eldorado of the 175-ers."[58] But this was just the beginning. That spring, the SPD-backing *Munich Post* began a series of front-page attacks on Röhm that spread throughout the left-wing press.

The SPD was the homosexual emancipation movement's oldest supporter among Germany's political parties. Yet the SPD's stand against Paragraph 175 did not preclude it from publicizing the homosexuality of its opponents for political gain. The Social Democrats had a long history of doing so. August Bebel's Reichstag speech against Paragraph 175 in 1898 seemed an important step forward to homosexual emancipationists, and yet in it, Bebel made a veiled threat. He gave as a reason for repealing Paragraph 175 the fact that homosexual sex went on in high social circles and that if this became public, national scandal would ensue.[59] A few years later, Social Democrats and their allies made good on this threat when they exposed the alleged homosexuality of officials in the highest levels of the kaiser's regime during the Krupp and Eulenburg-Moltke scandals.[60]

Nor was sexual denunciation of political enemies unusual in Weimar-era politics. In fact, it was a favourite tactic of the Nazis. They were notorious for dredging up salacious details and marshalling them to defame their enemies in print.[61] Goebbels printed and circulated hundreds of thousands of copies of a picture of Prussian Minister of the Interior and leading SPD figure Carl Severing with a young woman sitting on his lap. The photo, which was more than a decade old by the time Goebbels got a hold of it, had hardly resulted from an affair. Severing had assembled for a group portrait at an event and without warning, a stranger had jumped onto his lap just before the shutter clicked.[62]

Social Democrats thus employed a familiar tactic when in April 1931, the *Munich Post* began to publish allegations of Röhm's homosexuality and of widespread homosexuality in the SA. These were based on leaks from within the NSDAP, despite the fact that the *Munich Post* was a tenacious opponent of Nazism.[63] The first article purported to be a report from an unnamed former Nazi on a "clique" of SA leaders that included Röhm and Edmund Heines, who would later attack Klotz in the Reichstag cafe.[64] The informant claimed they were "175-ers" with whom Hitler happily marched "arm in arm."[65] A second article described Röhm's affair with a male prostitute.[66] Next, an article on "Sex Life in the Third Reich" charged the Nazi Party with "abhorrent hypocrisy" for claiming to carry on "a battle against sodomy" while tolerating "the shameless practice of sodomy in its own ranks." This article reported that Hitler had heard the many complaints about Röhm's sex life yet kept him in his post.[67] The basics of that last charge were true. Months earlier, Hitler had rejected a formal complaint within the NSDAP against Röhm because of his sexuality.[68] The *Munich Post* continued in this vein for months with article after article, revealing the primary source of its scandalous information to be letters between Röhm and a man named Eduard Meyer. Other Social Democratic and Communist newspapers picked up the story and flaunted the accusations under headlines like "The Third Sex Greets the Third Reich!"[69] In working-class Berlin, people read newsletters charging that Hitler himself was an effeminate homosexual and demanding, "Are such people – they can hardly be called men – renewers of the Reich? Are they the revivers of our youth?"[70] The Nazi leadership fretted, and NSDAP organs responded that these were fabrications by Jews and Marxists.[71] "The scandal around Röhm is becoming grotesque," Goebbels wrote in his diary.[72] Röhm claimed in the pages of the NSDAP's main newspaper, the *Völkischer Beobachter*, that the Meyer letters were fakes. And it turned out, to the relief of the Nazis, that he was telling the truth: the Meyer letters were fakes.[73] Röhm successfully sued, Meyer committed suicide in jail, and the furore about Röhm's sexuality in the left-wing press died down, although the rumours did not.[74]

Yet Röhm was hardly in the clear. Powerful figures within the SPD watched from the sidelines as the *Munich Post*'s muckraking failed and decided to see if they could get their hands on authentic incriminating letters and drum up a Paragraph 175 charge against Röhm.[75] The Berlin police, which in 1931 was under the jurisdiction of Severing's Prussian Interior Ministry, somehow got wind of the existence of the Heimsoth letters. The police were probably tipped off by NSDAP insiders who learned of the letters when Röhm, acting on a belated instinct for self-protection, unsuccessfully attempted to retrieve them from Heimsoth. The Berlin police were known for declining to enforce Paragraph 175, especially when blackmail was involved.[76] Yet they opened an investigation of Röhm based on a complaint made by the unemployed waiter who had tried to blackmail him. The police raided Heimsoth's lawyer's office and seized the letters.[77] Röhm's letters to Heimsoth were a far more dangerous thing to Röhm and his party than the *Munich Post* allegations. After Röhm's successful suit revealed that Meyer's letters were frauds, the *Munich Post* stories must have looked like libellous slander to anyone who had been following the story. But the letters to Heimsoth were real. The Social Democrat's immediate plans for the letters failed. They had wanted to charge Röhm under Paragraph 175, but neither the letters nor the subsequent interrogations of Röhm and Heimsoth turned up evidence for such a charge. Yet people within the SPD eventually realized that the letters themselves could do enormous damage to the Nazi Party.

When Hitler announced that he would run for president against Paul von Hindenburg in 1932, a man with ties to the SPD released the Heimsoth letters to the public in a well-orchestrated campaign.[78] He was Klotz, a former Nazi who had become a dedicated anti-fascist pamphleteer and Social Democrat. Social Democrats in the Prussian government gave Klotz the letters and encouraged him to publish them in order to hurt Hitler's campaign. Klotz wrote a brief introduction and put it and copies of Röhm's letters to Heimsoth into a pamphlet. He printed 300,000 copies. Just before the first round of voting for president in March 1932, Klotz mailed these pamphlets to politicians, army officers, doctors, teachers, notaries, and other important people all over Germany.[79] Klotz claimed that any party that tolerated homosexuality in its top ranks was morally corrupt and therefore poised to "poison the Volk[,] ... destroy [its] moral strength," and condemn Germany to "the fate of ancient Rome" if "responsible German citizens do not intervene."[80] Moreover, he claimed, the Nazi Party endangered German youth. Röhm also oversaw the Nazi youth organization, the Hitler Youth (*Hitler Jugend*), which was not yet formally separate from the SA.[81] The rhetoric that Klotz used was identical to moderate-conservative and right-wing attacks on homosexuality in public life, including those made by the Nazis themselves. The Social Democratic press pounced, publishing excerpts of the letters in newspapers across Germany.[82] Röhm quickly filed a lawsuit against Klotz to stop the distribution of the letters. But he could not claim that they were fraudulent. A Munich court noted this as it rejected Röhm's libel suit: because Röhm did not deny to the court that he had written the letters, there was nothing illegal about publishing authentic letters as evidence to support the contention that Röhm was unsuited to lead German youth.[83] Hitler once again stood by Röhm.[84] He also, however, made the Hitler Youth officially independent of the SA a few days after the brawl in the Reichstag building, in part to protect the youth organization from any future ban on the SA, and in part as a response to the publicity about Röhm's sexuality.[85]

Dismay and rising panic ran through party ranks as Röhm admitted to his fellow Nazis that he had written the letters.[86] Goebbels, meeting him a few days after the Heimsoth letters hit the press, found Röhm "bright-eyed" and wrote in his diary, "I don't understand it. I would be ashamed to the point of death."[87] Konstantin Hierl, later head of the Reich Labour Service (*Reichsarbeitsdienst*) and at the time a high-ranking party functionary, wrote to Hitler to warn him that the scandal would "break the faith of the masses in the strength and purity of the National Socialist Movement" and undermine the support of "tens of thousands," especially conservative voters whom Hitler needed to lure away from traditional conservatives such as Hindenburg.[88] To Goebbels the "Röhm Affair" was a crisis, and he sought to do what he could to alleviate it with campaign propaganda.[89] Other party members plotted to kill Röhm. The assassination plot failed and leaked to the press, which made the Nazis look even worse.[90] The conservatives who would appoint Hitler to the chancellorship in 1933, and whose support for Nazi power was necessary, received copies of the letters. President Hindenburg remarked privately that in the kaiser's day, one would have presented an officer like Röhm with a pistol (so that he could shoot himself).[91]

In another time, the scandal could have crippled the NSDAP. Allegations of homosexuality by the Social Democratic press had prompted the suicide of the kaiser's adviser and friend Friedrich Krupp in 1902.[92] A few years later, such allegations had destroyed the political career of Prince Eulenburg, a member of the kaiser's inner circle. After years of struggling in obscurity, it seemed to some Nazis that their party had risen near the heights of national power only to be hamstrung in 1932 by the Röhm scandal. This was precisely what the Social Democrats who fomented the scandal hoped would happen. Surely voters who cared about sexuality morality, homosexual seduction, and the protection of youth would think twice before they voted NSDAP in 1932.

Yet the Röhm scandal did not hamstring the Nazi Party. Although Hitler lost to Hindenburg by wide margins in the votes for president, his performance was a big improvement over the Nazis' last outing in a national election, in 1930, when they drew 18.3 per cent of the vote. In the first round of voting for president on 13 March 1932, Hitler came second in a field of four major candidates and got about 30 per cent of the vote. Hindenburg came first, with about 50 per cent. In the run-off election on 10 April, Hindenburg won about 53 per cent of the vote, Hitler about 37 per cent, and the KPD's Thälmann about 10 per cent.[93] In the July 1932 Reichstag elections, the NSDAP had its best-ever result in national elections, capturing 37.3 per cent of the national vote. Though they would poll no better than about 37 per cent, the sad reality was that in the Republic's endgame, a 37 per cent share of the electorate was large enough to inspire Hindenburg and the men around him to make Hitler chancellor.

The Rule of Fists in the Reichstag: Reporting on the Beating of Klotz and the Röhm Letters

Although the Röhm scandal did not affect the 1932 elections, it was not unimportant. This section examines how the national media reported the attack on Klotz in order to make two arguments. The first is that many voters knew about Röhm's sexuality when they cast their votes in 1932, including those who read liberal and conservative papers, and that this gave the lie to NSDAP claims to be especially poised to combat immorality. In major dailies like the *Deutsche Allgemeine Zeitung* and the *Frankfurter Zeitung*, there was abundant coverage of the bizarre and bloody climax of the scandal – the fracas in the Reichstag – and of the subsequent trials of Heines and the other Nazi deputies, in which Strasser was acquitted and

Heines and the others got three-month sentences.[94] And though doubt-less many people on the right considered the allegations of Röhm's homosexuality fraudulent, thanks to the failed libel suit the allegations could not be easily dismissed, even by some conservative media. General knowledge of the scandal made it hard for the NSDAP to claim a unique ability to renew Germany's morality. And as the next chapter shows, the NSDAP did not make issues of sexual morality a centrepiece of its propa-ganda in the early 1930s.

In addition, this section of the chapter makes a second argument: in print, many journalists were rather blasé about Röhm's sexuality. Röhm's homosexuality opened up a position from which to attack the NSDAP, but even diehard opponents of fascism, such as those at major liberal papers, declined to launch that sort of attack. Instead, they assigned other meanings to the bloody fisticuffs in the Reichstag. In examining these alternative narratives, my intention is not to make an argument about what journalists or readers *believed* about homosexuality and citizenship. That is, the fact that journalists at a diverse set of papers reported on the brawl as if Röhm's sexuality were unimportant does not necessarily indicate that they or their readers thought homosexuals could unprob-lematically be citizens. Rather, the project here is to examine what kinds of political rhetoric were possible and viable in this particular moment. Especially at conservative papers friendly to Nazism, journalists had self-serving reasons to minimize the importance of Röhm's sexuality. For conservative or liberal voters who were flocking to the NSDAP in this period, it was most likely a matter of ignoring the Röhm scandal and refusing to rethink their views on the NSDAP because of it, rather than deciding that in principle one's homosexuality did not preclude one's citizenship. Yet, whatever their reasons for so doing, journalists had the option of dismissing Röhm's sexuality as unimportant. This is a question of what it was possible to argue in a national debate. The notion that a person's homosexuality did not necessarily mean he ought to be imme-diately dismissed from his post at the head of a major party had enough credibility by 1932 that it could be asserted with a straight face, even by conservatives who otherwise opposed homosexual emancipation. At the same time, anti-fascist journalists at liberal papers chose not to attack the NSDAP for harbouring a known homosexual and instead attacked the NSDAP for introducing violence into the Reichstag chamber. What-ever they believed, conservative and liberal journalists assumed that they could act as if Röhm's sexuality was insignificant in politics and not lose all credibility with their readers, or – particularly in the case of journalists at liberal venues – they assumed that their readers would care less about the allegations of homosexuality than they would about the bloody pandemonium. Not surprisingly, the principle that a person's homosexuality did not preclude his citizenship, so long as he kept it private, was also apparent in the reactions of homosexual emancipationists to the scandal, although they differed in their interpretations of Nazism.

The attack on Klotz spread knowledge of the allegations about Röhm's sexuality, and reporting on the attack makes it apparent that journalists assumed that a lot of people had already heard those stories. A major conservative paper that was increasingly growing friendly to Nazism,[95] the *Deutsche Allgemeine Zeitung*, informed its readers that prior to the beating of Klotz, it had refrained from reporting on the Röhm "affair," although "for some time [the affair] has played a role in political discussion." Now, on the paper's front page, the whole story came out: Klotz had published accusations about Röhm's private life. Specifically, "Herr Röhm was accused of committing offences against Paragraph 175 of the criminal code, and if this is true, it certainly makes him unsuited to be a teacher of youth and a leader. The public does not know, however, whether such accusations are true." Ignoring the unsuccessful libel suit, the *Deutsche Allgemeine Zeitung* told readers that the truth was as yet undetermined: the "allegations ... cannot be verified by outsiders." Yet it certainly did not dismiss those allegations as untrue or as unimportant. It demanded that "after what happened yesterday," that is, the attack on Klotz, the NSDAP "clarify" whether the accusations were true.

To date, all Adolf Hitler has said about the matter is that he [Röhm] is and remains his chief of staff. It is more important for the public to know if there is anything to these slanderous accusations, and neither can the claims about other prominent National Socialists that are made in Lieutenant Klotz's pamphlet be rebutted by beating the publisher. One part of the population [*Volk*] thinks that all of the accusations are infamous lies, the other takes them to be absolutely true. We need to know once and for all what the objective reality is.[96]

This article frankly informed readers that Klotz had alleged that Röhm had engaged in homosexual sex. It also suggested that many people had already heard of these allegations. They had played a role in political debates "for some time," and one part of the population rejected them as lies while another part thought they were true. It faulted Hitler for failing to address the accusations against Röhm and other party members and called for the NSDAP to tell the public "what the objective reality is." In fact, the NSDAP had denied that the letters were real and continued to do so; the *Deutsche Allgemeine Zeitung*'s call for the party to reveal the truth thus suggested that the NSDAP's claims that the letters were fake were somehow insufficient. Finally, the article insisted that it mattered whether the charges against Röhm were true or not: if he had engaged in homosexual sex, he was unfit to be a youth leader or a political leader. In short, this coverage suggests relatively widespread knowledge of the accusations against Röhm. It also demonstrates that people were divided as to whether the stories were true. And it entertains the possibility that they could be true.

Other papers were less explicit about Röhm's sexuality in their coverage of the beating in the Reichstag and yet did not entirely avoid it. Moreover, their reporting often reflected the assumption that the claims about Röhm's sexuality had already circulated widely. The *Berliner Lokal-Anzeiger*, a major Alfred Hugenberg paper, had a circulation of around 200,000 and backed Hugenberg's conservative party, the DNVP.[97] It had not previously covered the rumours about Röhm's sexuality. But now its staff was forced to explain to readers why the NSDAP Reichstag delegation had attacked Klotz and to cover the trial at which Heines declared that he had beaten Klotz because "he published the Röhm letters."[98] The paper disparaged Klotz for his publication of the pamphlet about "the famous [*bekannt*] personal characteristics of Hitler's Chief of Staff, Captain Röhm,"[99] and printed the NSDAP's claim that Klotz had provoked the attack with his "outrageous" pamphlet.[100] Another article attacked Klotz for his "sleazy" publication.[101] *Berliner Lokal-Anzeiger* authors did not divulge the details of what Klotz's publication had alleged. Yet the line about "famous" characteristics suggests that the paper's staff assumed that many readers already knew about the scandal. The paper quoted a statement by the NSDAP that called Klotz insane and his allegations "outrageous and abusive" without specifying exactly what those allegations were.[102] But the *Berliner Lokal-Anzeiger* did not go so far as to call the stories about the "famous personal characteristics" fictions.

The liberal, anti-fascist, bourgeois *Vossische Zeitung*, which at the time had a circulation of about 50,000 and was one of Germany's newspapers of record, informed its readers that Klotz's accusations were true.[103] Although it did not repeat the details, it dropped ample hints pointing towards homosexuality. The paper's staff also seems to have assumed that many readers already knew about the scandal. Under a banner headline, "Nazi Act of Violence in the Reichstag," it reported that Klotz was the man "who made public the well-known letters by Röhm,"[104] which it also referred to as "the compromising letters by the SA Chief of Staff Röhm to a friend."[105] Another article explained how Klotz had published letters that "compromised Röhm personally" and that Klotz's decision to publish these letters was "certainly dictated by outrage over the hypocrisy" of the Nazis, which he sought to make plain by revealing "the moral qualities of Herr Röhm and the unusual friends who are close to him." The letters were real: Röhm had sued Klotz and lost, so "the authenticity of the letters Klotz published is a verified fact [*gerichtsnotorisch*]."[106] A reader who had not already heard of the letters could easily surmise that Röhm had been caught in some kind of sex scandal, one that involved "unusual friends," most probably homosexuality.

Other major bourgeoisie, liberal papers were more circumspect. Yet their staffs also seem to have assumed that many readers knew about the Röhm scandal. On its front page, the *Frankfurter Zeitung* described Klotz as the publisher of SA chief Röhm's "famous letters."[107] Its coverage made it clear that Klotz's publication of these letters prompted the attack on him, and it quoted Klotz at the trial of the Nazi deputies as having said, "I do not deny that I published the letters that Röhm wrote to someone else."[108] Another major bourgeoisie paper, the *Münchner Neueste Nachrichten*, took a similar line, telling readers only that Klotz was "known as the publisher of brochures ... that made serious accusations about the backgrounds [*Vorleben*]" of top Nazis and that contained "in particular, facsimile [*faksimilierte*] letters of Captain Röhm, which played a large role in the public discussion of the 'Röhm Affair.'"[109] As opaque as this reference was in comparison to the coverage in the *Deutsche Allgemeine Zeitung* or even the *Vossische Zeitung*, it nevertheless suggests that the "Röhm Affair" was getting national attention prior to the attack on Klotz.

Catholic papers did the most to eschew even the hint of sexual scandal. Given the theory of the dangers of mentioning homosexuality in print to which the Centre Party subscribed, this tacit approach is not a surprising editorial choice. Centre Party–affiliated *Germania* let on only that Klotz had published a pamphlet that various Nazis felt defamed them.[110] Readers of the *Kölnische Volkszeitung* learned only that Heines believed Klotz had slandered him and that Klotz had published "the Röhm letters."[111]

However, a good deal of the coverage of the attack on Klotz in the conservative and liberal press either strongly suggested or stated outright that Klotz had accused Röhm of homosexuality. Even more of this coverage referred to widespread knowledge of the accusations about Röhm's sexuality. Awareness of the accusations appears, therefore, to have been relatively common despite the fact that beyond the left-wing press, most journalists were not covering the Röhm scandal before the beating of Klotz. Not everyone thought the letters Klotz had published were real, however. The Nazis dismissed the Klotz pamphlet as a fiction, and apparently a not-insignificant number of people believed them: as the *Deutsche Allgemeine Zeitung* put it, "One part of the population thinks that all of the accusations are infamous lies."[112] At the same time, "the other takes them to be absolutely true."[113] Some people clearly did believe the stories. As the *Vossische Zeitung* reported, Röhm's failed libel suit had confirmed the authenticity of the letters. Even the *Deutsche Allgemeine Zeitung*, which in 1932 had a lot of sympathy for the NSDAP, treated the accusations of homosexuality as plausible. In short, it seems that by 1932, a lot of people knew that Röhm had been accused of homosexuality and that, in particular, Klotz's pamphlet had brought attention to these accusations. In addition, by no means were the stories of Röhm's sexuality being universally dismissed as lies. Finally, especially the reactions of major conservative and moderate papers demonstrate that even in conservative and moderate circles, there were many who acknowledged that the Röhm-Heimsoth letters were real. A prominent figure on the Far Right – Erich Ludendorff – even used the scandal to attack Hitler. He published a pamphlet titled "General Ludendorff Says: Let's Get Out of This Brown Swamp!" (*Heraus aus dem braunen Sumpf! Sagt General Ludendorff*) – brown being identified with the NSDAP and "swamp" being a favourite Weimar-era metaphor for sexual immorality – in which he harangued the Nazi leader for tolerating Röhm's homosexuality.[114]

Sources on public opinion surrounding the murder of Röhm some years later, after the Nazis took power, likewise indicate that in the Weimar years a lot of people heard about his homosexuality. In 1934, Hitler had Röhm shot during a purge of the SA and of non-fascist conservatives known as the "Night of the Long Knives."[115] Among the victims was Röhm's deputy Edmund Heines, the instigator of the brawl in the Reichstag café. The dictatorship claimed that Röhm and the others had been murdered because the SA plotted to overthrow Hitler, and also because it had come to Hitler's attention that the SA was led by a clique of homosexual men, including Röhm and Heines – the Nazi press reported that when the SS burst into Heines's room to arrest him, they found him in bed with another man.[116] Thus, according to the party press and to statements made by Nazi leaders, the murders were both a defence against a putsch and a moral cleansing action.[117] The trope of male homosexuals as treacherous conspirators tied together the two varieties of allegations.[118] I bring up the purge of the SA because the Röhm scandal of 1931–2 came up in the public reaction to the 1934 killings. The SPD in exile (SOPADE) had a clandestine service that canvassed public opinion, and SPD informants recorded what people said in the wake of the murders. A SPD source in Saxony reported that he or she was hearing it said frequently that "it is an extremely underhanded thing to do [*ein Schuftigkeit*] to blame the murders on the abnormal inclinations of the victims, while the whole mess had been known about for years." This SPD reporter went on to describe a local incident that had drawn a great deal of chatter: people had gathered around a newspaper that was posted in a public area to read coverage of the purge of the SA. Someone in the crowd called out that the newspaper would have gotten things right if it had published the Röhm letters years ago.[119] A SPD informant in Pomerania reported that in discussions of the murders, some people mentioned that the SPD had raised the issue of Röhm's sexuality earlier.[120] In Berlin, according to one SPD reporter there, one frequently heard people say, "The SPD has been saying that for five years"; another Berlin informant made a similar report.[121] Not only had many people, according to these reports, already heard allegations about Röhm's sexuality, many of them associated them specifically with the period before 1933 and with the SPD – that is, with the scandal of 1931–2. Considering that the scandal was an SPD creation, informants for the SPD in exile could be expected to emphasize it in their reports. But these informants did not only seek public opinion in leftist circles. Their reports included information about what people in Nazi, Catholic, and conservative circles were saying.

The coverage of the attack on Klotz, together with the SOPADE reports, shows that wide swathes of the population had heard allegations that Röhm was homosexual by 1933. Whether they believed them is a separate question. But the scandal drew enough attention that it was difficult, if not impossible, for the Nazis to make their claim to be a force for the renewal of sexual morality a centrepiece of their campaigns in the late Weimar years.

There is, in addition, a theme in the liberal and conservative press's reactions to the attack on Klotz that seems to have helped the NSDAP weather the Röhm scandal: much of the commentary reflected the assumption that Röhm's personal homosexuality was not a political matter. Even people on the right who opposed homosexual emancipation adhered to this view, at times self-servingly. Many journalists treated the issue of homosexuality as of secondary or even tertiary import in comparison with other issues, such as the rule of law and the fate of democracy. To a considerable portion of the press, the key message was that with the attack, Nazism had made a spectacular display of its brutality, its preference for the "rule of fists" (*Faustrecht*) over the rule of law, and its contempt for democratic institutions.

For people with affiliations from the SPD to even as far to the right as the DNVP, the Klotz attack seemed a microcosm of the Nazi assault on democracy and the rule of law. This was the Klotz beating's true significance, according to observers. "Nazi Rule of Fists Breaks Up the Reichstag," ran a front-page headline in the Centre Party's *Germania*.[122] At the trial of the four Nazi Reichstag deputies, a prosecutor charged that their actions amounted to the "rule of fists."[123] When he sentenced the three Nazis, the judge echoed this. They had lawful avenues to express their "disgust" with Klotz, he noted: they could have sued. If they rejected these and instead chose personal violence as a defence of honour, they ought not to have done so within the Reichstag. The judge then voiced a rousing defence of democratic institutions, condemning the accused for hooliganism within the Reichstag itself, "which for millions of Germans is so holy as the site of the people's sovereignty that it is like a house of God or a cemetery is for religious people. It is not the house of National Socialism, as they sought to make it by following the rule of force rather than the rule of law."[124] As a survey of right-wing journalists' responses in the *Vossische Zeitung* shows, a lot of papers on the right justified the attack on Klotz and did not echo the judge's defence of democracy.[125] Yet to the liberal *Vossische Zeitung* and *Münchner Neueste Nachrichten*, as well as to the Centre Party–backing *Kölnische Volkszeitung*, all of which quoted at length the denunciations of Nazi violence made by the prosecutor and judge at the trial, the incident illustrated the thuggish character of Nazism and the threat it posed to democratic institutions.[126] In an article in *Vorwärts*, the SPD Reichstag president Paul Löbe made this point: the attack on Klotz was a symbol of the violent assault on democracy that Nazism was mounting across Germany.[127] The liberal *Frankfurter Zeitung*'s coverage of the brawl made a similar argument. It repeatedly quoted Nazi threats to abolish the parliament once they took power.[128] As did many other papers, it described the NSDAP Reichstag delegation's frenzied antisemitism in reaction to the arrival of Deputy Police President Weiss.[129] It quoted a Bavarian People's Party deputy decrying the attack on Klotz as "brutality" and a deputy of the right-liberal German People's Party (DVP) calling on the leaders of the NSDAP to condemn the attack.[130] The lead story on the front page on 15 May opined that Nazism was a "regression into barbarism – as the events of the last several days have made plain in a gruesome manner."[131] But fascism had no staying power, the *Frankfurter Zeitung* assured its readers.[132]

Even some major conservative press venues that were sympathetic to Nazism criticized the attack on Klotz for similar reasons, playing to a long-standing unease among traditional conservatives about Nazism being disreputable, a movement of street brawlers. The *Berliner Lokal-Anzeiger* held that "above all the Reichstag building is not the right place to take revenge or vengeance with a series of ear-boxings," even if what Klotz did was "not particularly delectable behaviour, in both the human and the political sense."[133] An editorial in the conservative *Deutsche Allgemeine Zeitung* called the beating "political stupidity."[134] The following day, a second editorial expressed support for Nazism but disapproved of the beating and suggested that some NSDAP Reichstag deputies were unfit to serve in their vaunted positions.[135]

The criticisms of the NSDAP reflected the parameters of what both opponents and friends of Nazism thought it was possible to criticize and what they thought would resonate with their readers. It is significant that all of these journalists chose to make an issue of Nazi violence, Nazi disreputableness, Nazi antisemitism, or Nazi disrespect for democracy – and not of Röhm's sexuality. Röhm's sexuality also offered a position from which to criticize the NSDAP. The *Deutsche Allgemeine Zeitung* used it, in a circumspect way that contrasted with the lavish homophobia on display in leftist organs such as the *Munich Post* or the KPD's *Rote Fahne*, which called the NSDAP a hotbed of homosexuality and accused Röhm of sexually abusing young men.[136] But other journalists, even opponents of fascism, elected not to use it. Moreover, some also expressed the view that Klotz had done something wrong when he published Röhm's private correspondence. It is not surprising that some right-wing and nationalist media denied the stories about Röhm and dismissed Klotz as a "slanderer" who deserved a pummelling for his fraudulent assault on Nazi honour.[137] What is noteworthy, however, is that people who did not deny the authenticity of the letters also condemned Klotz for publishing them.

A lot of the press coverage implied that not only was Röhm's sexuality not a salient issue, but Klotz was wrong to have sought to make it one. The *Berliner Lokal-Anzeiger* called Klotz's brochure "sleazy."[138] (This was quite a contrast with this paper's reaction decades earlier, in 1909, to revelations of the existence of private gatherings of homosexual women in

Berlin: then, it railed against lesbian seduction of "normal" women and against lesbian literature.)[139] The judge who sentenced the three Nazi Reichstag delegates implied that Klotz's actions were tasteless, though irrelevant.[140] The *Vossische Zeitung* defended Klotz but stopped short of arguing that what he had done was ethical, opining rather, "Whether it was noble to bring [Röhm's letters] to light is beside the point."[141] This indictment of Klotz for sleaze, apparent in both conservative and liberal treatments of the scandal, proceeds from the assumption that one ought not to publicize a political opponent's homosexuality for political gain. Bracketing the question of what these journalists and their readers believed about homosexuality and citizenship, it is clear that in 1932, to use an opponent's private homosexuality as a political weapon was to open oneself to allegations of disreputable behaviour.

The leftist journalist Kurt Tucholsky described a principle that seems to have guided many of the more restrained comments from journalists on the beating of Klotz. (Tucholsky admittedly did not often speak for a wide swathe of the chattering classes, but in this case he seems to have done so.) Writing to urge the left-wing press to break off its attacks on Röhm on account of his homosexuality, Tucholsky noted that Röhm himself had kept his sexuality private and had respected other sexual conventions that by now will be familiar to readers of this book: he did not flaunt his sexuality in public, he did not corrupt youth, and he did not knowingly infect others with venereal disease. "[Röhm's] inclination does nothing to undermine the man," wrote Tucholsky in the unaffiliated leftist magazine *Die Weltbühne*.

> He can be thoroughly respectable so long as he is not abusing his position to drag people onto his couch ... Did Röhm commit a public scandal? No. Has he abused young boys? No. Has he consciously transmitted venereal diseases? No. Such and only such can justify public criticism – everything else is his affair.[142]

Tucholsky was describing the reformist ideal of sexuality, the Weimar settlement on sexual politics. He echoed some of the tenets of the proposed reform of Paragraph 175 – Röhm must not pressure underlings to have sex and must not pursue children – as well as the new law on venereal disease. Röhm had acted as Weimar-era reformist sexual politics would have dictated. Therefore, his "abnormal" desires ought to be left in private. They were not a political matter. Klotz might be criticized for sleaze and Heines and other NSDAP members for violence. But Röhm's sexuality in and of itself was of little consequence. Incidentally, Röhm's own position on the matter was probably very much like this. Eleanor Hancock argues that he advocated a strict separation of public and private life. She notes his decree of September 1933 that the SA not get involved in decisions about peoples's private lives, including questions about whether women ought to smoke or wear makeup.[143] In contrast, most Nazis considered supposedly private matters like sexuality intensely public and political. It was in part thanks to homosexual emancipation's many decades of agitation that this idea of a public/private separation for homosexuality had credibility in 1932.

The reaction of the homosexual emancipation movement itself to the Röhm scandal was bifurcated: on the one hand, homosexual emancipationists believed that Röhm's sexuality ought not to matter; on the other hand, some – though not all – perceived the NSDAP as a looming peril. Friedrich Radszuweit's reaction focused on the principle that his organization, the League for Human Rights, had long endorsed: if homosexuals retained their respectability, their sexuality ought not to matter; they were citizens. Radszuweit defended Röhm as a "capable" political leader.[144] He also expressed frustration with the attacks by the Social Democrats, whom, Radszuweit wrote, he had supported for many years. Now, in contrast, Radszuweit felt respect for Hitler because, he wrote, Hitler had appointed Röhm in full knowledge of his sexuality and was refusing to dismiss him in the midst of the scandal. This was not unmitigated support for the NSDAP on Radszuweit's part; he qualified his sentiments with this: "I'd be the last to support the Hitler party." Yet he continued, "This trust that Hitler has placed in Röhm actually honours Hitler in a way ... and shows us that Hitler views sexual orientation as more of a private matter than one would have formerly assumed." Radszuweit suggested that Hitler in fact had nothing against "respectable homosexual people" but only had a problem with "disreputable" public displays of homosexuality. He thought the scandal would force the Nazi Party to desist from its attacks on homosexuals.[145] It is shocking to see Radszuweit so misread Hitler, who would later announce that he had had Röhm shot on account of his homosexuality, among other reasons. Perhaps it ought not to be shocking: by the early 1930s Radszuweit was expressing openness to the prospect of common ground with fascism similar to what Heimsoth and others in Brand's circle sought. Though antisemitism was otherwise largely absent from *Girlfriend* magazine and from the *Journal for Human Rights*, Radszuweit invoked it in a 1931 defence of the Nazis.[146] He wrote that they were not against homosexuality per se, but rather were against "Jewry (especially Magnus Hirschfeld)," Jews – and Hirschfeld in particular – being responsible for overstepping the public/private divide, for dragging "human sex lives in front of the public in such an unpleasant way."[147] Radszuweit's anti-semitism assisted him in misreading Hitler's refusal to fire Röhm; he misrecognized in it the model of homosexual citizenship that he and the League for Human Rights advocated. In this misreading, Radszuweit was also influenced by the Weimar settlement – he assumed that like most Weimar-era politicians, Hitler, too, thought that the division between public and private was important in sexual-political questions. In any event, Radszuweit's contention that Röhm's sexuality ought not to matter was not out of the mainstream: a lot of the press acted as if Röhm's sexuality was not a public concern.

The Scientific Humanitarian Committee was in a different position from Radszuweit. Its leadership, in which Jews and leftists were prominent, had no illusions about the NSDAP's stand on homosexuality.[148] WhK leaders had other reasons to oppose fascism as well, and yet felt an obligation to defend Röhm's privacy. The WhK had long argued that the private homosexuality of a citizen ought not to matter so long as he adhered to certain conventions of respectability. It rejected sexual denunciation as a tactic. The WhK seems to perhaps have been offered the opportunity by the SPD to leak Röhm's letters before Klotz published them, though it is impossible to say for sure. The WhK had learned of Röhm's letters to Heimsoth as early as 1931 from figures in the Prussian government and had alluded to their existence in print, threatening the Nazis with denunciation if they did not back away from their anti–homo-sexual agitation.[149] When Röhm's letters did emerge, the WhK took a sophisticated, and perhaps overly complicated, position: sexual denunci-ation was a tasteless and risky tactic, something the WhK itself would not do. The Nazi Party, however, was hypocritical because it railed against homosexuality and yet had a homosexual in its leadership. Furthermore, now that other people had published various materials about Röhm's sexuality, the matter was of scientific interest. WhK leaders thus under-took what is still the most extensive examination of the Röhm scandal, republishing most of the relevant materials and setting out both the Nazi and SPD sides in the WhK magazine. This effort seems to have been led by Linsert, who authored the articles.[150] WhK leaders also denounced the SPD and KPD campaigns against Röhm, writing a series of cease-and-desist letters to Social Democratic and Communist newspapers that were attacking him for his sexuality. They urged the SPD to respect Röhm's privacy: by dragging "into the public eye the most private characteristics of one's opponent ... one steps across the boundaries of good taste." They also warned the Social Democrats to reflect on the risks of sexual denunciation: "People who sit in glass houses shouldn't throw stones."[151]

The attack on Klotz in the Reichstag building brought allegations about Röhm's sexuality to national attention in papers of diverse political persuasions. Press coverage demonstrates that a lot of people were already talking about the Röhm scandal before Nazi Reichstag deputies beat Klotz. Not everyone believed that Röhm's letters to Heimsoth were real. But apparently a lot of people did. The next chapter contends that the Röhm scandal, together with other factors, made sexual politics an issue on which the Nazis could not profitably campaign in the late Weimar elections. In addition, in their coverage of the beating of Klotz, many journalists did not make an issue of Röhm's sexuality. Some did. But liberal as well as conservative papers attacked the NSDAP not for homosexuality but for hooliganism. Klotz came in for a lot of criticism for making Röhm's letters public. A substantial number of journalists therefore basically adhered to – or made strategic use of, in the case of Nazi-friendly conservative media – a key principle of homosexual emancipation. That is, a homosexual could be a respectable citizen so long as he confined his homosexuality to the private sphere. This was part of the Weimar settlement on sexual politics. It helped the NSDAP survive the Röhm scandal. It is not the case that everyone who went to the polls in the late Weimar elections thought Röhm was indeed homosexual and ignored the fact. But surely some did, including some readers of major conservative papers like the *Berliner Lokal-Anzeiger* that did not make an issue of Röhm's sexuality, or of major liberal papers like the *Vossische Zeitung*, which frankly reported that Röhm was homosexual and refrained from making his sexuality a political issue. Many conservative and liberal voters moved to the NSDAP during this period. Thanks to the Weimar settlement, a conservative or liberal voter who was attracted to the NSDAP and read about the scandal in these venues had a narrative ready at hand that would help him or her to ignore Röhm's sexuality when he or she voted.

German homosexual emancipation had been effective enough by the early 1930s that when a leading figure in an officially anti-homosexual party was revealed to be homosexual, there was a set of ideas about privacy, sexuality, and citizenship readily available to many people seeking to make sense of this. It is an ironic tragedy that the success of the Weimar settlement and of homosexual emancipation helped the NSDAP. The Nazis went on to establish a dictatorship that convicted 50,000 men of the "crime" of sodomy and sent between 5,000 and 15,000 alleged homosexuals to concentration camps, where many were murdered.[152]

6 The Politics of "Immoral" Sexuality in the Fall of the Weimar Republic and the Rise of the Nazis

On 6 May 1933, six weeks after the Enabling Act made Germany a dictatorship under Nazi Party control, trucks bearing scores of Nazi students and a brass band pulled up in front of the Institute for Sexual Science. The students banged on the door. They demanded Dr Hirschfeld. "You can search the whole house, from top to bottom," the Institute's housekeeper told them. "Dr Magnus Hirschfeld is not home."[1] Hirschfeld had left Germany on an international lecture tour. He never returned.

The students ransacked the Institute. They rifled through its many rooms, tearing pictures from the walls and overturning inkwells onto carpets. They threw a life-sized model of the human body and an exhibition display on sexual intermediaries out of windows. Meanwhile, the band played in front of the Institute's doors, and a crowd gathered. Inside, the students pulled the thousands of books in the library from their shelves and piled them on the floor. Amid the destruction they had wrought, the students posed for propaganda photographs. In the afternoon, SA men helped load the contents of the Institute onto trucks. They carted away the library, the archive, photographs, slides, and a bust of Hirschfeld. A few days later, students fed the contents of the Institute for Sexual Science into the flames of a bonfire on the plaza beside Berlin's opera house, surrounded by a cheering crowd. The thousands of books were burned because the students deemed sexual science, as well as the works of novelists and political thinkers that they also threw on the fire, "un-German." They paraded the bust of Hirschfeld through the crowd and dumped it into the flames. Shortly after the book burning, the new government officially dissolved the Institute for Sexual Science.[2]

The fire at the opera house plaza was a dramatic signal of the new fascist state's attack on "immorality." In the first months of Hitler's chancellorship, gay, lesbian, and transvestite bars and clubs like the Magic Flute

Nazi students raid the Institute for Sexual Science on 10 May 1933. They are loading the Institute's library into the truck to transport it to the book burning. Bundesarchiv.

and the Eldorado were shuttered, magazines like *Girlfriend* and *Friendship* forced out of business, books like *Berlin's Lesbian Women* snatched from the shelves of bookstores.[3] The new authorities banned the public display of "filthy" images at street kiosks and shut down the nudity movement, the sex reform movement, and the fight against the abortion law.[4] In 1933, police arrested male and female prostitutes en masse. Although the regime eventually brought back regulated female prostitution with a vengeance, upsetting conservatives and feminists alike, it always ruthlessly suppressed street soliciting by women and imposed ten-year prison sentences on men convicted of selling sex.[5] In 1935, the new regime made Paragraph 175 far stricter.[6] The Gestapo orchestrated a massive hunt for gay men and sent thousands to prisons and concentration camps, where many were murdered.[7]

The campaign against public immorality pleased people like Adolf Sellmann, the head of the Protestant West German Morality League. He wrote approvingly that when Hitler became chancellor, "In one fell swoop everything in Germany was different. All filth and trash [*Schmutz und Schund*] disappeared from public view. The streets of our cities were clean again."[8] Sellmann was not alone in this sentiment. In an October 1933 letter to his congregation, the Catholic Bishop of Münster, Clemens August Graf von Galen, wrote, "We thank the Lord our God for his loving guidance, which has enlightened and strengthened the great leaders of our Fatherland such that they have recognized the horrible danger threatening our beloved German Volk through the open propaganda for godlessness and immorality and now seek to eradicate it with a strong hand."[9] The reactions of both Protestant and Catholic conservatives to the events of 1933 make it seem possible that the fascists rode to power on a "backlash" against the Republic's relative toleration of immorality. This idea of a backlash has been reiterated a good deal in recent scholarship and seems on track to become the consensus. But it rests on shaky ground.

This chapter argues against the backlash thesis, examines why it has so much resonance for historians and for the general public, and finally offers a brief consideration of the perennial question of continuity or discontinuity between Weimar and Nazi Germany. Weimar-era sexual politics did not drive significant numbers of voters towards the NSDAP and did not convince formerly democratic factions, such as the leadership of the Centre Party, to support Nazism. The attack on the Institute for Sexual Science symbolized a Nazi crackdown on immorality in the public sphere that conservatives welcomed. But it happened after Hitler became chancellor. Sexual politics did not do all that much to help the Nazis take power aside from helping the NSDAP weather the Röhm scandal. Why, in that case, has the backlash thesis had such appeal? That is, if sex did not cause the fall of the Weimar Republic in any appreciable way, why do we keep identifying sex as a significant cause of it? Finally, the chapter takes up the question of continuity or discontinuity across 1933. Without presenting an exhaustive analysis of this important issue, I emphasize discontinuity. The Nazi State repudiated Weimar-era progressivism on sexuality, and yet Nazi policies did not always mirror the positions for which Weimar-era conservatives had fought. In addition, for some of the advocates of reform, 1933 was a dramatic point of historical rupture, to say the least.

Backlash?

The backlash thesis is, essentially, that conservative discontent with the sexual libertinism established by the Weimar Republic helped the

Nazis take power and/or contributed to the dissolution of democracy. Recently, studies have argued that Weimar-era sexual politics helped the Nazis, asserting that the Nazis presented themselves as "determined purifiers of public morality"[10] and were "extremely successful in presenting themselves as a dynamic party that would resolve the Depression, reestablish morality, and restore German grandeur."[11] This image of the NSDAP as a force for morality "played a vital role in their ultimate political success."[12] Weimar-era conservatives recoiled from cabaret, birth control, and literature with erotic content, and "the Nazis came to power partly on a promise to 'clean up the streets.'"[13] Weimar-era democracy crumbled independently of the NSDAP's rise, although both happened in the period 1929–32, and the growth of the NSDAP further disrupted the already compromised parliament. Different studies identify backlash at work in both of these phenomena. Some historians argue that conservative anxiety about the Republic's liberated sexual politics drew voters to the NSDAP.[14] Others argue that it convinced moderate politicians to abandon democracy or to throw in their lot with the NSDAP. The suspected culprits here are the leaders of the Centre Party. Some studies contend that sexual politics pushed the Centre Party to the right, which destabilized democracy in the early 1930s, though they stop short of arguing that Centre politicians embraced Nazism because of sexual-political issues.[15] Other studies hold that frustration with progressive sexual politics played a major role in driving Centre politicians to make common cause with Nazism,[16] to back the then chancellor Franz von Papen's illegal coup against the Social Democratic government of Prussia in July 1932,[17] and to vote for the Enabling Act.[18]

An evaluation of backlash thus ought to examine whether sexual politics attracted voters to the NSDAP as well as whether the Centre Party despaired of democracy due to immorality. I begin by examining the question of Nazi voters. Then I discuss the Centre Party.

Considering Backlash I: The Nazi Vote

To understand the Nazi rise to power, one must make sense of the enormous swell of Nazi strength in national elections that began in 1930 and crested in July 1932, when 13.7 million people, about 37.3 per cent of the electorate, voted Nazi. The vast majority of the women and men who did so had not voted for the party prior to 1929. The NSDAP did not poll above 7 per cent of the national electorate until the elections of September 1930.[19] In 1932, voters made the NSDAP Germany's largest party. Electoral success alone did deliver the chancellorship to Hitler. But without it, the men around President Hindenburg would not have tried to co-opt the Nazi "movement" by appointing Hitler chancellor in an effort to bolster their own power and to establish their own dictatorship of the non-fascist right. The questions of who the Nazi voters of the 1930s were and of what motivated them have been the topics of major studies, many published in the 1980s and 1990s, which did not identify issues of sexuality as central motives behind electoral behaviour.[20] These studies identify as motives of Nazi voters economic distress, fear of Communist revolution, nationalism, and disgruntlement with the non-fascist conservative parties and with the "Weimar system." Rising numbers of Nazi voters came primarily at the expensive of the traditional conservatives (the DNVP) and the two liberal parties (the DDP and DVP), although to a lesser extent former SPD voters switched to the Nazis as well. Only Centre Party and Communist voters were largely immune, staying with their parties.[21] The NSDAP also attracted people who had not voted in previous elections. Among the demographic shifts in the Nazi electorate as it grew was an increase in gender diversity: the party benefited from an influx of female Protestant voters into what had been a male-dominated NSDAP electorate.[22]

It seems very unlikely that the growth in the NSDAP vote was due to sexual politics, because the NSDAP had no special advantage over conservative and moderately conservative parties on sexual-political issues. In fact, the NSDAP had a disadvantage: the Röhm scandal. Röhm's widely known homosexuality made it difficult for the Nazi Party to position itself as the standard-bearer of the struggle against immorality. And it had an additional weakness: its core position on sexual-political issues, which was basically that immorality was the product of a Jewish conspiracy to corrupt nation and race, did not have a lot of appeal beyond the Far Right, at least in the Weimar period. The theory of a Jewish conspiracy behind immorality was prominently featured in Nazi propaganda in the period when the party had extreme difficulty attracting voters beyond the *völkisch* Right. In the period of the NSDAP's electoral growth, the Nazis changed their line on sexual politics and began to sound much more like traditional conservatives. Even so, they had no appreciable advantage over traditional conservatives on these issues.

Prior to 1929, when the NSDAP was polling in the single digits – in the 1928 Reichstag election it won 2.6 per cent of the vote[23] – the view that Jews were orchestrating immorality was quite clear to anyone who bothered to read the party press. In 1928, *Der Angriff,* a major NSDAP paper, frequently reminded its readers that sexual disorder stemmed from a Jewish conspiracy.[24] Jews, *Der Angriff* authors claimed, saturated Germany with pornography and sabotaged the implementation of the obscenity law, Paragraph 184, and the Filth and Trash Law. Jews were also behind female prostitution. They masterminded the "white slave trade," and Berlin's Deputy Police President Bernhard Weiss of course denied its existence, being Jewish himself.[25] Under the headline "Sexual Orgy on Christmas Eve," the paper informed readers that a Jewish theatre in Berlin planned an obscene play to coincide with Christmas and that, indeed, the commercialism of Christmas was a trick of the Jewish department stores.[26] In Julius Streicher's *Der Stürmer*, another widely read party organ, Jewish men were hypersexual predators of "Aryan" women, and democracy allowed Jews led by Magnus Hirschfeld to spread homosexuality.[27] Goebbels ranted in 1928 that the Kurfürstendamm of West Berlin was an "abscess" of "sin, vice, and corruption," featuring female prostitution, drugs, cabaret, "the Israelites," and hawkers pedalling back issues of *Girlfriend*, the lesbian magazine, for only 10 pfg. a piece.[28]

This anti-immorality position was both too sexual and too antisemitic to have much appeal beyond the Far Right. For one thing, the NSDAP press's reporting on sexuality could veer into the pornographic, which did not help it make headway with conservatives, who were invested in keeping sexuality out of the public sphere. In addition, the rabid antisemitism was not an asset. Although many people who were conservative on issues of sexual politics were also antisemitic, their antisemitism was generally of a far more subdued, less colourful sort. Nazi antisemitism differed from more conventional, "polite" antisemitism, which Donald Niewyk describes as "moderate" antisemitism, "a vague sense of unease about Jews that stopped far short of wanting to harm them."[29] This sentiment took forms already apparent in the nineteenth century, such as the notion that Jews were over-represented in fields like publishing and medicine or that they were insufficiently assimilated.[30] Although people who harboured moderate antisemitic views such as these could grow comfortable with Nazi antisemitism, which was typically far louder and more grotesque, they could only do so if Nazi antisemitism shed some of its garishness and appeared more like their own conventional prejudice, *salonfähig*, and less like a déclassé obsession of the far-right fringe. Stories like "Sexual Orgy on Christmas Eve" marked the NSDAP as peripheral. In contrast, explicit antisemitism was largely absent from mainstream discussions of censorship and pornography, such as those that took place in major newspapers and in the Reichstag.[31] Very occasionally, the "white slave trade" story arose in conjunction with the question of female prostitution. But most public debate about female prostitution beyond the extreme right was entirely lacking in antisemitic themes.[32] As much was true of homosexuality. The NSDAP leadership eventually realized that the party needed to put a lid on its "rabid antisemitism" in order to become a mass party.[33]

After 1929, the NSDAP's propaganda on sexual politics began to sound much more like that of the conventional conservatives, such as those in the DNVP. But even so, sexual politics does not seem to have been a major draw for new Nazi voters. That is because in the early 1930s, when voters were flocking to the NSDAP, immorality was no longer a prominent issue in its propaganda. Indeed, it was rarely an independent issue. Now, when it appeared at all, it was often a relatively vague reference in a long list of grievances against the Republic. In this period, the national party press also deemphasized antisemitism, which in the Nazi worldview was connected to immorality. To unconverted voters, the NSDAP presented an antisemitism that was more conventional, less zealous, and less central to its message.[34]

In the 1930s, the *Völkischer Beobachter* and *Der Angriff* only rarely published articles that were chiefly about sexual-political questions; most often, they referred to sexual-political issues vaguely and lumped them in with other supposed problems of the Weimar era. There were scattered reports on Jews and media with sexual content.[35] These articles were not a daily feature, however: in one two-week period in 1932, the *Völkischer Beobachter* published one such article; in a different two-week period that year, it published three.[36] Additionally, in what turned out to be fruitless appeals to Centre Party voters, the NSDAP also occasionally claimed that the fact that the Centre Party went along with the SPD on sexual-political issues demonstrated that the Centre was really just as godless as the Social Democrats.[37] But far more typical was a 1932 front-page piece by Goebbels that launched a flurry of accusations against the SPD. Goebbels referred in a generalized way to sexual politics, attacking the SPD for "corrupt[ing] public life, poisoning the *Volksmoral*" and "betray[ing] the youth to the poison of demoralization [*Entsittlichung*]," as well as "destroy[ing] family life and mak[ing] religion a mockery."[38] In this same piece, he also laid a long list of additional bad deeds at the SPD's door. The Social Democrats were guilty of fomenting class warfare, destroying the economy, taking land from farmers, wrecking Germany's armed forces, being corrupt, censoring political opponents,[39] sabotaging Germany's military in the First World War, signing the Versailles treaty, beating down the middle class (*Mittelstand*),

and backing the Young Plan. Issues of immorality and family are in this list. But they are not the singular focus; rather, the list is a sort of grab bag of many issues that right-leaning people cared about. Similarly, an April 1932 piece condemned the Centre, the SPD, and the two liberal parties primarily for destroying Germany's economy and thereby bringing misery to farmers and the middle class. It also blamed them for political street violence. It ended with a brief reference to morality: the SPD and Centre were responsible for "the political, moral, and economic destruction of our Volk."[40] The allegation that the Weimar Republic brought "cultural Bolshevism" and the "poisoning" of the Volk's morality was present in this propaganda. But it was not a centrepiece of it.

Nor did NSDAP propagandists feel they needed to mention "cultural Bolshevism" and moral renewal in every list of what was wrong with the Republic. For example, one article alleged that the Revolution of 1918 had brought economic ruin and the enslavement of Germany by foreign powers but did not mention sexual politics.[41] A July 1932 article made no mention of sexuality or the family, instead informing readers that the NSDAP opposed the Versailles treaty, Marxism, "reaction," "exploitation," "enslavement," "the terror," violent fights between political parties, class warfare, and the Young Plan.[42] Another long list of grievances did not mention sexuality.[43]

One might expect to find the NSDAP portraying itself as a defender of morality in appeals to women in particular, as general opinion held that they had a special duty to protect morality. But the party's propaganda for women did not always refer to sexuality. One appeal to women denied that Hitler would send their sons to war and claimed that he would protect their jobs and rights, but had nothing to say about immorality.[44] Another appeal to women mentioned their misery and hunger but not the questions of sexual morality in which they were supposedly especially interested.[45] A portrait of Hitler's personal side that seems calculated to interest female readers discussed many of the future dictator's alleged positive character traits, such his particular affection for children, his avoidance of alcohol and tobacco, and his enjoyment in feeding birds, but it did not bring up any supposed special ability he might have had to fight immorality.[46] And when sexual-political issues were included in propaganda for women, they were relatively vague and were presented alongside other issues rather than held out as a centrepiece. For example,

Adolf Hitler is fighting for a clean, respectable [*geachtet*] Germany, free from corruption and Judeo-marxist soul-poisoning, free from traitors and pacifists. He fights for the renewal of the nation according to *völkisch* principles, for a real unity of the Volk, in which everyone – man and woman – is a member doing their part.[47]

This sort of unspecific reference to sexual politics presented alongside other issues – such as pacifism and domestic conflict in this example – was typical in propaganda for women. In her analysis of NSDAP propaganda directed at women in the 1932 elections, Julia Sneeringer found that rather than harp on specific issues, like abortion and sexual liberation, the NSDAP made only vague and coded references to them, subsuming them under the mantle of "cultural Bolshevism."[48] A call to German women to vote for Hitler for president in 1932 avowed that Hitler was fighting for women, for children, and for the "renewal and growth of a new German culture," but did not explicitly mention sexual politics.[49] In short, although sexual politics were represented in some appeals to women, they were not a focus of attention.

The NSDAP was not trumpeting its positions on sexual-political issues in the 1930s. If these issues were inspiring a lot of voters to back the NSDAP, the members of the NSDAP who were crafting the party's message were apparently unaware of that. In addition, the NSDAP seems to have had no obvious advantage in this area over the DNVP. On issues of morality, the NSDAP's propaganda in the Republic's final years was identical to the DNVP's.[50] If these two parties offered voters the same platform on these issues, DNVP voters would not have cause to desert their party for the NSDAP on this account. Indeed, the indictment of the Republic as immoral was a common currency of the Right and had been since the Republic's early days. The NSDAP did not campaign against specific reforms, such as the 1927 venereal disease law or the committee vote in 1929 to repeal the sodomy law. By changing its propaganda so that it sounded more conventional and more like the DNVP, the Nazi Party made itself more respectable, less like a far-right fringe movement. This made it easier for more people to vote Nazi. But at the same time, it seems very unlikely that large numbers of voters were moving to the NSDAP primarily because of its positions on sexual-political questions.

Considering Backlash II: The Catholic Centre Party

The second possible way that backlash supposedly brought down the Republic was by driving the Centre Party to the right, away from its democratic commitments. Historians do not argue that the Centre electorate moved to the right because of sexual politics; the Centre's voters proved quite loyal and did not desert it for the NSDAP.[51] The argument, rather, is that Centre politicians, not voters, betrayed democracy. Yet although the Centre Party cared about immorality, and although the Centre Party undermined democracy in certain instances, there is little evidence that sexual-political issues were among the top concerns driving Centre Party politicians towards authoritarianism. The Centre moved to the right in the early 1930s. As sexual-political issues were part of the Centre's program, this move to the right is also discernible in the party's behaviour when it came to sexual politics. But again, these issues were relatively insignificant to the Centre Party in this period compared to other concerns. The Centre Party did not move right in order to solve sexual-political questions to its satisfaction. Nor did it abandon democracy in order to do so.

First, a brief look at the Centre Party's democratic and anti-democratic tendencies. Though it was a staunchly democratic party in the 1920s, the Centre Party's commitment to democracy in the 1930s was less than inspiring. The Centre was a member of the governing coalition in every one of the Republic's governments based on parliamentary coalitions, from 1919 to 1930. It was the main support for Brüning's presidential regime (1930–2). The Weimar Republic was led by Centre Party chancellors for half of its existence.[52] The Centre arguably had more influence over national legislation than any other party. The party was also a dedicated critic of antisemitism.[53] It is worth emphasizing the distinction between nominal Catholics in general and the Centre Party's constituency. Some, but not all, Catholics voted Centre; women and churchgoers were over-represented among Centre voters.[54] There is, in addition, an important distinction to be made between Catholics in general and a relatively small minority within that group, people whom Larry Eugene Jones terms "Catholic conservatives." They opposed democracy, decried the secularism that had, they thought, been set loose in the world by the French Revolution, wanted a dictatorship of the authoritarian (but not fascist) right, and blamed Jews and Freemasons.[55] Most of the Catholic conservatives who fit this descripton were not to be found in the Centre Party's ranks because the Centre was too far to the left for them; many preferred the DNVP.[56] At the same time, the Centre had a weakness for authoritarianism, particularly during the economic crisis of the 1930s, when it was led by men who clearly preferred cooperation with forces to the Centre's right over cooperation with Social Democracy.[57] In addition, the Centre's right wing had come to power with Ludwig Kaas, who was elected to head the party in 1928. The Centre was however basically resistant to Nazism prior to Hitler's appointment as chancellor on 30 January 1933, if ineffective and bungling in its resistance and, moreover, guided by a preference for the radical Right over the radical Left.[58] In the early 1930s, bishops warned Catholics against the NSDAP because of what they took to be its anti-Catholicism and prohibited the faithful from joining the party.[59] Centre Party propaganda echoed the accusations of paganism in the NSDAP and claimed that among the Nazis there was fervour for a new anti-Catholic *Kulturkampf*.[60]

The Centre did, however, play a role in the destruction of the democratic system. One important instance of this was the ascent of Heinrich Brüning to head an unelected government. In the summer of 1930, the government of the SPD's Hermann Müller fell. Since the 1928 elections, Müller had headed a Great Coalition of the Social Democrats, the Centre Party, the two liberal parties (DVP and DDP), and the Bavarian People's Party (the regional offshoot of the Centre Party). When his coalition collapsed, instead of supporting new elections, President Hindenburg exercised his constitutional authority and called on Brüning, who was the head of the Centre Party's Reichstag delegation, to form a crisis government that was not based on the parties in the parliament, though it ruled with the support of some of them. Brüning's regime lasted two years. Later, the Centre Party also voted in favour of the Enabling Act.

Morality issues were important to the Centre Party. Germany's Catholic bishops specifically charged Catholic politicians with the responsibility to fight moral decline.[61] What Centre parlance termed "cultural politics," including sexual-political issues, were also key for the party because they cut across the divisions within its extremely diverse electorate, which was made up of, for example, wealthy factory owners as well as their struggling employees, who had little in common aside from the fact that they were churchgoing Catholics. The election of Kaas to lead the party, the first priest in the Centre's history to serve as party head, was a sign of the Centre's turn towards "worldview" as a source of unity.[62] The Centre was aware that it had a particular strength on morality issues. It was also aware of its particular weakness on morality issues. This was that the Centre Party's anti-immorality platform plank was not so different from the DNVP's, and yet as a party of the Republic, the Centre was liable to be more closely associated with reforms. In 1929, the president of a Centre Party local chapter wrote to the Reich Justice Ministry to complain because birth control flyers were being handed to children on the street near his home in Berlin and a book on birth control was on display in a shop window. The Republic was doing nothing to protect youth from "filth," he wrote, and it was therefore understandable "that often Christian circles abandon the republican parties and go to the German Nationals [the DNVP]."[63] In the long run, however, large numbers of Centre voters did not desert the party for its opponents to the right, though concerns about losing voters do account for some of the enthusiasm with which the Centre Party beat the anti-immorality drum.

Yet there is little evidence that the Centre Party undermined democracy because of sexual politics. In addition, sexual politics were not among its leadership's more urgent concerns during the periods in which the Centre did act to undermine democracy. One such instance identified by scholars is the Centre's alleged support for Franz von Papen's regime. In the spring of 1932, President Hindenburg withdrew his support for Brüning's semi-democratic chancellorship and replaced him with a Catholic aristocrat, Franz von Papen. Papen was a "Catholic conservative," in Jones's formulation, a conservative of the Far, but not fascist, Right. He was also an erstwhile Centre Party politician. His chancellorship had no support in parliament. Papen's regime lasted from late May to mid-November 1932. During that period, he illegally took over the government of Prussia, deposing an SPD–Centre Party coalition. It has been argued that the Centre Party came to support Papen because he cracked down on immorality in public.[64] But the Centre Party was not a supporter of Papen's regime. Papen had belonged, uncomfortably, to the Centre Party's right wing, but when he agreed to become chancellor following Brüning's fall (a move the Centre Party opposed), the party repudiated him and the breach never healed.[65] Nor was the Centre happy about Papen's deposition of the government of Prussia. After Papen's coup in Prussia, the Centre Party there joined the SPD in an ultimately futile legal action to reverse the takeover.[66]

When Papen was chancellor, his moves against immorality in public were in fact rather limited. The chief one was a ban on nude bathing and nude dancing.[67] This decree mandated that men's and women's swimsuits in Prussia cover a certain amount of skin, something the Catholic Church had been demanding for years.[68] After much public debate, Papen's regime also shut down Adolf Koch's Berlin "body culture" (*Körperkultur*) school, known for nude gymnastics and dance.[69] Papen's reforms are most notable for what he did not dare attempt. He did not issue a general ban on women's street soliciting, although some of the municipal police chiefs he brought in did ban street soliciting by prostitutes in their cities – Cologne, Neuss, Münster, and Dortmund.[70] Under

Papen, the Prussian Interior Ministry directed police to try to use the obscenity law, Paragraph 184, to ban homosexual periodicals and other material with sexual content. This resulted in a concerted effort to do so, though the unwillingness of courts to convict hampered the effort, and the homosexual press was not shut down.[71]

The new head of the Berlin police under Papen, Kurt Melcher, presided over an attempt to curtail Berlin's homosexual subcultures. But it was far from ambitious. In September 1932, police in Berlin's Mitte district refused to renew the permits for dance events held by several homosexual clubs. This meant that when the permits expired the clubs could no longer host dances. The police did not, however, shut down the clubs, despite rumours that they planned to do so.[72] When the League for Human Rights wrote to Melcher to complain about the ban on dances, the head of the police replied with a remarkably conciliatory letter. He wrote that the ban "in no way restricts the rights of same-sex orientated people." The clubs in question, he wrote, could still hold dances, so long as "the events are open only to a closed circle of people, so that the events do not cause a sensation among sexually normal people or offend sexually normal people."[73] Melcher's explanation of the dance ban conformed to the Weimar settlement. Homosexuals could have clubs, and could even hold dances, so long as they were not in the public eye. He told a newspaper reporter something very similar, though in his statements for the mainstream press, he did not acknowledge the equal rights of homosexuals: "The public shenanigans [*Treiben*] of homosexuals that are particularly annoying and conspicuous will be combated. In the future, dance clubs that have a homosexual clientele will not receive dance permits; male and female prostitution will be energetically suppressed."[74] That is, public manifestations of "immorality" that were "conspicuous" would be repressed by the police. Melcher oversaw efforts to drive male prostitutes from central Berlin in September and November 1932, which included taking 251 men into police custody; it is unclear whether he moved against female prostitutes.[75] Though the Papen government's morality reforms were in keeping with conservative positions on sexual politics, they were not extensive. Lacking a base of political support, and with the threat of a general strike hanging over his regime, Papen likely could not do as much as he would have liked. The shuttering of the Koch school was controversial enough. In his letter to the League for Human Rights, Melcher even tacitly acknowledged that homosexuals had rights, although not the right to a robust public sphere.

Papen's limited morality reforms did not win the Centre Party over to his vision of an authoritarian state headed by the non-fascist right.[76] Although the Centre Party's organ *Germania* praised the Papen regime's moves against nude dancing and skimpy bathing suits, at the same time it levelled an implicit criticism. It reminded its readers that police measures were bound to be ineffective and that the real solution to the problem of "moral degeneration" was a resurgence of Catholic culture in public life. *Germania* also took the opportunity to declare that among Germany's political parties, the Centre Party was most committed to the fight against immorality, unlike unnamed others, who acted against immorality only out of political calculation.[77] And the Centre Party did not rally behind Papen. On the contrary: its leadership's loathing of Papen has been faulted for blinding them to the nature of the political situation in the Republic's final year.[78]

There is likewise little evidence that sexual politics influenced the Centre Party Reichstag delegation's infamous vote for the Enabling Act on 23 March 1933. The vote came after Hitler had been chancellor for several months. The Enabling Act suspended the Weimar Constitution and granted Hitler dictatorial powers. Prior to the vote, the Centre's Reichstag delegation had a heated debate about whether to back the law, and if sexual-political issues came up, that was not recorded in the meeting minutes.[79] The Centre Party also delivered a list of conditions for its support for the Enabling Act to Hitler, and sexual-political issues were not on the list.[80] Moreover, Hitler explicitly assured the Centre that he would not use the Enabling Act to change anything in the realm of "cultural politics," which for the Centre Party included schools, youth organizations, and state-church matters and encompassed sexual politics.[81] This makes it seem unlikely that the Centre supported him because they hoped he would act on sexual politics. One basis for the contention that sexual politics played a role in the Enabling Act vote is the rambling speech that Hitler gave to the rump Reichstag outlining his plans for his dictatorship on the day the Enabling Act passed.[82] He mentioned "moral renewal" several times. However, "morality" was not a major theme in this long speech. And when Hitler did mention it, he did not sound at all like he was appealing to non-fascist conservatives on sexual-political issues. For example, his description of the "moral purging of the German *Volkskörper*" seemed to be as much about high art and race as about filthy and trashy media. Later, he said that the churches might oppose the Nazi plan for "moral regeneration" and warned them to "respect" it.

Such a statement would hardly have mollified Centre Party fears about what the position of the Catholic Church would be under fascism.[83]

Historians still debate why the Centre Party voted for the Enabling Act.[84] A number argue that party leader Kaas and the intra-party constituency that he represented were won over to the idea that the Centre ought to support the new regime in exchange for a concordat with the Vatican.[85] Other historians emphasize in contrast the views that the Centre's Reichstag delegates expressed when they debated the bill.[86] Although a minority within the party hoped to win some influence over the new fascist regime through quick cooperation, a pessimistic majority feared fascist violence if they resisted.[87] Many, if not all, also believed that they were ultimately powerless to stop fascism: in the last round of elections in early March, which were not held under completely free conditions, the NSDAP had secured 43.9 per cent of the vote, which together with its then-ally the DNVP's 8 per cent gave Hitler's regime over 50 per cent of the national vote. The Centre Party polled 11.2 per cent in those elections.[88] In light of what Centre Party politicians took to be the unstoppable rise of fascism, they sought to protect a narrow range of Catholic interests such as the Church, Catholic schools, and the jobs of Catholic civil servants. The Centre also asked for and received guarantees from Hitler that he would respect the power of the president, Hindenburg. He assured them that he would use the Enabling Act for certain purposes only, foremost to destroy communism.[89] Questions about this vote, an odious mark on the history of political Catholicism to be sure, may never be answered. Nevertheless, there is relatively little evidence that sexual politics were a significant motivator.[90]

Perhaps the most promising place to search for a decisive, anti-democratic influence exercised by the politics of sex on the Centre Party is the conflict between it and the Social Democrats. The Centre Party and the SPD were the two largest democratic parties. Together with the left-liberal DDP, which was always smaller and which dwindled away over the course of the 1920s, they formed the Weimar Coalition, which in 1919 controlled the drafting of the Weimar Constitution. Cooperation between the Centre and SPD was good for democracy; the fact that they only rarely came together to form majority governments was not.[91] In the crisis of the early 1930s – economic depression, mass unemployment, the rise of anti-democratic parties on the left and right, street violence – SPD-Centre discord was not auspicious for the Republic's survival. Sexual politics could drive the Centre and SPD apart, as in 1926 when the Reichstag passed the Filth and Trash Law. The SPD objected to the law because it feared that vague provisions in it would be used to censor art and political speech, and as a result declined to join the governing coalition.[92] This has been identified as an instance of sexual politics pushing the Centre towards the DNVP and away from the democratic middle ground.[93] Yet this was no decisive blow against the democratic system. Democracy survived after the passage of the 1926 law. The Centre Party and SPD cooperated the following year on the reform of the laws on female prostitution and venereal disease. The DNVP did not become a new go-to coalition partner for the Centre Party, although it did join a governing coalition in 1927. In fact, by the mid-1920s, prior to its rightward swing to a pronounced anti-Republic stance after Alfred Hugenberg was elected to head it in 1928, the DNVP was essentially a republican party, though pragmatically, not in its rhetoric.[94] Overall, conflict in and of itself did not necessarily bode ill for democracy; the democratic system was designed to channel conflict and to create compromise.[95] And though sexual politics did not help matters, there were many other sources of conflict between the SPD and the Centre.[96]

The case in which Centre Party–SPD strife about sexual politics most clearly spilled over into a conflict that threatened the Republic came in 1930 when the government of the SPD's Hermann Müller was replaced by that of the Centre Party's Heinrich Brüning. This was also one of the clearest cases of the Centre Party's poor defence of democratic institutions. Müller's government fell on 27 March 1930 over a deadlock between the SPD and the right-liberal DVP about unemployment benefits, which were a signature piece of Social Democratic welfare. With mass unemployment, unemployment insurance had become hugely expensive and the DVP sought to cut it.[97] Elections did not follow Müller's fall. Instead, Hindenburg appointed Brüning. Although Brüning had the backing of the Centre Party, he did not head a Reichstag coalition. Rather, he relied on the president's power under Article 48 of the Constitution to rule somewhat independently of the parliament; he was, however, still vulnerable to a no-confidence motion in the Reichstag. Brüning's regime was "semi-parliamentary" government.[98] It was a step towards dictatorship, although dictatorship does not seem to have been what Brüning sought, and Brüning's chancellorship was within the bounds set by the Constitution.[99] An important piece of the context for Brüning's regime was the long-standing interest among Weimar-era moderates in hybrids between democracy and dictatorship. The Weimar Constitution incorporated some of these ideas.[100] Frustration with the inability of the coalition parties to reach a compromise on important questions during the economic crisis led a lot of moderates to call for the establishment of a chancellorship that would be somewhat independent of the parliament.[101] This is what Brüning's chancellorship was, a semi-dictatorial caretaker regime during a period of economic crisis and parliamentary dysfunction, or so Brüning and the Centre Party seem to have believed.[102] However, there proved to be no going back to a fully democratic parliamentary system.

At this fateful junction, in the months before Müller fell and Brüning accepted the chancellorship, the Centre Party, SPD, and liberals were locked in a bitter struggle over a sexual-political issue: divorce. For the entire Weimar period, the Centre Party's Reichstag delegation had fended off proposals from liberals, Social Democrats, and Communists to make it easier for people to dissolve their marriages.[103] By the winter of 1929, the Centre Party believed itself about to lose on this issue.[104] To its Reichstag delegation, the prospect was "intolerable."[105] Divorce violated Catholic dogma, but the Centre Party denied that this was why it opposed easier divorce. Rather, easier divorce threatened "monogamy and family," which the Centre Party's Helene Weber called "the great goal of humanity and also of the German Volk" in a Reichstag speech.[106] The Centre squelched an effort in Wilhelm Kahl's penal code reform committee to soften the divorce law. Then, it stalled any further efforts to revise the divorce law in order to make divorces easier to obtain by threatening to bring down Müller's government. In response to that threat, the coalition parties agreed to shelve the issue until after the government passed the Young Plan and dealt with the budget and financial reform.[107]

The win on divorce reform seemed to embolden Centre Party leaders to block other reforms brewing in the penal code reform committee, including the repeal of Paragraph 175. The Centre worked to stall the penal code reform committee through October 1931. The SPD and Centre delegates on that committee differed on the legality of human-animal sex, the death penalty, the use of religious oaths in court, and blasphemy. The issue of male homosexuality was reopened, with the Centre Party delegates favouring criminalization while the SPD favoured repeal. Their differences on these issues seemed "unbridgeable" to the SPD.[108] From the winter of 1931–2 onward, the Centre Party did not need to obstruct the penal code reform committee's work because the Nazis, the DNVP, and later the Communists obstructed it by refusing to take part.[109] When Kahl died in 1932, penal code reform died with him.

Yet the divorce fight does not seem to have had an important and negative effect on democracy at a key moment, even though it augmented Centre Party–SPD tensions.[110] The Centre Party did not bring Müller down. It is the case that the rise of Brüning to the chancellorship was a break between the Centre and SPD and that Brüning preferred conservatism to Social Democracy.[111] But the Centre seems to have acted in a conciliatory fashion during the deadlock on unemployment insurance and to have made genuine efforts to preserve Müller's government coalition.[112] To its constituents, the Centre Party portrayed itself as having fought to the last to keep Müller in power and to protect democracy.[113] A member of the SPD accused the Centre of bad faith in its attempts to save Müller, but those attempts do not in fact seem to have been insincere.[114] The Centre's behaviour in the divorce debate has been called obstructionist.[115] But it was not undemocratic. The problem of divorce reform was not, moreover, just a problem with the SPD. The Centre was bound to lose on the issue if it came to a vote because even right-liberals in the DVP backed divorce reform, as Centre Party leaders realized.[116]

One might speculate that the prospect of forestalling additional reforms on sexual-political issues entered the minds of Centre Party politicians as they contemplated a Brüning chancellorship, that the prospect cheered them, and that it provided them with another reason to support Brüning's move into the chancellor position. But this is just speculation. Centre Party politicians were thinking about sexual politics – especially as they affected marriage – when Brüning took power. But they were thinking about a lot of other things as well, and sexual politics were not a top priority. As Brüning was in negotiations to accept the chancellorship and to form a cabinet, the League of Catholic Women was organizing a mass rally in Berlin to effect "the rescue of the Christian family."[117] At that rally, leading Centre politicians repudiated the prospect of divorce reform.[118] Yet none of them said anything about the brand-new Brüning chancellorship being a solution to the threat to the family. The Centre's *Germania* drew no connections between sexual politics and Brüning's chancellorship. It rather portrayed Brüning's move into power as a means to overcome the parliamentary conflict, the "eternal arguing," and the irresponsibility of other parties, especially the SPD, that was dragging the country down in the midst of a crisis.[119] The Centre Party's Reichstag faction took the same position.[120] One article in *Germania* in the period just after Brüning took power called for an end to "cultural-political compromise" with the SPD and KPD, and the KPD's campaign for abortion rights was on the minds of Centre Party leaders.[121] Indeed, the most dire threat to the family, according to *Germania*, was Bolshevism, not Social Democracy.[122] In the spring of 1930, *Germania* was filled with stories of the alleged grotesqueries of family life in the USSR, as well as the violence and godlessness of the KPD, and spent far more space telling its readers of the dangers of communism than of those of fascism.[123] But around the same time, *Germania* also published a surprisingly conciliatory statement on sexual politics, one that was echoed later in its evaluation of Papen's regime. An author on literature and youth argued that only the quality of good literature could keep youth from reading filth and trash and it was misguided to think that law could shape the tastes of young people.[124] Culture, not the state, would rescue morality. Once in power, Brüning did not undertake major revisions of the reforms to laws on sexuality that had been achieved prior to 1930. Sexual politics were not among the foremost concerns of the Centre Party in this period and did not serve as a primary or secondary motive for Brüning to seek the chancellorship or for his party to support him in doing so.

One final example from *Germania* serves to illustrate the relatively low priority that the politics of sex had in Centre Party circles during the rise of Brüning. In relation to the following example, it is worth keeping in mind that the Centre Party electorate was disproportionally female and that women were supposed to have a particular interest in morality and family. Brüning became chancellor on 29 March 1930. The 30 March 1930 edition of *Women's World* (*Frauenwelt*), the weekly women's section of *Germania*, was devoted entirely to coverage of the League of Catholic Women's rally to save the Christian family. The next edition of *Women's World*, that of 6 April 1930, was devoted entirely to items about cooking for Easter. Immorality lacked the weighty significance to inspire even an additional week of coverage, even in a publication for women.

There are signs of the Centre Party shifting somewhat to the right on sexual-political issues in the 1930s. The Centre was partly reactive on sexual politics in this period. It was being pressed hard by liberals, Social Democrats, and Communists to revise laws on family and marriage – divorce and abortion – that it deemed inviolable. People in Centre Party circles were also unhappy with the persistence of "immorality" in public – that is, with female street soliciting and with the ineffectiveness of the 1926 law against trash and filth.[125] In a development that must have been influenced by this frustration, censorship seems to have gotten somewhat more strict under Brüning, with a handful of high-profile bans.[126] One of these came in 1931, when a Berlin court banned Hirschfeld's book *Moral History of the World War* (*Sittengeschichte des Weltkriegs*) under Paragraph

184, the obscenity law, though as Jens Dobler argues, there was no crackdown on gay and lesbian media in the Republic's final phase.[127] In addition, the Centre threw its weight behind an effort to stop the penal code reform committee's revision of the sodomy law. Homosexual emancipationists recognized that with Müller's fall, the chances of reforming Paragraph 175 dwindled.[128] Part of the Centre's aversion to the KPD, an aversion that informed the Centre Party's inept response to the threat of Nazism, was about sexual politics, though this was only one aspect of a comprehensive and pronounced anti-Communist position. In the late 1920s, the right wing of the national Centre Party was gaining influence.[129] But though the Centre moved to the right, sexual politics did not drive it to reject democracy. These issues were part of the Centre Party ideology. They played some role in the party's behaviour in the 1930s, yet that role was relatively minor.

To sum up this evaluation of the backlash argument, both as it pertains to Nazi electoral politics and as it pertains to the Centre Party's behaviour: surely the politics of sex influenced some voters in the elections of the 1930s. And sexual politics were not totally unimportant to Centre Party leaders. But sexual politics were not a primary or even secondary force in the Republic's destruction or in the success of Nazism. In addition, it is worth noting that though sexual-political issues were always among the anti-democratic themes of the Far Right, this does not seem at any point to have been instrumental in the Republic's fall. The Far Right hated the Republic from its beginning. The fact that large numbers of Germans opposed democracy ultimately helped to bring down the Republic. But sexual politics did not make opposition to democracy significantly more acute, nor did the politics of immorality sway large numbers of moderates towards the extreme right in the early 1930s.

Though sexual politics did not bring down the Weimar Republic, they did help the Nazis curry favour with conservatives like Adolf Sellmann and Bishop von Galen during the fascist regime's first months. The attack on the Institute for Sexual Science was a powerful symbol. It proclaimed the existence of common ground between the new Nazi state and conservative Christian foes of immorality. And though there was some common ground, there was not painless, complete agreement. Nazi sexual politics after 1933 were at times quite remote from what Sellmann and other religious morality activists would have preferred. In the immediate aftermath of Hitler becoming chancellor, the Nazis had to actively court people like Sellmann and von Galen, which they did by destroying the Institute and driving immorality from the streets.

And even after this purging of immorality from public life, Sellmann and some of his constituency remained sceptical. The bourgeoisie notions of morality they espoused did not line up exactly with Nazi sexual politics, as several scholars have noted.[130] At times, the new regime promoted "Aryan" heterosexual gratification outside of marriage.[131] It also liberalized the divorce law.[132] Conservative Christian commentators in Nazi Germany expressed dismay at casual premarital sex and at the decline of the institution of marriage.[133] Sellmann shared some of these anxieties. In a 1935 book, he praised the new regime and yet revealed some trepidation about Nazi sexual politics. He wrote that the West German Morality League was still on guard, specifically against the reintroduction of regulated female prostitution and brothels, the return of the nudity movement, the installation of condom-dispensing machines in public places, and, perhaps remembering the Röhm scandal, "pederasty and such perversions."[134]

Decadence and Cabaret: Why Do We Keep Identifying Sex as a Cause of the Weimar Republic's Fall?

The backlash thesis has a deep resonance for historians and for the wider public, despite a lack of evidence for it. This section of the chapter investigates why. Theories of how sex helped to bring down the Weimar Republic are almost as old as the Weimar Republic itself, and they garnered a lot of attention after the Republic fell. The backlash thesis is only one such theory, and it differs from older narratives. But the fact that many decades of scholarly and cultural production asserted a connection between sexual "decadence" and the fall of democracy lent credibility to the backlash thesis even though it rejected elements of the older theories. The backlash thesis also benefited from an additional asset: it helped to legitimate histories of sexuality.

When the Republic fell, conservative complaints about immorality that existed before 1933 provided fertile ground for historians' theories about what had gone wrong with democracy. In West Germany after 1945, the same conservative, Christian types who had found immoral sexuality so alarming in the Weimar years now looked back on the period and recognized sexual libertinism as a sign of the collapse of moral norms more generally that had, in hindsight, helped to pave the way for the amorality of Nazism.[135] West Germany's leading historians published explanations for the rise of Hitler that incorporated elements of the Weimar-era anti-immorality discourse as well as the new insight that immorality had given

Hitler a leg up. They identified an utter collapse of authority – political authority as well as moral and religious authority – in the years after the First World War.[136] This had led to fascism and to mass murder. In *The German Catastrophe* (*Die deutsche Katastrophe*, 1946), Friedrich Meinecke described how the French Revolution and nineteenth-century liberalism had initiated a long, relatively slow relaxation of "ethical ties" such as "family, custom, social stratification."[137] Christianity had formerly provided a moral framework, but with creeping secularization, conscience withered away.[138] This was "the moral degeneration of European society."[139] Without the authority of Christianity, people fell under the influence of demagogues.[140] This process began before the First World War but reached a nadir of "complete degeneration" in the Weimar years, thanks to materialism, growing irrationalism, and the Weimar state's lack of authority, among other things.[141] Nazism was very much a creature of the Weimar Republic in this formulation. The alleged collapse of moral norms, including those concerning family and sensuality, led to Hitler's political success. The Nazi mass murder programs were moreover evidence of a "radical breaking away from all moral restraints" that "climaxed" under Hitler's rule but had characterized the Weimar era as well.[142] Sexual impropriety is just one element of this breakdown, in Meinecke's description. Yet to him it was not insignificant. Ritter's argument in *Europe and the German Question*, discussed in the introduction, was similar.

Ritter also emphasized secularization, the "expulsion of the Church from the centre of life," as a precursor for Nazism.[143] In addition, the First World War disrupted tradition and undermined authority, creating a "political vacuum" (*Leerräume*), an unrestricted space for "new social and political experiments."[144] Only in such a morally unfettered atmosphere was the rise of Nazism possible, he wrote.[145] Denying that there was anything uniquely German about fascism, Ritter wrote that it rather belonged to a Europe-wide epoch of cultural degradation, spreading secularism, and "moral nihilism" that had set in in Germany around 1900 but had gotten worse in 1918.[146] Like Meinecke, Ritter informed his readers that fascism was in part a product of the licentiousness of the Weimar period, with immorality being one of the commonalities between the Weimar Republic and the Nazis.

Both of these arguments associated the Weimar period with the dissolution of Christian moral norms and blamed that dissolution for the rise of fascism, which they likewise associated with amorality. They fit within a larger trend in post-war West Germany, dominated as it was by the Christian Democratic Union (CDU): to understand Nazism's murderousness as "integrally linked," in Dagmar Herzog's words, to what Christians identified as its sexual libertinism.[147] Yet here Nazi amorality is connected not only to its own sexual immorality but also to the sexual immorality of the Weimar Republic.

Aside from West German historiography, a second powerful representation of a connection between Weimar-era libertinism and fascism existed in Christopher Isherwood's Berlin novels, and in the adaptations of them for stage and screen, particularly in the English-speaking world. Isherwood's depiction of happy hedonism in the shadow of Nazism had much in common with cultural production by other British intellectuals who spent time in Weimar-era Germany. Many of them viewed Berlin as more permissive towards sexuality than their own nation, which it was. But this vision of Berlin was not one of a city with a relatively progressive legal and police regime. Rather, British expatriates perceived orgiastic hedonism, a lack of any guidelines whatsoever.[148] Isherwood's novels, which were published after 1933, also convey a sense of doom that is typical of the retrospective views of British intellectuals who did not, for the most part, think the Republic doomed before 1933 but who projected that impression backward after democracy fell.[149] Many German émigrés likewise decided only in retrospect that the Republic was doomed.[150]

Probably the most widely consumed representation of Isherwood's Berlin is Bob Fosse's 1972 film *Cabaret*, which was nominated for ten Academy Awards.[151] *Cabaret* portrays a Berlin in which transvestitism, pornography, prostitution, abortion, homosexuality, and three-way sexual relationships are mundane and not uncommon. Rather than fascism coming to power on a wave of backlash against the libertinism of the Kit Kat Klub, the decadence of the cabaret embraces fascism, and vice versa. As in Meinecke's theory of amorality, the moral abandon of the cabaret is an avenue for fascism. This is best illustrated by the Master of Ceremonies, played by Joel Grey, a mysterious, sinister, androgynous, lecherous figure who urges the audience to forget their troubles. He delights in staging chaotic, dirty, gender-inverting violence – a mud-wrestling match between two women. At first, the cabaret appears hostile to fascism: an SA man is thrown out. In the mud-wrestling scene, the Master of Ceremonies mocks Hitler by mimicking him, painting a toothbrush moustache in mud on himself. But as the film progresses and the Nazi Party's strength grows, the mimicry loses its critical edge and begins to seem like simply falling in line, which is easy to do because in the cabaret, no moral norms exist to guide one away from the deep immorality

Perverse Germans into Nazis: the cabaret dancers, including the Master of Ceremonies in drag, morph into a troop of goose-stepping soldiers. From *Cabaret* (1972).

of fascism. A kick line of girls in brassieres – which includes the Master of Ceremonies, also in a brassiere – morphs into a company of goose-stepping, helmeted soldiers. Antisemitism creeps onto the stage when a gorilla serves as a metaphor for Jewish women. In the final scene, the Master of Ceremonies, sounding very much like the British commentator who in 1932 condemned Berlin's nightclubs as "waters of lethe" for those "unwilling to contemplate the future,"[152] speaks once again of how the beauty of the cabaret has made the audience forget their troubles. The camera pans to show that now, there are lots of men in SA uniforms in the audience. Amorality has opened the door to Nazism.[153]

But narratives of decadence and amorality rest on ahistorical premises. One is that fascism's amorality included sexual perversion.[154] Another is that under the Republic, immoral sexuality took the form of wanton, boundary-less frenzy. In the Weimar years, some Germans felt like that was the case, particularly in the big cities. But though the Republic had a relatively lax attitude towards homosexuality, female prostitution, and media with sexual content, its laxity was based in compromise, and it entailed a careful containment of these forms of immorality. So long as homosexuality, for example, stayed constrained in particular urban spaces like the Eldorado, it was tolerable to people as far to the right of the political spectrum as the right-liberal Wilhelm Kahl. Such toleration, however, may have seemed like an orgiastic frenzy to visiting Britons in the 1920s or to post-war West Germans. In its first decades, the Federal Republic was less tolerant of male homosexuality than the Weimar Republic had been.[155]

The recent work by historians on backlash has a different provenance from the work of Meinecke, Ritter, and Isherwood. Backlash studies appeared after the history of women and gender and the history of sexuality became academic sub-disciplines following the 1970s and 1980s feminist and gay liberation movements. The backlash thesis differs from older narratives like Meinecke's. He is disparaging of what he considers the abandonment of a God-given moral code. In contrast, proponents of the backlash concept celebrate sexual liberation and the agency of female prostitutes and gay men. Backlash narratives, moreover, see Nazism existing in opposition to Weimar-era sexual liberation, while the older narratives present the two periods as linked by moral degeneration. However, backlash shares a very general framework with older narratives of "decadence" or "amorality": it posits a causal relationship between the sexual liberation of the Weimar period and the rise of the Nazis. Backlash narratives thus present a new version of an old story.

Backlash narratives had an additional attribute that lent them staying power. As the history of sexuality emerged as a sub-discipline, it was often dismissed by established historians; indeed, studies of sexuality and gender are still marginalized by historians who treat them as divorced from political history.[156] The backlash narrative provided a path to legitimation by contending that the history of sexuality was a way to help understand one of the most important political questions in twentieth-century German history: how the Nazis came to power.[157] The legitimation of the field of the history of sexuality is a laudable outcome that, among other things, made this book possible. And yet, like older narratives, backlash rests on an ahistoricity. It assumes that sexual immorality was far more controversial in the Republic's final years than it actually was. With the exception of abortion, questions of sexual politics were settled by the Republic's end, that is, settled enough that a broad slice of the political spectrum could live with the bargains they had struck. Berlin's nightclubs may have been decadent, but the Republic was not. It forged a compromise position that controlled immorality, seeking above all to keep it from the public sphere.

1933 and After: Discontinuities between the Weimar and Nazi States on Sexual-political Questions and the Fates of Weimar-era Reformers

Historians have long debated the degree of continuity or discontinuity between Weimar-era and Nazi-era sexual politics, with waves of scholarship alternatingly asserting continuity or discontinuity, particularly with respect to bio-political issues.[158] Continuity existed. The people who designed and administered the Nazi State's programs had been adults during the Republic, and their views were influenced by Weimar-era politics and culture. The Nazi State did not reject all Weimar-era reforms; there was, for example, continuity on venereal disease policy.[159] However, it is useful to emphasize rupture or difference for the politics of sex. When contrasted with Weimar-era sexual politics, the sexual politics of Nazi Germany appear rather distinct. Once in power, the Nazis rejected much of the reformist position of the Weimar era, and to a certain extent, they rejected the conservative position as well. Though the Nazi State repudiated much of Weimar-era progressivism on sexuality, its programs did not always mirror the positions for which Weimar-era conservatives had fought.

A clear instance of this is female street and brothel prostitution. The Nazi State's policies on female prostitution were nothing like the Weimar Republic's. Moreover, Nazi prostitution policy was based on assumptions about the utility of the male heterosexual sex drive that would have horrified Weimar-era conservatives. After 1933, officials ruthlessly suppressed street soliciting. Female sex workers who drew the ire of those around them by soliciting in public could be labelled "asocial" and sent to concentration camps. Yet the Nazi leadership gradually brought back the regulated brothel, to the dismay of religious activists against immorality. Like all Nazi policies, this one had to do with race. Nazism valorized the reproductive heterosexuality of eugenically fit "Aryans" in the interest of strengthening the "Aryan" race. But pronatalism and eugenics were not the only goals of Nazi policies on sexuality: they also sought to stimulate and harness male heterosexual desire in order to cement the good feeling of citizens and make soldiers strong.[160] Top Nazis viewed the brothel as an antidote to male homosexuality. It was also, to them, a way to stimulate healthy male sexual expression and thereby help men be physically fit to be soldiers – a sort of welfare service. The Nazi State meted out harsh punishments for spreading venereal disease. Public services and public education were a far smaller part of the state's response to venereal disease than they had been under the Republic.[161]

The Nazi State went in directions that most conservative voices in Weimar-era debates had not dared to suggest and that many of those who had been conservative on sexual questions in the Weimar era did not welcome. In other respects though, Nazi policies were closer to what Weimar-era conservatives fought to achieve; this was true of the regime's initial move to drive lesbian, transvestite, and gay subcultures entirely from the public sphere. On lesbianism and transvestitism, the Nazi State then took something of an ambivalent, although certainly not friendly, stance.[162] At the same time, it enacted a murderous crackdown on male homosexuality that went far beyond what conservatives who were not of the Far Right had called for in the Weimar years. Gay men were subject to a centrally administered, national (and later, in areas under German occupation, international) effort to shut down their meeting places, to arrest them, and to intern or murder those of them who supposedly had no hope of reforming and rejoining the ranks of heterosexuals.

For many of the left-leaning activists who appear in this book, the Nazi takeover meant a radical break with the Weimar era. For some it also meant personal danger, although not for all. Those whom the new regime singled out for persecution were frequently targeted because they were not only activists for sexual freedom but also leftists, and in some cases Jews as well. Like so many members of the sex reform movement whom the Nazis drove into exile, Hirschfeld began a new life outside of Germany.[163] He settled in France but died of a stroke on 14 May 1935, almost exactly two years after the Institute for Sexual Science was destroyed.[164] The Gestapo came for Kurt Hiller shortly after the Nazis took power. He endured nine months in concentration camps and prisons in 1933–4.[165] Released, Hiller fled Germany. He returned to Hamburg after the war, where he continued to fight Paragraph 175, the draconian Nazi version of which was retained by the West German government.[166] Hiller lived to see some of the sodomy law's most onerous provisions repealed in 1969, although not the criminalization of male prostitution.[167] The paragraph was not entirely stricken from the criminal code until after German reunification.

Also arrested in 1933 were Lotte Hahm and Hilde Radusch. Hahm, the lesbian/transvestite activist and social club leader, was jailed for "seducing" a young woman into lesbianism in 1933 and eventually sent to the Moringen concentration camp.[168] Upon her release, Hahm returned to Berlin and organized some short-lived gatherings of lesbians. After 1945, she again took part in gay politics.[169] Radusch was arrested in 1933 on account of her membership in the KPD and imprisoned for six months.

She remained in Berlin after she was released, working at times with the underground Communist resistance. She left the Communist Party in 1946. She was active in the 1970s in L74, a lesbian group in West Berlin.[170]

Days after Hitler's appointment as chancellor, Richard Linsert came down with a flu that killed him suddenly, at thirty-three.[171] The loss devastated those around him, including Hiller.[172] KPD, WhK, and sex reform activists made up a large crowd at the funeral.[173] "His heart beat for the oppressed," a WhK leader told those assembled at the grave.[174] Some of the mourners consoled themselves with the thought that at least Linsert did not have to live through the Nazi takeover, "the triumph of reaction," as they did.[175] Nor did Friedrich Radszuweit live to see how futile were his pretensions to fellow-travel with Nazism. In the spring of 1932, just a few weeks after he published his defence of Ernst Röhm, Radszuweit succumbed to chronic illness.[176]

Other Weimar-era activists for sexual freedom quietly lived out their days under the Nazi State. They were not marked for persecution on account of Jewishness, leftism, or other characteristics. Ruth Roellig, the author of the lesbian guidebook to Berlin, lived through the Nazi years. She joined the Nazi writers' guild – membership was necessary in order to make a living as a writer – and published a novel with antisemitic themes.[177] Anna Pappritz resigned from her abolitionist organization. She may have been forced out because she was insufficiently enthusiastic about the new regime; she may have resigned out of bad health. She died in 1939.[178] Adolf Brand and his wife Elise (née Behrendt) were killed when a bomb struck their Berlin apartment building in 1945.[179]

The politics of immorality did not play a major role in the fall of the Weimar Republic or in the rise of the Nazis. The durability of notions to the contrary – that sex did help to bring down democracy in a significant way – is attributable to the ways in which the backlash thesis drew strength from a strong theme in post-war historiography and popular culture, though recent arguments about backlash differed in important ways from older ideas about decadence and amorality. Nazi sexual politics were in many cases quite distinct from both conservative and progressive positions under the Republic, though continuities existed.

Conclusion: The Weimar Settlement on Sexual Politics

Weimar-era reformers and conservatives arrived at a settlement – that is, an interrelated set of compromises that most of the parties could live with in relative calm, even if they did not love them and hoped to one day revisit them. The terms of the settlement tolerated some forms of non-normative sexuality so long as they remained largely out of the public eye; this supposedly contained them in an adult sub-population. The settlement moreover recognized the ability of certain people to make good choices about sexual expression on their own, without policing. Other people, in contrast, made bad choices, and they needed restraint. Scientific knowledge about degeneration and mental disability helped to identify them. This settlement did not extend to all sexual-political issues. Especially questions about the reproductive heterosexual couple, like divorce and abortion, remained unsettled. Yet the choices open to capable citizens were broadened, while the constraints on a minority changed in character and intensified. Here I offer a concluding description of the Weimar settlement. I consider an important limit to the settlement: abortion. I examine what the settlement meant for homosexual emancipation. Then, in two final sections – one on homonormativity and history, and a second on homosexual emancipation and German national identity today – I consider this study's implications for matters beyond Weimar-era Germany.

The Weimar Settlement

The Weimar settlement on sexual politics, and the type of freedom it established, was expressed in the legal reforms examined in this book. The Republic's censorship policies on media with sexual content were relatively lax, opening up space for queer sexual expressions and queer subcultures. The Republic did, however, restrict media about sexuality to a certain extent. Particularly, it made it less accessible to children, so that they would be protected from seduction into sexual abnormality; this would confine sexual abnormality to a relatively small group of adults. The new venereal disease law and the proposed reform of the sodomy law both mobilized bio-politics to keep sex work from the public eye. The 1927 venereal disease law deregulated and decriminalized female prostitution but also moved to greatly curtail it, focusing especially on street soliciting. Proponents of this law believed that it created sexual freedoms and public health duties that were aspects of citizenship. These were predicated on plans to constrain sex workers whom science had identified as incorrigible. The proposed reform of the sodomy law would have decriminalized private, non-commercial sex between adult men while cracking down on male prostitution and banning the seduction of a younger man by an older one. Proponents of the reform also hoped that it would cut down on homosexual "propaganda" – that is, homosexual emancipation media. This would keep male homosexuality from spreading. In addition, the proposed new law would give the police a means to move against men who sold sex, men whom the sciences had defined as dangerous, criminal, and degenerate. Some of the reforms discussed in this book did not become law, though they had broad support. Neither the preventative detention law that was intended as a companion to the venereal disease reform nor the revised version of the sodomy law ever passed. But even these failed initiatives reflected a consensus on the politics of sex. Principles of compromise were repeated in different contexts. They were put forward by a diverse set of actors who had realized that they could achieve portions of their agendas by catering to certain demands being made by the other side. The Weimar settlement did not help appreciably to bring down the Republic or to put the Nazis in power, although the fact that a consensus existed that sex between men in private was not a dire threat to the public good ended up helping the NSDAP manage the Röhm scandal.

Thus, at some expense to a small minority of people, most Germans – including many gay men and lesbians – came to enjoy greater toleration. This toleration was reflected by state policies and to a certain extent by social norms. Yet this was not exactly "liberation," though to many people, it felt liberating. Nor was it the complete dissolution of stigmas on non-normative sexualities. Rather, it was a shift in systems of regulation.[1] Over time, as political power rested increasingly with reformers, the Weimar state grew more involved, not less, with the sexuality of its citizens. Much of this new involvement was predicated on a moderate leftist reformist vision that prioritized science over religious mores. The Weimar welfare state also drew on eugenics and other bio-political and public health schemes to instrumentalize reproductive heterosexual sex, as other studies have shown.[2] This bio-political management also opened up realms of private and public space for queer sexualities that, although constrained, were unprecedented in German history and perhaps in world history.

Weimar-era eugenic programs also followed the pattern: they empowered thoughtful citizens to make good choices and sought to prevent incapable people from making bad ones. Eugenics is the science of improving a population of humans over time by managing reproduction through government programs intended to promote the births of babies with some traits and to discourage or eliminate the births of babies with other traits.[3] It had broad popular support in Weimar-era Germany from the Right, the moderate middle, and the Left, but at the same time, the versions of eugenics backed by the various political players differed quite widely.[4] Despite lots of support for eugenics in general, and lots of talk about eugenics, actual explicitly eugenic legislation and public policy initiatives were quite sparse.[5] There were only three programs: a pamphlet to be given to couples planning to marry, a proposed provincial sterilization law in Prussia, and a series of marriage and sex counselling clinics. The marriage and sex counselling clinics were a diverse lot and did far more than offer eugenic advice. Though the clinics were by far the largest of the three programs in terms of resources devoted and people affected, most of their clients were not all that interested in eugenics and rather sought help with practical matters such as fertility control.[6] It was the Left, the moderate left, and the centre that shaped Weimar-era eugenic initiatives, with the Centre Party and SPD wielding the most power in the politics of eugenics at the national level.[7] Leftist and moderate supporters of eugenics generally did not use race as a criteria to determine who ought to reproduce and who ought not to; on this question and others, they differed significantly from right-wing, racist eugenicists who later came into positions of influence under the Nazi regime.[8] For the most part, what emerged from a conflict between the Centre and the SPD over what form eugenic programs ought to take was an effort to educate the public to make better choices about reproduction, in the interest of the future physical and mental fitness of the national population. Public education was the main goal of the pamphlet and the clinics. They were part of the many Weimar-era public health education campaigns promoting salubrious living.[9]

Eugenic sterilization became a real political possibility only during the Depression, because of mounting anxieties about strapped welfare resources.[10] The authors of Prussia's 1932 draft law envisioned eugenic sterilization as a means to neutralize the threat to national well-being posed by "inferior" (*minderwertig*) people who, due to their supposed mental incapacities, could not be relied upon to refrain from having children and thereby passing on their bad hereditary stock. Among those to be sterilized according to this law were people with "hereditary mental illness" or "hereditary imbecility (*erblicher Geistesschwäche*)," which, according to the Prussian government's explanation of the law, included the "feebleminded" and "psychopaths."[11] As chapters 3 and 4 showed, these same designations were used to define "incorrigible" female prostitutes and blackmailing male prostitutes. The draft law – still in preparation when the Nazis took power and thus never passed – stipulated that eugenic sterilization be voluntary and said that institutionalized people could only be sterilized with the consent of their legal guardians.[12] But the plan was to pressure "inferior" people – especially those in institutions – to consent to sterilization or to easily gain the perfunctory consent of their legal guardians.[13]

Thus, taken as whole, Weimar-era eugenic programs were for the most part voluntary. They were aimed at a majority that was capable of making good choices, if provided with scientific information. Yet the sterilization law was an essentially compulsory measure to be used against a supposedly biologically inferior minority population that was deemed incapable of making good choices.[14]

Sex was among the most contentious of political matters that captured the nation's interest in the Weimar era, although there were other equally contentious matters like foreign policy and welfare.[15] It is surely worth meditating on the fact that despite how dramatically far apart conservative and reformist positions were on matters such as homosexuality and sexuality in media, conservatives and reformers used the democratic process to hash out several major legal reforms. And moreover, they did so in a parliamentary system that is famous for its dysfunction. I find persuasive the revisionist scholarship that holds that in fact, such infamy is unjustly assigned to the Weimar Republic, which increasingly appears (as McElligott puts it) not "weak, compromised, fragmented, and lacking in political authority," but rather as "a polity whose parliamentary institutions were resilient; its republican culture assertive; its civic identity robust."[16] When one looks only at the politics of immorality – albeit not a comprehensive view, to be sure – the Republic's democratic institutions seem to have been functioning rather well until 1930.[17] Instead of demonstrating any inherent weaknesses in the Weimar Republic, the politics of homosexuality, prostitution, media about sexuality, and venereal disease demonstrate how functional German democracy could be between 1919 and the early 1930s.

A Limit to the Settlement: Abortion

As democracy collapsed beginning with the Depression and the fall of Hermann Müller's Great Coalition, sexual politics exceeded compromises. The mass movement for abortion demonstrates this. The Weimar Republic relaxed restrictions on abortion and contraception, though abortion remained a crime and contraception remained difficult to get for many people. A 1926 SPD-backed reform to the abortion law together with a 1927 Reichsgericht decision gave Germany one of the world's "most liberal" abortion regimes, according to Cornelie Usborne, although abortion was still criminalized.[18] The 1926 reform to the abortion law had the support of the Social Democrats, the two liberal parties, and initially the KPD, although the KPD favoured more radical change. The Centre Party and the DNVP opposed it. The law decreased sentences for women who had had abortions, setting the minimum sentence at a single day, and made abortion a misdemeanour crime.[19] The following year, Germany's high court ruled that doctors could terminate pregnancies for medical reasons, making abortion even more accessible for those who could find and pay for a doctor willing to vouch for the medical necessity of a termination.[20] But many thousands of people were unsatisfied by the new abortion law.[21] The fact that during the Weimar period there was an enormous rise in convictions for abortion offences makes the 1926 reform seem insignificant and cannot have been unrelated to the widespread frustration with it.[22] Women who could not afford private clinics told of their miserable experiences seeking in vain doctors who would terminate their pregnancies.[23] The relatively liberal abortion law of 1926 was a moderate leftist reform and a compromise. It must however be counted as a failed compromise. It did not satisfy thousands of people, a good deal of whom were inspired to lend their support to an anti-democratic party, the KPD, at least temporarily.

The KPD's message on abortion was a rejection of democracy and of the Weimar state. In the Reichstag, the Communists condemned the Republic for failing to protect the rights of proletarian women and called for a new state that would liberate women and empower workers and farmers, as Russia had done.[24] In 1931, the KPD mobilized tens of thousands in a popular front campaign against the abortion law, Paragraph 218. Willi Münzenberg's mass-circulation newspapers fanned frustrations with Paragraph 218 and with the obscenity law, Paragraph 184, which restricted contraception.[25] Although KPD-led, the campaign included a broad spectrum of people who fell in line with sex reform and feminism. The KPD saw the campaign as a means to attract much-needed female voters.[26] Atina Grossmann describes how ultimately, the KPD proved too ambivalent towards women's organizing and women's issues to successfully capitalize on the abortion movement.[27] Party ranks swelled during the campaign, but joining dropped off when it waned.[28] The abortion movement petered out in 1931; Grossmann suggests that in the midst of economic and political crisis, people lacked the energy for activism on this issue.[29] Yet the abortion campaign lent at least the appearance of strength to the KPD in a moment when fear of the KPD was driving people to support the NSDAP. Even many who were wary of Nazism saw the KPD as the greater threat and hoped that the Nazis would crush the Communists; this sentiment was apparent even as early as the spring of 1930 in the Centre Party's *Germania*, with its frequent accounts of KPD violence and sexual anarchy. At the same time, sexual-political issues were not the foremost reason that moderates feared communism, and in addition, the swell in KPD support during the Depression is not due primarily to the movement for abortion.

The Weimar settlement was a compromise hammered out by contending parties in a democracy, and it was a functioning compromise in many respects. Yet it did not encompass the right to abortion that protesters in the 1930s demanded. They wanted a freedom that the settlement could not stretch far enough to include. The campaign against the abortion law did not, however, play a primary role in the collapse of democracy.

German Homosexual Emancipation and the Weimar Settlement

For the German homosexual emancipation movement, the Weimar settlement on sexual politics established an expanded realm of sexual freedom for people who could fulfil the settlement's terms. It meant liberation for some men who had sex with men. That liberation came at the expense of other men who had sex with men. It also meant liberation for gay men, lesbians, and transvestites at the price of agreeing to curtail public representations of queerness. Yet even under these restrictions, gay male, lesbian, and transvestite subcultures were allowed limited public space in publications and in certain urban centres. This albeit constrained public sphere was indispensable to the growth of gay male, lesbian, and transvestite subcultures and political movements. Both with respect to censorship politics and with respect to the sodomy law, the Weimar settlement offered toleration, even acceptance, to a certain kind of queer subject. This subject could conceal his or her sexuality and/or gender transgression, displaying it only in private or in the limited queer subcultural sphere. She or he possessed middle-class respectability and could successfully perform the duties of citizenship.[30]

This expansion of sexual freedom was possible only because it was accompanied by schemes to manage and restrict the disreputable queer sexuality of people who did not meet these qualifications, foremost among them sex workers. They were identified according to markers of disability, degeneration, and class. The expansion of freedom for some depended upon curtailing these others. Politicians only voted to allow the queer press to operate, to deregulate female prostitution, and to repeal the sodomy law because all three reforms contained schemes to curb excesses and, in the second two cases, were planned to coincide with measures that would have physically constrained people who sold sex in public.

The settlement thus affected various people who had queer sex differently. They had different answers to the question of whether the terms of the settlement were acceptable. For many homosexual emancipationists who were themselves respectable types and who, aside from their sexuality, could hope to perform good citizenship, these terms of liberation were fine. Among these activists were Hirschfeld and Radszuweit, and doubtless many members of their respective organizations, the WhK and the League for Human Rights. People who engaged in queer sex and who did not like the terms of this settlement included female prostitutes who worked on the streets and complained after 1927 of harassment by state officials and social workers. People who disliked the settlement probably also included many men who sold sex. For sex workers who solicited on the streets, or for women who worked in police-regulated brothels, keeping one's sexuality out of the public sphere was not an option. Of the leaders of homosexual emancipation, Hiller and Linsert most clearly rejected the terms of the Weimar settlement when they dedicated the WhK to fight the proposed repeal of the sodomy law because it cracked down on male prostitutes. Hiller as well seemed to chafe against the confines of one central term of the settlement – to keep one's sexuality relatively private – when in the Republic's early years he called for tactics that depended upon being frank about one's sexuality, such as a mass declaration or a homosexual political party.

There is not a single type of queer sexual freedom that waxes and wanes over time. Rather, several basic types of sexual freedom have come into being in European culture, science, and politics since the eighteenth and nineteenth centuries gave us the contemporary senses of "freedom" and "sexuality."[31] The Weimar settlement on sexual politics represents one such convention. The kind of freedom that it produced was freedom of sexual expression in private and in subcultural spaces cordoned off from the mainstream. It offered the opportunity for some people who had queer sex to be included in respectability and citizenship. It was not only a liberal freedom to be left alone, but also a positive freedom to become a certain kind of subject, to name oneself as an upstanding citizen and to be recognized as such. At the same time, one's queerness would remain concealed. Transvestites sought to pass. The homosexual emancipation movement's central demands did not include the freedom to be open about one's sexuality in spaces beyond the subcultures, such as in the workplace.[32]

In addition, Europeans did not simply become progressively more tolerant of "sexual minorities" over time. A period of relative openness and forbearance could be followed by one of violent repression in which many of the gains won by activists in the former period were quickly nullified, as Weimar-era reforms were in the Nazi period. This is true in the broader European context as well. In the 1950s, capitalist Western Europe, including West Germany, saw the reassertion of Christian ideas about marriage and gender. This later period brought diminished toleration of sexual diversity in comparison to the Weimar years.[33]

Beyond Homonormativity

Since the early twenty-first century, Lisa Duggan's concept of homonormativity has been enormously influential in the interdisciplinary analysis of queer sexualities.[34] It has also been very useful. On the basis of this study of the Weimar Republic, I nevertheless want to suggest specifically to historians that they work towards an analytic beyond homonormativity. Homonormativity and similar analytics are productive for history. They draw attention to just how conservative political movements for sexual freedom can be. And yet they also have the potential to confound historical analysis because they depend on misrememberings of history. These misrememberings may be strategic. But because of them, when the concept of homonormativity is put to use in the practice of history, analysis tends to collapse. In moving beyond homonormativity, the history of sexuality could offer different analytics that could lead to more complex conclusions. There are two misrememberings of history upon which scholarship on homonormativity often depends. The first is the idea that assimilationist, not-all-that-radical gay politics are new and aberrant in the history of homosexuality. The second is the neglect of the ways in which "radical" is historical, which is related to the narrow definition of homonormativity.

Current scholarship often presents queer conservatism as an historical aberration. For Duggan, homonormativity in the United States in the 1990s was unique. Even the homophile movement of the 1950s had not been as conservative as was the homonormativity of the first decade of the following century, she argues, because homophile activists sought not only private sexual rights but also access to a limited public sphere and, moreover, freedom from harassment in the workplace on account of one's sexuality. David Eng names relatively conservative queer politics in the United States in the early twenty-first century "queer liberalism."[35] He writes that, "paradoxically, prior historical efforts" on the part of queer radicals who rejected "state oppression" and "state regulation of family and marriage" have now "given way to the desire for state legitimacy, sanction, and authorization of same-sex marriage."[36] There is a sense here that conservative gay politics is not just a disturbing contrast with radical gay liberation of the 1970s or leftist queer activism of the 1980s and 1990s. It is, rather, a more fundamental betrayal of the queer past, a category mistake, as if conservative queerness is an oxymoron. Describing the earlier movement as "paradoxically" giving way to the later one implies that there was something properly, inherently queer about the earlier radicalism that the later conservatism violated.[37] One also gets the impression from Duggan that politics for homosexual liberation tend by definition to be radical and left. She writes that the project of homonormativity to "redefine gay equality ... as access to the institutions of domestic privacy, the 'free' market, and patriotism" is "a big job given the history of gay rights activism in the United States." The job is big because "the overall goals" of queer politics "have been relatively consistent: the expansion of a right to sexual privacy against the intrusive, investigatory labeling powers of the state, and the simultaneous expansion of gay public life through institution building and publicity."[38] In this depiction, homonormativity diverts the momentum of many decades of activism. It is historical rupture.

But relatively conservative movements for queer sexual freedom are not new. In German-speaking Europe since the nineteenth century, there have been homosexual emancipationist movements that met many of the criteria of homonormativity or queer liberalism. Activists in these movements claimed citizenship, trumpeted their patriotism, turned to the state to affirm their rights, and deployed liberalism in their defence. They created a queer form of respectability and embraced it in the hope that once they did so, some of the mainstream social stigma on queerness would dissipate, which it often did not. They also at times fought towards their goals by denigrating other queers whom they deemed too disreputable and too public. In the Weimar period, they used bio-politics to separate themselves from other queers. As many other scholars have noted, queer sex is not necessarily connected to a given political tradition.[39] Yet it seems that historically, *most* activists for queer sexual freedom in North America and Western Europe from the nineteenth century to the end of the twentieth did gravitate to a given political tradition: liberalism. And in that time period and in those places, liberalism was not always radical. Yet, at the same time, it was rarely homonormative, either.

The second manner in which homonormativity threatens to confound the practice of history results from its definition, which is quite narrow. Relatively conservative movements that drew on liberalism have only very rarely – if ever – been homonormative by Duggan's definition. In most times and places, it was not possible to have a public queer culture that was depoliticized. Nor was it possible to have a depoliticized private queer existence. The survival of queer publics and queer privates were political questions, as this book has demonstrated. For queers, no matter how far to the right they happened to be, the personal could never *not* be political, as Ernst Röhm discovered to his dismay. Though he was invested in a conventional and racialized form of masculinity that most people considered heterosexual, Röhm's ideas about homosexuality nevertheless contested what Duggan terms "dominant heteronormative assumptions."[40] Röhm's belief that men who had sex with men were masculine violated the norms of his day. Röhm was a fascist who simply wanted a private queer existence and a very limited subcultural queer sphere. If he does not qualify as homonormative, the concept's utility for historians seems limited.

What is misremembered in homonormativity's definition is the fact that radical is historical. Activism that would later be identified as less radical, such as seeking legal marriage, had a much better claim to radicalness in the 1920s and even in the 1970s.[41] To take certain conservative, heteronormative, exclusionary, or racist elements in gay politics in the past and to identify them as roots of a homonormativity that would come into full bloom in the present, as recent scholarship has done, is to perhaps miss an opportunity to reach a more profound conclusion.[42] We need a theoretical apparatus that allows us to pay attention to how movements for sexual freedom could pose real challenges to norms of gender and sexuality and yet, at the same time, totally endorse other norms.

I would offer the following as an alternative: since the advent of modern notions of sexuality, the state, and freedom, movements for queer emancipation have arisen within a variety of political frameworks. They always exist within encompassing frameworks. Claims to queer emancipation are never made divorced from broader political projects. This is the case even when they allege that they are indeed isolated from broader projects. Take Hirschfeld, Hiller, and Linsert as examples. Hirschfeld's politics were scientific and wedded to Social Democracy, which itself was steeped in modern science and bio-politics. Hiller's politics during the Republic defy easy categorization. A liberal and an elitist, he was also immersed in causes of the unaligned left, such as pacifism. By the early 1930s, Linsert was a Communist. The political principles of these three men influenced how they sought sexual freedom, even though the group that they led, the WhK, nominally had a very narrow focus on the persecution and exploitation of homosexuals. All three men, at various times, made claims about citizenship. But they had different understandings of what citizenship was. All three were radical in their particular time and place. Their radicalisms had different contents and worked towards different outcomes. Some were more radical than others – that is, Hiller and Linsert called for changes that would have changed German state and society more than the reforms that Hirschfeld called for would have. It is crucial to consider the politics surrounding a given person's struggle for sexual freedom. Not all claims on citizenship and the state are the same.

In addition, the dilemma posed by the Weimar settlement for Hirschfeld and Hiller is a dilemma that has been endemic to queer sexual politics as they took on their characteristic, indelible shape since the last third of the nineteenth century, in Europe as well as in North America and elsewhere. Without attempting a full account of the first half-century of homosexual emancipation, I would note that a narrower movement, based in claims to citizenship and respectability, is apparent from the nineteenth century into the present. It existed in the publications and activism of Ulrichs in the second half of the nineteenth century and in WhK petitions prior to 1918.[43] This type of activism, which I am terming "narrower," was quite radical in its day. It challenged fundamental norms of gender and sexuality. It would be hard to call Ulrich's public speech against the sodomy law before the Congress of German Jurists in 1867 anything but radical.[44] Yet by the Weimar period, if not sooner, the constituency for a broader movement that challenged other norms in addition – such as those of class, criminality, disability, and respectability – was apparent. It was expressed by Linsert and Hiller and by sex workers who advocated a politics that conflicted with the Weimar settlement. This more radical movement was in part made up of people for whom a respectable existence in the private sphere was not possible. After 1945, reconstituted homosexual emancipation groups in Germany and elsewhere tended to be narrower in their rhetorics and agendas.[45] The late 1960s and early 1970s saw the rise of a more radical movement in West Germany, although it also had factions of "integrationists" (*Integrationisten*).[46] Similar movements in North America in that period were also broader and more radical, challenging patriarchy and rejecting respectability. Following the initial AIDS crisis, a sometimes acrimonious split between more radical queer factions and factions that cleaved more closely to the Weimar settlement happened in Western Europe and North America. This coincided with the success of some of the narrower tradition's central demands. People who wanted a more radical movement critiqued the narrower tradition, which became the larger and more powerful faction. But the narrower tradition was not new; it had been there from the beginning.

Rather than seek signs of homonormativity in the past, historians could trace the various incarnations of this dilemma, the split between more and less radical factions. Since the 1920s, if not before, the major principles structuring the debate about sexual freedom have often reoccurred and have been close to what they were for German homosexual emancipation under the Weimar Republic. The dilemma – the choice between a more radical movement and a narrower one based on respectability, privacy, assimilation, and citizenship claims – is, arguably, always present when movements in the tradition of German homosexual emancipation are present. This dilemma ought to be recognized as characteristic of queer politics in the twentieth and early twenty-first centuries. It was not, in fact, the turn of queer activism away from radicalism and towards respectability after the heyday of the 1970s that produced the tensions of the 1990s and the following decade. Those tensions were apparent from the beginning of "homosexuality" and of activism for homosexual emancipation. They were fully developed in the 1920s. They arose from the interactions between models of sexuality such as Hirschfeld's and the conditions of liberal, democratic politics. When one adopts a model such as Hirschfeld's, something like the Weimar settlement can be on offer, though the Weimar settlement is no longer possible in the exact form that it took in the 1920s. In the final decades of the twentieth century, social movements such as those of feminists, people with disabilities, people of colour, colonized people, and sex workers shifted the terms of what was possible in sexual politics, at least in Germany. But even as the settlement shifts over time, its basic tenets offer moderates much that they like. The Weimar settlement functions well in democratic, liberal states. Under the Weimar Republic, such a settlement brought liberation at a price, and not only at the price of forgoing a more profound critique: it came at a direct price for some queers.

Homosexual Emancipation and German National Identity

Since 2010, many Germans have claimed homosexual emancipation as an important part of their national history. More and more people are celebrating the fact that Germany seems to have been the home of the world's first gay rights movement. Hirschfeld himself has once again been made the face of homosexual emancipation, as he was for most of his adult life. In 2011, the Bundestag endowed a national Magnus Hirschfeld Foundation. The Foundation's purpose is to memorialize queer victims of the Nazis, to promote the history of gay men and lesbians in Germany and Hirschfeld's history in particular, and to fight the persecution of gay men and lesbians in Germany today.[47] In 2013, the Lesbian and Gay Union of Berlin-Brandenburg (*Lesben- und Schwulenverband Berlin-Brandenburg*) and the Alliance Against Homophobia (*Bündnis gegen Homophobie*) campaigned for a national memorial to homosexual emancipation in Berlin, where there is already a street named for Hirschfeld, a park named for Hiller, and a monument on the site of the Institute for Sexual Science.

In the summer of 2013, posters advertising a fundraiser for the planned national memorial graced bus stops in Berlin. The poster features an image of five "New Women" of the 1920s standing before the Brandenburg Gate, which is a central symbol of the German nation. The photo has been altered so that a rainbow banner is woven among

VON BERLIN AUS STARTETE EINE SCHWARZE ZEIT FÜR DIE WELT. ABER AUCH DIE BUNTESTE BEWEGUNG, DIE ES JE GAB.

SENDEN SIE PER SMS
DENKMAL
AN DIE RUFNUMMER
81190
UND HELFEN SIE
MIT 5 EURO*

WIR BAUEN IN DANKBARKEIT UND IM GEDENKEN AN DR. MAGNUS HIRSCHFELD

 Bündnis gegen Homophobie

EIN DENKMAL FÜR DIE ERSTE HOMOSEXUELLE EMANZIPATIONS BEWEGUNG

DENKMAL-FUER-BERLIN.DE   STOPP-HOMOPHOBIE.DE

Einmalig Spenden: BLSB e.V., Konto: 082 44 33 01, Deutsche Bank, BLZ: 100 700 24. Stichwort: Denkmal. Oder per SMS.
*Von den 5 EUR gehen 4,83 EUR direkt an das Denkmal-Projekt. Kosten zzgl. einer Standard-SMS.

"A black time for the world came from Berlin. But so did the most colourful movement that there had ever been." 2013 poster campaign to raise money for a memorial to Magnus Hirschfeld and homosexual emancipation. © LSVD Berlin-Brandenburg e.V.

the women. Text imposed on the photograph reads, "A black time for the world came from Berlin. But so did the most colourful movement that there had ever been. [*Von Berlin aus startete eine schwarze Zeit für die Welt. Aber auch die bunteste Bewegung, die es je gab.*]"

This poster fashions homosexual emancipation into a "usable past" for Germans.[48] It contrasts homosexual emancipation – positive, "colourful" – with the "black time," that is, the Nazi years. Homosexual emancipation here helps to portray a tolerant Berlin that is positioned as a foil to Nazi Germany. Nazism came from Berlin, "but so did" homosexual emancipation. Berlin was capable of producing good as well as evil. Homosexual emancipation is thus offered as a positive national achievement that is even worth mentioning in the same breath as Nazism. Beyond this poster, the celebration of Hirschfeld also has the effect of bringing public attention to German-Jewish history, which is laudable. But Hirschfeld's Jewishness tends to be mentioned near the top of press releases and websites, in a manner that seems to present homosexual emancipation as a contrast to the racism of Nazism. Overall, these moves to claim Weimar-era homosexual emancipation as a source of national pride are part of reunified Germany's efforts to find positive achievements in German national history, to construct a national past with which contemporary Germans can identify without the difficulties that had previously beset such identification thanks to the national reckonings with the Nazi crimes that began in the 1960s.[49] These efforts are troubling to those on the left who have long insisted that Germans abandon conventional nationalism altogether.

Even if one is comfortable with a project to build national identity by prioritizing some historical narratives over other, darker ones, making homosexual emancipation into one of the prioritized narratives is a fraught endeavour. Magnus Hirschfeld does not make a bad hero. If one is a moderate leftist, Hirschfeld's moderate-left politics, his pacifism, his courageous struggle on behalf of queer people, and his critiques of racism, imperialism, and fascism will all recommend him for the post above many other candidates. Hirschfeld himself may not have wanted the job: he was no nationalist, and he may have asked some of the same questions about the project of reclaiming a conventional German national identity that the contemporary Left asks. Yet there is a larger problem. The history of homosexual emancipation in the Weimar years is troubled by violences, exclusions, and hierarchies that many Germans would not want to associate with Germany in the twenty-first century. Hirschfeld wholeheartedly supported a moderate eugenics program, as did most of his contemporaries. Antisemitism was not absent from Weimar-era homosexual emancipation – think of Brand, Radszuweit, even Röhm. The movement's gender politics were fraught, and the poster erases this, seeking as it does to use an image of women to raise money for a memorial that will apparently focus on groups dominated by men. Nor was homosexual emancipation devoid of class prejudice, belief in "degeneration," support for eugenics, efforts to exclude transvestites and prostitutes, and suspicion of democracy – on this last count, think not only of Brand but of Hiller. One might add that it is ironic to see homosexual emancipation claimed as a national achievement by the German state, a state that, despite homosexual emancipation, retained a version of the sodomy law into the 1990s – though not as long as did other states, such as the United States, which struck down its sodomy laws only in 2003.

All of this must haunt any project to make Hirschfeld a national hero or to claim homosexual emancipation as a national achievement. It ought to. I do not make this point in order to condemn Hirschfeld or his contemporaries. Rather, we in the present would gain far more from our relationship with the past – with the history of homosexual emancipation – if that relationship encompassed the complexity and ugliness of homosexual emancipation, because of what that more sophisticated relationship would help us to perceive about our own politics.

From the perspective of the history narrated here, it is to be hoped that the national memorial to homosexual emancipation and to Hirschfeld will reflect the debates within homosexual emancipation and the compromises that the movement made in the Weimar years. The movement contained more and less radical strands. Like all movements for sexual freedom, it was flawed and conflicted. Ultimately, its achievements under the Weimar Republic were more in keeping with a relatively narrow tradition of activism that shied away from radical claims to public space and, in addition, rejected a broader form of sexual freedom that would have included more people. And its achievements came at a price to a small and relatively disadvantaged group of people, who have since been largely forgotten. Hopefully in the public attention to homosexual emancipation in the twenty-first century, they, too, will be remembered.

Notes

Introduction: The Opening Night of the Institute for Sexual Science, July 1919

1 "Aus der Bewegung," *Jahrbuch für sexuelle Zwischenstufen unter besonderer Berücksichtigung der Homosexualität* [*JfsZ*] 19 (January/April 1919): 52. Unless otherwise noted, translations are my own.

2 Detlev Peukert, *The Weimar Republic: The Crisis of Classical Modernity*, trans. Richard Devenson (New York: Hill and Wang, 1993), 132–3. "Welfare state" was a term of derision at the time; people rather referred to the "social state": David Crew, *Germans on Welfare: From Weimar to Hitler* (New York: Oxford University Press, 1998), 10–11.

3 "Aus der Bewegung," *JfsZ* (January/April 1919): 52–3. The singer was Leo Gollanin. There is footage of him singing the Kol Nidre in 1932: United States Holocaust Memorial Museum, Steven Spielberg Film and Video Archive, http://www.ushmm.org/online/film/display/detail.php?file_num=1325&tape_id=8dea86ca-551c-4e4b-bf47-07643d1c689d&clip_id=&media_type=mp4 (accessed 20 February 2015).

4 He denounced racism and imperialism: Magnus Hirschfeld, *Racism*, trans. Eden and Cedar Paul (Port Washington, NY: Kennikat Press, 1973). His reputation was compromised by Moll, for example: Ivan Crozier, "'All the World's a Stage': Dora Russell, Norman Haire, and the 1929 London World League for Sexual Reform Congress," *Journal of the History of Sexuality* 12, no. 1 (2003): 32–3.

5 "Aus der Bewegung," *JfsZ* (July/October 1920).

6 "Aus der Bewegung," *JfsZ* 19 (January/April 1919): 53.

7 Magnus Hirschfeld, *Sappho und Sokrates oder wie erklärt sich die Liebe der Männer und Frauen zu Personen des eigenen Geschlechts?* 3rd ed. (Leipzig: Max

Spohr (Ferd. Spohr), 1922), 24; the 1st edition was 1896. For more detail on Hirschfeld's model, see Hirschfeld, *Sappho und Sokrates*; Hirschfeld, *Die Homosexualität des Mannes und des Weibes* (Berlin: Louis Marcus Verlagsbuchhandlung, 1920); Edward Ross Dickinson, *Sex, Freedom, and Power in Imperial Germany, 1880–1914* (New York: Cambridge University Press, 2014), 157–60.

8 Hirschfeld, *Homosexualität*, 372–3.
9 Hirschfeld, *Sappho und Sokrates*, 32.
10 Ibid.
11 Hirschfeld, *Homosexualität*, 1026.
12 Manfred Herzer, *Magnus Hirschfeld: Leben und Werk eines jüdischen, schwulen und sozialistischen Sexologen* (Frankfurt: Campus, 1992), 29.
13 On the meaning of "transvestite" in this time and place, see pp. 59–61. On my use of "lesbian" see chapter 2, note 3. "Gay" is used here, and occasionally throughout this study, ahistorically: in the Weimar period, its German equivalent, *schwul*, existed but was rarely used in print and did not have the same meanings that it does today. Historians of sexuality have argued that it is important to use only the terms that people in the past would have used to describe their lives, in order to avoid making unwarranted assumptions about their self-conceptions, such as that they conceived of "sexuality" as a feature of their self. I agree that this is important. I am however writing about a period in which sexual identity existed, though it was not meaningful for everyone. My reason for using "gay" is that a term that historical actors used, "homosexual," has a pejorative meaning today that it did not have in the early twentieth century. There is no vocabulary that can relieve a historian of the conflict between making the past legible for one's readers and not obscuring the meanings that prevailed in the past. This sort of translation cannot be perfect. That being acknowledged, "gay" is not a terrible translation of what "homosexual" meant to many male and female homosexuals in the 1920s, when "homosexual" was a term of positive self-definition, an alternative to "pederast" (*Päderast*), although it differs, especially in that "homosexual" harkened to sexology. (Indeed, some of the leaders of the homosexual emancipation movement, such as Adolf Brand and Kurt Hiller, disliked "homosexual"; Brand and his circle preferred "homoerotic" as a noun.) Using "gay" together with historical terms moreover has the advantage of not normalizing the use of "homosexual" as a neutral term in the present, as "homosexual" has become an offensive and alienating term for many people in the contemporary moment. Therefore, I use "gay" throughout the study to designate people who termed themselves "homosexuals," "inverts," or "homoerotics." I use the historical terms as well. I hope that this will not confuse readers, but rather that in my use

of several terms they will perceive the attempt to make the past legible for the present, an attempt that will necessarily be flawed. See Clayton Whisnant, *Male Homosexuality in West Germany: Between Persecution and Freedom, 1945–69* (New York: Palgrave Macmillan, 2012), xii. Mine is not a standard approach; compare for example Stefan Micheler, *Selbstbilder und Fremdbilder der "Anderen": Männer begehrende Männer in der Weimarer Republik und der NS-Zeit* (Konstanz: UVK, 2005), 9–10.

14 By "queer," I mean sexualities and forms of gender expression deemed by hegemonic understandings to be outside of the boundaries of "normal": David Eng with Judith Halberstam and José Esteban Muñoz, "What's Queer about Queer Studies Now?" *Social Text* 23 (2005): 1–17. "Queer" is used ahistorically as a term of analysis, and yet, in the Weimar era, both conservative and left-leaning people understood the distinction between "moral" and "immoral," "normal" and "abnormal" sexualities as fundamental and did use terms like "abnormal" to describe sexual outsiders, including homosexuals and some prostitutes.

15 Regarding brain slides, fetish items, masturbation statistics, see "Aus der Bewegung," *JfsZ* 19 (January/April 1919): 55. For the other items, see Christopher Isherwood, *Christopher and His Kind* (New York: Farrar, Straus, Giroux, 1976), 16–17.

16 Isherwood, *Christopher*, 16–17.

17 Although Hirschfeld's homosexuality was something of an open secret, he was not, as Evans asserts, "openly homosexual": Richard Evans, *The Coming of the Third Reich* (New York: Penguin, 2003), 128. In the course of their investigation of the Institute, the Berlin police reported to Prussian officials that Hirschfeld was regarded in "general opinion" as having homosexual tendencies: Police to Prussian Welfare Minister, 24 July 1920, Geheimes Staatsarchiv Preußischer Kulturbesitz [GStAPK], I. HA Rep. 76 VIII B Nr. 2076, 7–8.

18 Kurt Hiller, "Sexualfreiheit und Proporz," *Vierteljahrsberichte des Wissenschaftlich-humanitären Komitees während der Kriegszeit* [*Vierteljahrsberichte*] 18 (April–July 1918): 83–7.

19 Ibid., 87. On proportional representation, see Thomas Childers, *The Nazi Voter: The Social Foundations of Fascism in Germany, 1919–1933* (Chapel Hill: University of North Carolina Press, 1983), 42.

20 Kurt Hiller, "Ethische Aufgaben der Homosexuellen," *JfsZ* 13, no. 4 (July 1913): 406–7.

21 Hirschfeld, *Homosexualität*, 1003. Mass declaration was also used by campaigners for abortion rights in 1931: Atina Grossmann, *Reforming Sex: The German Movement for Birth Control and Abortion Reform, 1920–1950* (New

York: Oxford University Press, 1997), 84, 86. In 1971, West German women used a similar tactic to challenge the criminalization of abortion: Ute Frevert, *Women in German History: From Bourgeois Emancipation to Sexual Liberation*, trans. Stuart McKinnon-Evans (Oxford: Berg, 1989), 294. Inspired by that abortion action, hundreds of gay men declared their sexuality in a national magazine in 1978: Bernhard Rosenkranz and Gottfried Lorenz, *Hamburg auf anderen Wegen: Die Geschichte des schwulen Lebens in der Hansestadt* (Hamburg: Lambda, 2005), 157.

22 Hirschfeld, *Homosexualität*, 1003–4.

23 Ibid., 973–7, 1004.

24 Matt Houlbrook, *Queer London: Perils and Pleasures in the Sexual Metropolis, 1918–1957* (Chicago: University of Chicago Press, 2005), 241–63.

25 For a review of the debate on whether homophile organizations were more radical than initial histories claimed, see David Churchill, "Transnationalism and Homophile Political Culture in the Postwar Decades," *GLQ: A Journal of Lesbian and Gay Studies* 15, no. 1 (2009): 33.

26 Lisa Duggan, "The New Homonormativity: The Sexual Politics of Neoliberalism," in *Materializing Democracy*, ed. Russ Castronovo and Dana D. Nelson (Durham, NC: Duke University Press, 2002), 179.

27 Robert Beachy, "The German Invention of Homosexuality," *Journal of Modern History* 82, no. 4 (2010), 801–38.

28 Jennifer Evans and Jane Freeland, "Rethinking Sexual Modernity in Twentieth-century Germany," *Social History* 37, no. 3 (2012): 317–18; this entire article is a useful discussion of work on sexuality and citizenship that informs this book.

29 Dickinson's article on crime statistics looks at several aspects of "immorality" together; on Dickinson's argument, see Conclusion, note 1. Edward Ross Dickinson, "Policing Sex in Germany, 1882–1982: A Preliminary Statistical Analysis," *Journal of the History of Sexuality* 16, no. 2 (2007): 204–50.

30 I use the conservatives' term rather than "abnormal" because "immoral" included a broader field and was more widely understood.

31 Gisela Bock, "Keine Arbeitskräfte in diesem Sinne," in *"Wir sind Frauen wie andere Auch!": Prostituierte und ihre Kämpfe*, ed. Pieke Biermann (Hamburg: Rowohlt, 1980), 70–106; Elisabeth Meyer-Renschhausen, "The Bremen Morality Scandal," in *When Biology Became Destiny: Women in Weimar and Nazi Germany*, ed. Renate Bridenthal, Atina Grossmann, and Marion Kaplan (New York: Monthly Review Press, 1984), 87–108; Grossmann, *Reforming Sex*; Michaela Freund-Widder, *Frauen unter Kontrolle: Prostitution und ihre staatliche Bekämpfung in Hamburg vom Ende des Kaiserreichs bis zu den Anfängen der Bundesrepublik* (Münster: Lit Verlag, 2003); Cornelie Usborne, *The Politics*

of the Body in Weimar Germany: Women's Reproductive Rights and Duties (Ann Arbor: University of Michigan Press, 1992); Usborne, *Cultures of Abortion in Weimar Germany* (New York: Berghahn, 2007); Victoria Harris, *Selling Sex in the Reich: Prostitutes in German Society, 1914–1945* (Oxford: Oxford University Press, 2010); Julia Roos, *Weimar through the Lens of Gender: Prostitution Reform, Women's Emancipation, and German Democracy, 1919–1933* (Ann Arbor: University of Michigan Press, 2010); Annette Timm, *The Politics of Fertility in Twentieth-century Berlin* (New York: Cambridge, 2010); Dorothy Rowe, *Representing Berlin: Sexuality and the City in Imperial and Weimar Germany* (Burlington, VT: Ashgate, 2003); Jill Suzanne Smith, *Berlin Coquette: Prostitution and the New German Woman, 1890–1933* (Ithaca, NY: Cornell University Press, 2013). There were also women who sold sex to women, but this form of sex work seems to have been a very small market and was almost entirely absent from public discussions of prostitution. For an example of an unusual personal ad in which a woman seeks a female client, see the ad by the Fraulein from Austria in *Die Freundin*, 27 January 1932. On female prostitutes with female clients, see also Ruth Margarete Roellig, "Lesbierinnen und Transvestiten," in *Das lasterhafte Weib*, ed. Agnes Eszterházy (Vienna: Verlag für Kulturforschung, 1930), 72.

32 The following list of prominent studies is by no means exhaustive: James Steakley, *The Homosexual Emancipation Movement in Germany* (Salem, NH: Ayer, 1993); Hans-Georg Stümke, *Homosexuelle in Deutschland: Eine Politische Geschichte* (Munich: Beck, 1989); *Eldorado: Homosexuelle Frauen und Männer in Berlin 1850–1950: Geschichte, Alltag und Kultur* (Berlin: Edition Heinrich, 1992); Marita Keilson-Lauritz, *Die Geschichte der eigenen Geschichte: Literatur und Literaturkritik in den Anfängen der Schwulenbewegung* (Berlin: Verlag Rosa Winkel, 1997); *Invertito: Jahrbuch für die Geschichte der Homosexualitäten* 2 (2000); Florian Mildenberger, *... in der Richtung der Homosexualität verdorben: Psychiater, Kriminalpsychologen und Gerichtsmediziner über männliche Homosexualität 1850–1970* (Hamburg: MännerschwarmSkript, 2002); Elke-Vera Kotowski and Julius H. Schoeps, eds., *Der Sexualreformer Magnus Hirschfeld: Ein Leben im Spannungsfeld von Wissenschaft, Politik und Gesellschaft* (Berlin: be.bra wissenschaft verlag, 2004); Ralf Dose, *Magnus Hirschfeld: Deutscher – Jude – Weltbürger* (Teetz: Hentrich & Hentrich, 2005); Micheler, *Selbstbilder und Fremdbilder*; Rosenkranz and Lorenz, *Hamburg auf anderen Wegen*; Jens Dobler, *Von anderen Ufern: Geschichte der Berliner Lesben und Schwulen in Kreuzberg und Friedrichshain* (Berlin: Bruno Gmünder Verlag, 2003); Jens Dobler, *Zwischen Duldungspolitik und Verbrechensbekämpfung: Homosexuellenverfolgung durch die Berliner Polizei von 1848 bis 1933* (Frankfurt: Verlag für Polizeiwissenschaft/Lorei, 2008); Elena Mancini, *Magnus Hirschfeld and the Quest for*

Sexual Freedom (New York: Palgrave Macmillan, 2010); Beachy, "German Invention." Those focused on the Republic are James Kollenbroich, *Our Hour Has Come: The Homosexual Rights Movement in the Weimar Republic* (Germany: VDM, 2007); Glenn Ramsey, "The Rites of Artgenossen: Contesting Homosexual Political Culture in Weimar Germany," *Journal of the History of Sexuality* 17 (2008): 85–109. Robert Beachy's *Gay Berlin: Birthplace of a Modern Identity* (New York: Alfred A. Knopf, 2014) was published when this book was in press and I am therefore unfortunately unable to engage with it.

33 Ilse Kokula, *Weibliche Homosexualität um 1900 in zeitgenössischen Dokumenten* (Munich: Verlag Frauenoffensive, 1981); Kokula, *Jahre des Glücks, Jahre des Leids: Gespräche mit älteren lesbischen Frauen: Dokumente* (Kiel: Frühlings Erwachen, 1986); Lillian Faderman and Brigitte Ericksson, *Lesbians in Germany: 1890's–1920's* (Tallahassee, FL: Naiad Press, 1990); Kirsten Plötz, *Einsame Freundinnen? Lesbisches Leben während der zwanziger Jahre in der Provinz* (Hamburg: MännerschwarmSkript Verlag, 1999); Claudia Schoppmann, *Der Skorpion: Frauenliebe in der Weimarer Republik* (Hamburg: Frühlings Erwachen, 1985); Schoppmann, "Vom Kaiserreich bis zum Ende des Zweiten Weltkrieges," in *In Bewegung bleiben: 100 Jahre Politik, Kultur und Geschichte von Lesben*, ed. Gabriele Dennert, Christiane Leidinger, and Franziska Rauchut (Berlin: Querverlag, 2007), 12–26; Heike Schader, *Virile, Vamps und wilde Veilchen: Sexualität, Begehren und Erotik in den Zeitschriften homosexueller Frauen im Berlin der 1920er Jahre* (Königstein im Taunus: Ulrike Helmer Verlag, 2004); Marti Lybeck, *Desiring Emancipation: New Women and Homosexuality in Germany, 1890–1933* (Albany: State University of New York Press, 2014); Lybeck, "Writing Love, Feeling Shame: Rethinking Respectability in the Weimar Homosexual Women's Movement," in *After "The History of Sexuality": German Genealogies With and Beyond Foucault*, ed. Scott Spector, Helmut Puff, and Dagmar Herzog (New York: Berghahn, 2012), 156–68; Katie Sutton, *The Masculine Woman in Weimar Germany* (New York: Berghahn, 2011), 90–125.

34 On transvestitism, see Rainer Herrn, *Schnittmuster des Geschlechts: Transvestitismus und Transsexualität in der frühen Sexualwissenschaft* (Gießen: Psychosozial-Verlag, 2005); Katie Sutton, "'We Too Deserve a Place in the Sun': The Politics of Transvestite Identity in Weimar Germany," *German Studies Review* 35, no. 2 (2012): 335–54; Sutton, *Masculine Woman*, 111–25. On male prostitution, see Martin Lücke, *Männlichkeit in Unordnung: Homosexualität und männliche Prostitution in Kaiserreich und Weimarer Republik* (Frankfurt: Campus, 2008).

35 The exception is Jens Dobler, "Zensur von Büchern und Zeitschriften mit homosexueller Thematik in der Weimarer Republik," *Invertito: Jahrbuch für die Geschichte der Homosexualitäten* 2 (2000): 85–104. For a citation of works on censorship and the Republic, see chapter 1.

36 Herbert Heinersdorf, "Akten zum Falle Röhm," *Mitteilungen des Wissen-schaftlich-humanitären Komitees* [*WhKM*], January/March 1932 and following.
37 Eng with Halberstam and Muñoz, "What's Queer," 3 (paraphrasing Michael Warner's introduction to *Fear of a Queer Planet*). See also Sharon Marcus, *Between Women: Friendship, Desire, and Marriage in Victorian England* (Princeton: Princeton University Press, 2007), 13.
38 Gerhard Ritter, *Europa und die deutsche Frage: Betrachtungen über die geschichtliche Eigenart des deutschen Staatsdenkens* (Munich: Münchner Verlag, 1948), 199.
39 Ritter, *Europa und die deutsche Frage*, 192.
40 For reviews of this revisionist wave and of the literature to which it responded, see Jochen Hung, "Beyond Glitter and Doom: The New Paradigm of Contingency in Weimar Research," in *Beyond Glitter and Doom: The Contingency of the Weimar Republic*, ed. Jochen Hung, Godela Weiss-Sussex, and Geoff Wilkes (Munich: IUDICIUM, 2012), 9–15; Nadine Rossol, "Chancen der Weimarer Republic," *Neue politische Literatur* 55, no. 3 (2010): 393–419.
41 A key work here is Karl-Dietrich Bracher's classic *Die Auflösung der Weimarer Republik: Eine Studie zum Problem des Machtverfalls in der Demokratie* (Ring: Stuttgart and Düsseldorf, 1955), which emphasizes constitutional weaknesses, though Bracher also spends a good deal of energy analysing events after 1930. Hans Mommsen, too, stresses factors present in 1919 – such as in his discussion of the Constitution: *The Rise and Fall of Weimar Democracy*, trans. Elborg Forster and Larry Eugene Jones (Chapel Hill: University of North Carolina Press, 1996), 87 – though he denies that fascist dictatorship was "inevitable" in 1919: *Rise and Fall*, vii. Peter Fritzsche also locates causality early in his argument about voter realignment in 1924–5: *Germans into Nazis* (Cambridge, MA: Harvard University Press, 1998), 160–1. For reviews of other works that emphasize early causation, see Anthony McElligott, *Rethinking the Weimar Republic: Authority and Authoritarianism 1916–1936* (London: Bloomsbury, 2014), 2.
42 Evans, *Coming of the Third Reich*, 77–153; Horst Möller, *Die Weimarer Republik: Eine unvollendete Demokratie* (Munich: Deutscher Taschenbuch Verlag, 2004), 255–86; Richard Bessel, *Germany after the First World War* (Oxford: Oxford University Press, 1993), 254–5.
43 Eberhard Kolb and Dirk Schumann, *Die Weimarer Republik* (Munich: Oldenbourg, 2013), 255–64. See also Peukert's famous call to study the Weimar period in its own right: Peukert, *Weimar Republic*, xii.
44 Eric Weitz, "Weimar Germany and Its Historians," *Central European History* 43 (2010): 581–91.
45 Kathleen Canning writes that the Republic's history "can neither be forgotten nor assigned significance in shaping the history that followed it":

"Introduction: Weimar Subjects/Weimar Publics: Rethinking the Political Culture of Germany in the 1920s," in *Weimar Publics/Weimar Subjects: Rethinking the Political Culture of Germany in the 1920s*, ed. Kathleen Canning, Kerstin Barndt, and Kristin McGuire (New York: Berghahn, 2010), 2.

46 Steakley, *Homosexual Emancipation*, 73; Herzer, *Hirschfeld*, 29–30.

47 McElligott, *Rethinking*, 1–2; McElligott, "Political Culture," in *Weimar Germany*, ed. Anthony McElligott (Oxford: Oxford University Press, 2009), 26–49; Dirk Schumann, *Political Violence in the Weimar Republic 1918–1933: Fight for the Streets and Fear of Civil War*, trans. Thomas Dunlap (New York: Berghahn, 2009), 305–6; Manuela Achilles, "With a Passion for Reason: Celebrating the Constitution in Weimar Germany," *Central European History* 43 (2010): 666–89; Michael Dreyer, "Weimar as a 'Militant Democracy,'" in *Beyond Glitter and Doom: The Contingency of the Weimar Republic*, ed. Jochen Hung, Godela Weiss-Sussex, and Geoff Wilkes (Munich: IUDICIUM, 2012), 69–86; Rossol, "Chancen."

48 Alexander Gallus, "Einleitung," in *Die vergessene Revolution von 1918/19*, ed. Alexander Gallus (Göttingen: Vandenhoeck & Ruprecht, 2010), 7–13; McElligott, *Rethinking*, 29–30; for a thorough review of the debate, see also Kolb and Schumann, *Weimarer Republik*, 166–78.

49 Thomas Mergel, *Parlamentarische Kultur in der Weimarer Republik: Politische Kommunikation, symbolische Politik und Öffentlichkeit im Reichstag* (Düsseldorf: Droste, 2005). Mergel argues, however, that in its functionality and civility the Reichstag did not accurately reflect German society and that ultimately in the Depression years this helped to undermine it: 479–80.

50 Eric Weitz, *Weimar Germany: Promise and Tragedy* (Princeton: Princeton University Press, 2007), 2. This is also true, arguably, about women, citizenship, and politics. See Canning's critique of arguments that assert that female citizenship did not change politics or gender relations: Canning, "Das Geschlecht der Revolution – Stimmrecht und Staatsbürgertum 1918/1919," in Gallus, *Die vergessene Revolution von 1918/19*, 84–116; Canning, "Claiming Citizenship: Suffrage and Subjectivity after the First World War," in Canning, Barndt, and McGuire, *Weimar Publics/Weimar Subjects*, 122–5.

51 For an analysis of this trend in recent publications, see chapter 6.

52 An example of this is the Centre Party's claim that the SPD acted "irresponsibly" in 1930. See p. 191.

53 Regarding unemployment insurance, see Mommsen, *Rise and Fall*, 226–7, 290–1; Donna Harsch, *German Social Democracy and the Rise of Nazism* (Chapel Hill: University of North Carolina Press, 1993), 51–9. Regarding welfare, see Crew, *Germans on Welfare*, 206; Young-Sun Hong, *Welfare, Modernity, and the Weimar State, 1919–1933* (Princeton: Princeton University Press, 1998), 6;

Edward Ross Dickinson, *The Politics of German Child Welfare from the Empire to the Federal Republic* (Cambridge, MA: Harvard University Press, 1996), 202.

54 See chapter 6.

55 Pamela Swett, *Neighbors and Enemies: The Culture of Radicalism in Berlin* (Cambridge: Cambridge University Press, 2004); Childers, *Nazi Voter.*

56 Mark Mazower, *Dark Continent: Europe's Twentieth Century* (New York: Vintage, 2000), 3–5.

57 Schumann, *Political Violence*, 313; Harsch, *German Social Democracy*; Weitz, *Weimar Germany*, 331–60; Detlef Junker, *Die Deutsche Zentrumspartei und Hitler 1932/33* (Stuttgart: Ernst Klett, 1969), 231.

58 "Achievement" is a reference to Weitz, who includes "sexual experimentation" among the "great achievements of Weimar": *Weimar Germany*, 331.

59 On homosexual emancipation's beginnings, see p. 24.

60 In 1917, the left wing of the SPD split off to form the Independent Socialist Party of Germany (*Unabhängige Sozialistische Partei Deutschlands*, USPD) because of the majority's support for the war. The USPD withdrew from the revolutionary interim government prior to the elections for the National Assembly (Eric Weitz, *Creating German Communism, 1890–1990: From Popular Protest to Socialist State* (Princeton: Princeton University Press, 1997), 86). Much of its membership went over to the new KPD. The USPD reunified with the Social Democratic Party in 1922 (Harsch, *German Social Democracy*, 19). Between 1917 and 1922, the SPD was known as the Majority Social Democrats (*Mehrheitssozialdemokratische Partei Deutschlands*, MSPD). However, because the split between MSPD and USPD does not come up in this book, to avoid confusion I do not use the MSPD designation and instead refer to the main Social Democratic Party as the SPD or "Social Democrats" in the period 1917–22.

61 Weitz, *Creating German Communism*, 234–43.

62 Quoted in Georg May, *Ludwig Kaas: Der Priester, der Politiker und der Gelehrte aus der Schule von Ulrich Stutz*, Vol. 3 (Amsterdam: B.R. Grüner, 1982), 9–10. On Stutz, see Michael Grüttner, "Der Lehrkörper 1918–1932," in *Geschichte der Universität Unter den Linden: Die Berliner Universität zwischen den Weltkriegen 1918–1945*, ed. Rüdiger vom Bruch and Heinz-Elmar Tenorth (Berlin: Akademie, 2012), 154.

63 "Aus der Bewegung," *JfsZ* 19 (January/April 1919): 58.

64 Ibid.

65 *Staatsbürger-Zeitung*, 10 August 1919. Wilhelm Bruhn, a member of the right wing of the German National People's Party (DNVP), edited the *Staatsbürger Zeitung*. Lewis Hertzman, *DNVP: Right-wing Opposition in the Weimar Republic, 1918–1924* (Lincoln: University of Nebraska Press, 1963).

66 GStAPK I. HA Rep. 76 VIII B Nr. 2076, 2–3.

67 McElligott, *Rethinking*, 130.

68 Statistischen Reichsamt, ed., *Statistisches Jahrbuch für das Deutsche Reich* (Berlin: Reimar Hobbing, 1926), 1.

69 Ibid.

70 I draw especially on Grossmann, *Reforming Sex*; Usborne, *Politics*; Usborne, *Cultures*.

71 Fatima El-Tayeb, *Schwarze Deutsche: Der Diskurs um "Rasse" und nationale Identität 1890–1933* (Frankfurt: Campus, 2001), 149–62.

72 Julia Roos, "Nationalism, Racism, and Propaganda in Early Weimar Germany: Contradictions in the Campaign against the 'Black Horror on the Rhine,'" *German History* 30, no. 1 (2012): 45–74; Roos, "Women's Rights, Nationalist Anxiety, and the 'Moral' Agenda in the Early Weimar Republic: Revisiting the 'Black Horror' Campaign against France's African Occupation Troops," *Central European History* 42, no. 3 (2009): 473–508.

73 Reiner Pommerin, *Sterilisierung der Rheinlandbastarde: Das Schicksal einer farbigen deutschen Minderheit 1918–1938* (Düsseldorf: Droste Verlag, 1979), 92–3.

74 Reichskolonialamt an den Königlich Preußischen Minister des Innern, June 1916, BArch R 1001/4457/6, 121.

75 Katharina Oguntoye, *Eine afro-deutsche Geschichte: Zur Lebenssituation von Afrikanern und Afro-Deutschen in Deutschland von 1884 bis 1950* (Berlin: Hoho, 1997), 21–3, 27–9. See also Peter Jelavich, *Berlin Cabaret* (Cambridge, MA: Harvard University Press, 1993), 165–75.

76 El-Tayeb, *Schwarze Deutsch*, 149–52.

77 Rowe, *Representing Berlin*; Sutton, *Masculine Woman*, 159–68.

78 Plötz, *Einsame Freundinnen?* 64–6, 84.

79 "Adressen-Verzeichnis einzelner Ortsgruppen des B.f.M., E.V.," *Blätter für Menschenrecht*, October/November 1932.

80 Sutton, *Masculine Woman*, 173–7.

81 Timm, *Politics*, 67–8. About Oktoberfest: Staatsarchiv München Pol. Dir. Nr. 4054, Report of 20 September 1922, "Überwachung der Ausstellung zur Hebung der Volksgesundheit und Bek. ansteckender Krankheiten auf der Oktoberfestwiese am 19. 9. 1922."

82 Usborne, *Cultures*, 26–53, 163–200, quotation at 163.

1 Homosexual Emancipation, Censorship, and the Revolution of 1918–1919

1 Stephan Heiß, "Die Polizei und Homosexuelle in München zwischen 1900 und 1933: Schlaglichter auf ein schwieriges Verhältnis zwischen Obrigkeit

und Subkultur," in *Polizeireport München*, ed. Michael Farin (Munich: Belleville, 1999), 194–207.

2 Münchner Freundschaftsbund, "Ziel und Zweck des Bundes," undated, Staatsarchiv München Pol. Dir. (Polizeidirektion Sachakten) Nr. 3573.

3 Linsert to Amtsgericht Registergericht, München, 31 January 1922, Staatsarchiv München Pol. Dir. Nr. 3573.

4 Polizeidirektion München an die Regierung von Oberbayern, Kammer des Innern, 28 February 1922, Staatsarchiv München Pol. Dir. Nr. 3573.

5 Entscheidung des Bayerischen Verwaltungsgerichtshofs, 11 October 1922, Staatsarchiv München Pol. Dir. Nr. 3573.

6 Max H. Danielsen, "Mehr Mut – mehr Idealismus," *Die Freundschaft* Nr. 18, Jahrg. 1 (1919).

7 Its first issue came out in August 1919: Hans Leu, "Ein Jahr siegreichen Kampfes!" *Die Freundschaft* Nr. 32, 14–20 August 1920.

8 Regarding Kassel: Entscheidung des Bayerischen Verwaltungsgerichtshofs, 11 October 1922, Staatsarchiv München Pol. Dir. Nr. 3573. For other places: "Komitee-Mitteilungen," *JfsZ* 20, nos. 3/4 (July/October 1920): 181. On the friendship leagues, see also Ramsey, "Rites"; Ramsey, "Erotic Friendship, Gender Inversion, and Human Rights in the German Movement for Homosexual Reform, 1897–1933" (PhD diss., Binghamton University, State University of New York, 2004).

9 Unfortunately space permits only a cursory look at imperial sex and gender politics. A selection of the considerable literature on the topic includes Dickinson, *Sex*; Dickinson, "'A Dark, Impenetrable Wall of Complete Incomprehension': The Impossibility of Heterosexual Love in Imperial Germany," *Central European History* 40 (2007): 467–97; Dickinson, "'Must We Dance Naked?': Art, Beauty, and Law in Munich and Paris, 1911–1913," *Journal of the History of Sexuality* 20 (January 2011): 95–131; Dickinson, "Biopolitics, Fascism, Democracy: Some Reflections on Our Discourse about 'Modernity,'" *Central European History* 37 (2004): 1–48; Dickinson, "Reflections on Feminism and Monism in the Kaiserreich, 1900–1913," *Central European History* 34 (2001): 191–230; Dickinson, "The Men's Christian Morality Movement in Germany, 1880–1914: Some Reflections on Politics, Sex, and Sexual Politics," *Journal of Modern History* 75 (2003): 59–110; Dickinson, "Domination of the Spirit over the Flesh: Religion, Gender and Sexual Morality in the German Women's Movement before World War I," *Gender & History* 17 (2005): 378–408; Dickinson, "Not So Scary After All? Reform in Imperial and Weimar Germany," *Central European History* 43 (2010): 149–72; Dickinson, "Policing Sex"; Dickinson, "Sex, Masculinity, and the 'Yellow Peril': Christian von Ehrenfels' Program for a Revision of

the European Sexual Order, 1902–1910," *German Studies Review* 25 (2002):
225–84; Andrew Lees, *Cities, Sin, and Social Reform in Imperial Germany* (Ann
Arbor: University of Michigan Press, 2002); Tracie Matysik, *Reforming the
Moral Subject: Ethics and Sexuality in Central Europe, 1890–1930* (Ithaca, NY:
Cornell University Press, 2008); Gary Stark, *Banned in Berlin: Literary Censor-
ship in Imperial Germany, 1871–1918* (New York: Berghahn, 2009); Philippe
Weber, *Der Trieb zum Erzählen: Sexualpathologie und Homosexualität, 1852–1914*
(Bielefeld: transcript, 2008); Ramsey, "Rites"; Ramsey, "Erotic Friendship";
Beachy, "German Invention"; Keilson-Lauritz, *Geschichte*; John Fout, "Sexual
Politics in Wilhelmine Germany: The Male Gender Crisis, Moral Purity, and
Homophobia," *Journal of the History of Sexuality* 2, no. 3 (1992): 388–421;
Fout, "The Moral Purity Movement in Wilhelmine Germany and the
Attempt to Regulate Male Behavior," *Journal of Men's Studies* 1 (1995): 5–32;
Ann Taylor Allen, "German Radical Feminists and Eugenics, 1900–1908,"
German Studies Review 11 (1988): 31–56; Taylor Allen, *Feminism and Motherhood in Germany 1800–1914* (New Brunswick, NJ: Rutgers University Press,
1991); Ute Planert, *Antifeminismus im Kaiserreich: Diskurs, soziale Formation
und politische Mentalität* (Göttingen: Vandenhoeck & Ruprecht, 1998);
Richard Evans, *The Feminist Movement in Germany, 1894–1933* (London: Sage,
1976); Kirsten Leng, "Contesting the 'Laws of Life': Feminism, Sexual Science and Sexual Governance in Germany and Britain, c. 1880–1914" (PhD
diss., University of Michigan, 2011).
10 Dickinson, *Sex*, 302.
11 Ibid., 314.
12 Dickinson, "Men's Christian Morality Movement," 75. There were however
limits to the SPD's support for the women's movement: Frevert, *Women*, 140–1.
13 Dickinson, "Men's Christian Morality Movement," 75; Dickinson, *Sex*, 144.
See also Dickinson, *Sex*, 137–51; Jean Quataert, *Reluctant Feminists in German
Social Democracy, 1885–1917* (Princeton: Princeton University Press, 1979).
14 Marion Kaplan, *The Jewish Feminist Movement in Germany: The Campaigns of the
Jüdischer Frauenbund, 1904–1938* (Westport, CT: Greenwood Press, 1979); Frevert, *Women*; Nancy Reagin, *A German Women's Movement: Class and Gender in
Hanover, 1880–1933* (Chapel Hill: University of North Carolina Press, 1995).
15 Frevert, *Women*, 113.
16 Dickinson, *Sex*, 44.
17 On the German Society for Combating Venereal Diseases, see Dickinson,
Sex, 177–89; Timm, *Politics*, 52–3.
18 "Guidelines of the German Association for the Protection of Mothers"
(1922), in *The Weimar Republic Sourcebook*, ed. Anton Kaes, Martin Jay, and
Edward Dimendberg (Berkeley: University of California Press, 1995), 697–8;
Dickinson, *Sex*, 190–241; Kristin McGuire, "Feminist Politics Beyond the

Reichstag: Helene Stöcker and Visions of Reform," in Canning, Barndt, and McGuire, *Weimar Publics/Weimar Subjects*, 138–52.

19 Matysik, *Reforming*, 55–78. On Stöcker's ideas see also Dickinson, *Sex*, 190–241; Dickinson, "Reflections on Feminism and Monism"; Ian Grimmer, "The Politics of *Geist*: German Intellectuals and Cultural Socialism, 1890–1920" (PhD diss., University of Chicago, 2010), 231–72.

20 Grossmann, *Reforming Sex*, 16–17, 56–7.

21 Grimmer, "Politics of *Geist*," 233, 256.

22 Helene Stöcker, "Havelock Ellis und sein Werk," *Die Neue Generation* 25, no. 2 (February 1929): 49–55, quotation at 51.

23 Ibid., 54.

24 Ramsey, "Erotic Friendship," 87–98; Manfred Herzer, "Opposition im 19. Jahrhundert," in *Goodbye to Berlin? 100 Jahre Schwulenbewegung* (Berlin: Verlag Rosa Winkel, 1997), 27.

25 Beachy, "German Invention," 810–13; Weber, *Der Trieb zum Erzählen.*

26 Karl Heinrich Ulrichs, *Forschungen über das Rätsel der mannmännlichen Liebe* (New York: Arno Press, 1975); Ulrichs, *The Riddle of "Man-Manly" Love: The Pioneering Work on Male Homosexuality*, trans. Michael A. Lombardi-Nash (Buffalo, NY: Prometheus Books, 1994); Hubert Kennedy, *Ulrichs* (Boston: Alyson, 1998).

27 Hirschfeld, *Homosexualität*, 973.

28 On this translation of *Der Eigene*, see Keilson-Lauritz, *Geschichte*, 74.

29 Richard Linsert and Kurt Hiller, eds., *Für Magnus Hirschfeld zu seinem 60. Geburtstage als Beigabe zu den "Mitteilungen" des W.H.K.E.V.* (Berlin: Verlage des Wissenschaftlich-humanitären Komitees, 1928), xxvii, reprinted in Walter v. Murat, ed. *Mitteilungen des Wissenschaftlich-humanitären Komitees 1926–1933* (Hamburg: C. Bell, 1985).

30 See also Dickinson, *Sex*, 162–3.

31 Keilson-Lauritz, *Geschichte*, 95; on this translation of "Eigene," see Keilson-Lauritz, *Geschichte*, 74.

32 "Komitee-Mitteilungen," *JfsZ* 14, no. 3 (July 1914): 373.

33 Kai Sommer, *Die Strafbarkeit der Homosexualität von der Kaiserzeit bis zum Nationalsozialismus* (Frankfurt: Peter Lang, 1998), 119–20; Herzer, *Hirschfeld*, 35–7.

34 Isabel Hull, *The Entourage of Kaiser Wilhelm II, 1888–1918* (Cambridge: Cambridge University Press, 1982); James Steakley, "Iconography of a Scandal: Political Cartoons and the Eulenburg Affair in Wilhelmin Germany," in *Hidden from History: Reclaiming the Gay and Lesbian Past*, ed. Martha Vicinus, Martin Duberman, and George Chauncey (New York: Meridian, 1989), 233–63; Norman Domeier, *Der Eulenburg-Skandal: Eine politische Kulturgeschichte des Kaiserreichs* (Frankfurt: Campus, 2010); Dickinson, *Sex*, 170–2.

35 Fout, "Moral Purity Movement"; Dickinson, "Men's Christian Morality Movement"; Dickinson, *Sex*, 13–113. There were also Jewish moral purity activists, but they only rarely appear in the literature. An example is found in Dickinson, *Sex*, 131.

36 Dickinson, *Sex*, 281.

37 Ibid., 58–76.

38 Dickinson, "Men's Christian Morality Movement," 64.

39 Ibid., 80; Robin Lenman, "Art, Society, and the Law in Wilhelmine Germany: The Lex Heinze," *Oxford German Studies* 8 (1973): 86–113, esp. 91.

40 Dickinson, "Men's Christian Morality Movement"; Gary Stark, "Pornography, Society, and the Law in Imperial Germany," *Central European History* 14 (1981): 211–12.

41 Dickinson, *Sex*, 282.

42 Ibid., 70–1, 111.

43 Ibid., 300, 314–15, 133.

44 Mary Louise Roberts, *Civilization without Sexes: Reconstructing Gender in Postwar France, 1917–1927* (Chicago: University of Chicago Press, 1994); Carolyn Dean, *The Frail Social Body: Pornography, Homosexuality, and Other Fantasies in Interwar France* (Berkeley: University of California Press, 2000); Joanna Bourke, *Dismembering the Male: Men's Bodies, Britain, and the Great War* (Chicago: University of Chicago Press, 1996); Victoria de Grazia, *How Fascism Ruled Women: Italy, 1922–1945* (Berkeley: University of California Press, 1992); Susan Kingsley Kent, *Making Peace: The Reconstruction of Gender in Interwar Britain* (Princeton: Princeton University Press, 1993).

45 Although Usborne's analysis of how this perception played out differs from my argument, she too describes a sense of rupture shared by Left and Right: *Politics*, 69–101; Cornelie Usborne, "The Christian Churches and the Regulation of Sexuality in Weimar Germany," in *Disciplines of Faith: Studies in Religion, Politics and Patriarchy*, ed. Jim Obelkevich, Lyndal Roper, and Raphael Samuel (London: Routledge & Kegan Paul, 1987), 100.

46 On this newspaper, see Donald Niewyk, *The Jews in Weimar Germany* (Baton Rouge: Louisiana State University Press, 1980), 166; Corey Ross, *Media and the Making of Modern Germany: Mass Communications, Society, and Politics from the Empire to the Third Reich* (Oxford: Oxford University Press, 2008), 148.

47 "Eros vor Gericht," *Kölnische Zeitung*, 23 April 1924.

48 On this see also Weitz, *Weimar Germany*, 328.

49 Dickinson, *Sex*, 14. On Weber, see Lees, *Cities, Sin, and Social Reform*, 84–8.

50 Quoted in Adolf Sellmann, *50 Jahre Kampf für Volkssittlichkeit und Volkskraft: Die Geschichte des Westdeutschen Sittlichkeitsvereins von seinen Anfängen bis heute (1885–1935)* (Schwelm [Westphalia]: G. Meiners, 1935), 70.

51 Lisa Todd, "'The Soldier's Wife Who Ran Away with the Russian': Sexual Infidelities in World War I Germany," *Central European History* 44 (2011): 257–78; Jason Crouthamel, *An Intimate History of the Front: Masculinity, Sexuality, and German Soldiers in the First World War* (New York: Palgrave Macmillan, 2014); Sellmann, *50 Jahre Kampf*, 73–9.

52 Sellmann, *50 Jahre Kampf*, 79.

53 Ibid., 81.

54 Dickinson, *Sex*, 58; for more on why, see 58–65.

55 Sellmann, *50 Jahre Kampf*, 81–2.

56 Ibid., 84.

57 "Kampf um die Volksmoral: Das presse-Echo der Braucht'schen Sittlichkeitserlasse," *Germania: Zeitung für das deutsche Volk* [hereafter *Germania*], 26 August 1932.

58 Quoted in F. Frank, "Der Zuhälter," *Die Weltbühne*, 1 September 1931, 325–8. See also "Verwilderung durch den Umsturz. Klassenjustiz und Sittlichkeit," *Volksstimme* (Frankfurt am Main) Nr. 48, 26 February 1930.

59 Max Bauer, "Die moderne Frau (Die neueste Zeit)," in Johannes Scherr, *Weib, Dame, Dirne: Kultur- und Sittengeschichte der deutschen Frau*, ed. Max Bauer (Dresden: Paul Aretz, 1928), 311–22.

60 "Die homosexuelle Seuche: Anmerkung zum Haarmannprozeß," *Völkischer Kurier* 28–9 (1924).

61 Timm, *Politics*, 80–1; Usborne, *Politics*, xi–xiv; Grossmann, *Reforming Sex*, 3–13.

62 Canning, "Introduction," 5. See also Rüdiger Graf, *Die Zukunft der Weimarer Republik: Krisen und Zukunftsaneignungen in Deutschland 1918–1933* (Munich: Oldenbourg, 2008).

63 Quoted in McGuire, "Feminist Politics Beyond the Reichstag," 145. See also McGuire's argument here about Stöcker's hopes for the Republic in its early phase.

64 Quoted in Manuela Achilles, "Reforming the Reich: Democratic Symbols and Rituals in the Weimar Republic," in Canning, Barndt, and McGuire, *Weimar Publics/Weimar Subjects*, 175–6.

65 Anna Mosegaard writing in *Die Gleichheit*, quoted in Roos, *Lens*, 144. Roos's translation.

66 "Eine Bubikopftragödie," *Die Freundin*, 15 April 1925.

67 Ibid.

68 Kokula, *Jahre*, 76.

69 Magnus Hirschfeld, "Situationsbericht," *Vierteljahrsberichte* 17 (October 1918–March 1919): 159–60.

70 Ruth Roellig, *Berlins lesbische Frauen* [1928], in Adele Meyer, ed., *Lila Nächte: Die Damenklubs im Berlin der Zwanziger Jahre* (Berlin: Edition Lit. Europe, 1994), 13.

71 Marie Weis, "Über die inneren Voraussetzungen der Anerkennung des transvestitischen Menschen seitens der Öffentlichkeit," *Garçonne* 2 (1931). On Weis, see Schader, *Virile*, 246.

72 Herrn, *Schnittmuster*, 143.

73 Hans-Walther Siegele, "Die Lösung des europäischen Problems," *Die Freundschaft* 16 (1919).

74 Kurt – Leipzig, "Von der Freiheit!" *Die Freundschaft* Nr. 6, Jahrg. 5, 10 February 1923.

75 S., "Aufhebung des §175?" *Die Freundschaft* Nr. 1, Jahrg. 1 (1919); O. Mann to Reich Justice Ministry, BArch R 3001/5774 (§175 1907–1929), 363; on Hirschfeld with respect to this issue, see the introduction.

76 WhK to Justice Ministry, 21 February 1919, BArch R 3001/5775, 121–2.

77 On the municipal level, see Grossmann, *Reforming Sex*, 13.

78 Ibid., 46–77.

79 The Lex Heinze affair is a good example of how conservatism did not reign prior to 1913. See Lenman, "Art, Society, and the Law in Wilhelmine Germany"; Stark, "Pornography."

80 On censorship of media with sexual content under the Republic, see also Dobler, "Zensur"; McElligott, *Rethinking*, 134–44; Margaret Stieg, "The 1926 German Law to Protect Youth against Trash and Dirt: Moral Protectionism in a Democracy," *Central European History* 23 (1990): 22–56; Klaus Petersen, "The Harmful Publications (Young Persons) Act 1926: Literacy, Censorship, and the Politics of Morality in the Weimar Republic," *German Studies Review* 15 (1992): 505–25. On the Republic's censorship of media without sexual content, see Dieter Breuer, *Geschichte der literarischen Zensur in Deutschland* (Heidelberg: Quelle und Meyer, 1982); Klaus Petersen, *Zensur in der Weimarer Republik* (Stuttgart: J.B. Metzler, 1995); Karl Christian Führer, "A Medium of Modernity? Broadcasting in Weimar Germany, 1923–1932," *Journal of Modern History* 69 (1997): 722–53; McElligott, *Rethinking*, 139–44.

81 Stark, *Banned*, 263–4; Ross, *Media*, 63–86; Lees, *Cities, Sin, and Social Reform*, 77–119; Kara Ritzheimer, "Protecting Youth from 'Trash': Anti-*Schund* Campaigns in Baden, 1900–1933" (PhD diss., Binghamton University, State University of New York, 2007).

82 I will not keep the words "filth" and "trash" or "filthy" and "trashy" in quotations throughout the book; I trust readers will understand that I have done so in order to avoid over-using quotation marks, not because I agree with these characterizations.

83 Breuer, *Geschichte der literarischen Zensur*, 210–18; Martin Kitchen, *The Silent Dictatorship: The Politics of the German High Command under Hindenburg and Ludendorff, 1916–1918* (New York: Holmes & Meier, 1976), 273–4; Ross, *Media*, 70–5.

84 Stark, *Banned*, 266.
85 Belinda Davis, *Home Fires Burning: Food, Politics, and Everyday Life in World War I Berlin* (Chapel Hill: University of North Carolina Press, 2000), 104–5; Gary Stark, "All Quiet on the Home Front: Popular Entertainments, Censorship, and Civilian Morale in Germany, 1914–1918," in *Authority, Identity and the Social History of the Great War*, ed. Frans Coetzee and Marilyn Shevin-Coetzee (Providence, RI: Berghahn, 1995), 57–80.
86 Berlin police list of publications banned by military order in April 1916, GStAPK I. HA Rep. 77 Tit. 380 Nr. 7 Bd. 11; "Nachtrag zu unserer Berichten 'Aus der Kriegszeit,'" *Vierteljahrsberichte* 17 (October 1918–March 1919); Reichsminister des Innern, report on meeting on Schundliteratur, 23 October 1919, GStAPK I. Rep 84a Justizministerium (D) Nr. 1998, Bd. 1.
87 Usborne, *Politics*, 21.
88 Von Jacobi's comments, 14 October 1919 meeting on Schund, BArch R 3001/6216.
89 Reichsminister des Innern an den Reichstag, Entwurf eines Gesetzes zu Bewahrung der Jugend vor Schund- und Schmutzschriften, Berlin, 6 August 1925, *Verhandlungen des Reichstags*, Wahlperiode 1924/1925, Band 404, Nr. 1461.
90 Paul Lerch, Berliner Verein zur Bekämpfung der öffentlichen Unsittlichkeit to Interior Ministry, 2 September 1919, GStAPK I. HA Rep. 77 Tit. 380 Nr. 7 Bd. 11, 455–6; Lerch to Interior Ministry, 15 September 1919, GStAPK I. HA Rep. 77 Tit. 380 Nr. 7 Bd. 11, 457–8; September 1919 report, Polizeipräsidium Berlin, Div. III, GStAPK I. HA Rep. 77 Tit. 380 Nr. 7 Bd. 11, 464–6.
91 Polizeipräsidium to Interior Ministry, 30 October 1919, GStAPK I. HA Rep. 77 Tit. 2772 Nr. 2 Bd. 1.
92 Modris Eksteins, *The Limits of Reason: The German Democratic Press and the Collapse of Weimar Germany* (Oxford: Oxford University Press, 1975), 70–1; James Steakley, "Cinema and Censorship in the Weimar Republic: The Case of *Anders als die Andern*," *Film History* 11, no. 2 (1999): 189–90.
93 Usborne, "Christian Churches," 100.
94 Berlin POLUNBI report, 5 April 1919, Staatsarchiv München Pol. Dir. Nr. 7420.
95 GStAPK I. HA Rep. 77 Tit. 2772 Nr. 2 Bd. 1. See also the report on the meeting on Schundliteratur, 23 October 1919, GStAPK I. Rep. 84a Nr. 1998, 268–71.
96 Steakley, "Cinema and Censorship," 188. On *Anders als die Andern* see also Peter Jelavich, *Berlin Alexanderplatz: Radio, Film, and the Death of Weimar Culture* (Berkeley: University of California Press, 2006), 139–42.
97 Steakley, "Cinema and Censorship," 191.

98 "Der Kampf gegen den Schmutzfilm," *Frankfurter Zeitung* 2 November 1919; "Wer hat die 'Aufklärungs'-Filme eingeführt?" *Der Tag*, 17 January 1920.

99 Steakley, "Cinema and Censorship," 189.

100 Gary Stark, "Aroused Authorities: State Efforts to Regulate Sex and Smut in the German Mass Media, 1880–1930" (paper presented at Popular Sex: Mass Media and Sexuality in Germany, University of Calgary, Calgary, Alberta, 7–9 January 2011), 18.

101 For information on Brunner, see Steakley, "Cinema and Censorship," 191; Ross, *Media*, 67–70; Dickinson, *Sex*, 32–3.

102 Karl Brunner, "Ein verkehrtes Gesetz," *Deutsche Allgemeine Zeitung*, 2 June 1928.

103 Dickinson, *Sex*, 30–42.

104 W.H. Bruford, *The German Tradition of Self-Cultivation: "Bildung" from Humboldt to Thomas Mann* (Cambridge: Cambridge University Press, 1975); Jennifer Jenkins, *Provincial Modernity: Local Culture and Liberal Politics in Fin-de-Siècle Hamburg* (Ithaca, NY: Cornell University Press, 2003); Stark, *Banned*, 261.

105 "Filmzensur," *Dresdner Anzeiger*, 28 February 1920.

106 Berliner Verein zur Bekämpfung der öffentlichen Unsittlichkeit to Prussian Justice Ministry, 12 March 1920, GStAPK I. HA Rep. 84 a Nr. 8100, 1911–27.

107 Königsberg to Ministerium for Kunst, 5 July 1919, GStAPK I. HA Rep. 77 Tit. 380 Nr. 7 Bd. 11, 434.

108 Leicht and comrades, Antrag, 15 January 1925, *Verhandlungen des Reichstags*, Wahlperiode 1924, Band 398, Nr. 346.

109 Prussian Landtag, Grobe Anfrage Nr. 43, 3 April 1925, Porsch et al. GStAPK I. HA Rep. 84 a. Nr. 8100, 349.

110 Prussian Ministry of the Interior to Porsch et al., 27 June 1925, GStAPK I. HA Rep. 84 a. Nr. 8100, 351–6.

111 Grzesinski, 20 April 1926, GStAPK I. HA Rep. 84 a. Nr. 8100, 362–7. See also a similar exchange in 1927: GStAPK I. HA Rep. 84 a. Nr. 8100, 232–41.

112 Stieg, "1926 German Law," 33–4; Steakley, "Cinema and Censorship," 190.

113 Stark, *Banned*, 191.

114 Usborne, "Christian Churches," 105; Usborne, *Politics*, 11.

115 Stark, *Banned*, 195.

116 Eksteins, *Limits*, 70–2; Dennis E. Showalter, *Little Man, What Now? Der Stürmer in the Weimar Republic* (Hamden, CT: Archon Books, 1982), 52–3; Bernhard Fulda, *Press and Politics in the Weimar Republic* (Oxford: Oxford University Press, 2009), 62.

117 Steakley, "Cinema and Censorship," 189–92.

118 Ibid., 191–2. Though Moll had been an ally of homosexual emancipation in the imperial period, he turned against the movement. See Dickinson, *Sex*, 155–6, 171, 250, 275. On Placzek, see "Siegfried Placzek, Neurologist, Dies: German-Born Pioneer in Study of Effects of Altitudes also Was Sexology Authority," *New York Times*, 9 March 1946.

119 Ross, *Media*, 78–81.

120 Führer, "A Medium of Modernity?" 722–53; Steakley, "Cinema and Censorship."

121 See Stieg, "1926 German Law"; Petersen, "The Harmful Publications (Young Persons) Act 1926."

122 Stieg, "1926 German Law."

123 "'Ecce Homo' unter Anklange!" *Vorwärts*, 3 January 1924; "Der Kampf gegen Georg Groß," *Vossische Zeitung*, 3 January 1924; "Unzüchtigkeit aus lauteren Motiven," *Vorwärts*, 1 November 1921; Stieg, "1926 German Law," 39.

124 Paul Fechter, "Die Freiheit der Kunst," *Deutsche Allgemeine Zeitung*, 10 October 1925; "Eine 'Lex Heinze' in Sicht?" *Berliner Tageblatt*, 14 January 1921; Wolfgang Heine, "Zurück zur Zensur. Eine Warnung," *Vossische Zeitung*, 11 November 1925.

125 Stieg, "1926 German Law," 47.

126 Ibid., 52–5; Brunner, "Ein verkehrtes Gesetz."

127 See the proceedings of the Munich board – GStAPK I. HA Rep. 77 Tit. 2772 Nr. 3f – and those of the Berlin board – GStAPK I. HA Rep. 77 tit. 2772 Nr. 3e Bd. 1; GStAPK I. HA Rep. 77 tit. 2772 Nr. 3E Bd. 2.

128 Staatsarchiv München Pol. Dir. 7331; Staatsarchiv München Pol. Dir. 7419.

129 Nr. 772, Reichstag IV, Wahlperiode 1928, *Verhandlungen des Reichstags*, Band 434.

130 Peter Jelavich, "Paradoxes of Censorship in Modern Germany," in *Enlightenment, Passion, Modernity: Historical Essays in European Thought and Culture*, ed. Mark S. Micale and Robert L. Dietle (Stanford: Stanford University Press, 2000), 273; McElligott, *Rethinking*, 135–6; Paul Schleisinger, "Nachttänze," *Vossische Zeitung*, 23 January 1922.

131 A. Hellwig, "Der Kampf gegen die Schundfilme," *Der Tag*, 18 October 1919.

132 Corey Ross, *Media and the Making of Modern Germany: Mass Communications, Society, and Politics from the Empire to the Third Reich* (Oxford: Oxford University Press, 2008), 73–4.

133 Hellwig, "Der Kampf gegen die Schundfilme."

134 McElligott, "Political Culture," 26.

135 See the letters sent in the fall of 1918 to the Prussian Interior Ministry from municipal authorities in Köningsberg, Allenstein, Marienwerder, Potsdam, Frankfurt an der Oder, Stettin, Köslin, Stralsund, Bromberg, and

a number of other cities, all in GStAPK I. HA Rep. 77 Tit. 380 Nr. 7 Fasz. zu Bd. 11.

136 "Die Mucker triumphieren," *Die Rote Fahne*, 1 November 1921.

137 "Der beleidigte Professor Brunner," *Berliner Tageblatt*, 2 June 1923.

138 "Gegen jüdische Verleumdung," *Deutsche Zeitung*, 27 April 1923; "Aus dem Freistaat Preußen," *Das Deutsche Tageblatt*, both collected in GStAPK I. HA Rep. 77 Tit. 2772 Nr. 5 Beiakten 1.

139 "Betreff: Czudnochowsky," 9 November 1931; see also the response by officials in the Prussian Justice Ministry and other bureaucrats: GStAPK I. HA Rep. 84a Nr. 8101 Bd. X, 99–113. On the case against the Mosse publishing company in 1931, see GStAPK I. HA Rep. 84a Nr. 8101 Bd. X, 171 and following.

140 Sellmann, *50 Jahre Kampf*, 84. This term, which can also be translated as "usury," often had an antisemitic connotation: Nicola Wenge, *Intergration und Ausgrenzung in der Städtischen Gesellschaft: Eine Jüdisch-Nichtjüdische Beziehungsgeschichte Kölns 1918–1933* (Mainz: Phillip von Zabern, 2005), 298.

141 Berliner Verein zur Bekämpfung der öffentlichen Unsittlichkeit, 2 September 1919, to Prussian Interior Ministry, GStAPK I. HA Rep. 77 Tit. 380 Nr. 7 Bd. 11, 455–6. See also Steakley, "Cinema and Censorship," 190–1.

142 Dickinson, *Sex*, 72–4, 112.

143 On how the war changed homosexual emancipation, see also Crouthamel, *Intimate History of the Front*, 128–45.

144 For example, see Hirschfeld on Krafft-Ebing's argument about this: *Homosexualität*, 969.

145 Canning, "Claiming Citizenship," 117. See also Kathleen Canning, "'Sexual Crisis' and the Writing of Citizenship and the State of Emergency in Germany, 1917–1920," in *Staats-Gewalt: Ausnahmezustand und Sicherheitsregimes: Historische Perspektiven*, ed. Alf Lüdtke and Michael Wildt (Göttingen: Wallstein, 2008), 168–211.

146 Davis, *Home Fires*, 238. See also Ute Daniel, *Arbeiterfrauen in der Kriegsgesellschaft: Beruf, Familie und Politik im Ersten Weltkrieg* (Göttingen: Vandenhoeck & Ruprecht, 1989).

147 "Aus der Kriegszeit (IV. Teil)," *Vierteljahresberichte*, October 1915, 103–19, quotation at 116.

148 "Aus der Kriegszeit (VI. Teil)," *Vierteljahresberichte*, April 1916, 51–65, quotations at 55, 60.

149 Hans Georg, "Der Invertierte und die Politik," *Der Freund* [*Freundschaft*] Nr. 3 Jahrgang 1 [1919].

150 "Anträge zum Bundestag," *Blätter für Menschenrecht* Nr. 4, 1 April 1923.

151 Danielsen, for example, had ties to the WhK: Max H. Danielsen, "Mehr Mut – mehr Idealismus," *Die Freundschaft* Nr. 18, Jahrgang 1 [1919].

152 Magnus Hirschfeld with Richard Linsert, "Die Homosexualität," in *Sittengeschichte des Lasters: Die Kulturepochen und Ihre Leidenschaften*, ed. Leo Schidrowitz (Vienna and Leipzig: Verlag für Kulturforschung, 1927), 309. Linsert may have been convinced of this by 1927 after his experience with the League for Human Rights in the early 1920s.

153 Ramsey, "Rites," 95, 100; Andreas Sternweiler, "Die Freundschaftsbühne – eine Massenbewegung," in *Goodbye to Berlin?* 95–104. See also Ramsey, "Erotic Friendship."

154 Landesarchiv Berlin [LA] A Rep. 358–01 Mf. Nr. A 836–837; GStAPK I. HA Rep. 77 tit. 2772 Nr. 3E Bd. 1, 27–31. The League for Human Rights, run for most of its lifetime by Friedrich Radszuweit, ought not to be confused with the German League for Human Rights (*Deutsche Liga für Menschenrechte*), a leftist pacifist and human rights group with which Hiller was affiliated. See Otto Lehmann-Russbüldt, *Der Kampf der Deutschen Liga für Menschenrechte, vormals Bund Neues Vaterland, für den Weltfrieden 1914–1927* (Berlin: Hensel & Co, 1927).

155 Hans Janus, "Wen wählen wir?" *Die Freundschaft* Nr. 21 (1920); René Stelter, "Politik," *Die Freundschaft* Nr. 8, Jahrgang 5, 19 May 1923.

156 Ramsey, "Rites," 94. See also Steakley, *Homosexual Emancipation*, 74–6.

157 Hirschfeld quoted in Steakley, *Homosexual Emancipation*, 78. Steakley's translation.

158 Max H. Danielsen, "Unsere Presse," *Die Freundschaft* Nr. 17, 1–7 May 1920; Hans Leu, "Ein Jahr siegreichen Kampfes!" *Die Freundschaft* Nr. 32, 14–20 August 1920.

159 Hans Leu, "Die gesellschaftliche Ächtung," *Die Freundschaft* Nr. 9, 1920 (26 February–3 March).

160 "Briefkasten," *Die Freundschaft* 1, no. 2 [1919].

161 Willi Sagen, "Die Jugendfreunde," *Die Freundschaft* 2, no. 1 [1919].

162 Hirschfeld with Linsert, "Die Homosexualität," in Schidrowitz, *Sittengeschichte des Lasters*, 310.

163 Beachy, "German Invention"; Stark, *Banned*, 192–3.

164 Keilson-Lauritz, *Geschichte*, 99. See also Stark, "Pornography, Society, and the Law," 222–6. Initially, Brand's magazine had a public circulation, but after two convictions for obscenity, he and others founded the *Gemeinschaft der Eigenen* and restricted the magazine's circulation to members. The need to have a closed circle of readers, which made the magazine less onerous to police, was the purpose of founding the *Gemeinschaft*: Keilson-Lauritz, *Geschichte*, 95. See also Keilson-Lauritz's discussion of Adolf Brand's three obscenity trials: *Geschichte*, 85–99. For a more detailed examination of how late-imperial Germany's censorship policies differed from those of the Weimar Republic, see Laurie Marhoefer, "'The Book Was a

Revelation, I Recognized Myself in It': Lesbian Sexuality, Censorship, and the Queer Press in Weimar-era Germany," *Journal of Women's History* 27 (2015): 64–7.

165 Dickinson, *Sex*, 161.

166 "Nachtrag zu unserer Berichten 'Aus der Kriegszeit,'" *JfsZ* 17 (October 1918–March 1919).

167 Auswärtiges Amt to Ministry of Interior, 26 August 1919, GStAPK I. HA Rep. 77 Tit. 380 Nr. 7 Bd. 11, 462.

168 Karl Schultz, "Die 'Freundschaft' verboten! Warum?" *Der Freund* Nr. 3 Jahrgang 1 (1919).

169 Karl Schultz, "*Die Freundschaft* freigegeben!" *Die Freundschaft* Nr. 14, 1919.

170 GStAPK I. HA Rep. 77 Tit. 380 Nr. 7 adhib. 3, 46–55.

171 Reich Economics Ministry to Reich Interior Ministry, 18 May 1920, GStAPK I. HA Rep. 77 Tit. 380 Nr. 7 adhib. 3, 46; Hirsch, Reich Economics Ministry, to Prussian Ministry of Interior, 22 October 1920, GStAPK I. HA Rep. 77 Tit. 380 Nr. 7 adhib. 3, 59–60.

172 Polizeipräsident to Ministry of Interior, 8 September 1920, GStAPK I. HA Rep. 77 Tit. 380 Nr. 7 adhib. 3, 49–50.

173 Polizeipräsident, Abteilung III, POLUNBI, to Ministry of Interior, 24 December 1920, GStAPK I. HA Rep. 77 Tit. 380 Nr. 7 adhib. 3, 66–9; see also the offending issue of *Der Galgen* at 20–3.

174 Polizeipräsident Abteilung III (Szczesny and Brunner) to Ministry of Interior, 4 November 1920, GStAPK I. HA Rep. 77 Tit. 380 Nr. 7 adhib. 3, 61–2.

175 Brunner an Medizinabteilung, 23 December 1920. GStAPK I. HA Rep. 76 VIII B Nr. 2076, 15.

176 An Polizeipräsidenten, 26 January 1921, GStAPK I. HA Rep. 76 VIII B Nr. 2076, 19–22.

177 Ibid.

178 Mildenberger, … *in der Richtung der Homosexualität verdorben*, 111.

179 Gert Hekma, Harry Ooterhuis, and James Steakley, "Leftist Sexual Politics and Homosexuality: A Historical Overview," *Journal of Homosexuality* 29, nos. 2–3 (1995): 22; Albert Moll, *Behandlung der Homosexualität: Biochemisch oder psychisch?* (Bonn: A. Marcus & E. Weber, 1921), 35.

180 Quoted in "Die Verhandlungen des Strafrechtsausschusses des deutschen Reichstages über die Strafwürdigkeit der Homosexualität" (85. Sitzung, 16 October 1929), *WhKM* Nr. 24, September/October 1929, 182–3.

181 Ratibor Hahn et al., *§175 muß bleiben! Denkschrift des Verbandes zur Bekämpfung der öffentlichen Unsittlichkeit an den Deutschen Reichstag* (Cologne: Koltz & Kreuder, 1927), 32–3 (in GStAPK I. HA Rep. 84a Nr. 8101 Bd. X). The age of consent for girls was sixteen years.

182 Elizabeth Harvey, *Youth and the Welfare State in Weimar Germany* (Oxford: Clarendon Press, 1993), 103; Swett, *Neighbors and Enemies*, 117–19; Detlev Peukert, *Grenzen der Sozialdisziplinierung: Aufstieg und Krise der deutschen Jugendfürsorge von 1878 bis 1932* (Cologne: Bund, 1986), 166–7.

183 For example, Ratibor Hahn, "Die Irrlehre der Homosexuellen," in Hahn et al., *§175 muß bleiben!*, 32–3 (in GStAPK I. HA Rep. 84a Nr. 8101 Bd. X).

184 Siegfried Placzek, *Homosexualität und Recht* (Leipzig: Georg Thieme, 1925), 11.

185 Ibid., 81.

186 Ibid., 60–1.

187 Ibid., 60–1.

188 Hahn, "Die Irrlehre der Homosexuellen," 31.

189 Ibid., 37. The Haarmann case was used by a number of opponents of homosexual emancipation: Sommer, *Strafbarkeit*, 194–5.

190 Hahn, "Die Irrlehre der Homosexuellen," 22–3, quoting Placzek, *Homosexualität*, 60, 136, where Placzek quotes Berlin Criminal Commissioner von Tresokow.

191 Hahn, "Die Irrlehre der Homosexuellen," 30.

192 Anna Clark, *Desire: A History of European Sexuality* (New York: Routledge, 2008), 143–4; Erin Carlston, "Secret Dossiers: Sexuality, Race, and Treason in Proust and the Dreyfus Affair," *Modern Fiction Studies* 48, no. 4 (2002): 937–68; Leela Gandhi, *Affective Communities: Anticolonial Thought, Fin-de-Siècle Radicalism, and the Politics of Friendship* (Durham, NC: Duke University Press, 2006), 51.

193 Max Danielsen, "Der 2tägige Prozess gegen die 'Freundschaft,'" *Die Freundschaft*, 2–8 July 1921.

194 Moll, *Behandlung*, 22; Iwan Bloch, *The Sexual Life of Our Time*, trans. M. Eden Paul (New York: Falstaff Press, 1937) [German edition 1907], 455–66, 533.

195 Dobler, "Zensur," 103.

196 Danielsen, "Der 2tägige Prozess."

197 Prussian Justice Ministry to Reich Interior Ministry, 22 September 1931; meeting report 19 October 1931; Prussian Justice Ministry, 1 October 1931; all in GStAPK I. HA Rep. 84a Nr. 8101 Bd. X. On the campaigns against the "small advertisements," see in addition GStAPK I. HA Rep. 77 Tit. 2772 Nr. 11 Bd. 1; GStAPK I. HA Rep. 77 Tit. 380 Nr. 7 adhib. 3, among others. It was the Lex Heinze that made these prosecutions for pimping possible: Stark, "Pornography, Society, and the Law."

198 Meeting report 19 October 1931, GStAPK I. HA Rep. 84a Nr. 8101 Bd. X, 110–12.

199 "Was ist unzüchtig? 'Solange 175 St.-G.-B. besteht …'!" *Volks Zeitung* 7 January 1922, in GStAPK I. HA Rep. 77 Tit. 380 Nr. 7 adhib. 3, 117.

200 Reichsgericht decision, GStAPK I. HA Rep. 77 Tit. 380 Nr. 7 adhib. 3, 130–46.

201 Danielsen, "Der 2tägige Prozess."

202 Walter Bahn, "Bericht: Der Prozeß gegen die 'Freundschaft,'" *Die Freundschaft*, 19 May 1923.

203 René Stelter, "Unser Weg: Zur Einstellung der 'Freundschaft,'" *Die Freundschaft*, 5 May 1923; Bahn, "Bericht."

204 Friedrich Radszuweit, "Unsere Stunde ist gekommen!" *Blätter für Menschenrecht*, 15 February 1923; "Nachrichten des Hauptvorstandes," *Blätter für Menschenrecht*, 15 February 1923; Falk, "Nachricht des Hauptvorstandes zum Bundestag," *Blätter für Menschenrecht*, 15 March 1923.

205 Paul Weber, "Friedrich Radszuweit ist tot," *Die Freundin*, 13 April 1932.

206 "Filth and Trash Law" boards did use these criteria, however.

207 Walter, "Er kam zu mir des Nachts," *Freundschaft* Nr. 13 [1920 or 1921]. Reprinted in the Reichsgericht decision on *Freundschaft*: GStAPK I. HA Rep. 77 Tit. 380 Nr. 7 adhib. 3, 130–46.

208 GStAPK I. HA Rep. 77 Tit. 2772 Nr. 6 Bd. 1, 154–8; Schader, *Virile*, 44.

209 Dobler, "Zensur," 102. An exception to this is the 1931 prosecution of Hirschfeld's *Moral History of the World War* (*Sittengeschichte des Weltkrieges*), discussed in chapter 6.

210 Schneider, Ministerium für Volkswohlfahrt, 19 May 1928, GStAPK I. HA Rep. 77 Tit. 2772 Nr. 3D Bd. 2.

211 Kokula, *Jahre*, 78–9.

212 Dobler, "Zensur," 101.

213 Dickinson, "Policing Sex," 224–5; Stümke, *Homosexuelle in Deutschland*, 90–1.

214 Compare Dickinson, "Policing Sex."

215 Heiß, "Die Polizei," 196.

216 "In Erpresserhänden," *Berliner Stadtblatt*, 23 December 1926.

217 See chapter 2.

218 POLUNBI 1925 report, Staatsarchiv München Pol. Dir. 7419.

219 Magnus Hirschfeld, "Die männliche Prostitution," in *§ 297.3 "Unzucht Zwischen Männern"? Ein Beitrag zur Strafgesetzreform*, ed. Richard Linsert (Berlin: Neuer Deutscher Verlag, 1929), 22.

220 Weigand, report of 27 August 1921, Staatsarchiv München Pol. Dir. 7983.

221 Gerthard Daniel to Hintermeister, undated [1921], Staatsarchiv München Pol. Dir. 7983.

222 Linsert to the Amtsgericht Registergericht, München, 31 January 1922, Staatsarchiv München Pol. Dir. 3573.

223 For more on which acts Paragraph 175 covered, see chapter 2.
224 Polizeidirektion München an die Regierung von Oberbayern, Kammer des Innern, 28 February 1922, Staatsarchiv München Pol. Dir. Nr. 3573.
225 "Aufruf!" *Blätter für Menschenrecht*, 15 March 1923.
226 Falk, "Nachricht des Hauptvorstandes zum Bundestag."
227 "Anträge der Ortsgruppen," *Blätter für Menschenrecht*, 15 March 1923.
228 Friedrich Radszuweit and Paul Weber to Jeckel, 3 November 1923, Staatsarchiv München Pol. Dir. 3573.

2 Lesbianism, Reading, and Law

1 Vitho, "Hilde," *Die Freundin*, 3 December 1930.
2 Curt Moreck, *Führer durch das "lasterhafte" Berlin* (Leipzig: Verlag moderner Stadtführer, 1996 [1931]); G.F. Salmony, "Kaschemmenbummel mit Bancroft," *BZ am Mittag*, 18 October 1929. Portions of this chapter were included in Marhoefer, "'The Book Was a Revelation.'" Thanks to the *Journal of Women's History* for permission to reprint. This book's cover image is a drawing by Paul Kamm for Moreck's *Führer*.
3 A note about the terms "lesbian" and "transvestite": female authors in the Weimar years who wrote about women's same-sex sexuality, and who themselves had relationships with women, often called themselves by terms that had special meaning in their subcultures but vaguer meaning in the world beyond. These included "girlfriend" and "one of the 'others.'" They less frequently used terms that circulated in the wider public discourse on female same-sex sexualities in sexology and popular media such as the "moral histories" (*Sittengeschichte*). These included "female homosexual," "lesbian woman," and rarely, "lesbian" (*Lesbierin*; see Roellig, "Lesbierinnen und Transvestiten," 67–80). In short, the women I am writing about used "lesbian," but they did so rarely. However, I am writing on the other side of a movement in English to claim "lesbian" as a term of positive self-identification. For my readers, it is a relatively close translation of "girlfriend." Therefore, I use it. For a different approach, albeit about the imperial period, see Tracie Matysik, "In the Name of the Law: The 'Female Homosexual' and the Criminal Code in Fin de Siècle Germany," *Journal of the History of Sexuality* 13, no. 1 (2004): 27n4. Also compare Lybeck, *Desiring*, 10–12. "Transvestite" had a flexible meaning in the 1920s. It was used to self-identify by people who were in transition from their birth sex to their true sex. It was also used by people who cross-dressed or had nonconformist gender presentations but who were not transitioning from one sex to another. On the category "transvestite," see pp. 59–61.

4 On the Weimar-era lesbian subcultures, see also especially Lybeck, *Desiring*, 151–88; Schader, *Virile*; Plötz, *Einsame Freundinnen?*

5 Schader, *Virile*, 61.

6 Ibid., 41.

7 In two cases, women ran the entire operation: Selli Engler's *Blätter Idealer Frauenfreundschaft* and the final 1932 issues of *Garçonne* (see below): Schader, *Virile*, 59–60, 74–5. Engler's magazine eluded archiving: Schader, *Virile*, 74–5.

8 For circulation information, see Radszuweit's lawyer's statement, Berlin board session of 24 April 1928, GStAPK I. HA Rep. 77 tit. 2772 Nr. 3E Bd. 1, 85–90.

9 Schader, *Virile*, 43–4, 51.

10 Decision of 21 April 1931, Prüfstelle in Berlin für Schund- und Schmutzschriften, GStAPK I. HA Rep. 77 tit. 2772 Nr. 3E Bd. 2.

11 Schader, *Virile*, 59–60. Schader thinks there may be more publications, now lost, that were not linked to the two large organizations, the League for Human Rights and DFV: *Virile*, 42n1.

12 Roellig, *Berlins lesbische Frauen*, 11–55.

13 On Roellig, see Claudia Schoppmann, *Days of Masquerade: Life Stories of Lesbians During the Third Reich*, trans. Allison Brown (New York: Columbia University Press, 1996), 133–44.

14 Roellig, *Berlins lesbische Frauen*, 13.

15 Schader, *Virile*, 7–8, 36–9, 253–4n120. On the film, see Jelavich, *Berlin Alexanderplatz*, 141–2.

16 Th. von Rheine, *Die lesbische Liebe: Zur Psychologie des Mannweibes* (Berlin-Charlottenburg: Verlag Aris & Ahren, 1933), 64. Von Rheine's book appears to have been completed and published in the Republic's final months. Its introduction is dated fall 1932, and its copyright is dated 1932. In addition, the copy currently held by the Staatsbibliothek zu Berlin is marked with a sticker from the Martin Radszuweit Buchhandlung, which seems to indicate that the library bought the copy from Radszuweit's bookstore, and the bookstore would not have sold such material after the Nazi crackdown on gay and lesbian subcultures.

17 Von Rheine, *Die lesbische Liebe*; Erich Wulffen, *Irrwege des Eros* (Leipzig: Avalun-Verlag, 1929); Heinz Marteneau, *Sappho und Lesbos* (Leipzig: Eva-Verlag, 1931); Franz Scheda, *Die lesbische Liebe*, vol. 1 of *Die Abarten im Geschlechtsleben* (Berlin: Schwalbe-Verlag, 1930). This book's cover image was initially published in a city guide to Berlin vice, Moreck's *Führer durch das "lasterhafte" Berlin*, which, while not technically a *Sittengeschichte*, conformed to the genre in many ways, including in the style of its illustrations.

18 *WhKM* Nr. 24, September/October 1929, 181.
19 Ursula Sillge, "Frauen im Wissenschaftlich-humanitären Komitee," in *Homosexualität: Handbuch der Theorie- und Forschungsgeschichte*, ed. Rüdiger Lautmann (Frankfurt: Campus, 1993), 124–6; Ulrike Krettmann, "Johanna Elberskirchen," in Lautmann, *Homosexualität: Handbuch*, 111–16; Christiane Leidinger, "'Anna Rüling': A Problematic Foremother of Lesbian History," *Journal of the History of Sexuality* 13 (2004): 477–99.
20 Plötz, *Einsame*, 64–84. She notes that most local chapters for women were in the north and east of Germany. Vienna chapter: *Frauenliebe* Nr. 50, 1927; Zurich chapter: *Garçonne* Nr. 1, 1932.
21 Lotte Hahm and Friedrich Radszuweit, "Bund für ideale Frauenfreundschaft," *Die Freundin*, 7 May 1930; Schader, *Virile*, 76, 79.
22 Friedrich Radszuweit, "Lehrreiche statistische Feststellungen!" *Blätter für Menschenrecht*, September/November 1926.
23 *Blätter Idealer Frauenfreundschaft* was seized as obscene by a Berlin court: Staatsarchiv München Pol. Dir. 7320.
24 Schader, *Virile*, 74–6; Claudia Schoppmann, *Nationalsozialistische Sexualpolitik und weibliche Homosexualität* (Pfaffenweiler: Centaurus, 1997), 171.
25 Schader, *Virile*, 80–1.
26 Schoppmann, *Days*, 96; "Der 'Damenklub,'" *Berliner Tageblatt*, 22 April 1909; see also Lybeck, *Desiring*, 103–8.
27 Schader, *Virile*, 76.
28 "Achtung Freundinnen!" *Die Freundin*, 23 July 1930.
29 Lotte Hahm, "Klubnachrichten über Violetta," *Die Freundin*, 31 July 1929.
30 Advertisement, *Die Freundin*, 3 December 1930. On the *Zauberflöte*, see Schader, *Virile*, 80.
31 For example, Roellig, *Berlins lesbische Frauen*, 21.
32 "Aufruf an alle homosexuell veranlagten Frauen!" *Die Freundin*, 1 March 1925. On Weber, see Schader, *Virile*, 44.
33 Steakley, *Homosexual Emancipation*, 78–81. See also Ramsey, "Rites," 98–9.
34 See Canning, "Das Geschlecht der Revolution," 91–5.
35 Ibid., 95.
36 Roellig, *Berlins lesbische Frauen*, 47.
37 Lybeck, *Desiring*, 174–6, quotation at 174.
38 In print, she went by "Karen": Lybeck, *Desiring*, 233n35.
39 Karen, "Aufruf zur Mitgliedschaft!" *Garçonne*, 23 December 1930.
40 Sutton, "We Too," 349. In addition to Sutton, the other major work on this under-studied movement is Herrn, *Schnittmuster*.
41 Sutton, "We Too," 339.
42 Ibid., 340–4.

43 Magnus Hirschfeld, *Transvestites: The Erotic Drive to Cross-Dress*, trans. Michael A. Lombardi-Nash (Amherst, NY: Prometheus Books, 1991). The rumour that Hirschfeld was a transvestite is a canard: Herrn, *Schnittmuster*, 31n1.

44 Sutton, "We Too," 337.

45 A third magazine for transvestites survived for only a few issues: Sutton, "We Too," 340.

46 Werner Kn., "Der Kampf der Transvestiten," *Die Freundin*, 2 April 1928.

47 Hirschfeld coined "transsexual" in 1923 but it took about thirty years to catch on: Herrn, *Schnittmuster*, 19–21.

48 Sutton, *Masculine Woman*, 116–17.

49 Ein älterer, wohlmeinender Transvestit und Akademiker, "Briefe, die man der 'Freundin' schreibt: Transsensiblen-Club?" *Die Freundin*, 19 March 1928.

50 Toni Fricke, "Aus dem Empfindungsleben eines 'Transvestiten'!" *Die Freundin*, 12 September 1924.

51 Toni Fricke, "Einiges über das Problem der Namensänderung für Transvestiten," *Der Transvestit/Die Freundin*, 15 May 1925; x., "Hat der Transvestit eine Existenzberechtigung?" *Der Transvestit/Die Freundin*, 1 March 1925.

52 Käte K., "Aus dem Leben der Transvestiten," *Der Transvestit/Die Freundin*, 1 March 1925; H.W. Burg, "Meine Weihnachten: Erinnerungen eines Transvestiten," *Der Transvestit/Die Freundin*, 1 January 1925; Lina Es, "Sternkieker," *Der Transvestit/Die Freundin*, 15 March 1925; Roellig, "Lesbierinnen und Transvestiten," 77–8.

53 "Mein Liebling heißt Kurty!" *Der Transvestit/Die Freundin*, 1 February 1925.

54 Sutton, "We Too," 344–5.

55 Herrn, *Schnittmuster*, 38–40; Sutton, "We Too," 344–5.

56 Sutton, *Masculine Woman*, 117. For a rare autobiography of a female-to-male person, see "Verzweiflungskampf eines weiblichen Transvestiten," *Ledige Frauen (Die Freundin)*, 28 May 1928.

57 Hirschfeld, *Transvestites*, 265–78; "Nur in Frauenkleidern glücklich," *Die Welt der Transvestiten/Die Freundin*, 16 April 1930; Roellig, "Lesbierinnen und Transvestiten," 78; Herrn, *Schnittmuster*, 65–6.

58 Herrn, *Schnittmuster*, 63–4.

59 Ibid., 103–4.

60 Joanne Meyerowitz, *How Sex Changed: A History of Transsexuality in the United States* (Cambridge, MA: Harvard University Press, 2004), 15.

61 Hirschfeld, *Transvestites*, 265–78.

62 Herrn, *Schnittmuster*, 126.

63 Ibid., 129–31.

64 Ibid., 126–9.

65 Regarding Lothar, see the advertisement in *Die Freundin*, 27 August 1930.

66 Roellig, *Berlins lesbische Frauen*, 47.

67 On Radszuweit directing transvestites, including male-to-female individuals, to join women's clubs rather than men's organizations, see *Die Welt der Transvestiten/Die Freundin*, 8 June 1932. For Radszuweit's fear that the visible presence of feminine men would harm homosexual emancipation, see Ramsey, "Rites," 85.

68 Lotte Hahm, "Transvestitenehe," *Die Welt der Transvestiten/Die Freundin*, 19 November 1930.

69 Hannchen, "Sehr geehrte Redaktion!" *Die Welt der Transvestiten/Die Freundin*, 12 November 1930.

70 [No title], *Die Welt der Transvestiten/Die Freundin*, 8 June 1932.

71 Lotte Hahm, "Geschäftliche Mitteilungen," *Die Freundin*, 29 June 1932.

72 Roellig, *Berlins lesbische Frauen*, 47.

73 Roellig, "Lesbierinnen und Transvestiten," 76.

74 "Verzweiflungskampf eines weiblichen Transvestiten"; Kokula, *Jahre*, 23.

75 See Sutton's argument in favour of taking an approach that does not focus on one of these identity categories to the exclusion of the other: *Masculine Woman*, 93–4.

76 Roellig, *Berlins lesbische Frauen*, 24.

77 Sutton, "We Too," 340–2.

78 It is difficult to select a pronoun to describe this person because it is unclear how the person self-identified. Hirschfeld refers to the person as "she." I have, however, refered to the person as "he"; since the person sought to live as a man, it seems more likely that the person used male pronouns.

79 Hirschfeld, *Transvestites*, 152–3.

80 E. Raven writing in *Die Welt der Transvestiten* in 1932, quoted in Sutton, "We Too," 342. Sutton's translation.

81 Lybeck, "Writing Love, Feeling Shame"; Lybeck, *Desiring*, 164–70.

82 Lybeck, *Desiring*, 178–80.

83 Ibid., 169.

84 Herrn, *Schnittmuster*, 148.

85 George Mosse, *Nationalism and Sexuality: Respectability and Abnormal Sexuality in Modern Europe* (New York: Howard Fertig, 1985), 22, quoted in Sutton, "We Too," 341.

86 Duggan, "The New Homonormativity," 179.

87 Irene von Behlau, "Die homosexuelle Frau und die Reichstagswahl," *Die Freundin*, 14 May 1928.

88 Kokula, *Jahre*, 66–7.

89 Roellig, *Berlins lesbische Frauen*, 15, 29, 47.

90 Kokula, *Jahre*, 67. Hilde Radusch is another example of a woman who took part in lesbian subcultures but devoted her political energies to the KPD: Schoppmann, *Days*, 32–3.

91 Roellig, *Berlins lesbische Frauen*, 16–17.

92 One exception to this underemphasis is Martin Meeker, *Contacts Desired: Gay and Lesbian Communications and Community, 1940s–1970s* (Chicago: University of Chicago Press, 2006).

93 On being unpaid, see Schader, *Virile*, 53, 45–6.

94 Helene Stock, "Die Ächtung der homosexuellen Frau," *Die Freundin*, 31 July 1929.

95 Roellig, "Lesbierinnen und Transvestiten," 70.

96 Mimi, "Was wir Transvestiten leiden," *Die Freundin*, 14 May 1928.

97 Schader, *Virile*, 91–106; Paulowna, "Für oder gegen den Bubikopf?" *Die Freundin*, 2 April 1928.

98 N. Lermann, "Die Freundin der Olga Diers," *Die Freundin*, 8 August 1924.

99 Schoppmann, *Days*, 31–2.

100 Ibid., 32–3.

101 Ibid., 147.

102 Ibid., 147. Freia Eisner was the stepdaughter of Kurt Eisner, head of the short-lived Bavarian Republic.

103 Von Rheine, *Die lesbische Liebe*, 17.

104 Elvira Karstens, "Erwiderung auf den Artikel 'Kann Transvestitismus aner-zogen werden?'" *Die Freundin*, 27 January 1932. For a similar story about a transvestite, see Roellig, "Lesbierinnen und Transvestiten," 79. See also Hannchen, "Sehr geehrte Redaktion!"

105 "Branda" is a pseudonym: Kokula, *Jahre*, 77.

106 Roellig, *Berlins lesbische Frauen*, 16; Sutton, *Masculine Woman*, 108–10.

107 Anny Dolder-Uhl, "Skizze," *Garçonne*, Nr. 25, 1931.

108 Schoppmann, *Days*, 92–4.

109 Sutton, *Masculine Woman*, 154–5.

110 Kokula, *Jahre*, 65–73, 74–6.

111 Ibid., 74.

112 Ibid., 69.

113 *Eros*, a magazine, was seized by Berlin police, but Munich police reported it was not for sale there: Staatsarchiv München Pol. Dir. 7327.

114 See the report of a raid on Karl Kebler's bookshop in 1929; it sold sex reform material. There had been a similar raid on another shop: Krim. Oberkomm. report, 20 June 1929, Staatsarchiv München Pol. Dir. 7178.

However, a court later determined that the raid on Kebler's shop was invalid: Amtsgericht München, Betreff: Kebler, Karl, Staatsarchiv München Pol. Dir. 7178.

115 Krim. Bezirk to Landesstelle z. Bek. Unz. Schriften, 16 July 1927, Staatsarchiv München Pol. Dir. 7331.

116 Alfred Mensi-Klarbach, Gutachten, 11 August 1927, Staatsarchiv München Pol. Dir. 7331.

117 Ibid.

118 See the POLUNBI reports in Staatsarchiv München Pol. Dir. 7419.

119 *Garçonne* Nr. 1, 1932.

120 Ibid.

121 Hauer, Betreff: Fremdenkontrolle, 13 August 1925, Staatsarchiv München Pol. Dir. 7974; records of arrests of 4 November 1924 and 13 July 1925, Staatsarchiv München Pol. Dir. 7974.

122 "Burschen in Mädchenkleidern," *Vorwärts*, 10 December 1923.

123 Kokula, *Jahre*, 78–9.

124 Radszuweit, "Lehrreiche statistische Feststellungen!"

125 von Behlau, "Die homosexuelle Frau und die Reichstagswahl."

126 Brigitte Eriksson, ed. and trans., "A Lesbian Execution in Germany, 1721: The Trial Records," in *Historical Perspectives on Homosexuality: The Gay Past*, ed. Salvatore Licata and Robert Petersen (New York: Haworth, 1981), 27–40.

127 Schoppmann, *Nationalsozialistische Sexualpolitik*, 80–1.

128 Ibid., 80–2; Schoppmann, *Verbotene Verhältnisse: Frauenliebe 1938–1945* (Berlin: Querverlag, 1999), 127–8.

129 Schoppmann, *Nationalsozialistische Sexualpolitik*, 81–2.

130 Matysik, "In the Name of the Law," 46.

131 On the debate on this in imperial Germany, see Matysik, "In the Name of the Law"; Lybeck, *Desiring*, 108–15.

132 On similar notions in an earlier period, see Lybeck, *Desiring*, 81.

133 "Die im Liebesleben und seinen Abarten vorkommenden häufigster Fremdwörter," Zusammengestellt von Krim. Komm. H. Eller, undated [late 1920s], Staatsarchiv München Pol. Dir. 7946.

134 See reports in GStAPK I. HA Rep. 77 Tit. 2772 Nr. 2A Bd. 1; reports in Staatsarchiv München Pol. Dir. Nr. 7419. See also Placzek, *Homosexualität*, 82–3; Roellig, "Lesbierinnen und Transvestiten," 69–70.

135 Quoted in Kartell für Reform des Sexualstrafrechts, ed., *Gegen-Entwurf zu den Strafbestimmungen des Amtlichen Entwurfs eines Allgemeinen Deutschen Strafgesetzbuch über geschlechtliche und mit dem Geschlechtsleben im Zusammenhang stehend Handlung* (Berlin: Verlag der Neuen Gesellschaft, 1927), 59.

136 Von Rheine, *Die lesbische Liebe*, 83, 101. Franz Scott makes the same assumption: *Das lesbische Weib: Eine Darstellung der konträrsexuallen weiblichen Erotik* (Berlin: Pergamon Verlag, 1931), 31.

137 Von Rheine, *Die lesbische Liebe*, 14.

138 Sommer, *Strafbarkeit*, 43.

139 Ibid., 50.

140 Ibid., 51–6.

141 Ibid., 52.

142 Staatsarchiv München, Disziplinarstrafkammer München Nr. 155.

143 Matysik, "In the Name of the Law," 34–7.

144 Matysik, *Reforming*, 160–1.

145 Von Guérard, as quoted in "Die Verhandlungen des Strafrechtsausschusses des deutschen Reichstages über die Strafwürdigkeit der Homosexualität," *WhKM* Nr. 24, September/October 1929, 185. The WhK's magazine reprinted the official text of the debate in the penal code reform committee on Paragraph 175. "Die Verhandlungen des Strafrechtsausschusses" is the debate during the 85th session, on 16 October 1929.

146 Von Rheine, *Die lesbische Liebe*, 101–2, 37.

147 Ibid., 101.

148 Ibid., 102–3.

149 Placzek, *Homosexualität*, 81.

150 Ibid., 11.

151 Marti Lybeck, "Gender, Sexuality, and Belonging: Female Homosexuality in Germany, 1890–1933" (PhD diss., University of Michigan, 2007), 309. On proponents of extending the law to women, see also Schoppmann, *Nationalsozialistische Sexualpolitik*, 84–6.

152 "Die Verhandlungen des Strafrechtsausschusses," 181.

153 Moll, *Behandlung*, 39; Hirschfeld, *Homosexualität*, 46; Placzek, *Homosexualität und Recht*, 10–11.

154 Bloch, *Sexual Life*, 540–1.

155 "Die Verhandlungen des Strafrechtsausschusses," 183.

156 Ministerialdirektor Schäfer, as recorded in the official text of the second day of debate on Paragraph 175 in the penal code reform committee, reprinted as "Deutscher Reichstag: Beratungen des Strafgesetzausschusses des Deutschen Reichstag über den §297 des Amtlichen Strafgesetzentwurfs," *WhKM*, Nr. 26, December 1929/January 1930, 214–15.

157 See the decisions in GStAPK I. HA Rep. 77 tit. 2772 Nr. 3E Bd. 1, 27–31, 34–7, 159; GStAPK I. HA Rep. 77 Tit. 2772 Nr. 3E Bd. 2, 14, 162.

158 Prussian Welfare Ministry, application to place *Die Freundschaft* and *Die neue Freundschaft* on the Schmutz and Schund list, 19 May 1928, GStAPK I. HA Rep. 77 Tit. 2772 Nr. 3D Bd. 2.

159 Prussian Welfare Ministry, application to put *Frauenliebe* on the Schmutz and Schund list, 16 March 1929, GStAPK I. HA Rep. 77 Tit. 2772 Nr. 3D Bd. 2.
160 Decision of 21 April 1931, GStAPK I. HA Rep. 77 Tit. 2772 Nr. 3E Bd. 2, 21.
161 Session of 11 June 1929, GStAPK I. HA Rep. 77 tit. 2772 Nr. 3E Bd. 1, 175.
162 For example, see *Die Freundschaft* decision, 23 November 1932, in GStAPK I. HA Rep. 77 Tit. 2772 Nr. 3D Bd. 2.
163 Session of 16 December 1927, GStAPK I. HA Rep. 77 tit. 2772 Nr. 3E Bd. 1.
164 Ibid.
165 Session of 10 January 1928, GStAPK I. HA Rep. 77 tit. 2772 Nr. 3E Bd. 1, 34–7.
166 Session of 16 December 1927.
167 The magazine ran personal ads for men and women because all of Radszuweit's papers often ran the same set of ads.
168 Session of 16 December 1927.
169 Wilhelm Kahl, "Paragraph 175 Ernstes aus dem Strafrechtsausschuß," *Vossische Zeitung*, 25 October 1929. See also chapter 4.
170 "Die Verhandlungen des Strafrechtsausschusses," 183.

3 Female Prostitution, Modern Heterosexuality, and the 1927 Venereal Disease Law

1 Anna Pappritz, *Handbuch der amtlichen Gefährdetenfürsorge* (Munich: Verlag von J.F. Bergmann, 1924), 74. Portions of this chapter appeared in Laurie Marhoefer, "Degeneration, Sexual Freedom, and the Politics of the Weimar Republic, 1918–1933," *German Studies Review* 34 (2011): 529–50. Thanks to *German Studies Review* for permission to reprint.
2 Ibid.
3 Ibid., 75.
4 M. Sieverts, "Nachgehende Fürsorge und Zusammenarbeit mit der freien Liebestätigkeit," in Pappritz, *Handbuch*, 144.
5 Pappritz, *Handbuch*, 75.
6 Ibid.
7 Sieverts, "Nachgehende Fürsorge," 144.
8 Roos, *Lens*, 3.
9 Pappritz, *Handbuch*, 74.
10 On its coercive aspects, see Freud-Widder, *Frauen*, 104–5; Harris, *Selling Sex*, 162–5. Roos considers the coercive aspects of the 1927 reform but emphasizes its emancipatory aspects: *Lens*, see especially 8, 91–2, 133; see also her discussions of coercive tendencies in reformist political circles: 129–33, 157–8, 162–70. Timm, whose interest is in venereal disease policy as it affected the general public, argues the law both created new welfare and public health benefits and set limitations on sexual expression: *Politics*, 2.

11 Freund-Widder, *Frauen*; Roos, *Lens*; Timm, *Politics*; Harris, *Selling Sex*. On German policy in a European context, see Peter Baldwin, *Contagion and the State in Europe, 1830–1930* (Cambridge: Cambridge University Press, 1999), 355–523.

12 A rare consideration of venereal disease and both male and female homosexual sex is in Bloch, *Sexual Life*, 368–9.

13 On regulation's various rules, which were more complex than I have space to describe, see Roos, *Lens*, 16–21.

14 Birgit Adam, *Die Strafe der Venus: Eine Kulturgeschichte der Geschlechtskrankheiten* (Pößneck: Orbis Verlag, 2001), 107–11, 148–94; Meyer-Renschhausen, "Bremen Morality Scandal."

15 Judith Walkowitz, *Prostitution and Victorian Society: Women, Class, and the State* (Cambridge: Cambridge University Press, 1982). On international abolitionism, see also: the special issue of *Women's History Review* 17 (2008), "Gender, Religion and Politics: Josephine Butler's Campaigns in International Perspective (1875–1959)"; Phillipa Levine, *Prostitution, Race, and Politics: Policing Venereal Disease in the British Empire* (New York: Routledge, 2003).

16 On female prostitution and abolitionism prior to 1918, see Richard Evans, "Prostitution, State and Society in Imperial Germany," *Past and Present* 70 (1976): 106–29; Kaplan, *Jewish Feminist Movement*, 103–45; Ann Taylor Allen, "Feminism, Venereal Diseases, and the State in Germany, 1890–1918," *Journal of the History of Sexuality* 4, no. 1 (1993): 27–50; Reagin, *A German Women's Movement*, 147–72; Dickinson, *Sex*, 21–9, 88–90, 177–89.

17 Katharina Scheven, "Die sozialen und wirtschaftlichen Grundlagen der Prostitution," in *Einführung in das Studium der Prostitutionsfrage*, ed. Anna Pappritz (Leipzig: Verlag von Johann Ambrosius Barth, 1919), 139–72; *Verhandlungen des Reichstages*, Bd. 391 (256 Sitzung, 21 January 1927), 8677; *Verhandlungen des Reichstages*, Bd. 391 (257 Sitzung, 22 January 1927), 8700, 8702, 8707.

18 LA A Pr Br Rep 031–03 #3103.

19 Walkowitz, *Prostitution*.

20 Kerstin Wolff, "*Herrenmoral*: Anna Pappritz and Abolitionism in Germany," *Women's History Review* 17 (2008): 234.

21 Agnes Neuhaus made this point in a 1927 speech: *Verhandlungen des Reichstages*, Bd. 391 (257 Sitzung, 22 January 1927), 8707. On Neuhaus, see p. 86.

22 Matysik, *Reforming*, 75–6. On Pappritz's views of female sexuality versus Stöcker's (and Hirschfeld's) prior to 1918, see Leng, "Contesting the 'Laws of Life,'" 90–1; Dickinson, *Sex*, 289.

23 Roos, *Lens*, 107; see also Reagin, *Women's Movement*, 149.

24 Hirschfeld, *Homosexualität*, 1011.

25 Von Rheine, *Die lesbische Liebe*, 13, 50.

26 Robert Gaupp, "Das Problem der Homosexualität," *Klinische Wochenschrift* 1, no. 21 (20 May 1922): 1036; E.F.W. Eberhard, *Die Frauenemanzipation und ihre erotischen Grundlagen* (Vienna and Leipzig: Wilhelm Braumüller, 1924), 508, 514; Albert Moll, "Die sozialen Formen der sexuellen Beziehungen," in *Handbuch der Sexualwissenschaften mit besonderer Berücksichtigung der kulturgeschichtlichen Beziehungen*, ed. Albert Moll (Leipzig: F.C.W. Vogel, 1921), 375.

27 Roellig, *Berlins lesbische Frauen*, 16–17.

28 Scheda, *Die lesbische Liebe*, 19–25.

29 Margit Göttert, "'Mir sind die frauenrechtlerischen Ideen direkt eingeboren': Anna Pappritz (1861–1939)," *Ariadne* 28 (1995): 50–5.

30 Lybeck, *Desiring*, 113. On female-female partnerships that appear to have been similar to that of Pappritz and Friedenthal, see Lybeck, *Desiring*, 77–8, 117–50; Estelle Freedman, "'The Burning of the Letters Continues': Elusive Identities and the Historical Construction of Sexuality," *Journal of Women's History* 9, no. 4 (1998): 181–200.

31 Matysik, *Reforming*, 166–8.

32 Pappritz, *Handbuch*.

33 For Jewish women's groups, see Elisabeth Wolf, Yearly Report of the Pflegeamte, 1 April 1927 to 31 March 1928, Frankfurt a.M., GStAPK I. HA Rep. 76 VIII B Nr. 3813 [hereafter "Wolf 1928 report"].

34 Roos, *Lens*, 35.

35 *Reichstagshandbuch* (1924, 3. Wahlperiode) (Berlin: Bureau des Reichstags, 1925), 318.

36 Pappritz, *Handbuch*, 1.

37 Roos, *Lens*, 37.

38 Ibid., 144.

39 Ibid., 35.

40 See for example Roos, *Lens*, 42.

41 Ibid., 8.

42 *Geschlechtskrankheiten* also referred to chanchroids (ulcus molle, or soft chancres) and lymphogranuloma inguinale (Nicholas-Favre disease), which had recently been distinguished from syphilis. These two conditions were, however, rare. Timm, *Politics*, 36.

43 A. Blaschko, "Die Bekämpfung der Geschlechtskrankheiten im Kriege," *Deutschen Medizinischen Wochenschrift* Nr. 40, 1914.

44 "Erschreckende Zunahme der Prostitution!" *National-Zeitung*, 17 April 1925.

45 *Verhandlungen des Reichstags* (258 Sitzung, 24 January 1927), Band 391, 8726.

46 *Verhandlungen des Reichstags* (256 Sitzung, 21 January 1927), Band 391, 8693.

47 Ibid., 8695.

48 Timm, *Politics*, 60–1.

49 Entwurf, Gesetz zur Bekämpfung der Geschlechtskrankheiten, Reich Minister of the Interior to the Reichstag, 6 June 1925, BArch R 86/4594.

50 Leo von Zumbusch, "Die gesundheitlichen Gefahren der Prostitution und die Verbreitung der Geschlechtskrankheiten," in Pappritz, *Einführung*, 107–33. See also Timm, *Politics*, 52–3.

51 Jadassohn, "Ansprache zur Eröffnung der Festsitzung der 25 Jahresversammlung der Deutschen Gesellschaft zur Bekämpfung der Geschlechtskrankheiten am 28 October 1927," *Mitteilungen der Deutschen Gesellschaft zur Bekämpfung der Geschlechtskrankheiten* Nr. 11/12 (1927).

52 Berlin Magistrat to Prussian Welfare Ministry, 9 July 1928, GStAPK I. HA Rep. 76 VIII B Nr. 3813.

53 The 1927 venereal disease law did this by allowing the discreet advertisement of products previously prohibited by the obscenity law, Paragraph 184, if they could prevent infection. Some of these products – notably condoms – also prevented conception: Grossmann, *Reforming Sex*, 33; Usborne, *Politics*, 111–10; Usborne, "Christian Churches," 104–5; James Woycke, *Birth Control in Germany 1871–1933* (London: Routledge, 1988), 113. The 1927 law was not an unmitigated win for birth control, however, because it attempted to block the work of midwives, homeopaths, and lay self-help birth control leagues: Grossmann, *Reforming Sex*, 11.

54 Roos, *Lens*, 31–57.

55 Ibid., 36–7.

56 Ibid., 38, 188–9.

57 Schatz, "Das Gesetz zur Bekämpfung der Geschlechtskrankheiten," *Völkischer Beobachter*, 11 February 1928; Nochmals das Gesetz zur Bekämpfung der Geschlechtskrankheiten," *Völkischer Beobachter*, 28 December 1927.

58 Pappritz, *Handbuch*, 3.

59 Clara Thorbecke, "Die Verwahrlosung der weiblichen Jugend," in Pappritz, *Einführung*, 184.

60 Frankfurt am Main to Prussian Welfare Ministry, 10 July 1928, GStAPK I. HA Rep. 76 VIII B Nr. 3813.

61 Christoph Sachße, "Social Mothers: The Bourgeois Women's Movement and German Welfare-State Formation, 1880–1929," in *Mothers of a New World: Maternalist Politics and the Origins of Welfare States*, ed. Seth Koven and Sonya Michel (New York: Routledge, 1993), 152.

62 *Verhandlungen des Reichstages*, Bd. 391 (257 Sitzung, 22 January 1927), 8707.

63 Ibid.

64 Seth Koven and Sonya Michel, eds., *Mothers of a New World: Maternalist Politics and the Origins of Welfare States* (New York: Routledge, 1993).

65 Hong, *Welfare*, 34.
66 Mommsen, *Rise and Fall*, 226–8.
67 Crew, *Germans on Welfare*, 10–11; Hong, *Welfare*, 5–6.
68 Prussian Welfare Ministry, 31 August 1927, GStAPK R 4901/549, 246–59; Evangelischer Oberkirchenrat, 29 August 1927, GStAPK R 4901/549, 244.
69 Freund-Widder, *Frauen*, 35–8.
70 Meyer-Renschhausen, "Bremen Morality Scandal," 99.
71 GStAPK I. HA Rep. 76 VIII B Nr. 3813. Thanks to Peter Randolph for pointing out the civic nature of these arguments.
72 Paul Mulzer, "Zur Bekämpfung der Geschlechtskrankheiten im Felde und in der Heimat," *Dermatologische Zeitschrift*, 1918 (reprint from vol. 25, no. 4).
73 "Ioshiwara im Zentrum Berlins," *Berliner Tageblatt*, 29 August 1923.
74 *Verhandlungen des Reichstags*, Bd. 391 (257 Sitzung, 22 January 1927), 8702.
75 *Reichstagshandbuch* (1924, 3. Wahlperiode), 355.
76 Roos, *Lens*, 161.
77 *Verhandlungen des Reichstags*, Bd. 391 (256 Sitzung, 21 January 1927), 8675.
78 Pappritz, *Handbuch*, 4–7.
79 "Die Schließung der Bordelle," *Leipziger Volkszeitung*, 23 November 1925.
80 Ibid.
81 Adolf Sellmann, *Das Gesetz zur Bekämpfung der Geschlechtskrankheiten* (Schwelm [Westphalia]: G. Meiners, 1927), 36–7.
82 Schatz, "Das Gesetz."
83 This concern is apparent in "Die Schließung der Bordelle" and "Wie sie zur Prostitution kamen: 35 Lebensfragmente bordellierter Mädchen," *Leipziger Volkszeitung*, 28 July 1928. Compare Roos on the Kern interviews: *Lens*, 92.
84 Pappritz, *Handbuch*, 74.
85 On reformatories, see Dickinson, *Politics*, 194–201.
86 Roos, *Lens*, 75.
87 Richard Wetzell, *Inventing the Criminal: A History of German Criminology, 1880–1945* (Chapel Hill: University of North Carolina Press, 2000), 297–8.
88 Ibid., 239.
89 Warren Rosenblum, *Beyond the Prison Gates: Punishment & Welfare in Germany, 1850–1933* (Chapel Hill: University of North Carolina Press, 2008), 4–5, 103–19, 141–99.
90 On Lombroso's reception in Germany, see Wetzell, *Inventing*, 40–59.
91 Thorbecke, "Die Verwahrlosung der weiblichen Jugend," 183–4; Ernst Delbanco and Annie Blumenfeld, "Das moderne Prostitutionswesen," in Pappritz, *Einführung*, 28.
92 Gustav Aschaffenburg, *Das Verbrechen und seine Bekämpfung*, vol. 3 (Heidelberg: Carl Winters, 1923), 104.

93 Pappritz, *Handbuch*, 1.
94 Rosenblum, *Beyond*, 152–3.
95 Scheven, "Die sozialen und wirtschaftlichen Grundlagen der Prostitution," 159. On this translation of "Anlage" and the use of the term in criminology, see Wetzell, *Inventing*, 159.
96 Scheven, "Die sozialen und wirtschaftlichen Grundlagen der Prostitution," 159.
97 On "incorrigibility" in the thinking of Aschaffenburg and others, see Wetzell, *Inventing*, 299.
98 Dickinson, *Politics*, 205–8, quotation at 205.
99 Wetzell, *Inventing*, 47.
100 Daniel Pick, *Faces of Degeneration* (Cambridge: Cambridge University Press, 1989).
101 Wetzell, *Inventing*, 47; Heinz Schott and Rainer Tölle, *Geschichte der Psychiatrie: Krankheitslehren, Irrwege, Behandlungsformen* (Munich: Verlag C.H. Beck, 2006), 103.
102 Wetzell, *Inventing*, 149.
103 Ibid., 48–9.
104 Ibid.
105 Ibid., 149; Schott and Tölle, *Geschichte*, 106.
106 Wetzell, *Inventing*, 145.
107 Reichstag Committee for Bevölkerungspolitik, 20 February 1918, BArch R 86/4594.
108 Schott and Tölle, *Geschichte*, 364–5.
109 A.H. Hübner, *Lehrbuch der forensischen Psychiatrie* (Bonn: A. Marcus & E. Weber, 1914), 734–5.
110 Ibid., 735.
111 Ibid., 737.
112 Kurt Schneider, *Studien über Persönlichkeit und Schicksal eingeschriebener Prostituierter* (Berlin: Julius Springer, 1921), 8, 227.
113 Moll, "Die sozialen Formen," 387; Moll, *Polizei und Sitte* (Berlin: Gersbach & Sohn, 1926), 63–4.
114 Wolf 1928 report.
115 Sächsisches Ministerium für auswärtige Angelegenheiten, 26 June 1924, BArch R 86/2374.
116 Hartkopf, "Das wissenschaftliche Für und Wider," *Kölnische Zeitung*, 1 November 1929; Otto Kankeleit, *Die Unfruchtbarmachung aus rassenhygienischen und sozialen Gründen* (Munich: J.F. Lehmanns Verlag, 1929), 55; Gertrud Moses, Review of *Zum Problem der sozialen Familienverwahrlosung unter besonderer Berücksichtigung der Verhältnisse im Krieg* and *Die Familie*

Kallikak: Eine Studie über die Vererbung des Schwachsinns, Mitteilungen der Deutschen Gesellschaft zur Bekämpfung der Geschlechtskrankheiten 19, no. 5 (1921): 124–5.

117 Aschaffenburg, *Das Verbrechen*, 151, 202, 203, 208–9; Wetzell, *Inventing*, 67, 145, 222.

118 Aschaffenburg, *Das Verbrechen*, 104.

119 Ibid.

120 Ibid., 215, quotation at 236.

121 Otto Kaus, "Der Fall Böters," *Das Tage-Buch*, 7 March 1925; Heinrich Boeters, "Die Unfruchtbarmachung der geistig Minderwertigen," *Zwickauer Tagesblatt*, circa 1923, in BArch R 86/2374.

122 Schneider, *Studien*, 226; Aschaffenburg, *Das Verbrechen*, 104.

123 Scheven, "Die sozialen und wirtschaftlichen Grundlagen der Prostitution," 160. On Scheven, see Wolff, "*Herrenmoral.*"

124 Pappritz, *Handbuch*, 9.

125 Scheven, "Die sozialen und wirtschaftlichen Grundlagen der Prostitution," 159–60; Pappritz, *Handbuch*, 8–9.

126 Pappritz, *Handbuch*, 9. Roos also notes this theme in abolitionists' views: *Lens*, 130–1.

127 Irmgard Jaeger, speaking in 1923. Quoted in Pappritz, *Handbuch*, 6.

128 Dickinson, *Politics*, 198.

129 Wolfgang Ayass, *Das Arbeitshaus Breitenau: Bettler, Landstreicher, Prostituierte, Zuhälter, und Fürsorgeempfänger in der Korrektions- und Landesarmenanstalt Breitenau (1874–1949)* (Stuttgart: Franz Steiner, 1987), 245–7.

130 Ingrid Richter, *Katholizismus und Eugenik in der Weimarer Republik und im Dritten Reich: Zwischen Sittlichkeitsreform und Rassenhygiene* (Paderborn: Ferdinand Schöningh, 2001), 177–91; Jochen-Christoph Kaiser, Kurt Nowak, and Michael Schwartz, eds., *Eugenik, Sterilisation, "Euthanasie": Politische Biologie in Deutschland 1895–1945, Eine Dokumentation* (Berlin: Buchverlag Union, 1992), 102.

131 Preventative detention finally became law in the Federal Republic in 1961. It was struck down as unconstitutional six years later. Matthias Willing, *Das Bewahrungsgesetz* (Tübingen: J.C.B. Mohr, 2003).

132 Ibid., 289–90.

133 Ibid., 291.

134 Ibid., 288–92.

135 Crew, *Germans on Welfare*, 197.

136 Willing, *Bewahrungsgesetz*, 292–3.

137 On her originating the idea, see Willing, *Bewahrungsgesetz*, 286. As its champion, see: Ayass, *Arbeitshaus Breitenau*, 248–9; Richter, *Katholizismus*

und Eugenik, 177; Dickinson, *Politics*, 198; Willing, *Bewahrungsgesetz*, 286–91; *Verhandlungen des Reichstages*, Bd. 391 (257 Sitzung, 22 January 1927), 8707.

138 *Verhandlungen des Reichstages*, Bd. 391, 8707.

139 An example of the SPD's position on this: *Verhandlungen des Reichstages*, Bd. 391 (260 Sitzung, 26 January 1927), 8757.

140 *Verhandlungen des Reichstages*, Bd. 391 (257 Sitzung, 22 January 1927), 8704.

141 Anna Pappritz, "Das Reichsgesetz zur Bekämpfung der Geschlechtskrankheiten vom Standpunkt der Frau," *Mitteilungen der Deutschen Gesellschaft zur Bekämpfung der Geschlechtskrankheiten* 25, nos. 11–12 (1927): 133.

142 Ibid.

143 Emma Bunge to Prussian Welfare Ministry, 25 November 1927, GStAPK I. HA Rep. 76 VIII B Nr. 3813. This incident happened before the 1927 law officially went into effect; the *Länder* (provinces) were authorized to implement interim measures mirroring the new law.

144 Polizeipräsident Berlin to Prussian Welfare Ministry, 10 December 1927, GStAPK I. HA Rep. 76 VIII B Nr. 3813.

145 Ibid.

146 Wolf 1928 report.

147 Timm, *Politics*, 64; for Timm's analysis of the Republic's venereal disease policy, see 35–79. Timm is especially interested in how the majority of Berliners received and shaped venereal disease measures and less interested in female prostitution and in the 1927 law's compulsory measures. In contrast, I am interested in female prostitutes and other people deemed "immoral": such people constituted a minority of those who were in contact with the public health system, but they were more likely to encounter its compulsory measures. Therefore, my portrait of venereal disease policy foregrounds compulsory measures, whereas Timm's foregrounds ordinary people's willing participation and gains.

148 Sellmann, *Das Gesetz zur Bekämpfung der Geschlechtskrankheiten*, 28.

149 Reichsgesundheitsamt, *Ratschläge an Ärzte über die Mitwirkung bei der Bekämpfung der Geschlechtskrankheiten* (Berlin: R.v. Decker), 41–8, in BArch R 4901/549. Germany had some mandatory controls on venereal disease before 1927. Several *Länder* granted compulsory treatment powers as early as the 1860s. Criminalizing knowingly spreading venereal disease was proposed in 1892 and in 1909 and enacted by emergency decree in 1918, but for the most part it was used rarely and only in cases of female prostitution: Committee for Bevölkerungspolitik, 20 February 1918, BArch R 86/4594; Paul Weindling, *Health, Race and German Politics between National Unification and Nazism 1870–1945* (Cambridge: Cambridge University Press, 1989), 357–8; Timm, *Politics*, 40–1.

150 Prussian Staatsministerium implementation orders for the 1927 law, BArch R 4901/549, 236.
151 *Verhandlungen des Reichstages*, Bd. 391 (257 Sitzung, 21 January 1927), 8682–3; Herbert Fuchs, "Die Bekämpfung der Geschlechtskrankheiten," *Die Weltbühne* 16, no. 19 (6 May 1920).
152 *Verhandlungen des Reichstages*, Bd. 391 (257 Sitzung, 22 January 1927), 6897.
153 Timm, *Politics*, 54–8, 71–7.
154 Ibid., 78.
155 Atina Grossmann, "The New Woman and the Rationalization of Sexuality in Weimar Germany," in *Powers of Desire: The Politics of Sexuality*, ed. Ann Snitow, Christine Stansell, and Sharon Thompson (New York: Monthly Review Press, 1983), 153–71.
156 Prussian Welfare Ministry, 31 August 1927, BArch R 4901/549, 246–59.
157 Ibid.
158 Reichsgesundheitsamt, *Ratschläge an Ärzte*, 265–88.
159 Reichsgesundheitsamt, *Ratschläge an Ärzte*.
160 Wolf 1928 report.
161 Ibid.
162 Timm, *Politics*, 64.
163 "Kampf den Geschlechtskrankheiten!" *Vorwärts*, 5 October 1928.
164 Jadassohn, "Ansprache zur Eröffnung der Festsitzung der 25 Jahresversammlung der Deutschen Gesellschaft zur Bekämpfung der Geschlechtskrankheiten"; Reichsgesundheitsamt, *Ratschläge an Ärzte*.
165 Magistrat Gesundheitsamt Berlin, 19 August 1927, GStAPK I. HA Rep. 76 VIII B Nr. 3813.
166 Bürger Verein von 1848, e.V. von Altona, 17 May 1927, GStAPK I. HA Rep. 76 VIII B Nr. 3813.
167 Timm, *Politics*, 36–7; Meyer-Renschhausen, "Bremen Morality Scandal."
168 Berlin Magistrat to Prussian Welfare Ministry, 9 July 1928, GStAPK I. HA Rep. 76 VIII B Nr. 3813.
169 Prussian Welfare Ministry, 31 August 1927, BArch R 4901/549, 246–59.
170 Ibid.
171 Ibid.
172 Entwurf, Gesetz zur Bekämpfung der Geschlechtskrankheiten, Reich Minister of the Interior to the Reichstag, 6 June 1925, BArch R 86/4594.
173 Prussian Welfare Ministry, 31 August 1927, BArch R 4901/549, 246–59.
174 Ibid.
175 Ibid.
176 Wolf 1928 report.
177 Reichsgesundheitsamt, *Ratschläge an Ärzte*.

178 Prussian Welfare Ministry to Dittmar, 18 July 1929, GStAPK I. HA Rep. 76 VIII B Nr. 3813.
179 Prussian Welfare Ministry, 31 August 1927, BArch R 4901/549, 246–59.
180 Reichsgesundheitsamt, *Ratschläge an Ärzte*.
181 *Verhandlungen des Reichstages*, Bd. 391 (256 Sitzung, 21 January 1927), 8688.
182 Reichsgesundheitsamt, *Ratschläge an Ärzte*.
183 "Kampf den Geschlechtskrankheiten!" See also Timm, *Politics*, 71–7.
184 Wolf 1928 report.
185 On these men and prostitution, see chapter 4. On the conflation of male homelessness and sexual disorder in a different context, see Seth Koven, *Slumming: Sexual and Social Politics in Victorian London* (Princeton: Princeton University Press, 2004), 70–87.
186 *Stenographischer Bericht des Reichstags*, 409, 24 March 1928, in BArch R 1501/126314, 6, 9.
187 Reichsgesundheitsamt, *Ratschläge an Ärzte*.
188 Graf to Prussian Welfare Ministry, 10 July 1928, GStAPK I. HA Rep. 76 VIII B Nr. 3813.
189 Reich Minister of Interior to Prussian Welfare Ministry, 10 November 1928, GStAPK I. HA Rep. 76 VIII B Nr. 3813.
190 Frankfurt a.M. Magistrate to Prussian Welfare Ministry, 5 March 1929; Regierungspräsident, Wiesbaden to Prussian Welfare Ministry, 7 May 1929, both in GStAPK I. HA Rep. 76 VIII B Nr. 3813. Quotations in Regierungspräsident, Wiesbaden.
191 Magnus Hirschfeld, *Geschlechtskunde* III (Stuttgart: Julius Püttmann, 1930), 349. This sentiment dovetails with Harris's findings: see *Selling Sex*. A more general note on where Harris and I diverge: I agree that for women who had been registered prostitutes prior to 1927 and who continued to work as prostitutes after 1927, the 1927 reform did not change much. I do not agree that the 1927 law was poorly enforced or that Weimar-era prostitution policy was not so different from Nazi-era prostitution policy: Harris, *Selling Sex*, 163–4, 183–4. For a convincing look at discontinuities between Weimar and Nazi prostitution policies, see Roos, *Lens*, 225–7; Julia Roos, "Backlash against Prostitutes' Rights: Origins and Dynamics of Nazi Prostitution Policies," in *Sexuality and German Fascism*, ed. Dagmar Herzog (New York: Berghahn, 2005), 67–94; see in particular 83–94.
192 Roos, *Lens*, 59.
193 Hirschfeld, *Geschlechtskunde* III, 358.
194 Julia Roos, "Between Normalization and Resistance: Prostitutes' Professional Identities and Political Organizations in Weimar Germany," in *After "The History of Sexuality": German Genealogies With and Beyond Foucault*, ed.

Scott Spector, Helmut Puff, and Dagmar Herzog (New York: Berghahn, 2012), 149–52.

195 Martha Schulz to Minister of the Interior, undated [1930], GStAPK Rep. 77 II Titel 435 Nr. 6, 239–40.

196 Police to Minister of the Interior, 26 May 1930, GStAPK Rep. 77 II Titel 435 Nr. 6, 241–3; Minister of Interior to Police, 27 June 1930, GStAPK Rep. 77 II Titel 435 Nr. 6, 244.

197 Roos, *Lens*, 177–216.

198 Bürger Verein von 1848, E.V., Altona, 17 May 1927; Haus- und Grundbesitzerverein Quedlinburg to Prussian Welfare Ministry, 30 April 1927; Haus- und Grundbesitzerverband Magdeburg to Minister of the Interior, 7 June 1927: all in GStAPK I. HA Rep. 76 VIII B Nr. 3813.

199 *Verhandlungen des Reichstages* III, Wahlperiode 1924 (Sitzung, 24 March 1928), 13697.

200 To the Preußischer Landtag's committee on venereal disease, 8 November 1927, GStAPK I. HA Rep. 76 VIII B Nr. 3813.

201 Rektor and Senat of Albertus University, Königsberg, 21 March 1927, BArch R 4901/549.

202 Official copy of the venereal disease law, *Ratschläge an Ärzte*, 41–8; Roos, *Lens*, 161–2.

203 Roos, *Lens*, 204.

204 *Verhandlungen des Reichstages*, Bd. 395 (409 Sitzung, 24 March 1928), 13697.

205 Ibid., 13682.

206 Ibid., 13700.

207 "Kampf gegen die Geschlechtskrankheiten," *Kölnische Zeitung*, 25 September 1932.

208 "Gegen die öffentliche Unsittlichkeit," *Kölnische Volkszeitung*, 19 June 1932.

209 Schroeder's views on this are clear in speeches she made to the Reichstag on the 1927 reform: *Verhandlungen des Reichstages*, Bd. 391 (256 Sitzung, 21 January 1927), 8699–700; (260 Sitzung, 26 January 1927), 8757. For Pappritz on this, see *Handbuch*, 3–7.

210 Preußisches Staatsministerium, implementation orders for the Reichsgesetz zur Bekämpfung der Geschlechtskrankheiten, BArch R 4901/549, "Bek. zur GK." On Pappritz's support for this role for police, see Anna Pappritz, "Schutz der Gefährdeten: Aufgaben der weiblichen Polizei," *Vossische Zeitung*, 27 January 1927.

211 Dickinson, *Sex*, 89.

212 Friederike Wieking, "Prostituierte und Bekämpfung der Geschlechtskrankheit von Standpunkt einer Polizeifürsorgerin," *Blätter für Wohlfahrtspflege in Pommern*, 6 June 1921, excerpted in Pappritz, *Handbuch*, 4.

213 *Verhandlungen des Reichstages*, Bd. 428 (177 Sitzung, 17 June 1930), 5528–30.

214 Ibid., 5529.

215 Lybeck, *Desiring*, 129. See also Ursula Nienhaus, *"Nicht für eine Führungsposition geeignet": Josefine Erkens und die Anfänge weiblicher Polizei in Deutschland, 1923–1933* (Münster: Westfälisches Dampfboot, 1999).

216 Roos, *Lens*, 202–3.

217 Mergel, *Parlamentarische Kultur*, 477.

218 Compare Roos, *Lens*, 199–205, which reviews a number of calls to ban female street soliciting. These, however, did not result in a national ban, even under Brüning or von Papen: see chapter 6.

219 Dickinson, "Policing Sex," 218. As discussed earlier, the 1927 law prohibited female prostitution under certain circumstances.

220 Roos, *Lens*, 215; Timm, *Politics*, 176.

221 Timm, *Politics*, 39–40.

222 Thanks to an anonymous reader for the American Council of Learned Societies for pointing this out.

4 Male Prostitution, Homosexual Emancipation, and the 1929 Vote to Repeal the Sodomy Law

1 Kurt Hiller, *Logos*, vol. 1 of *Leben gegen die Zeit* (Hamburg: Rowohlt, 1969), 11–19, 69–71. Portions of this chapter appeared in Marhoefer, "Degeneration, Sexual Freedom, and the Politics of the Weimar Republic."

2 Kurt Hiller, *Eros*, vol. 2 of *Leben gegen die Zeit* (Hamburg: Rowohlt, 1973), 50.

3 Ibid., 50–1.

4 Ibid., 52.

5 Ibid., 114; see also 30.

6 Ibid., 113–14.

7 Mark Blasius and Shane Phelan, eds., *We Are Everywhere: A Historical Sourcebook of Gay and Lesbian Politics* (New York: Routledge, 1997), 133–4; Wayne Dynes, "Magnus Hirschfeld," in *Gay and Lesbian Biography*, ed. Michael J. Tuyrkus (Detroit: St. James Press, 1997), 228; Kollenbroich, *Our Hour*, 2–3.

8 Fout, "Sexual Politics in Wilhelmine Germany," 268; Dose, *Hirschfeld*, 52; Beachy, "German Invention," 805.

9 For example, Steakley does not mention the incident in *Homosexual Emancipation Movement*, and Herzer refers only briefly to a conflict with Linsert in his biography of Hirschfeld: *Hirschfeld*, 49. Herzer considers Hirschfeld's resignation in more detail elsewhere: Herzer, "Schwule Preussen, warme Berliner," *Capri: Zeitschrift für schwule Geschichte* 2 (1988): 16–18. Other

studies that discuss Hirschfeld's resignation are Mancini, *Hirschfeld*, 124; Burkhard Jellonnek, *Homosexuelle unter dem Hakenkreuz: Die Verfolgung von Homosexuellen im Dritten Reich* (Paderborn: Ferdinand Schöningh, 1990), 48–9; Kollenbroich, *Our Hour*, 260–2; Dose, *Hirschfeld*, 62–3; Friedemann Pfäfflin, "Die Mitteilungen des Wissenschaftlich-humanitären Komitees 1926–1933," in *Mitteilungen des Wissenschaftlich-Humanitären Komitees 1926–1933*, ed. Walter v. Murat (Hamburg: C. Bell Verlag, 1985), ix–xv. With the exception of Pfäfflin's essay, none of these studies ascribe any weighty significance to the resignation.

10 Grimmer, "Politics of *Geist*," 126–77.

11 Hiller, *Eros*, 87.

12 Ibid., 88, 113.

13 Ibid., 88.

14 Kartell für Reform des Sexualstrafrechts, ed., *Gegen-Entwurf zu den Strafbestimmungen des Amtlichen Entwurfs eines Allgemeinen Deutschen Strafgesetzbuchs*.

15 Hiller, *Eros*, 101–2; Timothy Brown, "Richard Scheringer, the KPD and the Politics of Class and Nation in Germany, 1922–1969," *Contemporary European History* 14, no. 3 (2005): 328–9.

16 Hiller, *Eros*, 101.

17 Helmut Gruber, "Willi Münzenberg's German Communist Propaganda Empire 1921–1933," *Journal of Modern History* 38, no. 3 (1966): 278–97; Grossmann, *Reforming Sex*, 94, 108.

18 Hiller reports that Linsert felt some trepidation about joining the WhK and entering a world of "doctors, lawyers, and wealthy people" (*Eros*, 95).

19 Ibid., 101.

20 Grossmann, *Reforming Sex*, 78–106.

21 Quoted in Richard Linsert, "Der Strichjunge: Eine Darstellung von 100 Lebensläufen männlicher Prostituierter," in *§ 297.3 "Unzucht zwischen Männern"? Ein Beitrag zur Strafgesetzreform*, ed. Richard Linsert (Berlin: Neuer Deutscher Verlag, 1929), 44.

22 Hiller, *Logos*, 208–9.

23 Richard Linsert, "Einleitung," in Linsert, *Unzucht*, 10.

24 Abteilung für Sexualreform (Wissenschaftlich-humanitäres Komitee), "§267 des Amtlichen Entwurfs eines Allgemeinen Deutschen Strafgesetzbuchs 'Unzucht zwischen Männern' eine Denkschrift, gerichtet an das Reichsjustizministerium," *Sexus*, vol. 4 (Stuttgart: Verlag Julius Püttmann, 1925), 10–11.

25 Linsert, *Unzucht*, 115.

26 Linsert, "Strichjunge," 68.

27 Ibid.

28 Linsert, "Einleitung," 7.
29 Ibid., 9. Many of the Weimar era's penal reforms reflected this same notion: Rosenblum, *Beyond.*
30 Linsert, "Einleitung," 7.
31 Linsert, "Strichjunge," 67–8.
32 Ibid., 40, 46, 69.
33 George Chauncey, *Gay New York: Gender, Urban Culture, and the Making of the Gay Male World, 1890–1940* (New York: Basic Books, 1995).
34 Beachy, "German Invention." The Eulenburg scandal also put male homosexuality in the public eye: Domeier, *Der Eulenburg-Skandal,* 190.
35 Gaupp, "Das Problem der Homosexualität," 1034–5; Richard von Krafft-Ebing, *Psychopathia sexualis: A Medico-Forensic Study,* trans. Harry Wedeck (New York: G.P. Putnam's Sons, 1965), 296; Bloch, *Sexual Life,* 465–6, 540–1; Hirschfeld, *Homosexualität,* 46, 193–4.
36 Gaupp, "Das Problem der Homosexualität," 1035, 1037.
37 Hirschfeld, *Homosexualität,* 597.
38 Isherwood, *Christopher,* 2–3, quotation at 2.
39 Isherwood, *Christopher,* 30.
40 Ibid., 28.
41 Ibid., 42.
42 Ibid., 44.
43 Linsert, "Einleitung," 10.
44 Linsert, "Strichjunge," 49–51.
45 Hirschfeld, "Die männliche Prostitution," 21.
46 Linsert, "Strichjunge," 46–7; Hirschfeld, "Die männliche Prostitution," 17–18.
47 k. [*sic*], "Zwecke und Ziele," *Die Freundschaft* Nr. 11 Jahrgang 1 [1919]; Ramsey, "Rites," 97.
48 "Idioten," *Die Freundschaft* Nr. 7 Jahrgang 1 [1919].
49 Hirschfeld, "Die männliche Prostitution," 15–16, 32.
50 Micheler, *Selbstbilder,* 226; Friedrich Radszuweit, "Strich," *Die Freundin,* 24 February 1932.
51 Hiller, *Eros,* 104, 113.
52 Ibid., 113.
53 Ibid., 113–14.
54 Ibid., 108.
55 The WhK reprinted the official text of the two-day debate in the penal code reform committee on Paragraph 175: "Die Verhandlungen des Strafrechtsausschusses des deutschen Reichstages über die Strafwürdigkeit der Homosexualität" (which is the proceedings of the 85. Sitzung, 16 October 1929),

WhKM Nr. 24, September/October 1929, 176–91; "Deutscher Reichstag: Beratungen des Strafgesetzausschusses des Deutschen Reichstags über den §297 des Amtlichen Strafgesetzentwurfs" (which is the proceedings of the 86. Sitzung, 17 October 1929), *WhKM* Nr. 26 December 1929/January 1930, 209–23.

56 *Berliner Tageblatt*, 17 October 1929.

57 *Deutsche Zeitung*, 17 October 1929.

58 Herbert Lewandowski, "Aufklärung tut not!" in *Die lesbische Liebe*, vol. 1 of *Abarten im Geschlechtsleben*, ed. Franz Scheda (Berlin: Schwalbe-Verlag, 1930), 4.

59 Charlotte Wolff, *Magnus Hirschfeld: A Portrait of a Pioneer in Sexology* (London: Quartet Books, 1986), 438.

60 Evidence that the WhK had the best connections to the parliament and federal regime includes the fact that Hirschfeld had a personal meeting with Wilhelm Kahl to discuss the vote on Paragraph 175, and Linsert lobbied Communist leaders about it: Hiller, *Eros*, 102–4. In addition, in 1928 officials from the Reich Justice Ministry visited the Institute for Sexual Science to hear the WhK's position on the penal code reform and "spoke at length" with people at the Institute: "Um das neue Strafrecht," *Berliner Tageblatt*, 31 October 1928. Radszuweit headed the organization with the largest membership, but he did not have this kind of access, although he did meet with the Reich Justice Minister in 1924: Friedrich Radszuweit, "Führer," *Blätter für Menschenrecht*, July 1931. In comparison, Brand's influence was minimal.

61 Vorstand des W.H.K., "Der §175 nicht gefallen!" *WhKM*, December 1929/January 1930.

62 Ibid.

63 Kurt Hiller, "Gefängnis für männliche Prostituierte?" *WhKM*, November 1929, 201.

64 Reichstagshandbuch 1930 (5. Wahlperiode) (Berlin: Reichsdruckerei, 1930), 384.

65 Ernst Hauenstein, "Wilhelm Kahl," *WhKM* Nr. 33 April/August 1932, 382–7; Wilhelm Kahl, "§175 Ernstes aus dem Strafrechtsausschuß," *Vossische Zeitung*, 25 October 1929.

66 Kahl, "§175."

67 Ibid.

68 Details of the criticisms of Kahl are found in the SPD paper *Vorwärts* and may be exaggerated, but Kahl's own account makes it plain that he faced criticism. "Klub zum Schutze der Unzucht," *Vorwärts*, 5 September 1930; Kahl, "§175."

69 "Gerüchte um Professor Kahl," *Vossische Zeitung*, 23 July 1930.

70 "Die Verhandlungen des Strafrechtsausschusses," 186.

71 On the frequency of Paragraph 175 prosecutions, see Dickinson, "Policing Sex."

72 Kahl, "§175."

73 Ibid.

74 Grzesinski, Polizeipräsident report, 20 April 1926, GStAPK I. HA Rep. 84a, Nr. 8100, 362–7.

75 Kahl, "§175."

76 "Die Verhandlungen des Strafrechtsausschusses," 213.

77 Ibid., 214.

78 "In Erpresserhänden," *Berliner Stadtblatt*, 23 December 1926, in LA A Rep. 358–01, Mf. Nr. 718. See also Lücke's analysis of this case: *Männlichkeit*, 142–9.

79 Decision of 22 December 1926, LA A Rep. 358–01 Mf. Nr. 718.

80 "In Erpresserhänden."

81 Decision of 22 December 1926, LA A Rep. 358–01 Mf. Nr. 718.

82 "Die Verhandlungen des Strafrechtsausschusses," 218.

83 Hirschfeld, *Homosexualität*, 884–5, 897. On blackmail and homosexuality see also Angus McLaren, *Sexual Blackmail: A Modern History* (Cambridge, MA: Harvard University Press, 2002).

84 Berlin Police to Prussian Welfare Ministry, report on the investigation of the Institute for Sexual Science, 24 July 1920, GStAPK I. HA Rep. 76 VIII B Nr. 2076, 7–8.

85 "Hochkonjunktur in Erpressungen," *WhKM* Nr. 19, January 1929.

86 Hiller, *Eros*, 52.

87 Linsert, "Strichjunge," 62.

88 On this, see also Lücke, *Männlichkeit*, 124, 128–31, 139.

89 McElligott, *Rethinking*, 94.

90 Harvey, *Youth and the Welfare State*, 103; Swett, *Neighbors and Enemies*, 117–19.

91 See pp. 105–6.

92 Wetzell, *Inventing*, 75–6.

93 Wolff, *Hirschfeld*, 43.

94 Rosenblum, *Beyond*, 1–3.

95 Ibid., 3.

96 Wetzell, *Inventing*, 91; Lücke, *Männlichkeit*, 130–1; Max Alsberg, "Wilhelm Kahl," *Vossische Zeitung*, 15 May 1932.

97 "Das neue Strafrecht," *Dresdner Anzeiger*, 27 February 1930. On Liszt's influence on Kahl, see also Wetzell, *Inventing*, 90–5; Alsberg, "Wilhelm Kahl."

98 "Die Verhandlungen des Strafrechtsausschusses," 218.

99 Ernst Müller-Meinigen, "Reform des Strafrechts" [publication title illegible], 1930, in BArch R 3001/6033, 104.

100 "Die Verhandlungen des Strafrechtsausschusses," 211.
101 Köhler, "Staatsanwalt und §175," *Berliner Börsen-Courier*, 19 October 1929.
102 Wetzell, *Inventing*, 145.
103 Albert Moll, *Die Konträre Sexualempfindung* (Berlin: Fischers Medizin Buch-handlung, 1899), 250–1, 254.
104 Moll, "Die sozialen Formen der sexuellen Beziehungen," 385.
105 Ibid.
106 Placzek, *Homosexualität und Recht*, 79–80.
107 Gaupp, "Das Problem," 1033–4.
108 Hirschfeld, "Die männliche Prostitution," 16–17. See also Hirschfeld, *Homosexualität*, 712–13, where he makes the same point.
109 Hirschfeld, "Die männliche Prostitution," 19.
110 Ibid.
111 Lücke also notes this: *Männlichkeit*, 239, 242–3. On the film, see also p. 33.
112 Hirschfeld, *Homosexualität*, 713.
113 "Die Verhandlungen des Strafrechtsausschusses," 184; "Deutscher Reichs-stag: Beratungen des Strafgesetzausschusses," 213–14.
114 "Deutscher Reichstag: Beratungen des Strafgesetzausschusses," 222.
115 "Paragraph 175 gestrichen – und wieder eingeführt," *Die Rote Fahne*, 18 October 1928.
116 Schoppmann, *Nationalsozialistische Sexualpolitik*, 125. See also Gaupp, "Das Problem."
117 Kahl, "§175."
118 "Die Verhandlungen des Strafrechtsausschusses," 187.
119 Ibid., 185.
120 Schoppmann, *Nationalsozialistische Sexualpolitik*, 124–5. See also Florian Mildenberger, "Kraepelin and the 'Urnings': Male Homosexuality in Psy-chiatric Discourse," *History of Psychiatry* 18 (2007): 321–35. On mainstream psychiatry's generally critical reaction to Hirschfeld's work, see Milden-berger, ... *in der Richtung der Homosexualität verdorben*.
121 See p. 190.
122 "Deutscher Reichstag: Beratungen des Strafgesetzausschusses," 222.
123 Rudolf Olden, "Einmal hin, einmal her ...," *Berliner Tageblatt*, 3 January 1930.
124 "Kundgebung des Vorstandes des W.H.K. Der §175 nicht gefallen!" *WhKM* Nr. 26, December 1929/January 1930.
125 Hauenstein, "Wilhelm Kahl."
126 Hiller, *Logos*, 208–9, 388.
127 Magnus Hirschfeld, "An die Mitglieder des WHK," *WhKM* Nr. 25, Novem-ber 1929.

128 Karl Besser, "Magnus Hirschfeld und das WHK," *WhKM* Nr. 25, November 1929. On Besser see Richard Linsert, "Worte am Grabe Karl Bessers," *WhKM* Nr. 30, March/August 1931.

129 Besser, "Magnus Hirschfeld und das WHK." In the revised penal code, the sodomy paragraph would have been numbered 296.

130 Friedrich Radszuweit, "Kritisches über unsere Bewegung," *Blätter für Menschenrecht* 11, no. 8 (November 1930).

131 Linsert, "Worte am Grabe."

132 A few years later, Paul Weber alleged that members of the WhK had claimed the latter: Paul Weber, "Lügen haben kurze Beine," *Blätter für Menschenrecht*, October/November 1932.

133 "Die organisatorische Umstellung des WHK," *WhKM* Nr. 27, February/March 1930.

134 Ibid.; "Traurige Tatsachen," *WhKM* Nr. 28, April/August 1930.

135 "Organisatorische Mitteilungen," *WhKM* Nr. 29, September 1930/February 1931.

136 "Die organisatorische Umstellung"; "Traurige Tatsachen."

137 Hauenstein, "Wilhelm Kahl." For Hauenstein as a Hiller pseudonym, see Pfäfflin, "Mitteilungen," xii.

138 Hodann and Linsert to Brupacher, 26 February 1930, in Pfäfflin, "Mitteilungen," xii–xiii. On Hodann, see Grossmann, *Reforming Sex*, 96 and elsewhere.

139 "Die Verhandlungen des Strafrechtsausschusses," 187; League for Human Rights, resolution from 23 September 1929 meeting, letter of 9 October 1929, BArch R 3001/5775; riku, "Scharmutzel," *WhKM* Nr. 34, September 1932/February 1933; "Die Verhandlungen des Strafrechtsausschusses," 187; Hauenstein, "Wilhelm Kahl"; Weber, "Lugen."

140 Besser, WhK, to Kahl, 26 September 1929, BArch R 3001/5775. One aspect of this letter possibly conflicts with what Linsert and Hodann wrote: they claimed Hirschfeld sent the letter to Kahl, but this letter is signed by Karl Besser. However, Linsert and Hodann also claimed that Hirschfeld had hoodwinked a member of the executive committee about the letter before it went in the mail. It seems possible that by this they meant that he had somehow roped Besser into the operation without making Besser fully aware of what was going on: Hodann and Linsert to Brupacher, in Pfäfflin, "Mitteilungen," xiii.

141 Pfäfflin, "Mitteilungen," xii.

142 O. Juliusburger, "Zur 'Behandlungen' der Homosexualität," *WhKM* 27, February/March 1930.

143 On Gaupp's article being widely read, see Juliusburger, "Zur 'Behandlungen.'"
144 Gaupp, "Das Problem," 1038. For more on Gaupp, who was also a major
     proponent of sterilizing criminals, see Wetzell, *Inventing*, 243–4.
145 Wolff, *Hirschfeld*, 428.
146 Ingo-Wolf Kittel, "Arthur Kronfeld zur Erinnerung," in *Arthur Kronfeld
     1886–1941: Ein Pionier der Psychologie, Sexualwissenschaft und Psychotherapie*
     (Konstanz: Bibliothek der Universität Konstanz, 1988), 7–13.
147 Arthur Kronfeld, "Zur 'konstitutionellen Bedingtheit' der Homosexual-
     ität," *WhKM* Nr. 26, December 1929/January 1930.
148 Ibid.
149 Pfäfflin, "Mitteilungen," xii. Pfällin's is the only account that portrays the
     resignation as having a broad significance for the history of homosexual
     emancipation. After Hirschfeld, he writes, the WhK grew more political,
     struggled more overtly against the Nazis, entertained a greater diversity of
     scientific opinion, and even distanced itself from science. Pfäfflin notes
     a number of issues that, he argues, caused the resignation, including sci-
     ence, financial questions, and other factors. In contrast, I argue that surviv-
     ing sources point to science as the central problem.
150 James Steakley, "*Per scientiam ad justitiam*: Magnus Hirschfeld and the
     Sexual Politics of Innate Homosexuality," in *Science and Homosexualities*, ed.
     Vernon Rosario (New York and London: Routledge, 1997), 140.
151 This was the case after Iwan Bloch's death in 1922. Moll was the only other
     living German sexologist whose authority matched Hirschfeld's in 1929.
152 Hirschfeld, "An die Mitglieder des WHK."
153 Radszuweit, "Führer."
154 Friedrich Radszuweit, "Fort mit den Ausnahmegesetzen!" *Blätter für Men-
     schenrecht*, 15 October 1923; Radszuweit, "Sieg oder Niederlage," *Blätter für
     Menschenrecht* 3, no. 9 (September 1925); Radszuweit, "Falsche Weg: Män-
     nliche Kultur – oder – medizinische Wissenschaft?" *Blätter für Menschenrecht*
     3, no. 11 (November 1925); Ramsey, "Erotic Friendship," 260–1. See also
     Ramsey, "Rites."
155 Radszuweit, *Führer*.
156 For WhK criticism of the League for Human Rights, see riku, "Scharmützel."
     It seems possible that the byline on this piece, "riku," is a pseudonym for Lin-
     sert and Hiller. It is a combination of the first two letters of their first names.
157 Ramsey, "Erotic Friendship," 260–1.
158 Kurt Hiller, "Recht und sexuelle Minderheiten," *Das Tagebuch* 47, 19
     November 1921, 1400–1, 1435, translated and reprinted in Kaes, Jay, and
     Dimendberg, *Weimar Republic Sourcebook*, 696–7.

159 "Vorwort," *WhKM* Nr. 32, January/March 1932.

160 See pp. 6–7.

161 Hiller, "Gefängnis für männliche Prostituierte?"

162 Hiller, "Recht und sexuelle Minderheiten." See also Kurt Hiller, "Das neue Sexualstrafrecht und die schwarze Gefahr," *Die Weltbühne* Nr. 32, 5 August 1930, 191–6.

163 On this see also Ramsey, "Rites," 95.

164 On this see also Hirschfeld, *Sappho und Sokrates*, though note that he later repudiated some of what he wrote there: Hirschfeld, *Homosexualität*, 372.

165 On the debate, see Andreas Seeck, "Einführung," in *Durch Wissenschaft zur Gerechtigkeit? Textsammlung zur kritischen Rezeption des Schaffens von Magnus Hirschfeld*, ed. Andreas Seeck (Münster: Lit Verlag, 2003), 7–24; Herzer, *Hirschfeld*, 12–13.

166 Maurice van Lieshout, "Lucien von Römer," in Lautmann, *Homosexualität: Handbuch*, 141–6.

167 Hirschfeld, *Homosexualität*, 390.

168 Ibid., 391; see also 392.

169 Ibid., 391.

170 Ibid., 391–2; see also 42.

171 Ibid., 392–3.

172 Magnus Hirschfeld, *Women East and West: Impressions of a Sex Expert*, trans. O.P. Green (London: William Heinemann, 1935), 232. See also Hirschfeld, *Sappho und Sokrates*, foreword to the 1902 edition.

173 Herrn, *Schnittmuster*, 123–6.

174 League for Human Rights letter, 9 October 1929, BArch R 3001/5775.

175 Hirschfeld, "Die männliche Prostitution," 32.

176 Ibid., 24. See also Magnus Hirschfeld, "Aus der Erpresserpraxis," *JfsZ* 13, no. 3 (April 1913): 293–4.

177 Paul Weber, "Sind Homosexuelle Ausbeuter der Prostituierten?" *Die Freundin*, 13 January 1933. In this essay, Weber includes a long quotation of the piece by Hirschfeld defending male prostitutes, which apparently ran in a Berlin women's magazine.

178 Hirschfeld, *Geschlechtskunde* III, 351.

179 Hirschfeld, *Homosexualität*, 876.

180 "Komitee-Mitteilungen," *JfsZ* 21 (July/October 1921).

181 Radszuweit, who died at the age of fifty-six, had suffered for years from a chronic illness: Paul Weber, "Friedrich Radszuweit ist tot," *Die Freundin*, 3 April 1932.

182 Weber, "Sind Homosexuelle Ausbeuter der Prostituierten?"

183 Hirschfeld, *Geschlechtskunde* III, 350.

184 Besser, "Magnus Hirschfeld und das WhK," 200.

185 Hirschfeld, "An die Mitglieder des WHK."

186 Wolff, *Hirschfeld,* 228. In the article about the meeting of the *Obmannschaft* in the WhK's magazine, the vote to oppose the reform is reported before Hirschfeld's resignation, which gives the impression that Hirschfeld took part in the vote and then resigned. However, as he was in the process of being forced out of the leadership against his will, it seems more likely that he resigned and that then the remaining leaders determined the WhK's future: "Wichtige Beschlüsse der Obmannschaft des W.H.K. vom 24 November 1929," *WhKM* Nr. 25, November 1929.

187 On Linsert's influence, see Heinrich Stabel, "Vereinte Trauergenossen!" *WhKM* Nr. 34, September 1932/February 1933.

188 WhK to Reich Justice Minister, 4 July 1930, BArch R 3001/5775.

189 Pfäfflin, "Mitteilungen," ix–x.

190 Kollenbroich, *Our Hour,* 260–2. Kollenbroich also argues that the remaining WhK leadership wanted to distance itself from Hirschfeld's public image; I see no evidence for this.

191 Dose, *Hirschfeld,* 62–3.

192 Herzer, "Schwule Preussen," 16–18. Herzer's account has been used by other scholars: Mancini, *Hirschfeld,* 124; Jellonnek, *Homosexuelle,* 48–9.

193 Hodann and Linsert to Brupacher, in Pfäfflin, "Mitteilungen," xi; Wolff, *Hirschfeld,* 428; Hirschfeld to Haire, 23 June 1930, quoted in Wolff, *Hirschfeld,* 440; Weber, "Lügen."

194 Kurt Hiller, "Antwort an [anonymous]," *WhKM* Nr. 32, January/March 1932.

195 Two of Hirschfeld's supporters whom Wolff interviewed said as much: *Hirschfeld,* 428, 433.

196 About being relieved of financial duties: Hodann and Linsert to Brupacher, in Pfäfflin, "Mitteilungen," xi.

197 Hiller describes Linsert's communism as pragmatic: Hiller, *Eros,* 101–2. It seems likely that Linsert was not a diehard ideologue given his involvement with Münzenberg, who sought alliances with non-Communist leftists.

198 In addition, a Hirschfeld friend interviewed by Wolff who discussed Hirschfeld's resignation from the WhK did not report that debates about gender non-conformity played a role: *Hirschfeld,* 428.

199 Hirschfeld, *Homosexualität,* 30. On these disagreements, which were more acute prior to the First World War, see Herrn, *Schnittmuster,* 38–40; Ramsey, "Erotic Friendship," 278; Dose, *Hirschfeld,* 56; Dickinson, *Politics,* 169–70.

200 Kurt Hiller, "Die Homosexuelle Frage," in Murat, *Mitteilungen des Wissenschaftlich-humanitären Komitees 1926–1933,* i–iv.

201 Quoted in Ramsey, "Erotic Friendship," 260–1. Ramsey's translation.

202 Radszuweit, "Führer."

203 Adolf Brand, "Entgegnung," *Der Eigene* Nr. 8 vol. 11, no. 8 [probably 1927], 268–9.

204 Dickinson, *Sex*, 167–8.

205 Proponents of decriminalization also used this argument after 1945: Jennifer Evans, "Bahnhof Boys: Policing Male Prostitution in Post-Nazi Berlin," *Journal of the History of Sexuality* 12, no. 4 (2003): 605–36.

206 "Aus der Bewegung," *JfsZ* 19 (July/October 1919): 133.

207 Reichstag Antrag Nr. 346, 15 January 1925, in GStAPK I. HA Rep. 84a Nr. 8100, 318.

208 Hirschfeld, Hiller, Ferd. Frhr. V. Reitzenstein, Karsch-Haack, for the WhK, to the Reich Justice Minister, 29 January 1925, GStAPK I. HA Rep. 84a Nr. 8100, 320.

209 Hirschfeld has been posthumously criticized for unintentionally reifying harmful science, such as that which sought to cure homosexuality. See the discussion in Seeck, *Durch Wissenschaft zur Gerechtigkeit?*; see also Gunter Schmidt, "Allies and Persecutors: Science and Medicine in the Homosexuality Issue," *Journal of Homosexuality* 10, nos. 3–4 (1984): 127–40; Nancy Ordover, *American Eugenics: Race, Queer Anatomy, and the Science of Nationalism* (Minneapolis: University of Minnesota Press, 2003), 84–5. Hirschfeld was not, however, generally supportive of attempts to cure homosexuality. My aim here is not to amplify these critiques.

210 Dämon's letter of 28 October 1934, LA A Rep. 358–01 Mf. Nr. 718.

211 LA A Rep. 358–01 Mf. Nr. 718.

5 "The Third Sex Greets the Third Reich!": The Röhm Scandal, 1931–1932

1 Eleanor Hancock, *Ernst Röhm: Hitler's SA Chief of Staff* (New York: Palgrave Macmillan, 2008), 116–17.

2 "Nationalsozialistischer Gewaltakt im Reichstag," *Vossische Zeitung* (Abend), 12 May 1932.

3 "Gefängnisstrafe für drei NSDAP-Abgeordnete," *Berliner Lokal-Anzeiger* (Morgen), 14 May 1932.

4 "Der Überfall im Reichstag," *Vossische Zeitung* (Morgen), 14 May 1932.

5 "Nationalsozialistischer Gewaltakt im Reichstag"; "Der Überfall im Reichstag"; "Gefängnisstrafe für drei NSDAP-Abgeordnete"; "Nazi-Faustrecht sprengt Reichstag," *Germania*, 13 May 1932; "Der Prozeß gegen die vier Abgeordneten," *Vossische Zeitung* (Morgen), 14 May 1932.

6 On Weiss, see Hsi-huey Liang, *The Berlin Police Force in the Weimar Republic* (Berkeley: University of California, 1970), 158–61.

7 "Polizei erscheint im Sitzungs-Saal," *Münchner Neueste Nachrichten*, 13 May 1932.

8 "Nazi-Faustrecht sprengt Reichstag"; "Darstellung der Polizei," *Germania*, 13 May 1932.

9 Paul Weber, "Das alte und das neue Jahr," *Die Freundin*, 28 December 1932. When he wrote this article, Weber was the head of the League for Human Rights. He took on the position after Radszuweit's death.

10 Susanne zur Nieden, "Aufstieg und Fall des virilen Männerhelden: Der Skandal um Ernst Röhm und seine Ermordung," in *Homosexualität und Staatsräson: Männlichkeit, Homophobie und Politik in Deutschland 1900–1945*, ed. Susanne zur Nieden (Frankfurt: Campus, 2005), 147–88; Alexander Zinn, *Die soziale Konstruktion des homosexuellen Nationalsozialisten: Zu Genese und Etablierung eines Stereotyps* (Frankfurt: Peter Lang, 1997), 44–51; Jellonnek, *Homosexuelle*, 66–9; Eleanor Hancock, "'Only the Real, the True, the Masculine Held Its Value': Ernst Röhm, Masculinity, and Male Homosexuality," *Journal of the History of Sexuality* 8, no. 4 (1998): 628–35; Hancock, *Röhm*, 113–18.

11 Zur Nieden, "Aufstieg und Fall," 171–2. See also Jellonnek, who reports that the scandal was limited to the leftist press, which it was at first, but not after the brawl: *Homosexuelle*, 67–8.

12 Jellonnek, *Homosexuelle*, 68; zur Nieden, "Aufstieg und Fall," 175.

13 Hancock, *Röhm*, 34–5.

14 Ibid., 56.

15 Röhm to Heimsoth, 25 February 1929, in Herbert Heinersdorf, "Akten zum Falle Röhm" (II. Teil), *WhKM* Nr. 33, April/August 1932.

16 Hancock, *Röhm*, 89. On the Eldorado, see Roellig, *Berlins lesbische Frauen*, 42.

17 Friedrich Radszuweit, "Hauptmann a. D. Röhm," *Die Freundin*, 30 March 1932.

18 Hancock, *Röhm*, 90.

19 Ibid., 89.

20 Quoted in Steakley, *Homosexual Emancipation Movement*, 84. Steakley's translation.

21 "Homosexualität und Nationalsozialismus," *WhKM*, March 1929; Jellonnek, *Homosexuelle*, 140–71.

22 Zur Nieden, "Aufstieg und Fall," 153.

23 "Aus der Bewegung," *JfsZ* 20, nos. 3–4 (July/October 1920).

24 Friedrich Radszuweit, "Lehrreiche statistische Feststellungen!" *Blätter für Menschenrecht*, September/November 1926.

25 Steakley, *Homosexual Emancipation Movement*, 91.

26 Such as Karl Günter Heimsoth and Paul Harald Grävell, who wrote for a Nordic, male supremacist journal admired by Hitler: Steakley, *Homosexual Emancipation Movement*, 43, 66–7n34.

27 Ibid., 43–54; Kollenbroich, *Our Hour*, 25–39, 282–4. On antisemitism and proto-fascism in Brand's group, see Marita Keilson-Lauritz, "Tanten, Kerle und Skandale: Die Geburt des 'modernen Homosexuellen' aus den Flügelkämpfen der Emanzipation," in zur Nieden, *Homosexualität und Staatsräson*, 81–99; Manfred Herzer, "Antisemitismus und Rechtsradikalismus bei Adolf Brand," *Capri: Zeitschrift für schwule Geschichte* 21 (1996): 37–41.

28 Quoted in Hancock, *Röhm*, 90. Hancock's translation.

29 Zur Nieden, "Aufstieg und Fall," 152.

30 Röhm to Heimsoth, 12 March 1928, reprinted in Herbert Heinersdorf, "Akten zum Falle Röhm" (II. Teil), *WhKM* Nr. 33, April/August 1932, 391.

31 Zur Nieden, "Aufstieg und Fall," 155.

32 Ibid., 159–63.

33 Keilson-Lauritz, "Tanten, Kerle und Skandale," 91.

34 Anonymous, "Nationalsozialismus und Inversion," *WhKM* 32, January/March 1932; Hancock, "Only the Real."

35 Röhm's letters to Heimsoth are reprinted in Herbert Heinersdorf, "Akten zum Falle Röhm," *WhKM*, January/March 1932 and September 1932/February 1933.

36 Zinn, *Die soziale Konstruktion*; Anson Rabinbach, "Van der Lubbe – ein Lustknabe Röhms? Die politische Dramaturgie der Exilkampagne zum Reichstagsbrand," in zur Nieden, *Homosexualität und Staatsräson*, 193–216.

37 Zinn, *Die soziale Konstruktion*; Dagmar Herzog, *Sex after Fascism: Memory and Morality in Twentieth-century Germany* (Princeton: Princeton University Press, 2007), 12–13, 157; Paul Morrison, *The Explanation for Everything: Essays on Sexual Subjectivity* (New York: New York University Press, 2001), 140–73; Carolyn J. Dean, *The Fragility of Empathy after the Holocaust* (Ithaca, NY: Cornell University Press, 2004), 106–36.

38 See Dean's review of literature: *Fragility*, 109–11.

39 Klaus Mann, "Die Linke und das 'Laster,'" *Europäische Hefte* 36–7 (1934): 675–8; Harry Oosterhuis, "The 'Jews' of the Antifascist Left: Homosexuality and Socialist Resistance to Nazism," in *Gay Men and the Sexual History of the Political Left*, ed. Gert Hekma, Harry Oosterhuis, and James Steakley (Binghamton, NY: Haworth Press, 1995), 227–58.

40 Dean, *Fragility*, 108–9; Herzog, *Sex after Fascism*, 157–8. For other thoughts on why it persists, see Herzog, *Sex after Fascism*, 12–13; Morrison, *Explanation*, 140–73; Dean, *Fragility*, 106–36.

41 The evidence that Hitler was homosexual is speculative at best. It is based on slanders his enemies launched against him beginning in the campaigns of the Weimar era. A recent version of this canard received a lot of attention: Lothar Machtan, *The Hidden Hitler*, trans. John Brownjohn and Susanne Ehlert (New York: Basic Books, 2002); on Machtan's book, see Geoffrey Giles, "Lothar Machtan, *The Hidden Hitler*," *Washington Post*, 25 November 2001; Dean, *Fragility*, 110–11. On Hitler's sexuality, see Ian Kershaw, *Hitler: 1889–1936: Hubris* (New York: Norton, 1998), 43–6, 351–5.

42 Herzog, *Sex after Fascism*, 12–13; Morrison, *Explanation*, 156.

43 As Halberstam argues with respect to Röhm and Bersani and others have argued in general: Judith Halberstam, *The Queer Art of Failure* (Durham, NC: Duke University Press, 2011), 147–71, especially 148–51. I disagree with Halberstam's argument that fascist German homosexuals have been erased from history or that there is a history of significant "overlaps" (155) between homosexuality and fascism that ought to be presented alongside the history of the persecution of gay men by the Nazi State and often is not. Historians have in fact done a good deal of investigating the common ground between fascist masculinity and Brand's wing of the homosexual emancipation movement. But this connection is not so significant that to narrate the mass murders without mentioning it constitutes a grave omission. A useful analysis of affinities between homoerotic traditions and fascism is Andrew Hewitt, *Political Inversions: Homosexuality, Fascism, and the Modernist Imaginary* (Stanford: Stanford University Press, 1996).

44 Bruce Campbell, *The SA Generals and the Rise of Nazism* (Lexington: University of Kentucky Press, 1998), 85.

45 Quoted in zur Nieden, "Aufstieg und Fall," 154.

46 Röhm to Heimsoth, 12 March 1928.

47 Hancock, *Röhm*, 89.

48 Joseph Goebbels, *Die Tagebücher von Joseph Goebbels* Band 2/II (June 1931–September 1932), ed. Elke Fröhlich (Munich: K.G. Saur, 2004), 44.

49 Zur Nieden, "Aufstieg und Fall," 165.

50 Jellonnek, *Homosexuelle*, 60–1.

51 Geoffrey Giles, "The Institutionalization of Homosexual Panic in the Third Reich," in *Social Outsiders in Nazi Germany*, ed. Robert Gellately and Nathan Stoltzfus (Princeton: Princeton University Press, 2001), 233.

52 Heinrich Hoffmann, "Erzählungen," 1954, quoted in Jellonnek, *Homosexuelle*, 58.

53 Campbell, *SA Generals*, 85–6.

54 Giles, "Homosexual Panic," 234.

55 Ibid., 235–6, 248.

56 Ibid., 236; see also 242. For a homosexual Nazi's understanding of what he believed to be his party's toleration of certain types of homosexuality in 1932, consider Anonymous, "Nationalsozialismus und Inversion."

57 Zur Nieden, "Aufstieg und Fall," 165.

58 Ibid. As early as 1929, the Nazi Party was attacked for harbouring homosexuals, according to the WhK: "Homosexualität und Nationalsozialismus," *WhKM*, March 1929.

59 Sommer, *Strafbarkeit*, 119–20.

60 Domeier, *Eulenburg-Skandal*; Hull, *Entourage*, 133–45.

61 Richard Linsert, *Kabale und Liebe: Über Politik und Geschlechtsleben* (Berlin: Man Verlag, 1931), 52.

62 Carl Severing, *Mein Lebensweg*, vol. 2 (Cologne: Greven Verlag, 1950), 331–2.

63 Zur Nieden, "Aufstieg und Fall," 168–9; Jellonnek, *Homosexuelle*, 64–5.

64 Otto Strasser may have been the real source of these allegations and of the information about Heimsoth's letters that later reached the Prussian government. He knew Heimsoth and would have welcomed the chance to attack Hitler through Röhm: Jellonnek, *Homosexuelle*, 64–5.

65 "Stammtisch 175," reprinted in Heinersdorf, "Akten zum Falle Röhm," I. Teil, *WhKM*, January/March 1932.

66 "Rassehochzüchter," reprinted in Heinersdorf, "Akten zum Falle Röhm," I. Teil.

67 "Warme Brüderschaft im Braunen Haus," reprinted in Heinersdorf, "Akten zum Falle Röhm," I. Teil.

68 Zur Nieden, "Aufstieg und Fall," 165.

69 "Das Dritte Geschlecht grüßt das Dritte Reich," *Welt am Montag*, 17 August 1932.

70 Swett, *Neighbors and Enemies*, 95.

71 Goebbels, *Tagebücher*, 44–9, 74.

72 Ibid., 47.

73 Heinersdorf, "Akten zum Falle Röhm," I. Teil; zur Nieden, "Aufstieg und Fall," 166–7.

74 Zur Nieden, "Aufstieg und Fall," 167–9; Goebbels, *Tagebücher*, 74.

75 Zur Nieden, "Aufstieg und Fall," 170.

76 See the discussion of the Zöhn case in chapter 4. On the cooperation between the Berlin police and homosexual emancipation, see Dobler, *Zwischen*, 536–7.

77 Zur Nieden, "Aufstieg und Fall," 168.

78 Ibid., 170–1.

79 Herbert Linder, *Von der NSDAP zur SPD: Der politische Lebensweg des Dr. Helmuth Klotz (1894–1943)* (Konstanz: Universitätsverlag Konstanz, 1998), 168–73. In 1943, Klotz was murdered by the Nazis.

80 Quoted in Jellonnek, *Homosexuelle,* 67.

81 The Hitler Youth began as a recruitment arm of the SA and, until 1931, was "little more than a subdivision of the SA," according to Orlow. Although it gained some organizational independence that year, it was still technically a wing of the SA in April 1932 and was thus affected by the ban on the SA: Dietrich Orlow, *The History of the Nazi Party,* vol. 1, *1919–33* (Pittsburgh: University of Pittsburgh Press, 1969), quotation at 227, 197, 252.

82 Heinersdorf, "Akten zum Falle Röhm," I. Teil, II. Teil.

83 Linder, *Von der NSDAP zur SPD,* 173.

84 Ibid., 173–4.

85 Hancock, *Röhm,* 115. The Hitler Youth under Baldur von Schirach became officially independent of the SA on 13 May 1932.

86 Goebbels, *Tagebücher,* 235.

87 Ibid., 238.

88 Quoted in zur Nieden, "Aufstieg und Fall," 174; see also Orlow, *Nazi Party,* 251.

89 Goebbels, *Tagebücher,* 254.

90 Zur Nieden, "Aufstieg und Fall," 174; Hancock, *Röhm,* 115–16.

91 Zur Nieden, "Aufstieg und Fall," 173.

92 Hull, *Entourage,* 169–71; Margaret Lavinia Anderson, *Practicing Democracy: Elections and Political Culture in Imperial Germany* (Princeton, NJ: Princeton University Press, 2000), 273.

93 Eberhard Kolb, *The Weimar Republic* (New York: Routledge, 2004), 227.

94 "Schlägerei im Reichstagsgebäude," *Berliner Lokal-Anzeiger* (Abend), 12 May 1932; "Groener als Reichswehrminister zurückgetreten: Große Polizei-Aktion im Reichstag: Wie die Tagung aufflog," *Berliner Lokal-Anzeiger* (Morgen), 13 May 1932; "Gregor Straßer im D-Zug festgenommen," *Berliner Lokal-Anzeiger* (Abend), 13 May 1932; "Gefängnisstrafe für drei NSDAP-Abgeordnete"; "Der Prozeß gegen die vier Abgeordneten."

95 Heinz-Dietrich Fischer, "Deutsche Allgemeine Zeitung (1861–1945)," in *Deutsche Zeitungen des 17. bis 20. Jahrhunderts,* ed. Heinz-Dietrich Fischer (Pullach bei München: Verlag Dokumentation, 1972), 279.

96 F.K., "Aufgeflogen!" *Deutsche Allgemeine Zeitung,* 14 May 1932.

97 John Leopold, *Alfred Hugenberg: The Radical Nationalist Campaign against the Weimar Republic* (New Haven, CT: Yale University Press, 1977), 96.

98 "Gefängnisstrafe für drei NSDAP-Abgeordnete."

99 "30 Stimmen Mehrheit für Brüning: Schlägerei im Reichstagsgebäude," *Berliner Lokal-Anzeiger,* 12 May 1932.

100 "Groener als Reichswehrminister zurückgetreten."

101 Friedrich Huffong, "Der geborstene Reichstag," *Berliner Lokal-Anzeiger*, 13 May 1932.
102 "Groener als Reichswehrminister zurückgetreten."
103 Klaus Bender, "Vossische Zeitung (1617–1934)," in Fischer, *Deutsche Zeitungen*, 38–9.
104 "Nationalsozialistischer Gewaltakt im Reichstag."
105 "Wer ist Klotz?" *Vossische Zeitung* (Abend), 12 May 1932.
106 M.J., "Das Echo der Ohrfeigen," *Vossische Zeitung* (Abend), 14 May 1932.
107 "Ein nationalsozialistischer Roheitsakt im Reichstag," *Frankfurter Zeitung*, 13 May 1932.
108 "Der nationalsozialistische Überfall vor Gericht," *Frankfurter Zeitung*, 14 May 1932.
109 "Schlägerei im Restaurant und in der Wandelhalle," *Münchner Neueste Nachrichten*, 13 May 1932.
110 "Nazi-Faustrecht sprengt Reichstag"; "Die 'Ritter' des Faustrechts," *Germania*, 14 May 1932.
111 "Vor dem Schnellrichter," *Kölnische Volkszeitung*, 14 May 1932. See also "Politische Wochenschau," *Stuttgarter Neues Tagblatt*, 19 May 1932.
112 F.K., "Aufgeflogen!"
113 Ibid.
114 Erich Ludendorff, *Heraus aus dem braunen Sumpf! Sagt General Ludendorff* (Munich: Ludendorffs Volkswarte-Verlag, 1932).
115 On the Röhm purge see zur Nieden, "Aufstieg und Fall"; Giles, "Panic"; Jellonnek, *Homosexuelle*, 95–9; Hancock, *Röhm*, 141–66; Stefan Micheler and Patricia Szobar, "Homophobic Propaganda and the Denunciation of Same-Sex-Desiring Men under National Socialism," *Journal of the History of Sexuality* 11 (2002): 95–130.
116 Hancock, *Röhm*, 153.
117 Ibid., 162–4; zur Nieden, "Aufstieg und Fall," 178–87.
118 See p. 45.
119 *Deutschland-Bericht der Sozialdemokratischen Partei Deutschlands* (Salzhausen and Frankfurt am Main: Verlag Petra Nettelbeck und Zweitausendeins, 1980 [1934]), 198.
120 Ibid., 200.
121 Ibid., 201.
122 "Nazi-Faustrecht sprengt Reichstag."
123 "Der Überfall im Reichstag."
124 Masur, quoted in "Gefängnisstrafe für drei NSDAP-Abgeordnete."
125 M.J., "Das Echo der Ohrfeigen." See also "Gefängnisstrafe für drei NSDAP-Abgeordnete."

126 M.J., "Das Echo der Ohrfeigen"; "Der Prozeß gegen die vier Abgeordneten"; "Freiheitsstrafen für die Ruhestörer im Reichstag," *Münchner Neueste Nachrichten*, 14 May 1932; "Vor dem Schnellrichter."

127 Paul Löbe, "Der erste Schlag," *Vorwärts*, 15 March 1932.

128 "Die wüste Szene im Reichstag," *Frankfurter Zeitung*, 13 May 1932.

129 Ibid.

130 "Die nationalsozialistischen Exzesse vor dem Ältestenrat," *Frankfurter Zeitung*, 14 May 1932.

131 "Glaube oder Aberglaube?" *Frankfurter Zeitung*, 15 May 1932. Denouncing Nazism as "barbarism" did not necessarily have nothing to do with Röhm's sexuality. An old idea that was often evident in European imperialism blamed a lack of civilization for immoral sexuality, including male homosexuality. The accusation that male homosexuality was a regression into barbarism had been made during the Eulenburg Affair: Laurie Marhoefer, "Homosexuality and Theories of Culture," in *Was ist Homosexualität? Forschungsgeschichte, gesellschaftliche Entwicklungen und Perspektiven*, ed. Jennifer Evans, Florian Mildenberger, Rüdiger Lautmann, and Jakob Pastötter (Hamburg: Männerschwarm, 2014), 255–6; Domeier, *Eulenburg-Skandal*, 194.

132 Ibid.

133 "Gefängnisstrafe für drei NSDAP-Abgeordnete."

134 "Unsere Meinung," *Deutsche Allgemeine Zeitung*, 13 May 1932.

135 Ibid., 14 May 1932.

136 Herbert Heinersdorf, "Akten zum Falle Röhm" (III. Teil) *WhKM* Nr. 34, September 1932/February 1933, 423. On SPD attacks of this nature, see Usborne, *Politics*, 100; Julia Sneeringer, *Winning Women's Votes: Propaganda and Politics in Weimar Germany* (Chapel Hill: University of North Carolina Press, 2002), 253.

137 M.J., "Das Echo der Ohrfeigen."

138 Huffong, "Der geborstene Reichstag."

139 Lybeck, *Desiring*, 105–6.

140 "Gefängnisstrafe für drei NSDAP-Abgeordnete."

141 M.J., "Das Echo der Ohrfeigen."

142 Kurt Tucholsky, "Röhm," *Die Weltbühne* 17, 26 April 1932, 641, in Kaes, Jay, and Dimendberg, *Weimar Republic Sourcebook*, 714. Don Reneau's translation.

143 Hancock, *Röhm*, 133.

144 Friedrich Radszuweit, "Hauptmann a. D. Röhm," *Die Freundin*, 30 March 1932.

145 Ibid.

146 On antisemitism in *Girlfriend* see also Lybeck, "Writing Love," 165.

147 Quoted in Lybeck, "Gender, Sexuality, and Belonging," 380.
148 Hiller, "Antwort."
149 "Antworten," *WhKM* Nr. 31, September/December 1931.
150 Heinersdorf, "Akten." The byline on these articles, "Herbert Heinersdorf," is a Linsert pseudonym: Hiller, *Eros*, 107.
151 "Der Fall Röhm," *WhKM* Nr. 32, January/March 1932.
152 Jellonnek, *Homosexuelle*, 328.

6 The Politics of "Immoral" Sexuality in the Fall of the Weimar Republic and the Rise of the Nazis

1 Alexandra Ripa, "Hirschfeld privat: Seine Haushälterin erinnert sich," in *Magnus Hirschfeld: En Leben im Spannungsfeld von Wissenschaft, Politik und Gesellschaft*, ed. Elke-Vera Kotowski and Julius H. Schoeps (Berlin: be.bra wissenschaft verlag, 2004), 68.
2 Wolff, *Hirschfeld*, 376–9; "Nazi Students Raid Institute on Sex," *New York Times*, 7 May 1933; Jellonnek, *Homosexuelle*, 82; Gunter Grau, ed., *Hidden Holocaust? Gay and Lesbian Persecution in Germany 1933–45*, trans. Patrick Camiller (London: Cassell, 1993), 31–3.
3 Regarding *Berlin's Lesbian Women* being seized: Schoppmann, *Nationalsozialistische Sexualpolitik*, 173. For bars and clubs ordered to shut on 23 February 1933, see Dobler, *Zwischen*, 545; Grau, *Hidden Holocaust*, 27–8. On the first fourteen bars and clubs, including the Magic Flute, that were shut on 4 March 1933, see Dobler, *Zwischen*, 546. For the ban on publications: Grau, *Hidden Holocaust*, 29–30.
4 Sellmann, *50 Jahre Kampf*, 108–11; Grossmann, *Reforming Sex*, 135–7; Jellonnek, *Homosexuelle*, 80–2.
5 Roos, *Lens*, 214–27; Jessica Anderson Hughes, "Forced Prostitution: The Competing and Contested Uses of the Concentration Camp Brothel" (PhD diss., Rutgers University–New Brunswick, 2011); Schoppmann, *Nationalsozialistische Sexualpolitik*, 95.
6 Sommer, *Strafbarkeit*, 314–15; Jellonnek, *Homosexuelle*, 110–11; Grau, *Hidden Holocaust*, 64–6.
7 The following is a by-no-means-exhaustive list of studies on the Nazi persecution of men accused of homosexuality: Jellonnek, *Homosexuelle*; Micheler, *Selbstbilder und Fremdbilder*; Stefan Micheler, ed., *Invertito* Jahrgang 2 (2002), *Denunziert, verfolgt, ermordet: Homosexuelle Männer und Frauen in der NS-Zeit*; Grau, *Hidden Holocaust*; Burkhard Jellonnek and Rüdiger Lautmann, eds., *Nationalsozialistischer Terror gegen Homosexuelle: Verdrängt und ungesühnt* (Paderborn: Schöningh, 2002); Giles, "Homosexual Panic"; Giles, "The

Denial of Homosexuality: Same-Sex Incidents in Himmler's SS and Police,"
in *Sexuality and German Fascism*, ed. Dagmar Herzog (New York: Berghahn,
2005), 256–90; Giles, "A Gray Zone among the Field Gray Men: Confusion
in the Discrimination against Homosexuals in the *Wehrmacht*," in *Gray Zones:
Ambiguity and Compromise in the Holocaust and Its Aftermath*, ed. Jonathan
Petropoulos and John K. Roth (New York: Berghahn, 2005), 127–46; Giles,
"'The Most Unkindest Cut of All': Castration, Homosexuality and Nazi
Justice," *Journal of Contemporary History* 27, no. 1 (1992): 41–61; Giles, "Legislating Homophobia in the Third Reich: The Radicalization of Prosecution
against Homosexuality by the Legal Profession," *German History* 23 (2005):
339–54; Andreas Pretzel and Gabriele Roßbach, eds., *"Wegen der zu erwartenden hohen Strafe … ": Homosexuellenverfolgung in Berlin 1933–1945* (Berlin:
Verlag Rosa Winkel, 2000); Susanne zur Nieden, *Erbbiologische Forschung
zur Homosexualität an der Deutschen Forschungsanstalt für Psychiatrie während
der Jahre des Nationalsozialismus; zur Geschichte von Theo Lang* (Berlin: Max-
Planck-Ges. Zur Förderung der Wiss., 2005); zur Nieden, *Homosexualität und
Staatsräson*.

8 Sellmann, *50 Jahre Kampf*, 107.
9 Quoted in Gerhart Binder, *Irrtum und Widerstand: Die deutschen Katholiken
   in der Auseinandersetzung mit dem Nationalsozialismus* (Munich: J. Pfeiffer,
   1968), 1.
10 Roos, *Lens*, 10.
11 Weitz, *Weimar Germany*, 358. See also Weitz, "Weimar Germany and Its
   Historians," 582. Richard McCormick makes a similar point: *Gender and
   Sexuality in Weimar Modernity: Film, Literature, and "New Objectivity"* (New York:
   Palgrave Macmillan, 2001), 7.
12 Roos, *Lens*, 13.
13 Elizabeth Heineman, *Before Porn Was Legal: The Erotic Empire of Beate Uhse*
   (Chicago: University of Chicago Press, 2011), 13.
14 Evans, *Coming of the Third Reich*, 265, 125–9; Roos, *Lens*, 205–10; Mosse,
   Nationalism and Sexuality, 132.
15 Dirk Blasius, *Ehescheidung in Deutschland 1794–1945: Scheidung und Scheidungsrecht in historischer Perspektive* (Göttingen: Vandenhoeck & Ruprecht, 1987),
   185–6; Stieg, "1926 German Law," 47.
16 Andreas Pretzel, "Homosexuality in the Sexual Ethics of the 1930s: A Values
   Debate in the Culture Wars between Conservatism, Liberalism, and Moral-
   National Renewal," in *After "The History of Sexuality": German Genealogies With
   and Beyond Foucault*, ed. Scott Spector, Helmut Puff, and Dagmar Herzog
   (New York: Berghahn, 2012), 210–11.
17 Roos, *Lens*, 204.

18 Ibid., 213–14.
19 Kolb, *Weimar Republic*, 224–5. Here and elsewhere I set aside what some have argued are signs of a shift in the electorate prior to the Depression that ultimately favoured the NSDAP; my view on this is that absent economic crisis, it would not have led to a fascist dictatorship. Compare Childers, *Nazi Voter*, 190–1.
20 Such as J.W. Falter, *Hitlers Wähler* (Munich: Beck, 1991), and Childers, *Nazi Voter*. For a review of this research see Kolb and Schumann, *Weimarer Republik*, 269–73.
21 Kolb and Schumann, *Weimarer Republik*, 270.
22 Sneeringer, *Winning*, 266.
23 Kolb, *Weimar Republic*, 225.
24 "Vom jüdischen Arzt überfallen: Für deutsche Mädchen Spott und Hohn," *Der Angriff*, 18 June 1928; "So sieht er aus!" *Der Angriff*, 19 November 1928. See also Sneeringer, *Winning*, 108–9.
25 "Gibt es einen Mädchenhandeln?" *Der Angriff*, 15 October 1928; "Mädchenhändler am Werk," *Der Angriff*, 22 October 1928.
26 "Sexualorgien am Weihnachtsabend," *Der Angriff*, 24 December 1928.
27 Herzog, *Sex after Fascism*, 19–21. Another such NSDAP attack on Hirschfeld is described in Derek Hastings, *Catholicism and the Roots of Nazism* (New York: Oxford University Press, 2010), 96–7.
28 Joseph Goebbels, "Rund um die Gedächtniskirche," *Der Angriff*, 23 January 1928, reprinted in Kaes, Jay, and Dimendberg, *Weimar Republic Sourcebook*, 560–2. Don Reneau's translation.
29 Niewyk, *Jews in Weimar Germany*, 80. See also Doris Bergen, "Catholics, Protestants, and Christian Antisemitism in Nazi Germany," *Central European History* 27 (1994): 329–48.
30 On assimilation, see Donald Niewyk, "Solving the 'Jewish Problem': Continuity and Change in German Antisemitism, 1871–1945," *Leo Baeck Yearbook* (1990): 338–9.
31 It is possible that antisemitism is more apparent in the internal publications of conservative groups: Dickinson, *Sex*, 72.
32 Roos describes a rare exception: *Lens*, 207–9. On Jews and the "white slave trade" discourse see also Kaplan, *Jewish Feminist Movement*, 103–45; Dickinson, *Sex*, 72.
33 Sneeringer, *Winning*, 110. See also Orlow, *Nazi Party*, 117–21; Niewyk, *Jews in Weimar Germany*, 54; Fritzsche, *Germans into Nazis*, 8.
34 Sneeringer, *Winning*, 249–50; Niewyk, "Solving the 'Jewish Problem,'" 368–9; Childers, *Nazi Voter*, 267; Oded Heilbronner, "The Role of Nazi Antisemitism in the Nazi Party's Activity and Propaganda: A Regional Historiographical Study," *Leo Baeck Yearbook* (1990): 397–439.

35 "Die Filmjuden Kaufmann und Lasky," *Völkischer Beobachter*, 11–12 May 1930; "Die unmoralische Anstalt," *Völkischer Beobachter*, 9 January 1932; S., "Kampf um ein deutsches Schriftum," *Völkischer Beobachter*, 20 July 1932; "Skandal auf der Filmbörse," *Der Angriff*, 25 May 1932.

36 Between 1 and 14 January, the daily *Völkischer Beobachter* published only one article that linked Jews to "immorality": "Die unmoralische Anstalt." Between 15 and 31 July 1932, it published three: S., "Kampf um ein deutsches Schrifttum"; "Vom Kulturellbolschewismus zu Heinrich v. Kleist," *Völkischer Beobachter*, 20 July 1932; "Und dieser Rasse lieferte das System unser Vaterland aus!" *Völkischer Beobachter*, 28 July 1932. See also Arne von Röpenak's study, which found that immorality was not a major theme in Nazi propaganda: *KPD und NSDAP im Propagandakampf der Weimarer Republik: Eine inhaltsanalytische Untersuchung in Leitartikeln von "Rote Fahne" und "Angriff"* (Stuttgart: Ibidem-Verlag, 2002), 43.

37 "'Christentum ist Kannibalismus …': Die religiösfeindlichen Koalitionsbrüder des christlichen Zentrums," *Völkischer Beobachter*, 22 July 1932; "14 Jahre Kulturpolitik mit Gottlosen," *Völkischer Beobachter*, 23 July 1923; "Halt! Katholizismus und Nationalsozialismus!" *Völkischer Beobachter*, 27 July 1932; "Meine Überzeugung und damit mein Programm," *Der Angriff*, 5 April 1932.

38 Joseph Goebbels, "SPD – Schamloseste Partei Deutschlands," *Der Angriff*, 5 July 1932.

39 The NSDAP press was frequently banned in this period: Fulda, *Press and Politics*, 62, 200.

40 "Adolf Hitler bringt Chaos, Bürgerkrieg und Inflation!" *Der Angriff*, 4 April 1932.

41 "Adolf Hitlers Schlusswort vor dem Volksgericht: Kapitulieren? Niemals, niemals!" *Roter Alder [Der Angriff]*, 8 April 1932.

42 Heinrich Becker, "Warum nationalsozialistische Betriebszellen?" *Der Angriff*, 7 July 1932.

43 "Freiheit, Schönheit und Würde!" *Völkischer Beobachter*, 15 July 1932. This article does mention censorship, but the censorship to which it refers is the suppression of political speech by the government, not the suppression of media with sexual content.

44 "Aufruf! Parteigenossinnen! Volksgenossinnen!" *Völkischer Beobachter*, 30 July 1932.

45 "300,000 vor Adolf Hitler: Zweiter Tag des Deutschlandfluges; Der Führer zerschmettert die Lüge von der 'Entrechtung der Frau,'" *Der Angriff*, 5 April 1932.

46 Joseph Goebbels, "Adolf Hitler als Mensch," *Der Angriff*, 4 April 1932.

47 "Die deutsche Frau wählt nationalsozialistisch!" *Völkischer Beobachter*, 30 July 1932.

48 Sneeringer, *Winning*, 251.

49 "Deutsche Frauen wählen Hitler!" *Der Angriff*, 23 April 1932.

50 Sneeringer, *Winning*, 225.

51 Childers, *Nazi Voter*, 189, 258–60; Kolb and Schumann, *Weimarer Republik*, 270.

52 Karsten Ruppert, *Im Dienst am Staat von Weimar: Das Zentrum als regierende Partei in der Weimarer Demokratie 1923–1930* (Düsseldorf: Droste, 1992), 409. The limit of the Centre's commitment to democracy has been the topic of debate for a long time. For a review of some of that literature, see William Patch, *Heinrich Brüning and the Dissolution of the Weimar Republic* (Cambridge: Cambridge University Press, 1998), 1–4.

53 Niewyk, *Jews in Weimar Germany*, 28–9.

54 Bracher, *Die Auflösung der Weimarer Republik*, 91.

55 Larry Eugene Jones, "Franz von Papen, Catholic Conservatives, and the Establishment of the Third Reich, 1933–1934," *Journal of Modern History* 83, no. 2 (2001): 274–5.

56 Ibid., 273; Bracher, *Die Auflösung der Weimarer Republik*, 91. On the involvement of such Catholics in the NSDAP in Munich in the first half of the 1920s, see Hastings, *Catholicism*.

57 Ruppert, *Im Dienst*, 409–19; Patch, *Brüning*, 322; Rudolf Morsey, *Der Untergang des Politischen Katholizismus: Die Zentrumspartei zwischen christlichem Selbstverständnis und "Nationaler Erhebung" 1932/33* (Stuttgart: Belser Verlag, 1977), 221; Dietrich Orlow, *Weimar Prussia 1925–1933: The Illusion of Strength* (Pittsburgh: University of Pittsburgh Press, 1991), 16–17. One's assessment of the Centre Party's democratic commitments after 1930 depends on whether one sees Brüning's chancellorship as a final attempt to save democracy or as an irrevocable step in the dissolution of democracy. This has been a central point of debate for many decades: Kolb and Schumann, *Weimarer Republik*, 255–60.

58 Patch, *Brüning*, 278–91; Junker, *Deutsche Zentrumspartei*, 231–2; Morsey, *Untergang*, 219–20.

59 Junker, *Deutsche Zentrumspartei*, 216; Binder, *Irrtum*, 71–6.

60 Childers, *Nazi Voter*, 113–14.

61 "Sittlichkeit, Kunst und Sport: Der katholische Standpunkt," *Vossische Zeitung*, 3 August 1927.

62 Morsey, *Untergang*, 18. See also Junker, *Deutsche Zentrumspartei*, 32.

63 To the Reich Justice Ministry, BArch R 3001/6217, 8 June 1929, 101.

64 Roos, *Lens*, 203–5.

65 Jones, "Franz von Papen, Catholic Conservatives," 278–9; Rudolf Morsey, "Die Deutsche Zentrumspartei," in *Das Ende der Parteien 1933*, ed. Erich Matthias and Rudolf Morsey (Bonn: Droste, 1960), 306–11. See also Larry

Eugene Jones, "Franz von Papen, the German Center Party, and the Failure of Catholic Conservatism in the Weimar Republic," *Central European History* 38 (2005): 191–217.

66 Orlow, *Weimar Prussia*, 241–4.

67 Prussian Interior Ministry to Police, 30 September 1932, GStAPK I. HA Rep. 84a Nr. 8101 Bd. X, 212; see also Dobler, *Zwischen*, 534.

68 "Kampf um die Volksmoral: Das presse-Echo der Braucht'schen Sittlichkeitserlasse"; "Sittlichkeit, Kunst und Sport: Der katholische Standpunkt."

69 GStAPK I. HA Rep. 84a Nr. 8101 Bd. X, 178–216; "Körperkultur verboten!" *Vorwärts*, 4 January 1933.

70 Roos, *Lens*, 204. As I argued in chapter 3, a ban on street soliciting was not necessarily a rejection of the new law on female prostitution: pp. 106–10.

71 Memo of 6 December 1932; Minister of Interior to Justice Minister, 12 December 1932; Interior Minister to Justice Minister 15 September 1932, all in GStAPK I. HA Rep. 77 tit. 2772 Nr. 6 Bd. 2. See also Dobler, who argues that there was no crackdown on homosexual periodicals: "Zensur."

72 Dobler, *Zwischen*, 534–5. On the rumours see von Rheine, *Die lesbische Liebe*, 103.

73 Melcher to Bund für Menschenrecht, quoted in Paul Weber, "Moral gehoben werden soll!" *Die Freundin*, 12 October 1932.

74 Quoted in Weber, "Moral gehoben werden soll!"

75 Dobler, *Zwischen*, 536.

76 On the Centre's aversion to Papen's agenda, see Jones, "Franz von Papen, the German Centre Party," 211.

77 "Kampf um die Volksmoral: Das presse-Echo der Braucht'schen Sittlichkeitserlasse."

78 Morsey, *Untergang*, 219.

79 Rudolf Morsey, ed., *Die Protokolle der Reichstagsfraktion und des Fraktionsvorstands der deutschen Zentrumspartei 1926–1933* (Mainz: Matthias Grünwald, 1969), 629–32.

80 "Die Bedingungen des Zentrums für die Zustimmung zum Ermächtigungsgesetz und Hitlers Antwort in seiner Regierungserklärung," in Morsey and Matthias, *Das Ende*, 429–31. See also Morsey, *Protokolle*, 629–33; Morsey, *Untergang*, 134–41.

81 See Ludwig Kaas's reports of his negotiations with Hitler: Morsey, *Protokolle*, 626, 630; see also Morsey, *Untergang*, 132; Junker, *Deutsche Zentrumspartei*, 181.

82 Roos, *Lens*, 214.

83 Max Domarus, ed., *Hitler: Speeches and Proclamations 1932–1945*, vol. 1, trans. Mary Fran Gilbert (London: I.B. Tauris, 1990), 275–85.

84 For reviews of the literature on the Centre's vote for the Enabling Act, see Jones, "Franz von Papen, Catholic Conservatives," 291n70; Martin Menke, "Misunderstood Civic Duty: The Center Party and the Enabling Act," *Journal of Church and State* 51 (2009): 236–64. See also Patch, *Brüning*, 295–300; Josef Becker, "Dokumentation: Zentrum und Ermächtigungsgesetz 1933," *Vierteljahrshefte für Zeitgeschichte* 9 (1961): 195–210; Junker, *Deutsche Zentrumspartei*, 171–89.

85 For a review of these positions, see Menke, "Misunderstood Civic Duty," 239–42.

86 The following summary of these positions is drawn from Patch, *Brüning*, 295–9 (although Patch puts more emphasis on the Concordat than I have in this summary); Morsey, *Untergang*, 115–41; and Morsey, *Protokolle*, 625–33.

87 Patch, *Brüning*, 298. On the threat of violence see also Morsey, *Untergang*, 134.

88 Kolb, *Weimar Republic*, 224–5.

89 Morsey, *Untergang*, 131–2.

90 Kaas did pen a statement about "excessive freedom" leading to "degeneration" being one of several justifications for the vote for the Enabling Act. But given the utter lack of discussions of immorality in other Centre Party sources, it seems a mistake to overemphasize this source. "Der Weg des Zentrums," *Germania*, 5 April 1933. For Kaas as the author, see Junker, *Deutsche Zentrumspartei*, 177–9. Junker argues that Kaas wrote this article in the belief that the Nazi "revolution" was already complete and that Catholicism's role was to maintain the state and the rule of law. It therefore seems possible that rather than expressing a motivation in the period prior to the law's passage, Kaas was laying foundations for a rapprochement between Catholics and the new regime.

91 On this see Kolb, *Weimar Republic*, 69–71; Bracher, *Auflösung*, 92.

92 Stieg, "1926 German Law," 48.

93 Ibid., 47.

94 Mergel, *Parlamentarische Kultur*, 323–31, 478, 481. The DNVP joined a government coalition in 1925 as well: Kolb, *Weimar Republic*, 71, 79.

95 On how the Weimar parliamentary system did this, see Mergel, *Parlamentarische Kultur*.

96 See for example Thomas Knapp, "The German Center Party and the Reichsbanner," *International Review of Social History* 14 (1969): 159–79.

97 Patch, *Brüning*, 48–71; Harsch, *German Social Democracy*, 51–2.

98 Patch's term: *Brüning*, 72.

99 Patch, *Brüning*.

100 McElligott, *Rethinking*, 181–95.

101 Ibid., 190, 199.

102 Patch, *Brüning*, 322–5; Ruppert, *Im Dienst*, 407–8; "Brüning beauftragt," *Germania*, 28 March 1930; E.B., "Das neue Kabinett," *Germania*, 31 March 1930.

103 Blasius, *Ehescheidung*, 155–87. On divorce law in the Weimar period see also Werner Schubert, *Die Projekte der Weimarer Republik zur Reform des Nichtehelichen-, des Adoptions- und des Ehescheidungsrechts* (Paderborn: Ferdinand Schöningh, 1986), 82–91; Michelle Mouton, *From Nurturing the Nation to Purifying the Volk: Weimar and Nazi Family Policy, 1918–1945* (New York: Cambridge University Press, 2007), 71–86.

104 Morsey, *Protokolle*, 247.

105 Ibid., 230.

106 *Verhandlungen des Reichstags* IV. Wahlperiode 1928, Band 423 (Berlin: Reichsdruckerei, 1929), 587.

107 Schubert, *Projekte der Weimarer Republik*, 647.

108 "Das Schicksal der Strafrechtsreform," *Münchener Post*, 16 October 1931; "Das neue Strafrecht," *Vorwärts*, 17 October 1931; "Die Strafrechtsreform," *Berliner Tageblatt*, 18 October 1931.

109 "Die gescheiterte Strafrechtsreform," *Deutsche Zeitung*, 12 August 1932; Nöldeke, "Die Strafrechtsreform," [the name of the paper is obscured; it may be *Badische Presse*], 13 November 1931, in BArch R 3001/6003, 182; "Rechtsausschuß an der Arbeit," *Vossische Zeitung*, 12 January 1932.

110 Blasius argues the contrary, that is, that it did have an important and negative effect on democracy at a key moment: *Ehescheidung*, 185–6.

111 Patch, *Brüning*, 44–5.

112 On the Centre Party and Müller's fall, see Patch, *Brüning*, 64–73. The Centre's Reichstag delegation claimed at the time that it had done its utmost to preserve the coalition. It blamed the SPD: "Rücktritt des Reichskabinetts," *Germania*, 28 March 1930.

113 Ruppert, *Im Dienst*, 405.

114 Patch, *Brüning*, 72; Harsch, *German Social Democracy*, 57.

115 Rebecca Heinemann, *Familie zwischen Tradition und Emanzipation: Katholische und sozialdemokratische Familienkonzeptionen in der Weimarer Republik* (Munich: R. Oldenbourg, 2004), 181.

116 Morsey, *Protokolle*, 67, 338.

117 M.R., "Eine Hauptaufgabe des Katholischen Deutschen Frauenbundes: Die Rettung der christlichen Familie," *Germania* (*Frauenwelt*), 23 March 1930.

118 Ibid.; Helene Weber, "Die Sammlung der Kräfte," *Germania* (*Frauenwelt*), 30 March 1930; Bell, "Ehe und Familie, die Keimzelle auch des deutschen Volksstaates," *Germania* (*Frauenwelt*) 30 March 1930; "Sonntag

der christlichen Familie," *Germania*, 31 March 1930; Joos, "Unser Kampf um die deutsche Familie," *Germania*, 31 March 1930; Christian Schreiber, "Heiliger Dienst am Kinde," *Germania*, 31 March 1930.

119 "Brüning beauftragt," *Germania*, 28 March 1930; E.B., "Das neue Kabinett," *Germania*, 31 March 1930.

120 "Die Aussprache im Reichstag: Erklärung der Zentrumsfraktion," *Germania*, 2 April 1930.

121 "Methoden der Kulturzersetzung," *Germania*, 22 May 1930.

122 See for example Helene Weber's back-and-forth with KPD Reichstag delegates about family policies in the USSR in 1931: *Verhandlungen des Reichstags* V. Wahlperiode, 1930, Band 445 (Berlin: Reichsdruckerei, 1931), 1413–15.

123 For example, "Kommunistenangriff auf Struveshof: 90 Personen verhaftet," *Germania*, 24 March 1930; "Kirchen-Besudelung in Krefeld," *Germania*, 24 March 1930; Joos, "Unser Kampf"; "Das 'Paradises' der Sowjets," *Germania*, 31 March 1930; "Wider den Geist des Bolschewismus," *Germania*, 6 April 1930. In contrast, see "Kurie und Faschismus," *Germania*, 31 March 1930. Yet *Germania* was also critical of the NSDAP: "Frick für 'geistige Revolutionierung,'" *Germania*, 3 April 1930.

124 W. Schulte, "Buch und Jugend," *Germania*, 23 March 1930.

125 W. Elfes, "Bessere Gesetze her! Zur Wahrung der öffentlichen Sittlichkeit," *Kölnische Volkszeitung*, 31 May 1932.

126 McElligott, *Rethinking*, 143. Jelavich argues that in the period after 1930, people in film and radio self-censored, depoliticizing their programming out of fear of the NSDAP: *Berlin Alexanderplatz*.

127 LA A Rep 358 Acc 2636; Dobler, "Zensur," 83.

128 Pretzel, "Homosexuality in the Sexual Ethics of the 1930s," 210–12. At the same time, the discourse Pretzel examines was, for the most part, typical of conservative views for the entire Weimar period and did not constitute a "witch hunt" against homosexuals (210) nor a meaningful continuity with the Nazi period.

129 Orlow, *Weimar Prussia*, 16–17.

130 Herzog, *Sex after Fascism*, 10–63; Timm, *Politics*, 157–86; Morrison, *Explanation*, 155–6.

131 Herzog, *Sex after Fascism*, 28, 36, 52–3, 60–2; Timm, *Politics*, 159–61.

132 Herzog, *Sex after Fascism*, 52.

133 Herzog, *Sex after Fascism*, 33–4, 45–8.

134 Sellmann, *50 Jahre Kampf*, 115.

135 Heineman, *Before Porn*, 10; McCormick, *Gender and Sexuality*, 169–71.

136 On the broader discussion of the Republic's lack of authority that was the context for these assertions, see McElligott, *Rethinking*, 1–2.

137 Friedrich Meinecke, *The German Catastrophe*, trans. Sidney Fay (Boston: Beacon Press, 1963), 72–3.

138 Ibid., 38–9, 84, 86.

139 Ibid., 2.

140 Ibid.

141 Ibid., 32, 34–5, 89, quotation at 56.

142 Ibid., 89.

143 Ritter, *Europa und die deutsche Frage*, 43.

144 Ibid., 178, 191. See also 188.

145 Ibid., 192.

146 Ibid., 199.

147 Herzog, *Sex after Fascism*, 103.

148 Colin Storer, *Britain and the Weimar Republic: The History of a Cultural Relationship* (London: Tauris Academic Studies, 2010), 86.

149 Ibid., 72, 94, 148–72.

150 Weitz, "Weimar Germany and Its Historians," 583. See also Canning, "Introduction," 4; Evans and Freeland, "Rethinking Sexual Modernity," 316–17.

151 *Cabaret*, dir. Bob Fosse (1972; Burbank, CA: Warner Home Video, 2003).

152 Stewart Roddie, quoted in Storer, *Britain*, 88.

153 See also Linda Mizejewski, *Divine Decadence: Fascism, Female Spectacle, and the Makings of Sally Bowles* (Princeton: Princeton University Press, 1992), 3–4.

154 See Herzog, *Sex after Fascism*, 157.

155 Herzog, *Sex after Fascism*, 88–95; Whisnant, *Male Homosexuality*, 28–30, 104–7, 167.

156 This is reflected in a tendency to put questions of gender and sexuality in the category "culture" and to treat "culture" as separate from politics: Kolb and Schumann, *Weimarer Republik*, 221–2. See also Weitz's critique of Mommsen: Eric Weitz, "*The Rise and Fall of Weimar Democracy*" (Review), *Central European History* 31, no. 3 (1998): 273–7.

157 Dickinson argues that bio-politics narratives have worked in a similar way: "Biopolitics," 1.

158 See Grossmann, *Reforming Sex*, vi–vii; Dickinson, "Biopolitics." A recent argument for continuity is Harris, *Selling Sex*, 190.

159 Timm, *Politics*, 157–9.

160 Herzog, *Sex after Fascism*; Timm, *Politics*, 157–86; Roos, *Lens*, 217.

161 Timm, *Politics*, 157–86.

162 Schoppmann, *Days*; Schoppmann, *Nationalsozialistische Sexualpolitik*; Jane Caplan, "The Administration of Gender Identity in Nazi Germany," *History Workshop Journal* 72, no. 1 (2011): 171–80; Herrn, *Schnittmuster*, 157–65.

163 Grossmann, *Reforming Sex*, 166–88.
164 Wolff, *Hirschfeld*, 413.
165 Hiller, *Eros*, 123.
166 Rosenkranz and Lorenz, *Hamburg auf anderen Wegen*, 146–7; Whisnant, *Male Homosexuality*, 77–8, 196.
167 Whisnant, *Male Homosexuality*, 203. See also Evans, "Bahnhof Boys."
168 The charge appears to have been that Hahm violated the age of consent law: Schoppmann, *Nationalsozialistische Sexualpolitik*, 166; see also 205, 209.
169 Ibid., 165–6.
170 Schoppmann, *Days*, 33–40; Anna Rheinsberg, "Man bleibt, wo man gebraucht wird," *Fraunkfurter Rundschau*, 30 November 1985; Gabriele Dennert, Christiane Leidinger, and Franziska Rauchut, "Lesben in Wut: Lesbenbewegung in der BRD der 70er Jahre," in Dennert, Leidinger, and Rauchut, *In Bewegung bleiben*, 41–2. See also Hilde Radusch box, Spinnboden Lesbenarchiv.
171 Hiller, *Eros*, 105.
172 Ibid., 106.
173 Kurt Hiller, "Richard Linsert Tot," *WhKM* Nr. 34, September 1932/February 1933; "Die Totenfeier," *WhKM* Nr. 34, September 1932/February 1933.
174 Fritz Flato, "Verehrte Anwesende, Freunde, Genossen!" *WhKM* Nr. 34, September 1932/February 1933.
175 Ibid.
176 Paul Weber, "Friedrich Radszuweit ist tot," *Die Freundin*, 13 April 1932.
177 Schoppmann, *Nationalsozialistische Sexualpolitik*, 173–4; Schoppmann, *Days*, 139–44.
178 Göttert, "'Mir sind die frauenrechtlerischen Ideen direkt eingeboren,'" 55. Göttert writes that Pappritz's position on fascism is as yet unclear because her papers from that period have not been analysed.
179 Keilson-Lauritz, *Geschichte*, 64.

Conclusion: The Weimar Settlement on Sexual Politics

1 Compare Dickinson, "Policing Sex," 225–6. He argues that the overall trend of policing and legal reform with respect to sexuality under the Republic was, on the one hand, to defend the individual's "sexual autonomy" from coercion (rape, incest) and from the state itself (female prostitution) while, at same time, increasingly managing reproduction and the family, and hence prosecuting male homosexuality because it threatened the birth rate. But statistics do not tell the whole story. The new law on female prostitution was not only about sexual autonomy. The Republic

was rather tolerant of male-male sexuality, which was not often mentioned in conjunction with the birth rate. In general, the trend was towards management, management of a certain kind, conforming to the terms of the Weimar settlement. This did produce a form of sexual autonomy for some people.

2 Timm, *Politics*, 21–2; Michael Schwartz, *Sozialistische Eugenik: Eugenische Sozialtechnologien in Debatten und Politik der deutschen Sozialdemokratie 1890–1933* (Bonn: Verlag J.H.W. Dietz, 1995); Ingrid Richter, *Katholizismus und Eugenik in der Weimarer Republik und im Dritten Reich: Zwischen Sittlichkeitsreform und Rassenhygiene* (Paderborn: Ferdinand Schöningh, 2001).

3 The literature on eugenics in Germany is extensive, although most works do not concentrate on the Republic. A selection of studies follows: Sheila Faith Weiss, *Race Hygiene and National Efficiency: The Eugenics of Wilhelm Schallmayer* (Berkeley: University of California Press, 1987); Sheila Faith Weiss, "The Race Hygiene Movement in Germany," *Osiris*, 2nd ser., 3 (1987): 193–236; Jürgen Kroll, Peter Weingart, and Kurt Bayertz, *Blut und Gene: Geschichte der Eugenik und Rassenhygiene in Deutschland* (Frankfurt: Suhrkamp, 1988); Taylor Allen, "German Radical Feminists and Eugenics"; Weindling, *Health, Race and German Politics*; Kaiser, Nowak, and Schwartz, *Eugenik, Sterilisation, "Euthanasie"*; Michael Burleigh, *Death and Deliverance: "Euthanasia" in Germany c. 1900–1945* (Cambridge: Cambridge University Press, 1994); Christoph Schneider, *Die Verstaatlichung des Leibes: Das "Gesetz zur Verhütung erbkranken Nachwuchses" und die Kirche* (Konstanz: Hartung-Gorre Verlag, 2000); Grossmann, *Reforming Sex*; Richter, *Katholizismus und Eugenik*; Schwartz, *Sozialistische Eugenik*; Dickinson, "Biopolitics"; Ulrike Manz, *Bürgerliche Frauenbewegung und Eugenik in der Weimarer Republik* (Königstein im Taunus: Ulrike Helmer Verlag, 2007); Sharon Gillerman, *Germans into Jews: Remaking the Jewish Social Body in the Weimar Republic* (Stanford: Stanford University Press, 2009).

4 Schwartz, *Sozialistische Eugenik*, 22.

5 Dickinson makes a good point when he stresses the value of distinguishing between rhetoric and actual programs: "Biopolitics," 10–15.

6 On the clinics, see Timm, *Politics*, 80–117; Grossmann, *Reforming Sex*, 46–77; Richter, *Katholizismus und Eugenik*, 122–38; Schwartz, *Sozialistische Eugenik*, 210–53; Dickinson, "Biopolitics," 14.

7 Schwartz, *Sozialistische Eugenik*, 342; see also the numerous examples in Richter, *Katholizismus und Eugenik*, such as at 288.

8 Schwartz, *Sozialistische Eugenik*, 335–6; See also Schopohl report, 27 October 1932, GStAPK I. HA Rep. 84a Nr. 871 (MF 8535–8539), 71–5; Richter, *Katholizismus und Eugenik*; Dickinson, "Biopolitics," 16–17, 20–1.

9 Michael Hau, *The Cult of Health and Beauty in Germany: A Social History, 1890–1930* (Chicago: University of Chicago Press, 2003), 135–48; Timm, *Politics*, 67–71; Weindling, *Health, Race and German Politics*, 409–16.

10 Kaiser, Nowak, and Schwartz, *Eugenik, Sterilisation, "Euthanasie,"* 101–2 (justification for the 1932 draft law); Reichsgesundheitsamt to Reich Minister of Interior, 2 March 1932, BArch R 1501/126248, 78; Deutscher Ärztevereinsbund to Reich Ministry of Interior, 7 November 1932, BArch R 1501/126248, 101–2; Rudolf Lennhoff, "Freiwillige Sterilisierung," *Vossische Zeitung*, 2 December 1932; Weindling, *Health, Race and German Politics*, 578; Burleigh, *Death and Deliverance*, 33–4; Grossmann, *Reforming Sex*, 70–5, 143–5; Wetzell, *Inventing*, 252; Richter, *Katholizismus und Eugenik*, 290–3.

11 See the draft law and commentary in Kaiser, Nowak, and Schwartz, *Eugenik, Sterilisation, "Euthanasie,"* 100–2.

12 Ibid., 100–1.

13 Ebermayer, "Die Unfruchtbarmachung Minderwertiger," *Magdeburg Zeitung*, 27 July 1929, in BArch R 3001, 6094; Prussian Landesgesundheitsrat session of 2 July 1932, BArch R 3001, 6094.

14 On the mix in SPD rhetoric of voluntarism for a majority and compulsion for a minority, see Richter, *Katholizismus und Eugenik*, 171.

15 On foreign policy, McElligott, *Rethinking*, 35–68. On welfare, Hong, *Welfare*; Crew, *Germans*.

16 McElligott adds that its social policy contained a "strain of liberal authoritarianism" (*Rethinking*, 2). Some recent examples of arguments to the contrary, which stress the weaknesses of democracy back to its origins in 1918, are Evans, *Coming of the Third Reich*, 77–153; Möller, *Die Weimarer Republik*, 255–86; Bessel, *Germany after the First World War*, 254–84. For reviews of the debates on why the Republic collapsed, see Kolb and Schumann, *Weimarer Republik*, 255–78; Swett, *Neighbors and Enemies*, 8–15 (see also Swett's argument about the sources of working-class radicalism in the crisis period: 5–8, 294–300, and elsewhere); Peter Fritzsche, "Did Weimar Fail?" *Journal of Modern History* 68 (September 1996): 629–56; Anthony McElligott, "Political Culture," in *Weimar Germany*, ed. Anthony McElligott (Oxford: Oxford University Press, 2009); McElligott, *Rethinking*, 1–2.

17 Much of what Mergel describes as the accepted way of doing business in the Reichstag prior to the crisis years, a way of doing business ratified by politicians from the SPD to the DNVP, is apparent in debates about sexuality. Mergel argues that often differences were hammered out in committees or behind-the-scenes meetings among the factions, and that parties prioritized compromise and avoided burning bridges despite their disagreements: *Parlamentarische Kultur*, 227–9, 475–6.

18 Usborne, *Cultures*, 5.
19 Usborne, *Politics*, 171–3; Usborne, *Cultures*, 215.
20 Usborne, *Politics*, 177.
21 Grossmann, *Reforming Sex*, 83.
22 Dickinson, "Policing Sex," 226.
23 Grossmann, *Reforming Sex*, 84–5.
24 Blasius, *Ehescheidung*, 180.
25 Grossmann, *Reforming Sex*, 78–106; on Münzenberg, for whom Linsert worked: 36, 84–5.
26 Grossmann, *Reforming Sex*, 94. See also Sneeringer, *Winning*, 250–5.
27 Grossmann, *Reforming Sex*, 94–5, 108–16.
28 Ibid., 131, 255n105.
29 Ibid., 106.
30 On respectability in homosexual and transvestite politics, see also Ramsey, "Rites"; Ramsey, "Erotic Friendship"; Sutton, "We Too"; Lybeck, *Desiring*, 164–70; Lybeck, "Writing Love, Feeling Shame"; Mosse, *Nationalism and Sexuality*, 40–3.
31 Michel Foucault, *The History of Sexuality*, vol. 1, *An Introduction*, trans. Robert Hurley (New York: Random House, 1978).
32 For a rare call for civil service positions to be open to known homosexuals despite their sexual orientation, see Hans Georg, "Der Invertierte und die Politik," *Der Freund [Freundschaft]* Nr. 3, Jahrgang 1 [1919]. For an example of a political settlement in a later period that produced queer sexual freedom along the lines of the Weimar settlement, see Houlbrook, *Queer London*, 254–63.
33 On the 1950s, see Herzog, *Sex after Fascism*, 101–40; Robert Moeller, "'The Homosexual Man Is a 'Man,' the Homosexual Woman Is a 'Woman'": Sex, Society, and the Law in Postwar West Germany," *Journal of the History of Sexuality* 4, no. 3: 395–429; Anna Clark, *Desire: A History of European Sexuality* (New York: Routledge, 2008), 198–222. On the immediate post-war period see also Jennifer Evans, *Life among the Ruins: Cityscape and Sexuality in Cold War Berlin* (New York: Palgrave Macmillan, 2011). On queer sex in the German Democratic Republic, see Josie McLellan, *Love in the Time of Communism: Intimacy and Sexuality in the GDR* (Cambridge: Cambridge University Press, 2011); Jennifer Evans, "The Moral State: Men, Mining, and Masculinity in the Early GDR," *German History* 23 (2005): 355–70; Jennifer Evans, "Decriminalization, Seduction, and 'Unnatural Desire' in the German Democratic Republic," *Feminist Studies* 36 (2010): 553–77; Erik Huneke, "Morality, Law, and the Socialist Sexual Self in the German Democratic Republic, 1945–1972" (PhD diss., University of Michigan, 2013).

34 Duggan, "The New Homonormativity." For a useful overview of the histori-cal circumstances in which critiques of homonormativity arose, see Paisley Currah, "Homonationalism, State Rationalities, and Sex Contradictions," *Theory & Event* 16 (2013).

35 David Eng, *The Feeling of Kinship: Queer Liberalism and the Racialization of Inti-macy* (Durham, NC: Duke University Press, 2010).

36 Ibid., 27–8.

37 The question of the relationship of queer politics to family, kinship, and children is an important one that I will bracket; this question is central to Eng's concept of queer liberalism.

38 Duggan, "The New Homonormativity," 179–80.

39 Halberstam reviews and elaborates on this scholarship: *Queer Art of Failure*, 148–51.

40 Duggan, "The New Homonormativity," 179.

41 According to opponents of homosexual emancipation, a speaker at the Institute for Sexual Science advocated same-sex marriage: Hahn et al., *§175 muß bleiben!*, 36–7. For an example of a call for same-sex marriage in the early 1980s, see Ralf König, "Schwule in der Politik: Ein Comic aus dem Jahr 1982," in *Rosa Radikale: Die Schwulenbewegung der 1970er Jahre*, ed. Andreas Pretzel and Volker Weiß (Hamburg: Männerschwarm, 2012), 102.

42 Maxime Cervulle, "French Homonormativity and the Commodification of the Arab Body," *Racial History Review* 100 (2008): 171–9.

43 See for example "Petition to the Reichstag," in Wolff, *Hirschfeld*, 445–9.

44 Kennedy, *Ulrichs*, 106–8.

45 Raimund Wolfert, *Gegen Einsamkeit und "Einsiedelei": Die Geschichte der Interna-tionalen homophilen Welt-Organisation* (Hamburg: Männerschwarm, 2009), 7; Whisnant, *Male Homosexuality*, 70–6.

46 Holy's term: Michael Holy, "Jenseits von Stonewall – Rückblicke auf die Schwulenbewegung in der BRD 1969–1980," in Pretzel and Weiß, *Rosa Radikale*, 41; Cristina Perincioli, "Warum musste die Tomate so weit fliegen? Über 68erInnen, Anarchismus, Lesbianismus bis zum Frauenzentrum," in Dennert, Leidinger, and Rauchut, *In Bewegung bleiben*, 62–7; Gabriele Dennert, Christiane Leidinger, and Franziska Rauchut, "Kämpfe und Konflikte um Macht und Herrschaft: Lesbenbewegung in der BRD der 80er Jahre," in Dennert, Leidinger, and Rauchut, *In Bewegung bleiben*, 126–59.

47 "Gegen Diskriminierung: Bundesstiftung Magnus Hirschfeld nimmt Arbeit auf," *Frankfurter Allgemeine Zeitung*, 11 November 2011; "Satzung der Bundesstiftung Magnus Hirschfeld," http://mh-stiftung.de/wp-content/uploads/Satzung-derBundesstiftung-Magnus-Hirschfeld.pdf (accessed

18 June 2014). See also the Bundesstiftung Magnus Hirschfeld's website, http://mh-stiftung.de/; in English: http://mh-stiftung.de/en/.

48 On the uncomfortable position of the history of Nazism in German national identity after 1945 and 1990, see, among others, Geoff Eley, "Nazism, Politics and the Image of the Past: Thoughts on the West German Historikerstreit 1986–1987," *Past & Present* 121 (1988): 171–208; Robert Moeller, "War Stories: The Search for a Usable Past in the Federal Republic of Germany," *American Historical Review* 101 (1996): 1008–48; Moeller, *War Stories: The Search for a Usable Past in the Federal Republic of Germany* (Berkeley: University of California Press, 2001); Ruth Wittlinger and Steffi Boothroyd, "A 'Usable' Past at Last? The Politics of the Past in United Germany," *German Studies Review* 33 (2010): 489–502.

49 Wittlinger and Boothroyd, "A 'Usable' Past," 494–500; Moeller, *War Stories*, 171–98.

Bibliography

Archival Sources

Bundesarchiv Berlin – Lichterfelde

R 86 Reichsgesundheitsamt
R 1001 Reichskolonialamt
R 1501 Reichsministerium des Innern
R 3001 Reichsjustizministerium
R 4901 Reichsministerium für Wissenschaft, Erziehung und Volksbildung

Geheimes Staatsarchiv Preußischer Kulturbesitz

I. Hauptabteilung (HA) Rep. 84a Justizministerium
I. HA Rep. 84a Justizministerium (D)
I. HA Rep. 76 Kultusministerium
I. HA Rep. 77 Ministerium des Innern

Landesarchiv Berlin

A Pr. Br. Rep. 030 Polizeipräsidium Berlin
A Pr. Br. Rep. 030–03 Bezirksausschuss/Bezirksverwaltungsgericht
    Berlin – Ältere Streitverfahren
A Rep. 358 Generalstaatsanwaltschaft bei dem Landgericht Berlin
A Rep. 358–01 Generalstaatsanwaltschaft bei dem Landgericht
    Berlin – Strafverfahren 1919–33

Stadtarchiv München

Nr. 325/6 Bürgermeister und Rat
Nr. 134, 139, 140/1, 140/2, 144 Gesundheitswesen

Staatsarchiv München

Polizeidirektion Sachakten
Disziplinarstrafkammer München

Periodicals

Der Angriff
Blätter für Menschenrecht
Berliner Börsen-Courier
Berliner Tageblatt
Berliner Lokal-Anzeiger
BZ am Mittag
Dermatologische Zeitschrift
Deutsche Allgemeine Zeitung
Deutsche Zeitung
Deutschen Medizinischen Wochenschrift
Die Freundin
Die Freundschaft
Dresdner Anzeiger
Frankfurter Allgemeine Zeitung
Frankfurter Rundschau
Frankfurter Zeitung
Garçonne
Germania: Zeitung für das deutsche Volk [*Germania*]
Jahrbuch für sexuelle Zwischenstufen unter besonderer Berücksichtigung
    der Homosexualität
Kölnische Volkszeitung
Kölnische Zeitung
Leipziger Volkszeitung
Mitteilungen der Deutschen Gesellschaft zur Bekämpfung der Geschlechtskrankheiten
Mitteilungen des Wissenschaftlich-Humanitären Komitees
Münchner Neueste Nachrichten
Münchener Post

National-Zeitung
Die Neue Generation
New York Times
Reichstagshandbuch
Die Rote Fahne
Staatsbürger-Zeitung
Stuttgarter Neues Tagblatt
Der Tag
Das Tage-Buch
Verhandlungen des Reichstags
*Vierteljahrsberichte des Wissenschaftlich-humanitären Komitees während
    der Kriegszeit*
Völkischer Beobachter
Völkischer Kurier
Volksstimme (Frankfurt a.M.)
Vorwärts
Vossische Zeitung
Welt am Montag
Die Weltbühne

Books and Articles

Abteilung für Sexualreform (Wissenschaftlich-humanitäres Komitee). "§267 des
    Amtlichen Entwurfs eines Allgemeinen Deutschen Strafgesetzbuchs 'Unzucht
    zwischen Männern' eine Denkschrift, gerichtet an das Reichsjustizministe-
    rium." *Sexus*, vol. 4. Stuttgart: Verlag Julius Püttmann, 1925.
Aschaffenburg, Gustav. *Das Verbrechen und seine Bekämpfung.* Vol. 3. Heidelberg:
    Carl Winters, 1923.
Bauer, Max. "Die moderne Frau (Die neueste Zeit)." In Johannes Scherr, *Weib,
    Dame, Dirne: Kultur- und Sittengeschichte der deutschen Frau,* edited by Max
    Bauer, 311–22. Dresden: Paul Aretz, 1928.
Bloch, Iwan. *The Sexual Life of Our Time.* Translated by M. Eden Paul. New York:
    Falstaff Press, 1937.
Delbanco, Ernst, and Annie Blumenfeld. "Das moderne Prostitutionswesen." In
    Pappritz, *Einführung,* 20–46.
Deutschland-Bericht der Sozialdemokratischen Partei Deutschlands. Salzhausen and
    Frankfurt am Main: Verlag Petra Nettelbeck und Zweitausendeins, 1980 [1934].
Eberhard, E.F.W. *Die Frauenemanzipation und ihre erotischen Grundlagen.* Vienna
    and Leipzig: Wilhelm Braumüller, 1924.

Gaupp, Robert. "Das Problem der Homosexualität." *Klinische Wochenschrift* 1, no. 21 (20 May 1922): 1033–8.

Goebbels, Joseph. *Die Tagebücher von Joseph Goebbels.* Vol. 2. Edited by Elke Fröhlich. Munich: K.G. Saur, 2004.

Hahn, Ratibor, et al. *§175 muß bleiben! Denkschrift des Verbandes zur Bekämpfung der öffentlichen Unsittlichkeit an den Deutschen Reichstag.* Cologne: Koltz & Kreuder, 1927.

Hiller, Kurt. *Eros.* Vol. 2 of *Leben gegen die Zeit.* Hamburg: Rowohlt, 1973.

– *Logos.* Vol. 1 of *Leben gegen die Zeit.* Hamburg: Rowohlt, 1969.

– *Das Recht über sich selbst: Eine strafrechtsphilosophische Studie.* Heidelberg: Carl Winter, 1908.

Hirschfeld, Magnus. *Geschlechtskunde.* Vol. 3. Stuttgart: Julius Püttmann, 1930.

– *Die Homosexualität des Mannes und des Weibes.* Berlin: Louis Marcus Verlagsbuchhandlung, 1920.

– "Die männliche Prostitution." In *§ 297.3 "Unzucht Zwischen Männern"? Ein Beitrag zur Strafgesetzreform,* edited by Richard Linsert, 13–32. Berlin: Neuer Deutscher Verlag, 1929.

– *Racism.* Translated by Eden and Cedar Paul. Port Washington, NY: Kennikat Press, 1973.

– *Sappho und Sokrates oder wie erklärt sich die Liebe der Männer und Frauen zu Personen des eigenen Geschlechts?* 3rd ed. Leipzig: Max Spohr (Ferd. Spohr), 1922.

– *Transvestites: The Erotic Drive to Cross-Dress.* Translated by Michael A. Lombardi-Nash. Amherst, NY: Prometheus Books, 1991.

– *Women East and West: Impressions of a Sex Expert.* Translated by O.P. Green. London: William Heinemann, 1935.

Hirschfeld, Magnus, with Richard Linsert. "Die Homosexualität." In *Sittengeschichte des Lasters: Die Kulturepochen und Ihre Leidenschaften,* edited by Leo Schidrowitz, 253–318. Vienna and Leipzig: Verlag für Kulturforschung, 1927.

Hübner, A.H. *Lehrbuch der forensischen Psychiatrie.* Bonn: A. Marcus & E. Weber, 1914.

Isherwood, Christopher. *Christopher and His Kind.* New York: Farrar, Straus, and Giroux, 1976.

Kankeleit, Otto. *Die Unfruchtbarmachung aus rassenhygienischen und sozialen Gründen.* Munich: J.F. Lehmanns Verlag, 1929.

Kartell für Reform des Sexualstrafrechts, ed. *Gegen-Entwurf zu den Strafbestimmungen des Amtlichen Entwurfs eines Allgemeinen Deutschen Strafgesetzbuch über geschlechtliche und mit dem Geschlechtsleben im Zusammenhang stehend Handlung.* Berlin: Verlag der Neuen Gesellschaft, 1927.

König, Ralf. "Schwule in der Politik: Ein Comic aus dem Jahr 1982." In Pretzel and Weiß, *Rosa Radikale,* 101–9.

Krafft-Ebing, Richard von. *Psychopathia sexualis: A Medico-Forensic Study.* Translated by Harry Wedeck. New York: G.P. Putnam's Sons, 1965.

Lehmann-Russbüldt, Otto. *Der Kampf der Deutschen Liga für Menschenrechte, vormals Bund Neues Vaterland, für den Weltfrieden 1914–1927.* Berlin: Hensel & Co., 1927.

Lewandowski, Herbert. "Aufklärung tut not!" In *Die lesbische Liebe,* vol. 1 of *Abarten im Geschlechtsleben,* edited by Franz Scheda, 3–6. Berlin: Schwalbe-Verlag, 1930.

Lewis, Wyndham. *Hitler.* London: Chatto & Windus, 1931.

Linsert, Richard, ed. *§ 297.3 "Unzucht Zwischen Männern"? Ein Beitrag zur Strafgesetzreform.* Berlin: Neuer Deutscher Verlag, 1929.

– *Kabale und Liebe: Über Politik und Geschlechtsleben.* Berlin: Man Verlag, 1931.

Ludendorff, Erich. *Heraus aus dem braunen Sumpf! Sagt General Ludendorff.* Munich: Ludendorffs Volkswarte-Verlag, 1932.

Mann, Klaus. "Die Linke und das 'Laster.'" *Europäische Hefte* 36–7 (1934): 675–8.

Marteneau, Heinz. *Sappho und Lesbos.* Leipzig: Eva-Verlag, 1931.

Mayer, Joseph. *Gesetzliche Unfruchtbarmachung Geisteskranker.* Freiburg im Breisgau: Herder & Co., 1927.

Meinecke, Friedrich. *The German Catastrophe.* Translated by Sidney Fay. Boston: Beacon Press, 1963.

Moll, Albert. *Behandlung der Homosexualität: Biochemisch oder psychisch?* Bonn: A. Marcus & E. Weber, 1921.

– *Die Konträre Sexualempfindung.* Berlin: Fischers Medizin Buchhandlung, 1899.

– "Die sozialen Formen der sexuellen Beziehungen." In *Handbuch der Sexualwissenschaften mit besonderer Berücksichtigung der kulturgeschichtlichen Beziehungen,* edited by Albert Moll, 313–460. Leipzig: F.C.W. Vogel, 1921.

– *Polizei und Sitte.* Berlin: Gersbach & Sohn, 1926.

Moreck, Curt. *Führer durch das "lasterhafte" Berlin.* Leipzig: Verlag Moderner Stadtführer, 1996 [1931].

Murat, Walter von, ed. *Mitteilungen des Wissenschaftlich-humanitären Komitees 1926–1933.* Hamburg: C. Bell, 1985.

Pappritz, Anna. "Das Reichsgesetz zur Bekämpfung der Geschlechtskrankheiten vom Standpunkt der Frau." *Mitteilungen der Deutschen Gesellschaft zur Bekämpfung der Geschlechtskrankheiten* 25, nos. 11–12 (1927): 133.

– ed. *Einführung in das Studium der Prostitutionsfrage.* Leipzig: Verlag von Johann Ambrosius Barth, 1919.

– *Handbuch der amtlichen Gefährdetenfürsorge.* Munich: Verlag von J.F. Bergmann, 1924.

Placzek, Siegfried. *Homosexualität und Recht.* Leipzig: Georg Thieme, 1925.

Rheine, Th. von. *Die lesbische Liebe: Zur Psychologie des Mannweibes.* Berlin-Charlottenburg: Verlag Aris & Ahren, 1933.

Ritter, Gerhard. *Europa und die deutsche Frage: Betrachtungen über die geschichtliche Eigenart des deutschen Staatsdenkens.* Munich: Münchner Verlag, 1948.

Roellig, Ruth Margarete. *Berlins lesbische Frauen* [1928]. In *Lila Nächte: Die Damenklubs im Berlin der zwanziger Jahre,* edited by Adele Meyer, 233. Berlin: Edition Lit. Europe, 1994.

– "Lesbierinnen und Transvestiten." In *Das lasterhafte Weib,* edited by Agnes Eszterhazy, 67–80. Vienna: Verlag fur Kulturforschung, 1930.

Scheda, Franz. *Die lesbische Liebe.* Vol. 1 of *Die Abarten im Geschlechtsleben.* Berlin: Schwalbe-Verlag, 1930.

Scheven, Katharina. "Die sozialen und wirtschaftlichen Grundlagen der Prostitution." In Pappritz, *Einführung,* 139–72.

Schneider, Kurt. *Studien über Persönlichkeit und Schicksal eingeschriebener Prostituierter.* Berlin: Julius Springer, 1921.

Scott, Franz. *Das lesbische Weib: Eine Darstellung der konträrsexuallen weiblichen Erotik.* Berlin: Pergamon Verlag, 1931.

Sellmann, Adolf. *50 Jahre Kampf für Volkssittlichkeit und Volkskraft: Die Geschichte des Westdeutschen Sittlichkeitsvereins von seinen Anfängen bis heute (1885–1935).* Schwelm (Westphalia): G. Meiners, 1935.

– *Das Gesetz zur Bekämpfung der Geschlechtskrankheiten.* Schwelm (Westphalia): G. Meiners, 1927.

Severing, Carl. *Mein Lebensweg.* Vol. 2. Cologne: Greven Verlag, 1950.

Sieverts, M. "Nachgehende Fürsorge und Zusammenarbeit mit der freien Liebestätigkeit." In *Handbuch der amtlichen Gefährdetenfürsorge,* edited by Anna Pappritz, 142–5. Munich: Verlag von J.F. Bergmann, 1924.

Statistischen Reichsamt, ed. *Statistisches Jahrbuch für das Deutsche Reich.* Berlin: Reimar Hobbing, 1926.

Thorbecke, Clara. "Die Verwahrlosung der weiblichen Jugend." In Pappritz, *Einführung,* 173–86.

Ulrichs, Karl Heinrich. *Forschungen über das Rätsel der mannmännlichen Liebe.* New York: Arno Press, 1975.

– *The Riddle of "Man-Manly" Love: The Pioneering Work on Male Homosexuality.* Translated by Michael A. Lombardi-Nash. Buffalo, NY: Prometheus Books, 1994.

Wulffen, Erich. *Irrwege des Eros.* Leipzig: Avalun-Verlag, 1929.

Zumbusch, Leo von. "Die gesundheitlichen Gefahren der Prostitution und die Verbreitung der Geschlechtskrankheiten." In Pappritz, *Einführung,* 107–33.

Films

Anders als die Andern. Directed by Richard Oswald. 1919; New York: Kino Lorber Films, 2009.

Cabaret. Directed by Bob Fosse. 1972; Burbank, CA: Warner Home Video, 2003.

Secondary Literature

Achilles, Manuela. "Reforming the Reich: Democratic Symbols and Rituals in the Weimar Republic." In Canning, Barndt, and McGuire, *Weimar Publics/ Weimar Subjects*, 175–91.

– "With a Passion for Reason: Celebrating the Constitution in Weimar Germany." *Central European History* 43 (2010): 666–89.

Adam, Birgit. *Die Strafe der Venus: Eine Kulturgeschichte der Geschlechtskrankheiten.* Pößneck: Orbis Verlag, 2001.

Anderson, Margaret Lavinia. *Practicing Democracy: Elections and Political Culture in Imperial Germany.* Princeton, NJ: Princeton University Press, 2000.

Anderson Hughes, Jessica. "Forced Prostitution: The Competing and Contested Uses of the Concentration Camp Brothel." PhD diss., Rutgers University–New Brunswick, 2011.

Ayass, Wolfgang. *Das Arbeitshaus Breitenau: Bettler, Landstreicher, Prostituierte, Zuhälter, und Fürsorgeempfänger in der Korrektions- und Landesarmenanstalt Breitenau (1874–1949).* Stuttgart: Franz Steiner, 1987.

Baldwin, Peter. *Contagion and the State in Europe, 1830–1930.* Cambridge: Cambridge University Press, 1999.

Bauer, Heike. *English Literary Sexology: Translations of Inversion, 1860–1930.* Basingstoke, UK: Palgrave Macmillan, 2009.

– "Theorizing Female Inversion: Sexology, Discipline, and Gender at the Fin de Siècle." *Journal of the History of Sexuality* 18 (2009): 84–102.

Beachy, Robert. "The German Invention of Homosexuality." *Journal of Modern History* 82, no. 4 (2010): 801–38.

Becker, Josef. "Dokumentation: Zentrum und Ermächtigungsgesetz 1933." *Vierteljahrshefte für Zeitgeschichte* 9 (1961): 195–210.

Bender, Klaus. "Vossische Zeitung (1617–1934)." In *Deutsche Zeitungen des 17. bis 20. Jahrhunderts,* edited by Heinz-Dietrich Fischer, 25–39. Pullach Verlag Dokumentation, 1972.

Bergen, Doris. "Catholics, Protestants, and Christian Antisemitism in Nazi Germany." *Central European History* 27 (1994): 329–48.

Bessel, Richard. *Germany after the First World War.* Oxford: Oxford University Press, 1993.

Binder, Gerhart. *Irrtum und Widerstand: Die deutschen Katholiken in der Auseinandersetzung mit dem Nationalsozialismus.* Munich: J. Pfeiffer, 1968.

Blasius, Dirk. *Ehescheidung in Deutschland 1794–1945: Scheidung und Scheidungsrecht in historischer Perspektive.* Göttingen: Vandenhoeck & Ruprecht, 1987.

Blasius, Mark, and Shane Phelan, eds. *We Are Everywhere: A Historical Sourcebook of Gay and Lesbian Politics.* New York: Routledge, 1997.

Bock, Gisela. "Keine Arbeitskräfte in diesem Sinne." In *"Wir sind Frauen wie andere Auch!": Prostituierte und ihre Kämpfe*, edited by Pieke Biermann, 70–106. Hamburg: Rowohlt, 1980.

Bollinger, Ernst. *Pressegeschichte II 1840–1930: Die goldenen Jahre der Massenpresse.* Freiburg Schweiz: Universitätsverlag Freiburg Schweiz, 1996.

Bourke, Joanna. *Dismembering the Male: Men's Bodies, Britain, and the Great War.* Chicago: University of Chicago Press, 1996.

Boyarin, Daniel, Daniel Itzkovitz, and Ann Pellegrini, eds. *Queer Theory and the Jewish Question.* New York: Columbia University Press, 2003.

Bracher, Karl-Dietrich. *Die Auflösung der Weimarer Republik: Eine Studie zum Problem des Machtverfalls in der Demokratie.* Stuttgart and Düsseldorf: Ring, 1955.

Breuer, Dieter. *Geschichte der literarischen Zensur in Deutschland.* Heidelberg: Quelle und Meyer, 1982.

Bridenthal, Renate, Atina Grossmann, and Marion Kaplan, eds. *When Biology Became Destiny: Women in Weimar and Nazi Germany.* New York: Monthly Review Press, 1984.

Brown, Timothy. "Richard Scheringer, the KPD and the Politics of Class and Nation in Germany, 1922–1969." *Contemporary European History* 14, no. 3 (2005): 317–46.

Bruford, W.H. *The German Tradition of Self-Cultivation: "Bildung" from Humboldt to Thomas Mann.* Cambridge: Cambridge University Press, 1975.

Burleigh, Michael. *Death and Deliverance: "Euthanasia" in Germany c. 1900–1945.* Cambridge: Cambridge University Press, 1994.

Campbell, Bruce. *The SA Generals and the Rise of Nazism.* Lexington: University of Kentucky Press, 1998.

Canaday, Margot. *The Straight State: Sexuality and Citizenship in Twentieth-century America.* Princeton: Princeton University Press, 2009.

Canning, Kathleen. "Claiming Citizenship: Suffrage and Subjectivity after the First World War." In Canning, Barndt, and McGuire, *Weimar Publics/Weimar Subjects*, 116–37.

– "Das Geschlecht der Revolution – Stimmrecht und Staatsbürgertum 1918/1919." In Gallus, *Die vergessene Revolution von 1918/19*, 84–116.

– "Introduction: Weimar Subjects/Weimar Publics: Rethinking the Political Culture of Germany in the 1920s." In Canning, Barndt, and McGuire, *Weimar Publics/Weimar Subjects*, 1–28.

– "'Sexual Crisis' and the Writing of Citizenship and the State of Emergency in Germany, 1917–1920." In *Staats-Gewalt: Ausnahmezustand und Sicherheitsregimes: Historische Perspektiven*, edited by Alf Lüdtke and Michael Wildt, 168–211. Göttingen: Wallstein, 2008.

Canning, Kathleen, Kerstin Barndt, and Kristin McGuire, eds. *Weimar Publics/Weimar Subjects: Rethinking the Political Culture of Germany in the 1920s*. New York: Berghahn, 2010.

Caplan, Jane. "The Administration of Gender Identity in Nazi Germany." *History Workshop Journal* 72, no. 1 (2011): 171–80.

— *Government Without Administration: State and Civil Service in Weimar and Nazi Germany*. Oxford: Clarendon Press, 1988.

Carlston, Erin. "Secret Dossiers: Sexuality, Race, and Treason in Proust and the Dreyfus Affair." *Modern Fiction Studies* 48, no. 4 (2002): 937–68.

Cervulle, Maxime. "French Homonormativity and the Commodification of the Arab Body." *Racial History Review* 100 (2008): 171–9.

Chauncey, George. *Gay New York: Gender, Urban Culture, and the Making of the Gay Male World, 1890–1940*. New York: Basic Books, 1995.

Childers, Thomas. *The Nazi Voter: The Social Foundations of Fascism in Germany, 1919–1933*. Chapel Hill: University of North Carolina Press, 1983.

Churchill, David. "Transnationalism and Homophile Political Culture in the Postwar Decades." *GLQ: A Journal of Lesbian and Gay Studies* 15, no. 1 (2009): 31–66.

Clark, Anna. *Desire: A History of European Sexuality*. New York: Routledge, 2008.

Crew, David. *Germans on Welfare: From Weimar to Hitler*. New York: Oxford University Press, 1998.

Crouthamel, Jason. *An Intimate History of the Front: Masculinity, Sexuality, and German Soldiers in the First World War*. New York: Palgrave Macmillan, 2014.

Crozier, Ivan. "'All the World's a Stage': Dora Russell, Norman Haire, and the 1929 London World League for Sexual Reform Congress." *Journal of the History of Sexuality* 12, no. 1 (2003): 16–37.

Currah, Paisley. "Homonationalism, State Rationalities, and Sex Contradictions." *Theory & Event* 16 (2013).

Daniel, Ute. *Arbeiterfrauen in der Kriegsgesellschaft: Beruf, Familie und Politik im Ersten Weltkrieg*. Göttingen: Vandenhoeck & Ruprecht, 1989.

Davis, Belinda. *Home Fires Burning: Food, Politics, and Everyday Life in World War I Berlin*. Chapel Hill: University of North Carolina Press, 2000.

Dean, Carolyn. *The Fragility of Empathy after the Holocaust*. Ithaca, NY: Cornell University Press, 2004.

— *The Frail Social Body: Pornography, Homosexuality, and Other Fantasies in Interwar France*. Berkeley: University of California Press, 2000.

Decker, Hannah. "The Reception of Psychoanalysis in Germany." *Comparative Studies in Society and History* 24 (1982): 589–602.

Dennert, Gabriele, Christiane Leidinger, and Franziska Rauchut, eds. *In Bewegung bleiben: 100 Jahre Politik, Kultur und Geschichte von Lesben*. Berlin: Querverlag, 2007.

– "Kämpfe und Konflikte um Macht und Herrschaft: Lesbenbewegung in der BRD der 80er Jahre." In Dennert, Leidinger, and Rauchut, *In Bewegung bleiben*, 126–59.

– "Lesben in Wut: Lesbenbewegung in der BRD der 70er Jahre." In Dennert, Leidinger, and Rauchut, *In Bewegung bleiben*, 31–61.

Dickinson, Edward Ross. "Biopolitics, Fascism, Democracy: Some Reflections on Our Discourse about 'Modernity.'" *Central European History* 37 (2004): 1–48.

– "'A Dark, Impenetrable Wall of Complete Incomprehension': The Impossibility of Heterosexual Love in Imperial Germany." *Central European History* 40 (2007): 467–97.

– "Domination of the Spirit over the Flesh: Religion, Gender and Sexual Morality in the German Women's Movement before World War I." *Gender & History* 17 (2005): 378–408.

– "The Men's Christian Morality Movement in Germany, 1880–1914: Some Reflections on Politics, Sex, and Sexual Politics." *Journal of Modern History* 75 (2003): 59–110.

– "'Must We Dance Naked?': Art, Beauty, and Law in Munich and Paris, 1911–1913." Journal of the History of Sexuality 20 (January 2011): 95–131.

– "Not So Scary After All? Reform in Imperial and Weimar Germany." *Central European History* 43 (2010): 149–72.

– "Policing Sex in Germany, 1882–1982: A Preliminary Statistical Analysis." Journal of the History of Sexuality 16, no. 2 (2007): 204–50.

– *The Politics of German Child Welfare from the Empire to the Federal Republic*. Cambridge, MA: Harvard University Press, 1996.

– "Reflections on Feminism and Monism in the Kaiserreich, 1900–1913." *Central European History* 34 (2001): 191–230.

– *Sex, Freedom, and Power in Imperial Germany, 1880–1914*. New York: Cambridge University Press, 2014.

– "Sex, Masculinity, and the 'Yellow Peril': Christian von Ehrenfels' Program for a Revision of the European Sexual Order, 1902–1910." *German Studies Review* 25 (2002): 225–84.

Dikotter, Frank. "Race Culture: Recent Perspectives on the History of Eugenics." *American Historical Review* 103 (1998): 467–78.

Doan, Laura. *Fashioning Sapphism: The Origins of a Modern English Lesbian Culture*. New York: Columbia University Press, 2001.

Dobler, Jens. *Von anderen Ufern: Geschichte der Berliner Lesben und Schwulen in Kreuzberg und Friedrichshain*. Berlin: Bruno Gmünder Verlag, 2003.

– "Zensur von Büchern und Zeitschriften mit homosexueller Thematik in der Weimarer Republik." *Invertito: Jahrbuch für die Geschichte der Homosexualitäten* 2 (2000): 85–104.

– *Zwischen Duldungspolitik und Verbrechensbekämpfung: Homosexuellenverfolgung durch die Berliner Polizei von 1848 bis 1933.* Frankfurt: Verlag für Polizeiwissenschaft/Lorei, 2008.

Domarus, Max, ed. *Hitler: Speeches and Proclamations 1932–1945.* Vol. 1. Translated by Mary Fran Gilbert. London: I.B. Tauris, 1990.

Domeier, Norman. *Der Eulenburg-Skandal: Eine politische Kulturgeschichte des Kaiserreichs.* Frankfurt: Campus, 2010.

Dose, Ralf. *Magnus Hirschfeld: Deutscher – Jude – Weltbürger.* Teetz: Hentrich & Hentrich, 2005.

– "The World League for Sexual Reform: Some Possible Approaches." Translated by Pamela Selwyn. *Journal of the History of Sexuality* 12 (2003): 1–15.

Dreyer, Michael. "Weimar as a 'Militant Democracy.'" In *Beyond Glitter and Doom: The Contingency of the Weimar Republic,* edited by Jochen Hung, Godela Weiss-Sussex, and Geoff Wilkes, 69–86. Munich: IUDICIUM, 2012.

Duggan, Lisa. "The New Homonormativity: The Sexual Politics of Neoliberalism." In *Materializing Democracy,* edited by Russ Castronovo and Dana D. Nelson, 175–94. Durham, NC: Duke University Press, 2002.

Dynes, Wayne. "Magnus Hirschfeld." In *Gay and Lesbian Biography,* edited by Michael Tyrkus, 226–9. Detroit: St. James Press, 1997.

Eder, Franz. "Sexuelle Kulturen in Deutschland und Österreich, 18.–20. Jahrhundert." In *Neue Geschichten der Sexualität,* edited by Franz Eder and Sabine Frühstück, 41–68. Vienna: Turia und Kant, 2000.

Eksteins, Modris. *The Limits of Reason: The German Democratic Press and the Collapse of Weimar Germany.* Oxford: Oxford University Press, 1975.

Eldorado: Homosexuelle Frauen und Männer in Berlin 1850–1950: Geschichte, Alltag und Kultur. Berlin: Edition Heinrich, 1992.

Eley, Geoff. "Nazism, Politics and the Image of the Past: Thoughts on the West German Historikerstreit 1986–1987." *Past & Present* 121 (1988): 171–208.

El-Tayeb, Fatima. *Schwarze Deutsche: Der Diskurs um "Rasse" und nationale Identität 1890–1933.* Frankfurt: Campus, 2001.

Eng, David. *The Feeling of Kinship: Queer Liberalism and the Racialization of Intimacy.* Durham, NC: Duke University Press, 2010.

Eng, David, with Judith Halberstam and José Esteban Muñoz. "What's Queer about Queer Studies Now?" *Social Text* 23 (2005): 1–17.

Eriksson, Brigitte, ed. and trans. "A Lesbian Execution in Germany, 1721: The Trial Records." In *Historical Perspectives on Homosexuality: The Gay Past,* edited by Salvatore Licata and Robert Petersen, 27–40. New York: Haworth, 1981.

Espinaco-Virseda, Angeles. "'I Feel That I Belong to You': Subculture, Die Freundin and Lesbian Identities in Weimar Germany." *Spaces of Identity* 4, no. 1 (2004): 83–113.

Evans, Jennifer. "Bahnhof Boys: Policing Male Prostitution in Post-Nazi Berlin." *Journal of the History of Sexuality* 12, no. 4 (2003): 605–36.

– "Decriminalization, Seduction, and 'Unnatural Desire' in the German Democratic Republic." Feminist Studies 36 (2010): 553–77.

– *Life among the Ruins: Cityscape and Sexuality in Cold War Berlin.* New York: Palgrave Macmillan, 2011.

– "The Moral State: Men, Mining, and Masculinity in the Early GDR." *German History* 23 (2005): 355–70.

Evans, Jennifer, and Jane Freeland. "Rethinking Sexual Modernity in Twentieth-century Germany." *Social History* 37, no. 3 (2012): 314–27.

Evans, Richard. *The Coming of the Third Reich.* New York: Penguin, 2003.

– *The Feminist Movement in Germany, 1894–1933.* London: Sage, 1976.

– "Prostitution, State and Society in Imperial Germany." *Past and Present* 70 (1976): 106–29.

Faderman, Lillian, and Brigitte Ericksson. *Lesbians in Germany: 1890's–1920's.* Tallahassee, FL: Naiad Press, 1990.

Falter, J.W. *Hitlers Wähler.* Munich: Beck, 1991.

Fischer, Heinz-Dietrich. "Deutsche Allgemeine Zeitung (1861–1945)." In *Deutsche Zeitungen des 17. bis 20. Jahrhunderts,* edited by Heinz-Dietrich Fischer, 269–81. Pullach bei München: Verlag Dokumentation, 1972.

Foucault, Michel. *The History of Sexuality.* Vol. 1, *An Introduction.* Translated by Robert Hurley. New York: Random House, 1978.

Fout, John. "The Moral Purity Movement in Wilhelmine Germany and the Attempt to Regulate Male Behavior." *Journal of Men's Studies* 1 (1995): 5–32.

– "Sexual Politics in Wilhelmine Germany: The Male Gender Crisis, Moral Purity, and Homophobia." *Journal of the History of Sexuality* 2, no. 3 (1992): 388–421.

Freedman, Estelle. "'The Burning of the Letters Continues': Elusive Identities and the Historical Construction of Sexuality." *Journal of Women's History* 9, no. 4 (1998): 181–200.

Freund-Widder, Michaela. *Frauen unter Kontrolle: Prostitution und ihre staatliche Bekämpfung in Hamburg vom Ende des Kaiserreichs bis zu den Anfängen der Bundesrepublik.* Münster: Lit Verlag, 2003.

Frevert, Ute. *Women in German History: From Bourgeois Emancipation to Sexual Liberation.* Translated by Stuart McKinnon-Evans. Oxford: Berg, 1989.

Fritzsche, Peter. "Did Weimar Fail?" *Journal of Modern History* 68 (September 1996): 629–56.

– *Germans into Nazis.* Cambridge, MA: Harvard University Press, 1998.

Führer, Karl Christian. "A Medium of Modernity? Broadcasting in Weimar Germany, 1923–1932." *Journal of Modern History* 69 (1997): 722–53.

Fulda, Bernhard. *Press and Politics in the Weimar Republic.* Oxford: Oxford University Press, 2009.

Gallus, Alexander, ed. *Die vergessene Revolution von 1918/19.* Göttingen: Vandenhoeck & Ruprecht, 2010.

– "Einleitung." In Gallus, *Die vergessene Revolution von 1918/19*, 7–13.

– "Die vergessene Revolution von 1918/19 – Erinnerung und Deutung im Wandel." In Gallus, *Die vergessene Revolution von 1918/19*, 14–38.

Gandhi, Leela. *Affective Communities: Anticolonial Thought, Fin-de-Siècle Radicalism, and the Politics of Friendship.* Durham, NC: Duke University Press, 2006.

Gay, Peter. *Weimar Culture: The Outsider as Insider.* New York: Harper Torchbooks, 1970.

Giles, Geoffrey. "The Denial of Homosexuality: Same-Sex Incidents in Himmler's SS and Police." In *Sexuality and German Fascism*, edited by Dagmar Herzog, 256–90. New York: Berghahn, 2005.

– "A Gray Zone among the Field Gray Men: Confusion in the Discrimination against Homosexuals in the *Wehrmacht.*" In *Gray Zones: Ambiguity and Compromise in the Holocaust and Its Aftermath*, edited by Jonathan Petropoulos and John K. Roth, 127–46. New York: Berghahn, 2005.

– "The Institutionalization of Homosexual Panic in the Third Reich." In *Social Outsiders in Nazi Germany*, edited by Robert Gellately and Nathan Stoltzfus, 233–55. Princeton: Princeton University Press, 2001.

– "Legislating Homophobia in the Third Reich: The Radicalization of Prosecution against Homosexuality by the Legal Profession." *German History* 23 (2005): 339–54.

– "Lothar Machtan, *The Hidden Hitler.*" *Washington Post*, 25 November 2001.

– "'The Most Unkindest Cut of All': Castration, Homosexuality and Nazi Justice." *Journal of Contemporary History* 27, no. 1 (1992): 41–61.

Gillerman, Sharon. *Germans into Jews: Remaking the Jewish Social Body in the Weimar Republic.* Stanford: Stanford University Press, 2009.

Goodbye to Berlin? 100 Jahre Schwulenbewegung. Berlin: Verlag Rosa Winkel, 1997.

Göttert, Margit. "'Mir sind die frauenrechtlerischen Ideen direkt eingeboren': Anna Pappritz (1861–1939)." *Ariadne* 28 (1995): 50–5.

Graf, Rüdiger. *Die Zukunft der Weimarer Republik: Krisen und Zukunftsaneignungen in Deutschland 1918–1933.* Munich: Oldenbourg, 2008.

Grau, Gunter, ed. *Hidden Holocaust? Gay and Lesbian Persecution in Germany 1933–45.* Translated by Patrick Camiller. London: Cassell, 1993.

de Grazia, Victoria. *How Fascism Ruled Women: Italy, 1922–1945.* Berkeley: University of California Press, 1992.

Grimmer, Ian. "The Politics of *Geist*: German Intellectuals and Cultural Socialism, 1890–1920." PhD diss., University of Chicago, 2010.

Grossmann, Atina. "Continuities and Ruptures Sexuality in Twentieth-century Germany: Historiography and Its Discontents." In *Gendering Modern German History*, edited by Karen Hagemann and Jean Quataert, 208–27. New York: Berghahn, 2007.

‒ "The New Woman and the Rationalization of Sexuality in Weimar Germany." In *Powers of Desire: The Politics of Sexuality*, edited by Ann Snitow, Christine Stansell, and Sharon Thompson, 153–71. New York: Monthly Review Press, 1983.

‒ *Reforming Sex: The German Movement for Birth Control and Abortion Reform, 1920–1950.* New York: Oxford University Press, 1997.

Gruber, Helmut. "Willi Münzenberg's German Communist Propaganda Empire 1921–1933." *Journal of Modern History* 38, no. 3 (1966): 278–97.

Grüttner, Michael. "Der Lehrkörper 1918–1932." In *Geschichte der Universität Unter den Linden: Die Berliner Universität zwischen den Weltkriegen 1918–1945*, edited by Rüdiger vom Bruch and Heinz-Elmar Tenorth, 135–86. Berlin: Akademie, 2012.

Hackett, Amy. "Helene Stöcker: Left-wing Intellectual and Sex Reformer." In Bridenthal, Grossmann, and Kaplan, *When Biology Became Destiny*, 109–30.

Halberstam, Judith. *The Queer Art of Failure.* Durham, NC: Duke University Press, 2011.

Hancock, Eleanor. *Ernst Röhm: Hitler's SA Chief of Staff.* New York: Palgrave Macmillan, 2008.

‒ "'Only the Real, the True, the Masculine Held Its Value': Ernst Röhm, Masculinity, and Male Homosexuality." *Journal of the History of Sexuality* 8, no. 4 (1998): 616–41.

Harris, Victoria. "In the Absence of Empire: Feminism, Abolitionism and Social Work in Hamburg (c. 1900–1933)." *Women's History Review* 17 (2008): 279–98.

‒ *Selling Sex in the Reich: Prostitutes in German Society, 1914–1945.* Oxford: Oxford University Press, 2010.

Harsch, Donna. *German Social Democracy and the Rise of Nazism.* Chapel Hill: University of North Carolina Press, 1993.

Harvey, Elizabeth. *Youth and the Welfare State in Weimar Germany.* Oxford: Clarendon Press, 1993.

Hastings, Derek. *Catholicism and the Roots of Nazism.* New York: Oxford University Press, 2010.

Hau, Michael. *The Cult of Health and Beauty in Germany: A Social History, 1890–1930.* Chicago: University of Chicago Press, 2003.

Hecht, Cornelia. *Deutsche Juden und Antisemitismus in der Weimarer Republik.* Bonn: Dietz, 2003.

Heilbronner, Oded. "The Role of Nazi Antisemitism in the Nazi Party's Activity and Propaganda: A Regional Historiographical Study." *Leo Baeck Yearbook* (1990): 397–439.

Heineman, Elizabeth. *Before Porn Was Legal: The Erotic Empire of Beate Uhse.* Chicago: University of Chicago Press, 2011.

Heinemann, Rebecca. *Familie zwischen Tradition und Emanzipation: Katholische und sozialdemokratische Familienkonzeptionen in der Weimarer Republik.* Munich: R. Oldenbourg, 2004.

Heiß, Stephan. "Die Polizei und Homosexuelle in München zwischen 1900 und 1933: Schlaglichter auf ein schwieriges Verhältnis zwischen Obrigkeit und Subkultur." In *Polizeireport München,* edited by Michael Farin, 194–207. Munich: Belleville, 1999.

Hekma, Gert, Harry Ooterhuis, and James Steakley. "Leftist Sexual Politics and Homosexuality: A Historical Overview." *Journal of Homosexuality* 29, nos. 2–3 (1995): 1–40.

Herrn, Rainer. *Schnittmuster des Geschlechts: Transvestitismus und Transsexualität in der frühen Sexualwissenschaft.* Gießen: Psychosozial-Verlag, 2005.

– "Von Traum zum Trauma: Das Institut für Sexualwissenschaft." In *Der Sexualreformer Magnus Hirschfeld: Ein Leben im Spannungsfeld von Wissenschaft, Politik und Gesellschaft,* edited by Kotowski and Schoeps, 173–199.

Herzer, Manfred. "Antisemitismus und Rechtsradikalismus bei Adolf Brand." *Capri: Zeitschrift für schwule Geschichte* 21 (1996): 37–41.

– *Magnus Hirschfeld: Leben und Werk eines jüdischen, schwulen und sozialistischen Sexologen.* Frankfurt: Campus, 1992.

– "Opposition im 19. Jahrhundert." In *Goodbye to Berlin? 100 Jahre Schwulenbewegung,* 27–34.

– "Schwule Preussen, warme Berliner." *Capri: Zeitschrift für schwule Geschichte* 2 (1988): 3–25.

Hertzman, Lewis. *DNVP: Right-wing Opposition in the Weimar Republic, 1918–1924.* Lincoln: University of Nebraska Press, 1963.

Herzog, Dagmar. *Sex after Fascism: Memory and Morality in Twentieth-century Germany.* Princeton: Princeton University Press, 2007.

Hewitt, Andrew. *Political Inversions: Homosexuality, Fascism, and the Modernist Imaginary.* Stanford: Stanford University Press, 1996.

Holy, Michael. "Jenseits von Stonewall – Rückblicke auf die Schwulenbewegung in der BRD 1969–1980." In Pretzel and Weiß, *Rosa Radikale,* 39–79.

Hong, Young-Sun. *Welfare, Modernity, and the Weimar State, 1919–1933.* Princeton: Princeton University Press, 1998.

Houlbrook, Matt. *Queer London: Perils and Pleasures in the Sexual Metropolis, 1918–1957.* Chicago: University of Chicago Press, 2005.

Hull, Isabel. *The Entourage of Kaiser Wilhelm II, 1888–1918.* Cambridge: Cambridge University Press, 1982.

Huneke, Erik. "Morality, Law, and the Socialist Sexual Self in the German Democratic Republic, 1945–1972." PhD diss., University of Michigan, 2013.

Hung, Jochen. "Beyond Glitter and Doom: The New Paradigm of Contingency in Weimar Research." In *Beyond Glitter and Doom: The Contingency of the Weimar Republic,* edited by Jochen Hung, Godela Weiss-Sussex, and Geoff Wilkes, 9–15. Munich: IUDICIUM, 2012.

Invertito: Jahrbuch für die Geschichte der Homosexualitäten 2 (2000).

Jelavich, Peter. *Berlin Alexanderplatz: Radio, Film, and the Death of Weimar Culture.* Berkeley: University of California Press, 2006.

– *Berlin Cabaret.* Cambridge, MA: Harvard University Press, 1993.

– "Paradoxes of Censorship in Modern Germany." In *Enlightenment, Passion, Modernity: Historical Essays in European Thought and Culture,* edited by Mark S. Micale and Robert L. Dietle, 265–85. Stanford: Stanford University Press, 2000.

Jellonnek, Burkhard. *Homosexuelle unter dem Hakenkreuz: Die Verfolgung von Homosexuellen im Dritten Reich.* Paderborn: Ferdinand Schöningh, 1990.

Jellonnek, Burkhard, and Rüdiger Lautmann, eds. *Nationalsozialistischer Terror gegen Homosexuelle: Verdrängt und ungesühnt.* Paderborn: Schöningh, 2002.

Jenkins, Jennifer. *Provincial Modernity: Local Culture and Liberal Politics in Fin-de-Siècle Hamburg.* Ithaca, NY: Cornell University Press, 2003.

Jones, Larry Eugene. "Franz von Papen, Catholic Conservatives, and the Establishment of the Third Reich, 1933–1934." *Journal of Modern History* 83, no. 2 (2001): 272–318.

– "Franz von Papen, the German Center Party, and the Failure of Catholic Conservatism in the Weimar Republic." *Central European History* 38 (2005): 191–217.

Junker, Detlef. *Die Deutsche Zentrumspartei und Hitler 1932/33.* Stuttgart: Ernst Klett, 1969.

Kaes, Anton, Martin Jay, and Edward Dimendberg, eds. *The Weimar Republic Sourcebook.* Berkeley: University of California Press, 1995.

Kaiser, Jochen-Christoph, Kurt Nowak, and Michael Schwartz, eds. *Eugenik, Sterilisation, "Euthanasie": Politische Biologie in Deutschland 1895–1945, Eine Dokumentation.* Berlin: Buchverlag Union, 1992.

Kaplan, Marion. *The Jewish Feminist Movement in Germany: The Campaigns of the Jüdischer Frauenbund, 1904–1938.* Westport, CT: Greenwood Press, 1979.

Kappeler, Manfred. *Der schreckliche Traum vom vollkommenen Menschen: Rassenhygiene und Eugenik in der Sozialen Arbeit.* Marburg: Schüren, 2000.

Keilson-Lauritz, Marita. *Die Geschichte der eigenen Geschichte: Literatur und Literaturkritik in den Anfängen der Schwulenbewegung.* Berlin: Verlag Rosa Winkel, 1997.

– "Tanten, Kerle und Skandale: Die Geburt des 'modernen Homosexuellen' aus den Flügelkämpfen der Emanzipation." In zur Nieden, *Homosexualität und Staatsräson,* 81–99.

Kennedy, Hubert. *Ulrichs.* Boston: Alyson, 1998.

Kershaw, Ian. *Hitler: 1889–1936: Hubris.* New York: Norton, 1998.

Kingsley Kent, Susan. *Making Peace: The Reconstruction of Gender in Interwar Britain.* Princeton: Princeton University Press, 1993.

Kitchen, Martin. *The Silent Dictatorship: The Politics of the German High Command under Hindenburg and Ludendorff, 1916–1918.* New York: Holmes & Meier, 1976.

Kittel, Ingo-Wolf. "Arthur Kronfeld zur Erinnerung." In *Arthur Kronfeld 1886–1941: Ein Pionier der Psychologie, Sexualwissenschaft und Psychotherapie,* 7–13. Konstanz: Bibliothek der Universität Konstanz, 1988.

Knapp, Thomas. "The German Center Party and the Reichsbanner." *International Review of Social History* 14 (1969): 159–79.

Kohler, Eric. "The Successful German Center-Left: Joseph Hess and the Prussian Center Party, 1908–32." *Central European History* 23 (1990): 313–48.

Kokula, Ilse. *Jahre des Glücks, Jahre des Leids: Gespräche mit älteren lesbischen Frauen: Dokumente.* Kiel: Frühlings Erwachen, 1986.

– *Weibliche Homosexualität um 1900 in zeitgenössischen Dokumenten.* Munich: Verlag Frauenoffensive, 1981.

Kolb, Eberhard. *The Weimar Republic.* New York: Routledge, 2004.

Kolb, Eberhard, and Dirk Schumann. *Die Weimarer Republik.* Munich: Oldenbourg, 2013.

Kollenbroich, James. *Our Hour Has Come: The Homosexual Rights Movement in the Weimar Republic.* Saarbrücken: VDM, 2007.

Kotowski, Elke-Vera, and Julius H. Schoeps, eds. *Der Sexualreformer Magnus Hirschfeld: Ein Leben im Spannungsfeld von Wissenschaft, Politik und Gesellschaft.* Berlin: be.bra wissenschaft verlag, 2004.

Koven, Seth. *Slumming: Sexual and Social Politics in Victorian London.* Princeton: Princeton University Press, 2004.

Koven, Seth, and Sonya Michel, eds. *Mothers of a New World: Maternalist Politics and the Origins of Welfare States.* New York: Routledge, 1993.

Krettmann, Ulrike. "Johanna Elberskirchen." In Lautmann, *Homosexualität,* 111–16.

Kroll, Jürgen, Peter Weingart, and Kurt Bayertz. *Blut und Gene: Geschichte der Eugenik und Rassenhygiene in Deutschland.* Frankfurt: Suhrkamp, 1988.

Lautmann, Rüdiger, ed. *Homosexualität: Handbuch der Theorie- und Forschungsgeschichte.* Frankfurt: Campus, 1993.

Lees, Andrew. *Cities, Sin, and Social Reform in Imperial Germany.* Ann Arbor: University of Michigan Press, 2002.

Leidinger, Christiane. "'Anna Rüling': A Problematic Foremother of Lesbian History." *Journal of the History of Sexuality* 13 (2004): 477–99.

Leng, Kirsten. "Contesting the 'Laws of Life': Feminism, Sexual Science and Sexual Governance in Germany and Britain, c. 1880–1914." PhD diss., University of Michigan, 2011.

Lenman, Robin. "Art, Society, and the Law in Wilhelmine Germany: The Lex Heinze." *Oxford German Studies* 8 (1973): 86–113.

Leopold, John. *Alfred Hugenberg: The Radical Nationalist Campaign against the Weimar Republic.* New Haven, CT: Yale University Press, 1977.

Lerner, Paul. "Hysterical Cures: Hypnosis, Gender and Performance in World War I and Weimar Germany." *History Workshop Journal* 45 (1998): 79–101.

Levine, Phillipa. *Prostitution, Race, and Politics: Policing Venereal Disease in the British Empire.* New York: Routledge, 2003.

Liang, Hsi-huey. *The Berlin Police Force in the Weimar Republic.* Berkeley: University of California, 1970.

Lieshout, Maurice van. "Lucien von Römer." In Lautmann, *Homosexualität,* 141–6.

Linder, Herbert. *Von der NSDAP zur SPD: Der politische Lebensweg des Dr. Helmuth Klotz (1894–1943).* Konstanz: Universitätsverlag Konstanz, 1998.

Lücke, Martin. "Männerbilder zwischen Konsum und Kommunismus: Die Konstruktion homosexueller Männlichkeit bei den Homosexuellen-Aktivisten Friedrich Radszuweit und Richard Linsert." *Invertito* 10 (2008): 57–78.

– *Männlichkeit in Unordnung: Homosexualität und männliche Prostitution in Kaiserreich und Weimarer Republik.* Frankfurt: Campus, 2008.

Lybeck, Marti. *Desiring Emancipation: New Women and Homosexuality in Germany, 1890–1933.* Albany: State University of New York Press, 2014.

– "Gender, Sexuality, and Belonging: Female Homosexuality in Germany, 1890–1933." PhD diss., University of Michigan, 2007.

– "Writing Love, Feeling Shame: Rethinking Respectability in the Weimar Homosexual Women's Movement." In *After "The History of Sexuality": German Genealogies With and Beyond Foucault,* edited by Scott Spector, Helmut Puff, and Dagmar Herzog, 156–68. New York: Berghahn, 2012.

Machtan, Lothar. *The Hidden Hitler.* Translated by John Brownjohn and Susanne Ehlert. New York: Basic Books, 2002.

Mancini, Elena. *Magnus Hirschfeld and the Quest for Sexual Freedom.* New York: Palgrave Macmillan, 2010.

Manz, Ulrike. *Bürgerliche Frauenbewegung und Eugenik in der Weimarer Republik.* Königstein im Taunus: Ulrike Helmer Verlag, 2007.

Marcus, Sharon. *Between Women: Friendship, Desire, and Marriage in Victorian England.* Princeton: Princeton University Press, 2007.

Marhoefer, Laurie. "Degeneration, Sexual Freedom, and the Politics of the Weimar Republic, 1918–1933." *German Studies Review* 34 (2011): 529–50.

– "Homosexuality and Theories of Culture." In *Was ist Homosexualität? Forschungsgeschichte, gesellschaftliche Entwicklungen und Perspektiven,* edited by Jennifer Evans, Florian Mildenberger, Rüdiger Lautmann, and Jakob Pastötter, 255–70. Hamburg: Männerschwarm, 2014.

– "'The Book Was a Revelation, I Recognized Myself in It': Lesbian Sexuality, Censorship, and the Queer Press in Weimar-era Germany." *Journal of Women's History* 27 (2015): 62–86.

Matysik, Tracie. "In the Name of the Law: The 'Female Homosexual' and the Criminal Code in Fin de Siècle Germany." *Journal of the History of Sexuality* 13 (2004): 26–48.

– *Reforming the Moral Subject: Ethics and Sexuality in Central Europe, 1890–1930.* Ithaca, NY: Cornell University Press, 2008.

May, Georg. *Ludwig Kaas: Der Priester, der Politiker und der Gelehrte aus der Schule von Ulrich Stutz.* Vol. 3. Amsterdam: B.R. Grüner, 1982.

Mayer, Dieter. "Die Epoche der Weimarer Republik." In *Geschichte der deutschen Literatur vom 18. Jahrhundert bis zur Gegenwart,* vol. 3/1, edited by Viktor Žmegač, 1–185. Weinheim: Beltz Athenäum, 1994.

Mazower, Mark. *Dark Continent: Europe's Twentieth Century.* New York: Vintage, 2000.

Mazura, Uwe. *Zentrumspartei und Judenfrage 1870/1–1933.* Mainz: Matthias-Grünewald, 1994.

McCormick, Richard. *Gender and Sexuality in Weimar Modernity: Film, Literature, and "New Objectivity."* New York: Palgrave Macmillan, 2001.

McElligott, Anthony. "Introduction." In *Weimar Germany,* edited by Anthony McElligott, 1–25. Oxford: Oxford University Press, 2009.

– "Political Culture." In *Weimar Germany,* edited by Anthony McElligott, 26–49. Oxford: Oxford University Press, 2009.

– *Rethinking the Weimar Republic: Authority and Authoritarianism 1916–1936.* London: Bloomsbury, 2014.

McGuire, Kristin. "Feminist Politics Beyond the Reichstag: Helene Stöcker and Visions of Reform." In Canning, Barndt, and McGuire, *Weimar Publics/Weimar Subjects,* 138–52.

McLaren, Angus. *Sexual Blackmail: A Modern History*. Cambridge, MA: Harvard University Press, 2002.

McLellan, Josie. *Love in the Time of Communism: Intimacy and Sexuality in the GDR*. Cambridge: Cambridge University Press, 2011.

Meeker, Martin. *Contacts Desired: Gay and Lesbian Communications and Community, 1940s–1970s*. Chicago: University of Chicago Press, 2006.

Menke, Martin. "Misunderstood Civic Duty: The Center Party and the Enabling Act." *Journal of Church and State* 51 (2009): 236–64.

Mergel, Thomas. *Parlamentarische Kultur in der Weimarer Republik: Politische Kommunikation, symbolische Politik und Öffentlichkeit im Reichstag*. Düsseldorf: Droste, 2005.

Merke, Franz. *History and Iconography of Endemic Goitre and Cretinism*. Lancaster: MTP Press, 1984.

Meyer, Adele, ed. *Lila Nächte: Die Damenklubs im Berlin der Zwanziger Jahre*. Berlin: Edition Lit. Europe, 1994.

Meyer-Renschhausen, Elisabeth. "The Bremen Morality Scandal." In Bridenthal, Grossmann, and Kaplan, *When Biology Became Destiny*, 87–108.

Meyerowitz, Joanne. *How Sex Changed: A History of Transsexuality in the United States*. Cambridge, MA: Harvard University Press, 2004.

Micheler, Stefan, ed. *Invertito* Jahrgang 2 (2002), *Denunziert, verfolgt, ermordet: Homosexuelle Männer und Frauen in der NS-Zeit*.

– *Selbstbilder und Fremdbilder der "Anderen": Männer begehrende Männer in der Weimarer Republik und der NS-Zeit*. Konstanz: UVK, 2005.

Micheler, Stefan, and Patricia Szobar. "Homophobic Propaganda and the Denunciation of Same-Sex-Desiring Men under National Socialism." *Journal of the History of Sexuality* 11 (2002): 95–130.

Mildenberger, Florian. "Kraepelin and the 'Urnings': Male Homosexuality in Psychiatric Discourse." *History of Psychiatry* 18 (2007): 321–35.

– *... in der Richtung der Homosexualität verdorben: Psychiater, Kriminalpsychologen und Gerichtsmediziner über männliche Homosexualität 1850–1970*. Hamburg: MännerschwarmSkript, 2002.

Mizejewski, Linda. *Divine Decadence: Fascism, Female Spectacle, and the Makings of Sally Bowles*. Princeton: Princeton University Press, 1992.

Moeller, Robert. "The Homosexual Man Is a 'Man,' the Homosexual Woman Is a 'Woman': Sex, Society, and the Law in Postwar West Germany." *Journal of the History of Sexuality* 4 (1994): 395–429.

– "War Stories: The Search for a Usable Past in the Federal Republic of Germany." *American Historical Review* 101 (1996): 1008–48.

– *War Stories: The Search for a Usable Past in the Federal Republic of Germany*. Berkeley: University of California Press, 2001.

Möller, Horst. *Die Weimarer Republik: Eine unvollendete Demokratie.* Munich: Deutscher Taschenbuch Verlag, 2004.

Mommsen, Hans. *The Rise and Fall of Weimar Democracy.* Translated by Elborg Forster and Larry Eugene Jones. Chapel Hill: University of North Carolina Press, 1996.

Morrison, Paul. *The Explanation for Everything: Essays on Sexual Subjectivity.* New York: New York University Press, 2001.

Morsey, Rudolf. "Die Deutsche Zentrumspartei." In *Das Ende der Parteien 1933,* edited by Erich Matthias and Rudolf Morsey, 279–417. Bonn: Droste, 1960.

–, ed. *Die Protokolle der Reichstagsfraktion und des Fraktionsvorstands der deutschen Zentrumspartei 1926–1933.* Mainz: Matthias Grünwald, 1969.

– *Der Untergang des Politischen Katholizismus: Die Zentrumspartei zwischen christlichem Selbstverständnis und "Nationaler Erhebung" 1932/33.* Stuttgart: Belser Verlag, 1977.

Morsey, Rudolf, and Erich Matthias. *Das Ende der Parteien 1933.* Bonn: Droste, 1960.

Mosse, George. *Nationalism and Sexuality: Respectability and Abnormal Sexuality in Modern Europe.* New York: Howard Fertig, 1985.

Mouton, Michelle. *From Nurturing the Nation to Purifying the Volk: Weimar and Nazi Family Policy, 1918–1945.* New York: Cambridge University Press, 2007.

Müller, Christian. *Verbrechensbekämpfung im Anstaltsstaat: Psychiatrie, Kriminologie und Strafrechtsreform in Deutschland 1871–1933.* Göttingen: Vandenhoeck & Ruprecht, 2004.

Nagle, Jill, ed. *Whores and Other Feminists.* New York: Routledge, 1997.

Nieden, Susanne zur. "Aufstieg und Fall des virilen Männerhelden: Der Skandal um Ernst Röhm und seine Ermordung." In zur Nieden, *Homosexualität und Staatsräson,* 147–88.

– *Erbbiologische Forschung zur Homosexualität an der Deutschen Forschungsanstalt für Psychiatrie während der Jahre des Nationalsozialismus; zur Geschichte von Theo Lang.* Berlin: Max-Planck-Gesellschaft zur Förderung der Wissenschaft, 2005.

– ed. *Homosexualität und Staatsräson: Männlichkeit, Homophobie und Politik in Deutschland 1900–1945.* Frankfurt: Campus, 2005.

Nienhaus, Ursula. *"Nicht für eine Führungsposition geeignet": Josefine Erkens und die Anfänge weiblicher Polizei in Deutschland, 1923–1933.* Münster: Westfälisches Dampfboot, 1999.

Niewyk, Donald. *The Jews in Weimar Germany.* Baton Rouge: Louisiana State University Press, 1980.

– "Solving the 'Jewish Problem': Continuity and Change in German Antisemitism, 1871–1945." *Leo Baeck Yearbook* (1990): 335–70.

Oguntoye, Katharina. *Eine afro-deutsche Geschichte: Zur Lebenssituation von Afri-kanern und Afro-Deutschen in Deutschland von 1884 bis 1950*. Berlin: Hoho, 1997.

Oosterhuis, Harry. "The 'Jews' of the Antifascist Left: Homosexuality and Socialist Resistance to Nazism." In *Gay Men and the Sexual History of the Political Left*, edited by Gert Hekma, Harry Oosterhuis, and James Steakley, 227–58. Binghamton, NY: Haworth Press, 1995.

Ordover, Nancy. *American Eugenics: Race, Queer Anatomy, and the Science of Nationalism*. Minneapolis: University of Minnesota Press, 2003.

Orlow, Dietrich. *The History of the Nazi Party*. Vol. 1, *1919–33*. Pittsburgh: University of Pittsburgh Press, 1969.

– *Weimar Prussia 1925–1933: The Illusion of Strength*. Pittsburgh: University of Pittsburgh Press, 1991.

Patch, William. *Heinrich Brüning and the Dissolution of the Weimar Republic*. Cambridge: Cambridge University Press, 1998.

Perincioli, Cristina. "Warum musste die Tomate so weit fliegen? Über 68erInnen, Anarchismus, Lesbianismus bis zum Frauenzentrum." In Dennert, Leidinger, and Rauchut, *In Bewegung bleiben*, 62–7.

Petersen, Klaus. "The Harmful Publications (Young Persons) Act 1926: Literacy, Censorship, and the Politics of Morality in the Weimar Republic." *German Studies Review* 15 (1992): 505–25.

– *Zensur in der Weimarer Republik*. Stuttgart: J.B. Metzler, 1995.

Peukert, Detlev. *Grenzen der Sozialdisziplinierung: Aufstieg und Krise der deutschen Jugendfürsorge von 1878 bis 1932*. Cologne: Bund, 1986.

– *The Weimar Republic: The Crisis of Classical Modernity*. Translated by Richard Devenson. New York: Hill and Wang, 1993.

Pfäfflin, Friedemann. "Die Mitteilungen des Wissenschaftlich-humanitären Komitees 1926–1933." In *Mitteilungen des Wissenschaftlich-Humanitären Komitees 1926–1933*, edited by Walter v. Murat, v–xxiii. Hamburg: C. Bell Verlag, 1985.

Pick, Daniel. *Faces of Degeneration*. Cambridge: Cambridge University Press, 1989.

Planert, Ute. *Antifeminismus im Kaiserreich: Diskurs, soziale Formation und politische Mentalität*. Göttingen: Vandenhoeck & Ruprecht, 1998.

– "Kulturkritik und Geschlechterverhältnis: Zur Krise der Geschlechtserordnung zwischen Jahrhundertwende und 'Drittem Reich.'" In *Ordnung in der Krise: Zur politischen Kulturgeschichte Deutschlands 1900–1933*, edited by Wolfgang Hartwig, 191–214. Munich: R. Oldenbourg, 2007.

Plötz, Kirsten. *Einsame Freundinnen? Lesbisches Leben während der zwanziger Jahre in der Provinz*. Hamburg: MännerschwarmSkript Verlag, 1999.

Pommerin, Reiner. *Sterilisierung der Rheinlandbastarde: Das Schicksal einer farbigen deutschen Minderheit 1918–1938*. Düsseldorf: Droste Verlag, 1979.

Poore, Carol. *Disability in Twentieth-century German Culture*. Ann Arbor: University of Michigan Press, 2007.

Pretzel, Andreas. "Homosexuality in the Sexual Ethics of the 1930s: A Values Debate in the Culture Wars between Conservatism, Liberalism, and Moral-National Renewal." In *After "The History of Sexuality": German Genealogies With and Beyond Foucault*, edited by Scott Spector, Helmut Puff, and Dagmar Herzog, 202–15. New York: Berghahn, 2012.

Pretzel, Andreas, and Gabriele Roßbach, eds. *"Wegen der zu erwartenden hohen Strafe ... ": Homosexuellenverfolgung in Berlin 1933–1945*. Berlin: Verlag Rosa Winkel, 2000.

Pretzel, Andreas, and Volker Weiß, eds. *Rosa Radikale: Die Schwulenbewegung der 1970er Jahre*. Hamburg: Männerschwarm, 2012.

Quataert, Jean. *Reluctant Feminists in German Social Democracy, 1885–1917*. Princeton: Princeton University Press, 1979.

Rabinbach, Anson. "Van der Lubbe – ein Lustknabe Röhms? Die politische Dramaturgie der Exilkampagne zum Reichstagsbrand." In zur Nieden, *Homosexualität und Staatsräson*, 193–216.

Ramsey, Glenn. "Erotic Friendship, Gender Inversion, and Human Rights in the German Movement for Homosexual Reform, 1897–1933." PhD diss., Binghamton University, State University of New York, 2004.

– "The Rites of Artgenossen: Contesting Homosexual Political Culture in Weimar Germany." *Journal of the History of Sexuality* 17 (2008): 85–109.

Reagin, Nancy. *A German Women's Movement: Class and Gender in Hanover, 1880–1933*. Chapel Hill: University of North Carolina Press, 1995.

Richter, Ingrid. *Katholizismus und Eugenik in der Weimarer Republik und im Dritten Reich: Zwischen Sittlichkeitsreform und Rassenhygiene*. Paderborn: Ferdinand Schöningh, 2001.

Ripa, Alexandra. "Hirschfeld privat: Seine Haushälterin erinnert sich." In *Magnus Hirschfeld: En Leben im Spannungsfeld von Wissenschaft, Politik und Gesellschaft*, edited by Elke-Vera Kotowski and Julius H. Schoeps, 65–70. Berlin: be.bra wissenschaft verlag, 2004.

Ritzheimer, Kara. "Protecting Youth from 'Trash': Anti-*Schund* Campaigns in Baden, 1900–1933." PhD diss., Binghamton University, State University of New York, 2007.

Roberts, Mary Louise. *Civilization without Sexes: Reconstructing Gender in Postwar France, 1917–1927*. Chicago: University of Chicago Press, 1994.

Roos, Julia. "Backlash against Prostitutes' Rights: Origins and Dynamics of Nazi Prostitution Policies." In *Sexuality and German Fascism*, edited by Dagmar Herzog, 67–94. New York: Berghahn, 2005.

– "Between Normalization and Resistance: Prostitutes' Professional Identities and Political Organizations in Weimar Germany." In *After "The History of Sexuality": German Genealogies With and Beyond Foucault*, edited by Scott Spector, Helmut Puff, and Dagmar Herzog, 139–55. New York: Berghahn, 2012.

– "Nationalism, Racism, and Propaganda in Early Weimar Germany: Contradictions in the Campaign against the 'Black Horror on the Rhine.'" *German History* 30, no. 1 (2012): 45–74.

– *Weimar through the Lens of Gender: Prostitution Reform, Women's Emancipation, and German Democracy, 1919–1933*. Ann Arbor: University of Michigan Press, 2010.

– "Women's Rights, Nationalist Anxiety, and the 'Moral' Agenda in the Early Weimar Republic: Revisiting the 'Black Horror' Campaign against France's African Occupation Troops." *Central European History* 42, no. 3 (2009): 473–508.

Röpenak, Arne von. *KPD und NSDAP im Propagandakampf der Weimarer Republik: Eine inhaltsanalytische Untersuchung in Leitartikeln von "Rote Fahne" und "Angriff."* Stuttgart: Ibidem-Verlag, 2002.

Rosenblum, Warren. *Beyond the Prison Gates: Punishment & Welfare in Germany, 1850–1933*. Chapel Hill: University of North Carolina Press, 2008.

Rosenkranz, Bernhard, and Gottfried Lorenz. *Hamburg auf anderen Wegen: Die Geschichte des schwulen Lebens in der Hansestadt*. Hamburg: Lambda, 2005.

Ross, Corey. *Media and the Making of Modern Germany: Mass Communications, Society, and Politics from the Empire to the Third Reich*. Oxford: Oxford University Press, 2008.

Rossol, Nadine. "Chancen der Weimarer Republic." *Neue politische Literatur* 55, no. 3 (2010): 393–419.

Rowe, Dorothy. *Representing Berlin: Sexuality and the City in Imperial and Weimar Germany*. Burlington, VT: Ashgate, 2003.

Ruppert, Karsten. *Im Dienst am Staat von Weimar: Das Zentrum als regierende Partei in der Weimarer Demokratie 1923–1930*. Düsseldorf: Droste, 1992.

Sachße, Christoph. "Social Mothers: The Bourgeois Women's Movement and German Welfare-State Formation, 1880–1929." In *Mothers of a New World: Maternalist Politics and the Origins of Welfare States*, edited by Seth Koven and Sonya Michel, 136–58. New York: Routledge, 1993.

Schader, Heike. *Virile, Vamps und wilde Veilchen: Sexualität, Begehren und Erotik in den Zeitschriften homosexueller Frauen im Berlin der 1920er Jahre*. Königstein im Taunus: Ulrike Helmer Verlag, 2004.

Scheck, Raffael. *Mothers of the Nation: Right-wing Women in Weimar Germany*. New York: Berg, 2004.

– "Women on the Weimar Right: The Role of Female Politicians in the Deutschnationale Volkspartei (DNVP)." *Journal of Contemporary History* 36 (2001): 547–60.

Schipkowski, Birgit. "Lesbische Subkultur Im Berlin Der Zwanziger Jahre." In *Neue Frauen Zwischen den Zeiten*, edited by Petra Bock and Katja Koblitz, 236–43. Berlin: Edition Hentrich, 1995.

Schmidt, Gunter. "Allies and Persecutors: Science and Medicine in the Homosexuality Issue." *Journal of Homosexuality* 10, nos. 3–4 (1984): 127–40.

Schneider, Christoph. *Die Verstaatlichung des Leibes: Das "Gesetz zur Verhütung erbkranken Nachwuchses" und die Kirche.* Konstanz: Hartung-Gorre Verlag, 2000.

Schoppmann, Claudia. *Days of Masquerade: Life Stories of Lesbians during the Third Reich.* Translated by Allison Brown. New York: Columbia University Press, 1996.

– "Vom Kaiserreichs bis zum Ende des Zweiten Weltkrieges." In Dennert, Leidinger, and Rauchut, *In Bewegung bleiben*, 12–26.

– *Nationalsozialistische Sexualpolitik und weibliche Homosexualität.* Pfaffenweiler: Centaurus, 1997.

– *Der Skorpion: Frauenliebe in der Weimarer Republik.* Hamburg: Frühlings Erwachen, 1985.

– *Verbotene Verhältnisse: Frauenliebe 1938–1945.* Berlin: Querverlag, 1999.

Schott, Heinz, and Rainer Tölle. *Geschichte der Psychiatrie: Krankheitslehren, Irrwege, Behandlungsformen.* Munich: Verlag C.H. Beck, 2006.

Schubert, Werner. *Die Projekte der Weimarer Republik zur Reform des Nichtehelichen-, des Adoptions- und des Ehescheidungsrechts.* Paderborn: Ferdinand Schöningh, 1986.

Schumann, Dirk. *Political Violence in the Weimar Republic 1918–1933: Fight for the Streets and Fear of Civil War.* Translated by Thomas Dunlap. New York: Berghahn, 2009.

Schwartz, Michael. *Sozialistische Eugenik: Eugenische Sozialtechnologien in Debatten und Politik der deutschen Sozialdemokratie 1890–1933.* Bonn: Verlag J.H.W. Dietz, 1995.

Seeck, Andreas, ed. *Durch Wissenschaft zur Gerechtigkeit? Textsammlung zur kritischen Rezeption des Schaffens von Magnus Hirschfeld.* Münster: Lit Verlag, 2003.

– "Einführung." In Seeck, *Durch Wissenschaft zur Gerechtigkeit?* 7–24.

Senelick, Laurence. "The Homosexual Theatre Movement in the Weimar Republic." *Theatre Survey* 49 (2008): 5–35.

Showalter, Dennis. *Little Man, What Now? Der Stürmer in the Weimar Republic.* Hamden, CT: Archon Books, 1982.

Sillge, Ursula. "Frauen im Wissenschaftlich-humanitären Komitee." In Lautmann, *Homosexualität*, 124–6.

Smith, Jill Suzanne. *Berlin Coquette: Prostitution and the New German Woman, 1890–1933.* Ithaca, NY: Cornell University Press, 2013.

Sneeringer, Julia. *Winning Women's Votes: Propaganda and Politics in Weimar Germany.* Chapel Hill: University of North Carolina Press, 2002.

Sommer, Kai. *Die Strafbarkeit der Homosexualität von der Kaiserzeit bis zum Nationalsozialismus.* Frankfurt: Peter Lang, 1998.

Springman, Luke. *Carpe Mundum: German Youth Culture of the Weimar Republic.* New York: Peter Lang, 2007.

Stark, Gary. "All Quiet on the Home Front: Popular Entertainments, Censorship, and Civilian Morale in Germany, 1914–1918." In *Authority, Identity and the Social History of the Great War,* edited by Frans Coetzee and Marilyn Shevin-Coetzee, 57–80. Providence, RI: Berghahn, 1995.

– "Aroused Authorities: State Efforts to Regulate Sex and Smut in the German Mass Media, 1880–1930." Paper presented at Popular Sex: Mass Media and Sexuality in Germany, University of Calgary, Calgary, Alberta, 7–9 January 2011.

– *Banned in Berlin: Literary Censorship in Imperial Germany, 1871–1918.* New York: Berghahn, 2009.

– "Pornography, Society, and the Law in Imperial Germany." *Central European History* 14 (1981): 200–30.

Steakley, James. "Cinema and Censorship in the Weimar Republic: The Case of *Anders als die Andern.*" *Film History* 11, no. 2 (1999): 181–203.

– *The Homosexual Emancipation Movement in Germany.* Salem, NH: Ayer, 1993.

– "Iconography of a Scandal: Political Cartoons and the Eulenburg Affair in Wilhelmin Germany." In *Hidden from History: Reclaiming the Gay and Lesbian Past,* edited by Martha Vicinus, Martin Duberman, and George Chauncey, 233–63. New York: Meridian, 1989.

– "*Per scientiam ad justitiam*: Magnus Hirschfeld and the Sexual Politics of Innate Homosexuality." In *Science and Homosexualities,* edited by Vernon Rosario, 133–54. New York and London: Routledge, 1997.

Stein, Peter. *Die NS-Gaupresse 1925–1933: Forschungsbericht, Quellenkritik, neue Bestandsaufnahme.* Munich: K.G. Saur, 1987.

Sternweiler, Andreas. "Die Freundschaftsbünde – eine Massenbewegung." In *Goodbye to Berlin? 100 Jahre Schwulenbewegung,* 95–104.

Stieg, Margaret. "The 1926 German Law to Protect Youth against Trash and Dirt: Moral Protectionism in a Democracy." *Central European History* 23 (1990): 22–56.

Storer, Colin. *Britain and the Weimar Republic: The History of a Cultural Relationship.* London: Tauris Academic Studies, 2010.

Streubel, Christiane. *Radikale Nationalistinnen: Agitation und Programmatik rechter Frauen in der Weimarer Republik.* Frankfurt: Campus, 2006.

Stümke, Hans-Georg. *Homosexuelle in Deutschland: Eine Politische Geschichte.* Munich: Beck, 1989.

Sutton, Katie. *The Masculine Woman in Weimar Germany.* New York: Berghahn, 2011.

– "'We Too Deserve a Place in the Sun': The Politics of Transvestite Identity in Weimar Germany." *German Studies Review* 35, no. 2 (2012): 335–54.

Swett, Pamela. *Neighbors and Enemies: The Culture of Radicalism in Berlin.* Cambridge: Cambridge University Press, 2004.

Tatar, Maria. *Lustmord: Sexual Murder in Weimar Germany.* Princeton: Princeton University Press, 1995.

Taylor, Mara. "'We Too, Belong to This Group of Krafft-Ebingers!': Women and Sexological Discourse in *Psychopathia Sexualis* and *Are They Women? Novel about the Third Sex.*" *Germanistik in Ireland* 5 (2010): 45–66.

Taylor, Seth. *Left-wing Nietzscheans: The Politics of German Expressionism 1910–1920.* Berlin: Walter de Gruyter, 1990.

Taylor Allen, Ann. *Feminism and Motherhood in Germany 1800–1914.* New Brunswick, NJ: Rutgers University Press, 1991.

– "Feminism, Venereal Diseases, and the State in Germany, 1890–1918." *Journal of the History of Sexuality* 4, no. 1 (1993): 27–50.

– "German Radical Feminists and Eugenics, 1900–1908." *German Studies Review* 11 (1988): 31–56.

Thoenelt, Klaus. "Heinrich Manns Psychologie des Faschismus." *Monatshefte* 63 (1971): 220–34.

Timm, Annette. *The Politics of Fertility in Twentieth-century Berlin.* New York: Cambridge, 2010.

Todd, Lisa. "'The Soldier's Wife Who Ran Away with the Russian': Sexual Infidelities in World War I Germany." *Central European History* 44 (2011): 257–78.

Usborne, Cornelie. "Body Biological to Body Politic: Women's Demands for Reproductive Self-determination in World War I and Early Weimar Germany." In *Citizenship and National Identity in Twentieth-century Germany*, edited by Geoff Eley and Jan Palmowski, 129–45. Stanford: Stanford University Press, 2008.

– "The Christian Churches and the Regulation of Sexuality in Weimar Germany." In *Disciplines of Faith: Studies in Religion, Politics and Patriarchy*, edited by Jim Obelkevich, Lyndal Roper, and Raphael Samuel, 99–112. London: Routledge & Kegan Paul, 1987.

– *Cultures of Abortion in Weimar Germany.* New York: Berghahn, 2007.

– *The Politics of the Body in Weimar Germany: Women's Reproductive Rights and Duties.* Ann Arbor: University of Michigan Press, 1992.

Walkowitz, Judith. *Prostitution and Victorian Society: Women, Class, and the State.* Cambridge: Cambridge University Press, 1982.

Walther, Daniel. "Racializing Sex: Same-sex Relations, German Colonial Authority, and Deutschtum." *Journal of the History of Sexuality* 17 (2008): 11–24.

Weber, Philippe. *Der Trieb zum Erzählen: Sexualpathologie und Homosexualität, 1852–1914.* Bielefeld: transcript, 2008.

Weindling, Paul. *Health, Race and German Politics between National Unification and Nazism 1870–1945.* Cambridge: Cambridge University Press, 1989.

Weiss, Sheila Faith. *Race Hygiene and National Efficiency: The Eugenics of Wilhelm Schallmayer.* Berkeley: University of California Press, 1987.

– "The Race Hygiene Movement in Germany." *Osiris*, 2nd ser., 3 (1987): 193–236.

Weitz, Eric. *Creating German Communism, 1890–1990: From Popular Protest to Socialist State.* Princeton: Princeton University Press, 1997.

– "*The Rise and Fall of Weimar Democracy*" (Review). *Central European History* 31, no. 3 (1998): 273–7.

– "Weimar Germany and Its Historians." *Central European History* 43 (2010): 581–91.

– *Weimar Germany: Promise and Tragedy.* Princeton: Princeton University Press, 2007.

Wenge, Nicola. *Intergration und Ausgrenzung in der Städtischen Gesellschaft: Eine Jüdisch-Nichtjüdische Beziehungsgeschichte Kölns 1918–1933.* Mainz: Phillip von Zabern, 2005.

Wetzell, Richard. *Inventing the Criminal: A History of German Criminology, 1880–1945.* Chapel Hill: University of North Carolina Press, 2000.

Whisnant, Clayton. "Gay German History: Future Directions?" *Journal of the History of Sexuality* 17 (2008): 1–10.

– *Male Homosexuality in West Germany: Between Persecution and Freedom, 1945–69.* New York: Palgrave Macmillan, 2012.

Wickert, Christl. "Sozialistin, Parlamentarierin, Jüden: Die Beispiele Käte Frankenthal, Berta Jourdan, Adele Schreiber-Kreiger, Toni Sender und Hedwig Wachenheim." In *Juden und deutsche Arbeiterbewegung bis 1933: Soziale Utopien und religiös-kulturelle Traditionen*, edited by Ludger Heid and Arnold Paucker, 155–64. Tübingen: J.C.B. Mohr (Paul Siebeck), 1992.

Willing, Matthias. *Das Bewahrungsgesetz.* Tübingen: J.C.B. Mohr, 2003.

Wittlinger, Ruth, and Steffi Boothroyd. "A 'Usable' Past at Last? The Politics of the Past in United Germany." *German Studies Review* 33 (2010): 489–502.

Wolfert, Raimund. *Gegen Einsamkeit und "Einsiedelei": Die Geschichte der Internationalen homophilen Welt- Organisation.* Hamburg: Männerschwarm, 2009.

Wolff, Charlotte. *Magnus Hirschfeld: A Portrait of a Pioneer in Sexology.* London: Quartet Books, 1986.

Wolff, Kerstin. "*Herrenmoral:* Anna Pappritz and Abolitionism in Germany." *Women's History Review* 17 (2008): 225–37.

Women's History Review 17 (2008), special issue, "Gender, Religion and Politics: Josephine Butler's Campaigns in International Perspective (1875–1959)."

Woycke, James. *Birth Control in Germany 1871–1933*. London: Routledge, 1988.

Zinn, Alexander. *Die soziale Konstruktion des homosexuellen Nationalsozialisten: zu Genese und Etablierung eines Stereotyps*. Frankfurt: Peter Lang, 1997.

Index

German and European Studies

General Editor: Rebecca Wittmann